For Nana

Acknowledgments

Chino Abashidze; Sasha Abuladze; Ia Abulashvili; Zaza Alekhidze; Givi Alkhazishvili; Nancy Allisen; Valery Amashukeli; Magnus Bartlett; Irina Begizova; Rose Borton; Deke Castleman; Guram and Mariko Chitaladze; the Davitishvili family; Zura Davitashvili; Temuri Devishvili; Tsisana Djanashia; Manana Djindjikhashvili; Rebecca Dockery; Tedo Dondua; Vakhtang Dzhanaridze; Tamazi Dvali; Vova Djainai; Dali Ebralidze; Hermione Edwards; Jane Finden-Crofts; Temuri Gamtsemlidze; Gia Gikashvili; Tina Gogiashvili; Tatuna Grdzelidze; Zaal V. Gogsadze; Lia and Irina Gugushvili; David Halford; Lisa Kaestner; Manana Khvedelidze; Tedo Japaridze; Stephen Jones; Rejeb Jordania; Merab and Ketino Hvedelidze; Nana Kalandadze; Zurab Karumidze; Nodar Kavtaradze; Mary Kazalikashvili; Soso; Nino Kereselidze; Tamuna and the Khelashvili family; Saba Kiknadze; Zaliko Kikodze; Vakhushti Kotetishvili and family; Paata and Maya Ksovreli; Manana Kvirkvelia; Maya Maisuradze; Ketevan Markozashvili; Anatoli Mindiashvili; Nana, Eleanora, and Paata Mukhadze; Manana Nachkabia; Bill Newlin; Alla Nikiforova; Dato Ninidze; Lena, Nonna, and Arkadi Portnov; Timothy Richardson; Ketevan Rizhamadze; Caroline Robertson; Alex Rondeli; Niko Rtveliashvili; Anatol Rukhadze; Hana Sakai; Irina Saralidze; Dato Sazandrishvili; Madlein, Armen, Emma, and Natasha Shakhbagian; Gizo; Giorgi Shengelaya; Zaza Shengeliya; Toby Steed; Rowan Stewart; Marina Torosashvili; Lali Tsipuria; Tamaz Vasadze; Vano Vashakmadze; Irina Vatzadze; Vakhtang Zhgenti; Henry T. Wooster.

And a very special thanks to Otar Nodia and the Collegium for Literary Translation of the Georgian Writers' Union; Soso Khelashvili; Eldar and Nellie Shengelaya; and Tolik Portnov.

ROGER ROSEN has been fascinated by Georgia since he was a student in Leningrad in 1975. His numerous and extensive travels throughout Georgia, his years of research, and above all his many Georgian friends have made this book possible. A writer who makes his home in New York, he is also the president of The Rosen Publishing Group.

JEFFREY JAY FOXX is an ethnographic photographer based in New York. For over 25 years he has worked for museums, the United Nations, *Life*, and *National Geographic*. One trip resulted in a ten-year project that became the Abrams book *Living Maya*. It won the Annisfield-Wolf award for books that promote intercultural understanding.

GEORGIA
A Sovereign Country of the Caucasus

Roger Rosen

Photography by Jeffrey Jay Foxx

© 1999, 1991 Odyssey Publications Ltd
Maps © 1999, 1991 Odyssey Publications Ltd

Odyssey Publications Ltd, 1004 Kowloon Centre, 29–43 Ashley Road,
Tsim Sha Tsui, Kowloon, Hong Kong
Tel. (852) 2856 3896; Fax. (852) 2565 8004; E-mail: odyssey@asiaonline.net

Distribution in the United Kingdom, Ireland and Europe by
Hi Marketing Ltd, 38 Carver Road, London SE24 9LT, UK

Distribution in the United States of America by
W.W. Norton & Company, Inc., New York

Library of Congress Catalog Card Number has been requested.

ISBN: 962-217-502-3

Grateful acknowledgment is made to the following authors and publishers:
Ardis Publishers for *The Goatibex Constellation* by Fazil Iskander
Atlantic Monthly Press for *Where Nights are Longest* by Colin Thubron
Farrar Straus Giroux for *A Captive of the Caucasus* by Andrei Bitov © 1992
Transliterating Georgian by Professor Howard I Aronson, University of Chicago

Editor: Albert LaFarge.
Series Coordinators: Jane Finden-Crofts and Frank Murdoch
Design: Paul Perlow
Maps: Bai Yiliang, Au Yeung Chui Kwai and Tom Le Bas
Cover Concept: Margaret Lee
Index: Françoise Parkin

Photography by Jeffrey Jay Foxx

Additional photography/illustrations courtesy of Gruzinform, Tbilisi 32; David Halford 8, 67, 97, 109,
116, 127, 275, 281, 299, 300, 316; A. Kikodze 7; Museum of Georgian Art, Tbilisi 34, 121; Fondazione
Sella, Biella, Italy 88, 197

Production by Twin Age Ltd, Hong Kong
Printed in China

Contents

A bishop of the Georgian Orthodox Church

Mt. Ushba at 4,700 meters is one of the highest mountains in Svaneti

Young girls from all over Georgia come to attend a dance festival in Tbilisi (photo by David Halford)

Foreword

This book holds the heartbeat of Georgia, echoing between Georgia's distant past and its tumultuous present.

When you read this book you realize that Georgia's geopolitical position has profoundly influenced its fortunes and, one might say, its misfortunes as well. Perhaps it was Georgia's destiny to be at the crossroads of Europe and Asia; indeed, the Silk Road that connected China with Europe went through Georgia. This probably explains why so many different conquerors and invaders came through Georgia in the past. Now, for many of the same reasons, the same route promises to bring new opportunities to the nation.

Today, Georgia has great potential for economic development. Its extensive natural resources, excellent climate, and rich cultural historical heritage all offer favorable conditions for mutually beneficial partnerships, investments, and the development of tourism.

Still, everyone who has ever traveled to Georgia would agree with me that the country's greatest asset is its people; convivial, tolerant and hospitable, they embody the finest artistic and cultural traditions of both East and West.

Since the first edition of this book in 1991, Georgia has undergone one of the most turbulent periods in recent history. I am convinced, however, that these difficult years are behind us. The processes of democratic development have taken strong root in Georgia. They have now, in fact, become irreversible.

This would not have occurred without the help of friendly countries who have helped Georgia shoulder its difficult task of building a democratic state and society. This book is one more illustration of the friendly attitude that the American people and others have expressed toward Georgia, and I would like to thank the author, Roger Rosen, and his publishers for this.

Lastly, I would like to express my deep appreciation for the support of all Georgia's international friends and offer the hope that such relationships will continue to grow.

Eduard Shevardnadze
President of Georgia

Introduction

Old Soviet hands used to think of Georgia as two hours and 20 minutes from Moscow by plane and another world away—filled with magnificent food and wine; elegantly dressed, and hospitable, men and women; extraordinary church architecture; gorgeous countryside, and the mystery of the Caucasus.

Since Georgia gained independence from the Soviet Union in 1991, it is now perhaps only the Russians who still think of Tbilisi solely in terms of its relation to Moscow. Georgians themselves are looking westward, calculating the distance from Tbilisi to Atlanta, London, and Paris. Whether this small nation will be able to associate so freely remains to be seen. Certainly, the political drama being played out in the Caucasus, a continuation of the Great Game of the nineteenth century, is one of the more exciting and strategically critical events of modern times.

A mythical place, Georgia is the land of Colchis, where Jason found the Golden Fleece and fell in love with Medea. Many Georgian women are still named after her and share the charms and subtle beauty that she possessed. In the first century BC, the Greek geographer Strabo described a technique used in Georgia for getting gold from a river. The technique, involving a sheep fleece, is still known among the old men of Svaneti, thus giving substance to the legend. The Amazons are said to have lived beside the Tergi (Terek) River, and Prometheus chained to either Mt. Kazbek or to Mt. Elbrus. In Georgia, our archetypes are the stuff of their national history.

If Georgia's connection with the Greek and Roman worlds were its only claim to fame, this guide would be considerably thinner. Bordered by the Caucasus mountains to the north, the Black Sea to the west, Azerbaijan in the east, and Turkey and Armenia in the south, Georgia is at the crossroads of Europe and Asia, and as such also shares the complicated and turbulent history of the Middle East. It is a land whose geographical position combined with its exquisite beauty has attracted an excessive number of conquerors (by one count, Tbilisi, the capital, has been destroyed 29 times in its 1,500-plus-year history); and the evidence of Hittites, Assyrians, Scythians, Cimmerians, Persians, Arabs, Turks, and Mongols is certainly present. Despite these invasions and occupations of their land, Georgians have proved extraordinarily tenacious in maintaining their own culture, religion, language, and traditions.

This guide is designed to acquaint you with the full expression of these aspects throughout all the provinces of Georgia: from fifth-century basilicas in Kartli to centenarian choirs in Abkhazia, known in Georgian as Abkhazeti, from 11th-century cave monasteries in Javakheti to the magnificent wines of Kakheti. Where else but in cosmopolitan Tbilisi could you find a synagogue, a mosque, a Georgian

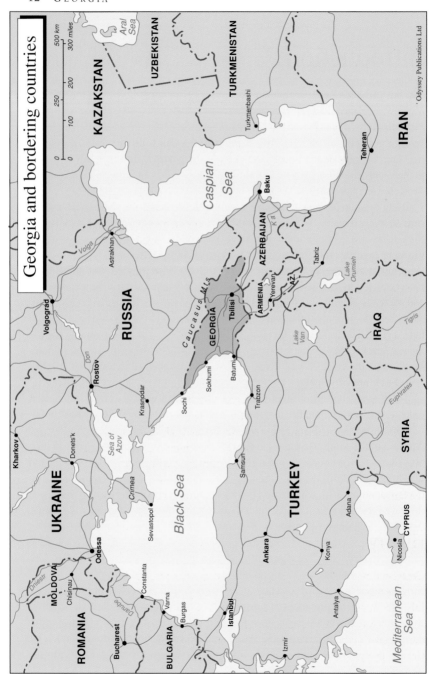

Georgia and bordering countries

basilica, an Armenian church, and a Zoroastrian temple all within a 15-minute walk of each other? And when you're tired, when you feel you've seen enough medieval Georgian churches, frescoes, icons, palaces, and fortresses—not to mention the paintings of Pirosmani, the Moorish Opera House, and the elegant 19th-century neoclassical streets—we'll take you to the baths in Tbilisi, about which Pushkin said, "Never in my life have I encountered either in Russia or in Turkey anything more luxurious than the Tiflis baths." And when you've had enough of that (and no one can ever have enough) we'll introduce you to a lavish Georgian dinner table.

Georgians believe that guests come from God. This belief, imbued by antique Caucasian mountain lore and the elegant verses of their 12th-century poet Shota Rustaveli, is quite simply the Georgian Constitution and Bill of Rights combined. Friendship, hospitality, and generosity are the codes by which Georgians live. These values have been tested in recent times. The independence wrested from the Soviet Union in 1991 has come at a high price. From 1991 until today Georgia has suffered a civil war and a series of conflicts in Abkhazia and Ossetia. More than 250,000 Georgian refugees have fled from their homes in Abkhazia. In a country of only five million people, everyone has lost someone dear to them in these years of fighting. There is a palpable sadness in the country, a sense of amazement at what the country has been forced to endure. But endurance is a trait not lacking in these people, and despite power and fuel shortages, unemployment, and other challenges emanating from a calcified body politic, many hold out hope that a new generation, equipped with diplomatic skills, Western business practices, and technological savvy, will be able to rebuild the country.

Before 1989 one encountered a country hermetically sealed since 1921 in its traditions and customs, but now you will encounter Baskin-Robbins in Tbilisi, Marlboro billboards, and the soon-to-be-constructed McDonald's. For those in search of new experiences in the next millennium, Georgia offers a ringside seat at the burgeoning syncretism of capitalism with ancient Caucasian tradition.

History

Georgians are not Russians, and their language is not Slavic. Georgian association with the Slavic world is of relatively recent vintage. Most historians choose the date July 24, 1783, as the symbolic beginning. That was the date on which Herekle II signed a treaty placing his small kingdom of Kartli-Kakheti under the protection of the Russian empire of Catherine the Great. Although Bolshevik annexation of Georgia by the Red Army in 1921 caused subsequent generations of Westerners to think of Georgia solely within the framework of the former USSR, the bulk of Georgian history and cultural identity has more to do with the shifting power struggles of the Middle East, reflecting the influence of Hittites, Assyrians, Scythians, Cimmerians, Greeks, Romans, Byzantines, Persians, Turks, Mongols and Russians on the resilient and uninterrupted indigenous culture of the Georgians.

Georgians themselves tell the following story about how they came to possess the land which they deem the most beautiful in the world. When God was distributing portions of the world to all the peoples of the Earth, the Georgians were having a party and doing some serious drinking. As a result they arrived late and were told by God that all the land had already been distributed. When they replied that they were late only because they had been lifting their glasses in praise of Him, God was pleased and gave the Georgians the part of Earth he had been reserving for himself.

Actually, Georgians do not call themselves Georgians but *Kartvel-ebi* and their land *Sa-kartvel-o*. These names are derived from a pagan god named Kartlos, said to be the father of all Georgians. The foreign name Georgia, used throughout western Europe, is mistakenly believed to come from the country's patron saint, St. George. Actually it is derived from the words *Kurj* or *Gurj,* by which Georgians are known to the Arabs and modern Persians. Another theory purports that the name comes from the Greek word *geos* (earth), because when the Greeks first came to Georgia they saw its inhabitants working the land. The classical world knew the people of eastern Georgia as Iberians, thus confusing the geographers of antiquity who thought this name applied only to the inhabitants of Spain.

TRIBES

Tracing the the origins of the Georgian nation proves as complex as considering the names by which this people has been known. Middle Paleolithic cave sites along the Black Sea coast of Abkhazia and Samegrelo indicate the presence of an indigenous people sometime between 100,000 and 40,000 BC. A greater quantity of archaeological evidence attests to a flourishing neolithic culture in the same area as well as in central and eastern Georgia in the fifth and fourth millennia BC. Early Bronze Age culture of the third millennium BC yields remains such as pottery, weapons, and domestic implements. These show the emergence of a distinctive Caucasian culture that had ties with other peoples of the Middle East. Georgian pottery of this period has been found in Syria and Palestine. The sophistication of metallurgy in Early Bronze Age Georgia was well known. Even The Bible makes mention of Tubal-cain, who is associated with a proto-Georgian tribe, as an "instructor of every artificer in brass and iron." (Genesis 4:22)

Toward the end of the third millennium BC an Indo-European people invading from the northern Caucasus and the Eurasian steppes introduced foreign elements to the relatively unified culture of the Early Bronze Age. This Maykop culture, also known as Kurgan, reveals its distinctive features through a vast array of gold, silver, and copper artifacts found in barrow burial shelters in the Kuban region of the Western Caucasus. Elements of this culture fused with those of indigenous groups to form the famous Bronze Age Trialeti culture of approximately 2100 BC, centered southwest of Tbilisi.

When the Sea Peoples who invaded Asia Minor from the Aegean and Mediterranean vanquished the Hittite Empire between 1200 and 1190 BC, various pre-Hittite people of Anatolia migrated northeast into the Caucasian isthmus. Forced to migrate not only by the "Sea Peoples" but also by the expansionist empire of the Assyrians in the south, these pre-Hittites merged with the indigenous populations to form the ethnic base from which the modern Georgians developed. Assyrian records tell us much about the many tribes of Transcaucasia and eastern Anatolia with which they came in contact. The Mushki tribe tried to take over land that formerly belonged to the Hittites and fought with the Assyrians. Upon their eventual defeat, one part of this tribe dispersed into southwestern Georgia to form the base of the present-day Meskhets. One of the Mushki kings, called Mita, is now thought to be none other than the famous King Midas of the golden touch. His wealth, however, didn't help him against the Cimmerian invaders who destroyed his empire (696–695 BC).

Another tribe associated with the Mushki (known as the Meshech in Ezekiel 38:1–4) are the Tubal, famous for their metalworking skills. This group settled in southwestern Georgia. The Greeks called this tribe the Tibareni, which may have given rise to the name Iberian, by which the classical world knew the eastern Georgians.

A tribe known to the Assyrians as the Daiaeni lived in the northeastern part of Anatolia, a region that was once part of Georgia. The Greeks called them the Taokhoi. The Georgians and Turks of today still refer to this region, which now belongs to present-day Turkey, as Tao. Many people there still speak Georgian.

The Colchians who lived in western Georgia are thought to be the Kilkhi mentioned in Assyrian inscriptions dating from the 12th century BC. They may have lived there since the Middle Bronze Age. It was in Colchis that Jason and his Argonauts found the Golden Fleece and sailed away with the Colchian princess and sorceress Medea. Strabo tells the legend of the Golden Fleece in his *Geography*, but the Medea legend is certainly older. In the *Odyssey,* Homer mentions both Jason and King Aeetes, who was Medea's father. Apollonius of Rhodes, in his *Argonautica* of the third century BC, describes the pre-Hellenic Colchis before the arrival of Greek colonists from Miletus in the seventh century BC. These colonists established many settlements along the Black Sea coast.

Beginning in 730 BC, the various tribal units inhabiting Caucasia came under attack from two nomadic warrior groups from the north. The Cimmerians migrated down the Black Sea coast and occupied Colchis. The Scythians crossed the Greater Caucasus along a route roughly equivalent to the present Georgian Military Highway into central Caucasia. From there they launched new campaigns south into Syria and Palestine and southwest into Phrygia. These invasions scattered some of the ancestral tribes of the Georgians into remoter mountainous regions and brought others under the protection of the Medes and Persians as subject peoples. Herodotus (484–420 BC) records taxes paid in silver by the Sasperoi, Moshkoi, Tibareni, and others to their Achaemenid rulers. He also mentions them as forming a part of Xerxes' army and describes their dress and weaponry. Yet by 400 BC the Achaemenid Persian Empire, weakened by dynastic infighting, no longer wielded much authority over the proto-Georgian tribes.

When Xenophon, as described in his *Anabasis*, marched toward the Black Sea with his thousands (401–399 BC), he encountered resistance from Colchians, Taochi, and other Georgian tribes who lived independently of any central authority and often in conflict with each other. By the time Alexander the Great crushed the Persians at Arbela in 331 BC, the Tibal (Tibareni) and Mushki had been established for many years in eastern Georgia in the Mtkvari (Kura) River valley. They had wrested this land from the Scythians and Cimmerians in hard-fought battles. Despite subsequent pressure from the new Armenian nation to the south—descendants of the people of the ancient state of Urartu—Tibal and Mushki tribes remained and merged with local tribes to form the peoples of Iberia.

GREECE AND ROME

Although Alexander the Great never invaded Georgia, Macedonian conquest extended across Asia Minor through Persia and Afghanistan to the borders of India. *The Georgian Chronicles (Kartlis Tskhovreba)*, the first national history, established the tradition that Alexander appointed Azon to be the administrator of the Mtskheta state (the name suggests a melding of this legend with that of Jason and the Argonauts). He ruled so harshly that the Georgians rose up against him under the leadership of Parnavazi, a descendant of Kartlos, supposedly the first Georgian. Parnavazi is credited with uniting the eastern Georgian kingdom of Kartli-Iberia and the western kingdom of Colchis-Egrisi to overthrow the hated Macedonian Azon. In so doing Parnavazi (estimated to reign from 299–234 BC) became the first king of Kartli-Iberia.

As part of the Kartli-Iberian kingdom, Colchis participated in the move from a purely agricultural economy to a partly commercial one. Greek goods brought to Colchis were transported over the Surami range to the Kura valley and across to the

Caspian Sea. There they were loaded on ships for Bactra, the town that was a transshipment point for the trade routes to China and India. Oriental wares came back the other way. Towards the end of the second century BC, however, Colchis-Egrisi drifted away from the Kartli-Iberian federation and came under the rule of the King of Pontus, Mithradates VI Eupator (111–63 BC). The Kingdom of Pontus, in northern Asia Minor, brought western Georgia more under the influence of the Hellenistic world, while eastern Georgia continued to have greater cultural ties with Persia.

This trend changed in 190 BC when the Romans, having extended their empire into eastern Anatolia, pushed forward into Persia and defeated the Seleucid King Antiochus III in the Battle of Magnesia. Armenia wasted no time in breaking away from the weakened Seleucid Empire to expand its own holdings, conquering parts of southern Georgia and later, in alliance with Mithradates VI, taking on the Romans and Persians to conquer Sophene. When in 66 BC Rome dispatched Pompey to deal with the situation in Transcaucasia, he also entered Iberia to fight the Georgians, who had allied themselves with the Armenians. Plutarch (c. AD 50–120) in his *Lives* describes the Iberians' defeat, after which all of Caucasia fell under Roman power.

Toward the end of the first century BC, however, Kartli-Iberia had sufficiently detached itself from Roman rule to be considered an ally rather than a subject state that had to pay taxes. While the Romans and the Parthians (the great Iranian dynasty of c. 240 BC–AD 226) fought over Armenia, the Georgians remained firmly allied with Rome for nearly three centuries of fighting. In AD 298, the Sassanids (the dynasty that overthrew the Parthians and ruled for another 400 years) signed the Peace of Nisibis with the Romans. This peace acknowledged Roman jurisdiction over both Kartli-Iberia and Armenia but recognized Mirian III (AD 284–361), the son of the King of Iran, as the king of eastern Georgia. With Mirian III began a new era, for he was the first ruler in Georgia to adopt Christianity.

CHRISTIAN GEORGIA

St. Nino of Cappadocia brought Christianity to Kartli-Iberia in AD 330. (Parts of western Georgia, primarily Greek colonies along the coast, were converted as early as the first century.) King Mirian's conversion strengthened the monarchy since it gave him a legitimate reason for suppressing the pagan priesthood, a class that had tremendous wealth and power at the time. Georgia's early acceptance of Christianity, however, had much greater implications: it meant an orientation toward Rome-Byzantium that would prove a decisive factor in the evolution of the national consciousness and culture.

By the middle of the fifth century AD, 30 bishops lived in Kartli-Iberia. King

Vakhtang Gorgasali further strengthened the Iberian Church by making it auto-cephalous (literally, self-headed), having secured permission from Constantinople to change the status of the bishop at Mtskheta to Catholicos. Mtskheta remains autocephalous and the seat of the bishop and the Georgian Orthodox Church to this day.

West Georgia in the sixth century was ruled by King Tsate of Lazica who, upon breaking his alliance with Iran, joined forces with the Byzantines. After his baptism, Christianity became the state religion in a territory that encompassed most of what had been ancient Colchis. Iran did not take their loss of influence in the region lightly, and when King Bakur III died in 580, the Iranians, who had been suppress-ing the monarchy since Vakhtang Gorgasali's death, now abolished it. Later the Byzantine Emperor Maurice restored it in 588 after his successful campaign against Iran in 582. Guaram became a reigning prince, not a king, and took the Byzantine title Curopalates. Guaram (588–602) and his heirs, Stepanoz I (602–627) and Stepanoz II (630–650) were caught in the middle as Iran and Byzantium struggled against each other for control of the region.

ARAB DOMINATION

The Arabs swept north through Iran after the death of Muhammad in 632. Under the caliphate of Omar (634–644), they defeated the Persians at Kadisiya in 637 and again at Nehawend in 641. They captured Tbilisi in 645 and installed an Arab emir there. Stepanoz II had no choice but to recognize the caliph as the ruler of Kartli-Iberia. The Arabs were not interested in colonizing eastern Georgia; instead they allowed Georgian princes to rule under the caliph's suzerainty. Georgian culture was able to flourish uninterrupted while the Arabs concentrated on trade, making Tbilisi thrive as an international center at the crossroads of several important trade routes.

At the beginning of the ninth century, the emir of Tbilisi was growing increas-ingly independent of his caliph. The caliph appointed Ashot I Bagrationi as prince of Kartli-Iberia to fight the rebellious emir. Ashot I (813–830) was ruler of the duchies in most of southern Georgia (Shida Kartli, Tao, Klarjeti, Samtskhe, Javakheti, Trialeti). He never succeeded in dislodging the powerful emir from Tbilisi but he did rule western Kartli-Iberia and the southern duchies, and was recognized as prince by the Byzantine Emperor Leo V. The Bagrationi dynasty ruled uninterrupted in Georgia for almost 1,000 years, finally ending with the Russian annexation of Kartli-Kakheti in 1801.

Early in the tenth century, Arab domination of eastern Georgia had weakened considerably and the Byzantine Empire was rapidly expanding. Although Bagrat III lost a portion of Tao to Byzantium's Emperor Basil II (972–1025), by 975 he had gained control of Shida Kartli, took over the Abkhazeti Kingdom in 976, and in 1008 Kartli-Iberia. He conquered Kakheti and Hereti in 1010. It is only with Bagrat III's reign that we are able to think about east and west Georgia as one entity. Georgia under Bagrat IV (1027–1072) became one of the major powers in Caucasia.

The relative stability established in the region through the gains of the Byzantines came to an end with the arrival of the Seljuk Turks, who moved out of Central Asia, captured most of Persia, and drove westward in the 1060s. They captured the Armenian capital of Ani in 1064, raided Javakheti and destroyed the town of Akhalkalaki in 1066, devastated Kartli in 1068, and crushed the Byzantine army at Mantzikert in 1071. King Bagrat IV died the year after the Byzantines were defeated and the reign passed to his son, Giorgi II (1072–1089). Giorgi II was unable to deal effectively with the constant onslaught of the Turks, and the throne was passed to his extraordinary 16-year-old son, David the Builder (1089–1125).

THE GOLDEN AGE

David's war against the Turks fortunately corresponded with the arrival of the Crusaders in Asia Minor and Syria. After winning several victories, he stopped paying tribute in 1096. He asserted the strength of the monarchy over those princes who would not submit to his authority. In 1105 he conquered Kakheti and annexed it to Georgia. He built up his army by adding 40,000 Kipchak mercenaries from the north Caucasian steppes, whom he settled in Georgia with their families. Between 1110 and 1122 he won many brilliant victories against the Turks, defeating them resoundingly on August 12, 1121, at the Battle of Didgori and capturing Tbilisi the following year. Humane treatment of the Moslem population in the capital set a standard for tolerance in his multi-ethnic kingdom that was a hallmark of his enlightened reign.

Using his military might, David extended Georgia's boundaries to include much of what is present-day Armenia and eastward to the Caspian Sea. He founded centers of learning at Gelati and Shiomghvime, and used the increased wealth and prestige of his monarchy to promote Georgian culture and political influence.

The 11th and 12th centuries were a Golden Age for Georgia, and the medieval monarchy reached its height under the reign of David the Builder's great-grand-daughter, Queen Tamara (1184–1212). A unique Georgian-Christian culture flourished between the reigns of David the Builder and Queen Tamara: this was the era of great building projects such as Gelati and Vardzia and the growth of a literary tradition revered to this day. It was to Queen Tamara that Shota Rustaveli dedicated his great epic poem, *The Knight in the Panther's Skin*, a poem which exemplifies all the virtues of chivalry and honor that were celebrated throughout the expanded Georgian kingdom in her reign.

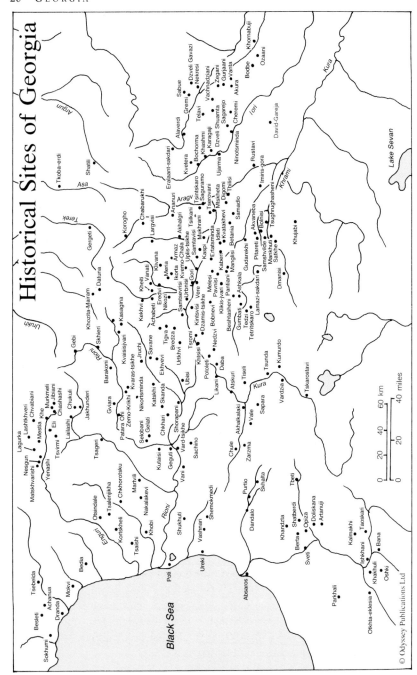

Historical Sites of Georgia

© Odyssey Publications Ltd

Queen Tamara left to her heir, Giorgi IV Lasha (1212–1223), a kingdom surrounded by tribute-paying states that filled the royal coffers to overflowing. King Giorgi was planning to join the Crusades to Palestine when he learned of the Mongol devastation of Armenia in 1220. Pushing north into Georgia, the Mongols were inexorable and even King Giorgi's 90,000 horsemen were no match for them. Giorgi Lasha himself died in battle against the Mongols in 1223. The Mongols invaded Georgia a third time in 1236, driving Queen Rusudan, Giorgi's sister, out of Tbilisi to take refuge in Kutaisi. The Mongols dominated Georgia for more than a century, splintering the Kingdom and sapping it through heavy taxation.

Only in the 14th century was there any relief from Mongol rule. Giorgi V (1314–1346), known as "the Brilliant," took advantage of his position as loyal vassal to a weakened il-Khan to rule over Georgia. Later when the il-Khan was assassinated, he stopped paying tribute and drove the Mongols out. He pursued a policy which led to a strengthened monarchy and the reclaiming of territory, conquering Samtskhe in 1334. He left his heirs, David VII (1346–1360) and Bagrat V (1360–1395), with a revitalized and expanded kingdom.

Tamerlane (1336–1405), the Mongol conquerer, invaded Georgia eight times. The first of Tamerlane's invasions occurred in 1386 and, following upon the horror of the Black Death that decimated Georgia in 1366, destroyed any hopes for a second Golden Age that Giorgi V's successors might have initiated. Tamerlane destroyed Tbilisi during his first incursion into Georgia and captured King Bagrat V in the process.

In 1453 the Ottoman Turks captured Constantinople, a development which, along with a change of trade routes from Europe to the Far East, seriously weakened Georgia economically. At the end of the 15th century, the rise of the Safavid Persians further threatened Georgia, which now found itself caught once more between two expanding empires.

During the 16th century the encroachment continued as the Persians under Shah Tahmasp invaded Georgia four times from 1541–1544. In 1548 the Safavids captured Tbilisi for the second time. Only Kakheti prospered during this century, thanks to the silk route to Astrakhan which passed through bazaar towns such as Gremi and Telavi. The Peace of Amasia in 1555 between the Ottoman Turks and the Safavid Persians divided Georgia into spheres of influence, giving the west to the Turks and the east to the Persians. For the next 250 years the kings of Kartli ruled only through the will of the Persian shahs. Many Georgian leaders tried to free the country from Persian rule, but to no avail. The defection of King Teimuraz I in Kakheti in the early 17th century brought terrible retribution from Shah Abbas in 1615 when he killed more than 60,000 Kakhetians and deported more than 100,000 to Iran.

Not until the 18th century were the father and son Bagrationi rulers, King Teimuraz II and Herekle II, able to rebuild Georgia in its own, and not Iran's, image. Surmounting numerous obstacles in the form of rebellious Georgian princes, raiding parties from the north Caucasus, and Moslem khans of east Caucasia, father and son ruled from 1744 to 1762 over Kartli and Kakheti respectively. Upon the death of Teimuraz II, Herekle II ruled a united Kartli-Kakheti from 1762 to 1798, during which time he forged the nucleus of a nascent Georgian Empire.

Convinced that his isolated Christian kingdom could not hold out indefinitely against its array of Moslem enemies, Herekle II forged an alliance with Catherine the Great of Russia. King Solomon II of Imereti, beleagured by constant Turkish incursions, also wanted to secure the help of his coreligionists to the north. On July 24, 1783, the Treaty of Georgievsk was signed by representatives of King Herekle and Catherine the Great, making Kartli-Kakheti a protectorate of the Russian Empire. Russia abrogated the conditions of that treaty when Catherine withdrew her troops from Georgia at the outbreak of the second Russo-Turkish War in 1787. King Herekle was forced to face a vastly superior force led by Shah Agha Mohammed Khan when the Persians invaded Kartli-Kakheti in 1795. Were it not for the 300 warriors of the Aragvi (*see* pages 106 and 295), King Herekle himself would have been captured. He managed to escape to Kakheti, where he died in 1798. Tbilisi, however, fared less well. Shah Agha Mohammed Khan burned it to the ground and killed more than 50,000 of its citizens.

King Herekle's son Giorgi XII (1798–1800) wanted, under certain conditions, to incorporate Georgia into the Russian Empire. Thus on December 18, 1800, Tsar Paul I annexed Georgia to Russia. Giorgi XII, the last of the Bagrationi kings, conveniently died that same year. In 1801, Tsar Paul's son and heir Tsar Alexander I (1801–1825) simply abolished the Kingdom of Kartli-Kakheti without even consulting Georgian representatives in St. Petersburg. The act was one of national humiliation for Georgia. After securing Kartli-Kakheti, the Russians incorporated the western provinces into their Empire: Samegrelo in 1803 and Imereti in 1804. King Solomon II signed an act of allegiance to Russia but was forced to abdicate his throne in 1810. During the Russo-Turkish War of 1806–1812, the Russians claimed Poti, Sokhumi, and Akhalkalaki. And in 1809 Abkhazeti's Prince Safar bey Sharvashidze left the Ottoman fold to receive Russian protection. In 1811 Guria became part of the Russian Empire.

GEORGIA UNDER THE TSAR
The agreement with the Russians left Georgian social and religious structures intact: the Georgian Church would retain its autocephalous nature, and the nobility its rank, possessions, and rights. Despite these initial guarantees, the Russian

government was determined to change the distinctive nature of the Georgian feudal system and make Georgia function according to the Russian social and administrative model. Military governors such as Generals Knorring, Tsitsianov, Ermolov, and Paskevich, along with latter-day viceroys such as Vorontsov, were sent to Tbilisi (called Tiflis by the Russians) to oversee the transformation. The Georgian Church lost its autonomy when the office of the Catholicos-patriarch was abolished in the east in 1811 and in the west in 1814. Ranks of nobility had to be proven and later their rights were redefined. New systems of taxation were instituted. Russian schooling and culture was introduced to Tiflis. All this did not occur without protest and, in some cases, outright revolt. By the end of the first half of the 19th century Georgia had been integrated into the Russian system.

The second half of the century saw the abolition of serfdom in Georgia (1864) and an ever-increasing Russification policy that touched every aspect of Georgian society. In reaction to the latter, one group of Georgian intellectuals, including Alexander Chavchavadze (1786–1846) and Grigol Orbeliani (1800–1883), plotted to break free. The conspiracy of 1832 ended in their arrest, but upon their later release the two led a romantic school of literature that concerned itself largely with the loss of Georgia's former glory. Ilya Chavchavadze (1837–1907) and Akaki Tsereteli (1840–1915), known as the "Men of the '60s," came back from Russian universities with a new spirit of social activism and democratic idealism that was reflected in their writing.

In the 1890s a second group of Georgian intellectuals returned to their homeland, having imbibed the new doctrine of Marxism while studying abroad. They were called the *tergdaleulni*, those who had drunk from the river Terek, which is to say, studied in Russia beyond the Terek River. One of these young men, Noe Zhordania (1868–1953), led the Georgian Social Democratic Movement in the years leading up to the Russian Revolution in 1917. In that year the Georgian Social Democrats, under Zhordania's leadership, took control of the Soviet in Tiflis, occupying the palace left by the last viceroy. The coalition of Mensheviks and Bolsheviks that, among other parties, formed the Social Democratic Movement, was unable to sustain a common platform because of their differing agendas and ideas regarding the future of Georgia. In June of 1917, the Bolsheviks, on Lenin's insistence, split from the Georgian Mensheviks. On May 26, 1918, the Menshevik government of Noe Zhordania raised the new national flag of Georgia over the Soviet and declared Georgia an independent state. Thus ended Georgia's 117-year official relationship with Russia.

Menshevik Georgia followed a moderate path between 1917 and 1920. Successfully avoiding the civil war that was being waged in Russia, it followed a system of land reform that allowed for more equitable distribution without depriving the nobility of its holdings. The Bolsheviks agitated among the peasantry and workers against the Menshevik "bourgeois" path and demanded an end to capitalism. In 1918, the Bolsheviks went underground to organize the overthrow of the Social Democratic state led by Zhordania. On April 28, 1920, the Red Army marched into Baku and proclaimed the creation of the Soviet Republic of Azerbaijan. The treaty of May 7, 1920, in which Soviet Russia and Social Democratic Georgia recognized each other's sovereignty, was broken on February 14, 1921, when the 11th Red Army crossed from Azerbaijan into Georgia. On February 25 they were in Tiflis driving the Menshevik government of Zhordania to Batumi. Three weeks later Noe Zhordania was forced to sail for France. The dream of a democratic, independent Georgia was short-lived. Georgia had been annexed by Bolshevik Russia.

Communist hegemony in Georgia brought this beleagured nation once more within the realm of foreign power. Between 1922 and 1936 Georgia was part of a single Transcaucasian republic. In 1936, it became one of the 15 republics of the Soviet Union. Despite the fact that Stalin and his chief of the secret police, Lavrenty Beria, were both Georgians, as were many prominent Bolsheviks, the Georgian people were given no reprieve under his repressive regime. In 1924, more than 5,000 were executed in retaliation for an attempted revolt led by the Georgian Mensheviks. The years 1936–1937 were particularly harsh, and many writers, scientists, and other intellectuals were purged, including the famous Georgian Symbolist poet, Titian Tabidze.

In October 1990, the first full-scale, multi-party elections since the 1920s were held in Georgia. The Communist Party leadership was voted out and the Roundtable Alliance led by Zviad Gamsakhurdia (son of the novelist Konstantine Gamsakhurdia) was voted in. Their platform called for the restoration of Georgia's independence as soon as possible. This motion was approved unanimously by the Georgian parliament on April 9, 1991.

GEORGIAN INDEPENDENCE

Georgian independence was not won without great struggle nor has it been sustained without enormous challenges. Zviad Gamsakhurdia was elected president in May 1991. He proved to be a more effective dissident, promoting the cause of Georgian rights and liberty under Soviet rule, than he was president of a sovereign country. His nationalistic agenda was perhaps not wholly incomprehensible in light of Georgia's newly found freedom and in reaction to the years of Soviet domination, but it frightened minority populations within the country who felt their rights could be abrogated.

Gamsakhurdia's policies created many problems between different social groups within Georgian society, as well as between different regions and cities. His initial rhetoric of "Georgia for the Georgians" was particularly inflammatory to certain national minorities, but these initial fires were certainly fanned by Moscow in the hopes of derailing Georgia's move to independence. The fact that Georgia's relations remained stable, with national minorities such as Russians, Azeris, Greeks, Jews, and Armenians living in Georgia, supports the belief that ethnic conflicts unfolding were not wholly a result of Georgian policy, nor of the Georgian mindset.

Most political analysts agree that the conflicts that arose in Abkhazia and South Ossetia were preprogrammed in Moscow as part of a plan to destabilize the country through ethnic infighting, and that these conflicts would have occurred regardless of the positions taken by Gamsakhurdia. The intensity of the Abkhazian and South Ossetian secessionist rumblings, fueled and abetted by Moscow, grew in 1989, culminating in horrible violence in the ensuing years. In the case of the former South Ossetia, the situation developed into full-scale civil war in 1990 and 1991, after which time the government in Tbilisi lost control of the region. The Abkhazian War, which will be discussed in greater detail later, exploded in 1992 and resulted in Georgia's loss of the territory in 1993.

Gamsakhurdia's miscalculations and Moscow's policies were devastating to the social fabric of the country, but political infighting was equally destructive. The variety of theories about why things unfolded as they did is mind-boggling, ranging from accusations that Gamsakhurdia was a KGB agent, to the belief that opposition to the legitimate government was sour grapes on the part of the former political elite. Whatever the truth, the result was civil war, called the Tbilisi War, which took place in the heart of the capital from December 21, 1991, until January 6, 1992. Led by Tengiz Sigua, the former Georgian prime minister, and Tengiz Kitovani, the head of the National Guard, the forces of this Military Council succeeded in dislodging Gamsakhurdia and his followers from power and forcing them to flee first to Armenia and later to Chechnya. The Military Council now found itself in the embarrassing position of having participated in a military coup against a president who, despite the fact that he might have been showing certain authoritarian predelictions, was nonetheless democratically elected. Clearly no government or international organization was likely to recognize the Military Council's legitimacy. Their solution was to invite Georgia's most recognized son to head the government. In March 1992 Eduard Shevardnadze, the former Minister of Foreign Affairs of the USSR, returned to Georgia to lead the State Council. Under his leadership, Georgia joined the United Nations and the country's independence was recognized internationally. In October 1992 Shevardnadze was elected chairman of the new parliament, which was followed by his election as Head of State. Georgia's democratic credentials had been restored.

But Georgia's problems were just beginning. In August 1992 Tengiz Kitovani, following Shevardnadze's orders, led a detachment of Georgian troops toward Abkhazia. He had the dual mission of securing the railway line to Samtredia that had been frequently attacked by Gamsakhurdia supporters acting as saboteurs, and of freeing the interior minister and other hostages whom Gamsakhurdia's forces had captured and reportedly spirited away to Abkhazia. When Georgian troops were fired upon by Abkhazian militia, Kitovani's troops marched into Sokhumi and the Abkhazian leadership fled to Gudauta. This action against Shevardnadze's orders led to civil war on August 14. There is still much controversy surrounding the events that precipitated this war. Some say that the leader of Abkhazia, Vladislav Ardzinba, had given the Georgians the right to pursue Gamsakhurdia's forces into Abkhazia. Others point out that the fighting between Gamsakhurdia supporters, the so-called Zviadists, and Shevardnadze's government suited the secessionist ambitions of Ardzinba perfectly, and that his ability to claim a violation of Abkhazia's self-proclaimed territorial integrity was part of a master plan.

Regardless of the behind-the-scenes reality, the result was full-scale war and the biggest tragedy to affect the Georgian people in recent history. The war pitted a people, the Abkhazians, who comprised only 1.8 percent of the entire population and less than 18 percent of the population in their own region, against the rest of the country, albeit a country already divided by the fighting going on between Gamsakhurdia's forces and those of Shevardnadze's government. Over the next year the Abkhazian forces assisted by Chechen coreligionists, other North Caucasian peoples, and most importantly the Russian military, fought a brutal war. Their successes culminated in the bombardment and siege of Sokhumi in September 1993.

While the Russian military and mercenaries from CIS countries fought in the trenches, the Russian government brokered two peace initiatives in September 1992 and July 1993. These negotiations called for both sides to disarm. While the Georgians abided by the terms, the Abkhazian troops used the opportunity to rearm. Most analysts of the war agree this factor was decisive in Abkhazia's success. On September 27, the Georgians were driven from Abkhazia, triggering the exodus of more than 250,000 refugees from the region. Charges of ethnic cleansing have been leveled against both sides. Retreating across the Enguri River into Samegrelo, the Georgian Army was attacked by Gamsakhurdia's forces. Gamsakhurdia had never committed his forces to helping his fellow Georgians fight in Abkhazia, and he chose this moment to try to recapture power. His forces were very close to capturing both Poti and Kutaisi when Shevardnadze made a last-ditch deal with Russia. In exchange for arms and other military assistance to fight Gamsakhurdia, Georgia would join the Commonwealth of Independent States (CIS) and the Russian military would be allowed bases on Georgian soil. This strategy, though unpopular at the time, gave Shevardnadze what he needed to defeat Gamsakhurdia, who either committed suicide or was killed in the mountains of Samegrelo on December 31, 1993. Shevardnadze's partial accommodation of Russian demands paved the way for a Russian peacekeeping force to operate along the Enguri River, between Abkhazia and western Georgia; its presence was meant to deter fighting and return refugees, especially to the Gali region. At the time of this writing, there are approximately 1,500 Russian peacekeepers operating under a CIS flag, but only a negligible number of refugees has returned.

The years between the loss of Abkhazia in September 1993 and the ratification of a new Georgian constitution in August 1995 were extremely difficult ones. The economy was at an all-time low and crime had reached near-anarchic proportions, with members of the various irregular units that had been formed to fight the war now terrorizing the countryside and streets of Tbilisi with automatic weapons. A failed assassination attempt on Shevardnadze in August 1995, as he was on his way to sign the new constitution, served as a galvinizing force that enabled him to deal with his political opposition, arresting Godfather-type figures like Jaba Ioseliani whose paramilitary group, Mkhedrioni, was thought to be responsible for much of the country's violence and corruption. In November 1995, Eduard Shevardnadze was elected president, garnering more than 70 percent of the vote.

In his ensuing years in office he has tried to rebuild the country by attracting foreign investment; cracking down on corruption; building a new generation of Western-oriented diplomats; positioning the country to reap the benefits of its strategic position at the crossroads of Europe and Asia; and securing loans from the World Bank, the International Monetary Fund and other international financial institutions. Just as the old Silk Road brought prosperity to Georgia as trade crossed its borders before moving across Central Asia to China, so can the much-discussed new Silk Road create the same favorable economic conditions. With the development of Caspian oil—a projected yield of 68 billion barrels—Azerbaijan is poised to become another Kuwait. The existing Baku-Batumi pipeline for early oil, as well as the likelihood of other transshipment arrangements, should all bring new sources of revenue to Georgia and wealth to the region.

At present, the plight of refugees and a solution to the situation in Abkhazia are foremost in people's minds. The government has achieved some notable victories on this front, most importantly Resolution 1096, adopted by the United Nations Security Council in 1997, wherein the following was resolved: "3. Reaffirms its commitment to the sovereignty and territorial integrity of Georgia, within its internationally recognized borders, and to the necessity of defining the status of Abkhazia in strict accordance with these principles, and underlies the unacceptability of any action by the Abkhaz leadership in contravention of these principles, in particular the holding on November 23, 1996, and December 7, 1996, of illegitimate and self-styled parliamentary elections in Abkhazia, Georgia. . . . And 8. Reaffirms the right of all refugees and displaced persons affected by the conflict to return to their homes in secure conditions in accordance with international law, and as set out in the Quadripartite Agreement of April 4, 1994 on voluntary return of refugees and displaced persons and condemns the continued obstruction of that return and stresses the unacceptability of any linkage of the return of refugees and displaced persons with the question of the political status of Abkhazia, Georgia."

Religion

Tradition has it that Christianity came to Georgia between AD 325 and 330 when St. Nino, a holy woman from Cappadocia, cured the Iberian Queen Nana of a strange illness, thus gaining her confidence. Nana's husband, King Mirian, was subsequently converted during a hunting trip when, suddenly enveloped in darkness, he called upon the Christian God, who restored the light. Numerous other legends mark this period. One concerns the erection of a church in the city of Mtskheta during which the central pillar of the church, too large to be raised by human means, suddenly levitated and landed in place by divine intervention. The distinctive shape of the Georgian Orthodox cross is also ascribed to St. Nino, who, upon entering Georgia, took two vine branches and tied them into a cross with strands of her own hair.

The advent of Christianity in Georgia replaced existing pagan beliefs which were based largely upon the pantheon of Greek gods (in west Georgia) and Iranian Zoroastrian beliefs in the east. Both of these had been combined with various Anatolian (probably Hurrian) cults whose followers included proto-Georgian tribes. The effect of Georgia's conversion to Christianity cannot be overestimated, for it turned the country toward the West and the centers of Orthodox Christian belief and away from the Mazdaism of Iran and the Islam of the Arab world.

At the end of the fifth century, King Vakhtang Gorgasali elevated the bishop of Mtskheta to Catholicos, thus making the Iberian Church autocephalous. Until the seventh century, the Iberian Church swung back and forth between supporting monophysitism and dyophysitism (differing doctrinal positions concerning the divine and human nature of Jesus Christ that arose out of the the Council of Chalcedon in 451). By 609 the Iberian Church definitively sided with the Chalcedonian position and became dyophysite, as opposed to the Armenian Church, which has remained monophysite.

When Russia annexed Georgia at the beginning of the 19th century, the Georgian church temporarily lost its independence, the position of Catholicos-patriarch was abolished, and the administration of the Church fell under the authority of the Russian Orthodox church. In 1917 the autocephalous nature of the church was reestablished and a new Catholicos-patriarch was selected. During the 1917–1920 civil war, the church supported the legitimate Menshevik government of Noe Zhordania. With the Bolshevik victory, the church was forced to take a position of loyalty to the Soviet government, and in 1943, after Stalin's intervention, the Russian Orthodox church recognized the autocephalous status of the Georgian Orthodox Church once again.

Like all religions throughout the Soviet Union prior to Gorbachev's reforms, the Georgian Church was supressed and many church buildings were destroyed or turned into museums or concert halls. As a national church, Georgian Orthodoxy has been a powerful rallying point for patriotic yearnings. In 1988, as a result of the new policies of the Kremlin toward religion, the present Catholicos, Ilya II, headquarted near Sioni Cathedral in Tbilisi, began consecrating formerly closed church buildings throughout Georgia. The Georgian Church has been very active in the restoration of these places of worship.

The Georgian Orthodox Church is also an important force in both the spiritual and temporal life of the country. Long concerned about some of the headway that proselytizing "Western Protestant" religions have been making in the country, and responding to growing pressure from concerned priests within his own church, in May 1997 Catholicos-Patriarch Ilya II withdrew his church from two major ecumenical bodies: the World Council of Churches and the Conference of European Churches.

Despite this recent move on the clergy's part, Georgians have always been highly tolerant of other peoples and religions. Tbilisi boasts a Christian cathedral, a mosque, and a synagogue all within walking distance of each other. Jewish communities exist throughout Georgia, especially in the cities of Kutaisi and Tbilisi. However, the war in Abkhazia and the ensuing economic problems have pressured many Jews into emigrating to Israel.

In the autonomous republics of Ajara and Abkhazia, many people follow Islam, having converted during Turkish dominion over these territories. Communities of Moslem Azeris also live in Georgia..

Armenians also comprise part of Georgia's ethnic make-up. Their church is also autocephalous and varies in points of doctrine and ritual from the Georgian Orthodox Church.

Children from the village of Sno on the Georgian Military Highway

People

ETHNIC GROUPS

Georgia has a population of 5.4 million, of which Georgians make up about 70 percent. More than 80 other nationalities make up the balance, including Armenians (8.1 percent), Russians (6.3 percent), Azeris (5.7 percent), Ossetes (3 percent), Greeks (1.9 percent), Abkhazians (1.8 percent), Jews (0.5 percent), and miscellaneous (2.6 percent).

Two minorities (the Abkhazians and the Ajars) have their own autonomous republics within the Georgian Republic. The Ajars, whose capital Batumi lies along the southern coast of the Black Sea bordering Turkey, are Georgians, some of whom are Moslems. The exact ethnic makeup and origins of the Abkhazians remains a hotly debated political issue. Most scholars trace the Abkhazians' ancestry back at least two millennia in Georgia. Abkhazians are a minority within Abkhazia, forming less than 20 percent of the population. At the time of Georgian independence, after a bitterly fought year-long war, Abkhazian separatists became increasingly vocal in their desire to have Abkhazia become a part of Russia. In September 1993, Abkhazian rebels captured the city of Sokhumi, compelling the Georgians to surrender the entire Abkhaz Autonomous Republic and forcing more than 250,000 Georgian refugees to flee the Abkhaz region.

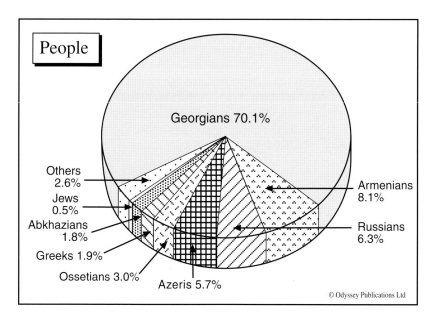

People

Georgians 70.1%

Others 2.6%

Jews 0.5%

Abkhazians 1.8%

Greeks 1.9%

Ossetians 3.0%

Azeris 5.7%

Armenians 8.1%

Russians 6.3%

© Odyssey Publications Ltd

The Ossetes, thought to be descended from the Alans and speaking an Iranian language, live in their own autonomous region. Some Ossetes also have nationalist ambitions and want to secede from Georgia. Georgians maintain that what is called the South Ossetian Autonomous Region is and has always been part of Shida Kartli (Inner Kartli). The Georgians maintain that the region was created by Stalin and the Bolsheviks in 1922 as part of a divide-and-rule policy in Georgia. On December 11, 1990, in reaction to a declaration by the Ossetian separatist movement to secede from Georgia, the Supreme Council of Georgia unanimously abolished the South Ossetian Autonomous Region as a political and administrative unit. (*See* page 138 for more information about this complicated conflict). The Ossetes' capital is Tskhinvali.

Others recently in the news are the Turks and Moslem Georgians who used to live in Meskheti, whom Stalin deported to Uzbekistan in 1945. Known as the Meskhets, they now want to return. Many Georgians are opposed to this because the region is now occupied by Armenians and Georgians and the potential for ethnic conflict would be enormous. (*See* page 256 for more information on the Meskhets).

THE GEORGIAN CHARACTER

Georgians are among the most hospitable people on Earth, with strong traditions of chivalry and codes of personal honor. Friendship is the greatest virtue. It is celebrated in Shota Rustaveli's national epic, *The Knight in the Panther's Skin*, in which a person's worth is judged not by wordly goods, but by the number of friends

(top) *Three young members of a Georgian dance troupe in Kutaisi*
(bottom) *Singers from a famous choir of centenarians*

he has. The Georgians are proud, passionate, and fiercely individualistic, yet deeply connected with each other through a shared sense of belonging to a greater Georgian family. Women are highly esteemed and are accorded a respect that is endowed with great courtliness. The statue of Mother Georgia (*Kartlis Deda*) that stands overlooking Tbilisi perhaps best symbolizes the national character: in her left hand she holds a bowl of wine with which she greets her friends, and in her right is a sword drawn against her enemies.

GEORGIAN CENTENARIANS

A television campaign in America for Dannon yogurt extolled the virtues of the product by attributing Georgian longevity to eating yogurt. Perhaps Madison Avenue didn't tell all, yet the centenarians in Georgia present a fascinating medical phenomenon that has attracted worldwide interest. In Tbilisi alone there are almost 100 people who are over 100 years old. The country as a whole claims 51 centenarians for every 100,000 inhabitants. Until the recent war in Abkhazia, longevity in that autonomous republic was particularly high. Indeed, the republic once sponsored a choir of centenarians that performed throughout Georgia (*see* page 236).

Before Georgia's recent travails, the reasons for longevity could, perhaps, have been the cuisine and the pristine countryside. These made life worth living and living . . . and living. Whether this phenomenon will continue, however, remains to be seen, particularly considering the heavy cigarette smoking to which so many are addicted and their kamikaze tendencies behind the wheel.

Art and Architecture

Georgian architecture must be regarded as the supreme expression of the nation's artistic vision and heritage. It is a direct result of the Georgians' affinity for and skill with stone. Certain edicts of Eastern Orthodoxy inhibited sculptural representation; but this did not restrict architechtural expression. The process further evolved from the people's need to build and rebuild monuments to their nation and their faith, following ceaseless incursions by conquerors. Whatever the underlying reason for such a magnificent 1,300-year tradition, the degree of artistry and creativity that gave birth to these treasures is awe-inspiring. The vagaries of fate, or perhaps the conscious will of some divine power, have left us many times more ecclesiastical buildings than secular ones by which to trace the flourishing of

Charming and fanciful animal reliefs adorn
the façades of many medieval Georgian churches

Pirosmani's painting Donkey Bridge from the Museum of Georgian Art

Georgian architectural genius. Every indication suggests, however, that secular and ecclesiastical buildings sprang from the same native roots and share many features.

Well into this century, Georgian art and architecture were often classified as Byzantine or derivative of the Armenian tradition. Although such classifications are now generally held to be erroneous, debate continues. Most Georgian scholars now claim that the bias toward Byzantium stems from a lack of sophistication on the part of Western travelers and scholars in the 19th century, who were unaware of the significance of certain key Georgian prototypical structures.

Scholars generally agree that the famous cupola structures that dominate Georgian ecclesiastical architecture can be traced to domestic dwellings with circular floor plans that date back to the fourth millennium BC. These dwellings ultimately evolved into the *darbazi* structures that have survived into modern times. Their significance lay in the transition of the square substructure into a beehive dome (*see* page 97). Ultimately, two major forms of ecclesiastical building developed in Georgia: the central domed structure and the basilica.

The basilica form came to Georgia primarily through the influence of the Roman and Hellenistic worlds. Its reformulation in Georgia blended Syrian influences with local traditions of construction found in prefeudal secular structures: markets, courtly halls, and audience chambers. The basilica itself has two forms in Georgia. The three-aisled basilica has no transept and is shaped like a hall, with middle and side naves of the same height covered by a common gabled ceiling. The only surviving example is the Sioni Basilica at Bolnisi. Variations on this style that are contemporary with Bolnisi or from a later date do exist but in a less pure form (see Anchiskhati, page 113, and Urbnisi, page 125). A second form of basilica, which evolved in the late sixth century and exists only in Georgia, is the triple-church basilica. It, too, has no transept, but—unlike the three-aisled basilica in which side naves are linked to the central nave by arcades—the side naves are shut off from the central aisle by walls, with access only through doors. Although all three aisles are barrel-vaulted, they are cut off from one another, creating three "separate" churches. In addition, the middle room is two or three times higher and wider than the side rooms. Kvemo Bolnisi is an excellent sixth-century example (see page 153); and a more sophisticated version can be seen at Nekresi which dates to the seventh century (see page 302).

Central domed churches appeared in Georgia in the early feudal period and evolved into many complex variations. By the fifth century they had already achieved a clearly individualized profile. Devoid of a dominant main axis, the central section is either square or hexagonal (later types such as the cross-cupola churches developed from these). The substructure acted as the base upon which the drum and ultimately the cupola rested. The transition from the room shape to the circular drum was achieved through the use of squinches, small arches that grow wider as they project in concentric arches across the interior corners of a square or polygonal room. In Georgia this technology reached a high degree of sophistication early on. The pendentive, which came to certain parts of Asia through the Greeks, was not used in Georgia until the ninth century. A pendentive is a kind of spandrel or triangular area at the corners of a square or polygonal room used to achieve the same effect as the squinch.

Variations on the central domed church appeared in the sixth and seventh centuries. "Free-cross" churches are cruciform in plan. At Idleti and Samtsevrisi the north, south, and west sections of the cruciform end in a quadrate with the eastern apse ending in a horseshoe. Another variation, also developed in the sixth century and extended in subsequent centuries into highly diverse formulations, was the tetraconch configuration (imagine a square surrounded by a clover leaf). The sixth-century Church of Dzveli-Gavazi is an early example. The Cathedral of Ninotsminda (sixth century) is the earliest surviving large centralized ecclesiastical building (see page 279).

The turn of the seventh century ushered in an epoch of extraordinary architectural achievement as the early tentative forms with which Georgian architects struggled to achieve their vision found harmonious completion. The tetraconch Church of Jvari is perhaps the shining example of this artistic triumph (*see* page 161). Original in design and conception, it soon became a model for many other architects. Ateni Sioni, Dzveli Shuamta, Martvili, and Dranda are all churches based on the Jvari type.

Although the second half of the seventh century saw the Arab invasion of Georgia, the foundation had already been laid for further expression of a decidedly Georgian aesthetic tradition. The Arab incursion affected the economic life of the population far more than the arts. Georgian architects moved away from city centers to work for individual rulers in the countryside. They thus felt free of the constraints of the classical rules that had governed previous building. As such, the eighth and ninth centuries were an interesting transitional period, a time of experimentation in which certain hybrid forms were achieved, such as the fusion of the central domed church and the triple-church basilica. The most notable surviving monuments of this kind are the Church of Vachnadziani and the double-domed Church of Kvelatsminda at Gurjaani (see page 298). These buildings served as important stepping-stones to the triumphs in grand-scale building that were to come in architecture's greatest period between the tenth and the 13th centuries.

In this epoch no single structural element came to dominate in a way that deflected an appreciation of the whole by absorption with details. The pendentive replaced the squinch as the means of choice for making the transition from the square substructure to the drum. The consequent increase in fluidity largely eliminated any vestiges of ponderousness that might have been felt in the interior. Exterior ornamentation reached a supreme level of artistic confidence. Fanciful use of a wide variety of decorative motifs—animal, vegetal, and geometric—worked in conjunction with architectonic devices to render a harmonious and powerful organic totality.

The Golden Age of Georgian culture came to an abrupt end in the 1240s with the Mongol invasion. The most important buildings erected under Mongol domination occurred in the province of Samtskhe under the rule of the Jakeli family. Through clever political stratagems, the clan leader, Sargis Jakeli, managed to stay on the right side of the Mongol khan, thereby managing to found the large domed Church of Zarzma in the early 1300s. This structure and a very similar church at Sapara are throwbacks to models from 100 years earlier, as was the case with structures going up in other provinces throughout Georgia at this time. As a rule, the particular brand of Georgian creativity that had flourished from the tenth to the early 13th centuries was in decline.

Despite many attempts by Georgia to throw off foreign dominance, Iranian influence was the strongest new element in Georgian architecture from the end of the 15th through the 17th centuries. Brick became the building material of choice, rather than stone, and the arrangement of bricks into patterns is distinctly Islamic, although the Georgians adapted the technique to serve their own Christian iconography. The province of Kakheti possesses the greatest number of excellent examples of Islam-influenced architecture. The Citadel of Gremi and the belltower of Ninotsminda (*see* pages 281and 301) show how Georgians interpreted the Persian style.

When Georgia was incorporated into the Russian Empire in the 19th century, Russian neoclassicism came to Tbilisi with a missionary fury. (The three-story belltower across from Sioni Cathedral, erected in 1812, is the oldest example.) Georgian culture was too strong, however, not to influence the Russian strict notions of classical order. Seduced by the charms of the Caucasus, the Russians' desire to impose a foreign aesthetic faltered: the resulting hybrids found in Tbilisi are one of the principal architectural joys of that city.

During the 20th century, Georgia did not escape the self-aggrandizing stone piles that marked the Stalinist era. Many municipal and state buildings were constructed in the 1950s to cow an already sorely tried populace into fearing the power of government. Although a tour of Georgia's outstanding contemporary buildings would not take up much time, one building, the Ministry for Highways in Tbilisi (*see* page 135) demonstrates that architectural creativity is alive and well in the land.

LITERATURE

In antiquity the Georgian oral tradition abounded in ballads, songs, legends, and proverbs. The legend of Amirani has come down to us through Apollonius of Rhodes, who makes reference to it in the third century BC.

After the development of writing, folk poetry flourished in Georgia. The earliest epigraphic monuments that have survived date from the first half of the fifth century AD. These literary examples are so highly developed that the existence of precursors cannot be doubted.

In the 470s, Jacob Tsurtaveli wrote *The Martyrdom of Saint Shushanik*, an original hagiographic work that demonstrates by its literary standards a pre-Christian writing tradition. Georgian literature over the next six centuries was exclusively religious in character, with writers primarily involved with translating biblical and scriptural texts into Georgian.

The 12th century is the classical period of Georgian medieval literature. *Amiran-Darejaniani*, ascribed to Mose Kheneli, is an adventure of derring-do and chivalrous acts that has its roots in the early folk tales surrounding Amirani. Much of this secular literature shares similarities with Moslem literature of the time. Tales written in Persian were recast in Georgian, most importantly *Shahname* by Firdausi and *Vis-o-Ramin* by Gurgani; the latter's plot is very similar to that of *Tristan and Isolde*.

Many of the best writers of the 12th century belonged to the courts of the Georgian kings, notably Shota Rustaveli, the most celebrated figure of Georgian culture. His major work, *The Knight in the Panther's Skin*, is regarded as the national epic.

The plot of the poem is long and complicated. An old Arabian king, Rostevan, has crowned his daughter, the wise and beautiful Tinatin, as regent. Tinatin is in love with Avtandil, the commander-in-chief of her father's army. One day when Avtandil and Rostevan are hunting they see a knight wrapped in a panther's skin, weeping inconsolably by a stream. Their repeated attempts to speak to him are unsuccessful, and eventually the knight vanishes. Rostevan takes this very badly so Tinatin commissions her champion, Avtandil, to find the mysterious knight at any cost. Avtandil readily accepts the will of his lady and after much hardship discovers the knight Tariel. Tariel tells his story: he is a prince and military leader to the King of India, Parsadan. Tariel is in love with Parsadan's daughter, Nestan-Darejan. The king, however, is determined to marry his daughter to the son of the King of Khwarazm, who would then succeed him to the throne. Nestan-Darejan persuades her lover, Tariel, to murder his rival and take power. Whereas he succeeds in the first, he fails in the second. Nestan-Darejan is severely punished for her love of Tariel and is spirited away from India. Tariel does not get to his lover before her abduction and despairs of ever finding her. He leaves India and goes to live alone in a cave. This is where Avtandil finds him. The two warriors become friends and together they set off to find Nestan-Darejan. After many adventures they finally locate her imprisoned in the fortress of Kajeti. Tariel, Avtandil, and a third knight and sworn brother, Phridon, capture the fortress and free Nestan-Darejan. Triumphant, the heroes return to their native countries.

During the 13th century Georgia was devastated by the Mongol invasions. With Tamerlane's death in 1405 the process of national renewal could begin, but it was not until the 16th century that a new literary spirit flowered. Patriotic in nature, the work of this period is marked by interpolations and sequels to *The Knight in the Panther's Skin*. The *Omaniani*, written at the beginning of the 17th century, follows the adventures of Tariel's grandson, Oman.

Georgian literature in the 16th century had renewed many of its ties with Moslem oriental verse. The major 17th-century poet and statesman, King Teimuraz I, was a great admirer of Persian poetry, having been brought up at the court of Shah Abbas I (1587–1629). He recast many Persian poems into Georgian. Despite his affection for their language, King Teimuraz suffered both personally and politically at the hands of the Persians. His long narrative poem, *The Martyrdom of Ketevan*, is about his mother's torture at the hands of Shah Abbas.

In the first part of the 18th century, King Vakhtang VI (1675–1737) was the central figure in Georgia's intellectual life. A monarch, scholar, and poet, he collected and edited many historical works and wrote his own laws, *The Code of Vakhtang*. He is responsible for setting up the first press to print books in Georgian in 1709; a 1712 edition of *The Knight in the Panther's Skin* contains his extensive commentary.

Eastern Georgia was incorporated into Russia in 1801. The literary school of Georgian romanticism that had been born in the exiled community of Vakhtang VI found full expression at the beginning of the 19th century in the work of Alexander Chavchavadze (1786–1846), the son of Garsevan, King Herekle II's ambassador to Russia. Chavchavadze's verse expressed his deep disappointment at Georgia's loss of independence.

Grigol Orbeliani (1804–1883) was Chavchavadze's artistic brother, a fellow Romantic who longed for the restoration of Georgia's independence. This patriotic movement reached its apogee with Nikoloz Baratashvili (1818–1845), who dreamed of liberty and independence for his motherland, while recognizing the futility of retreating into an idealized vision of past glory. In *Twilight on Mtatsminda* he found solace in nature, and in *Meditation on the Mtkvari's Bank* he focused on selflessly serving his countrymen.

In the 20th century, "the Blue Horns" were responsible for literary innovations as part of the symbolist movement. The group began publishing a magazine of the same name in 1916. Paolo Yashvili, Titian Tabidze, Galaktion Tabidze, Kolau Nadiradze, and Valerian Gaprindashvili thrived in the years of Georgia's independence between 1918 and 1921 but were suppressed in the years of Bolshevik domination.

Novelist Konstantine Gamsakhurdia (1891–1975) explored Georgia's past in his historical novels, *The Hand of the Great Builder*, *The Abduction of the Moon*, and *David the Builder*. They are still read widely throughout Georgia.

PAINTING

Georgian mural painting blossomed during the Middle Ages, particularly between the 11th and mid-13th centuries. National schools of a unique character developed through discovery and celebration of Georgian hagiography as well as through cultural contacts with neighboring countries. From the 14th century onward the imported Byzantine Paleologian style predominated. Interesting examples of Persian influence during the 16th and 17th centuries can be seen in the secular portraits of patrons. In the 19th century, when Russia annexed Georgia and the Georgian Orthodox Church lost its autocephalous character, many frescoes were whitewashed and irreparably damaged, leaving only a fraction of what had been.

The churches of Ateni Sioni, Udabno, Gelati, Vardzia, Timotes-Ubani, Kinstvisi and Nekresi contain the most notable surviving examples.

SCULPTURE

Large figurative sculpture was considered heretical by the Orthodox church and therefore never prospered in Georgia. The consummate artistry of Georgian stone carvers can be seen, however, in the relief work on building façades and capitals, and on altar screens. Carving techniques developed hand in hand with metalworking. Both traditions date to antiquity, when native skills had already reached a high level. Contact with the Roman and Hellenistic worlds also contributed to the evolution of a Georgian style. The early incorporation of Christian iconography with pagan motifs is an interesting element of fifth-century sculpture. In the sixth century the influence of Sassanid Iran can be seen in some of the forms. The altar screens demanded by Georgian liturgy within the church became a focal point of sculptural decoration from the early Middle Ages. From the 11th through 13th centuries, as mural painting gained in importance, attention to interior sculpture was almost wholly transferred to the façade.

Monumental sculpture is certainly a feature of Georgia's 20th-century artistic landscape. Only a small number are executed along the lines set down by the tenets of Socialist realism. The overwhelming majority of works, especially when celebrating Georgian themes, bear the distinctive features of a national sensibility where the lesser goal of faithful likeness is replaced by the search for the embodiment of Georgian archetypes. Particularly noteworthy are the monumental sculptures of Elguja Amashukeli throughout Tbilisi: the colossal Mother Georgia, the kneeling Pirosmani, and the equestrian statue of Vakhtang Gorgasali.

METALWORK

Georgian metalwork during the Middle Ages ranks among the country's greatest artistic achievements. The craft has an illustrious pedigree in the Caucasus that goes back to the third millennium BC. From the barrow graves in Trialeti we know that the ancestors of the Georgians were accomplished in smelting, forging, soldering, stamping, and embossing articles of the greatest delicacy as early as the Bronze Age (from the second millennium BC to the beginning of the first millennium BC). The numerous bronze belt buckles depicting fantastic animals, dating to the second half of the first millennium BC, bear similarities to the animal forms later associated with Scythian art. Examples of Georgian jewelry from the fourth and fifth centuries BC attest to high technical and aesthetic standards. Granulation, embossing, and delicate filigree work produced earrings, rings, and pendants on par with anything produced in the ancient world. The niello, gold, and silver icons, crosses, jewelry, and book covers that date from the eighth and ninth centuries AD are among the earliest examples of the medieval metalworker's skill. Pieces such as the Ishkhani Processional Cross from 973, the Khobi Icon of the Virgin Mary (tenth century), the Martvili Cross and the silver roundel of St. Mamai from Gelati (11th century), and the famous Khakhuli triptych (12th century) are on display in the treasury of the Museum of Georgian Art. These works were sometimes embedded with precious stones, or adorned with cloisonné enameling. Artists such as Beka Opizari set the standard for this work, using a wide variety of techniques and materials for achieving a high point of pictorial representation. As with Georgian architecture, the quality of metalworking declined in the late Middle Ages.

Flora

Despite Georgia's relatively small area, the country possesses an unusually diverse flora. This is a result of the variety of geographical and climatic zones, a topography of marked contrasts, and a territory that happens to be at the crossroads of a number of landscapes of differing origins.

Georgia has 5,000 types of wild vegetation and approximately 8,300 types of cryptogamous vegetation (5,000 types of mushroom, 2,000 types of seaweed, 600 types of moss, and 73 types of fern).

The flora of eastern and western Georgia are quite different, mostly due to the fact that the arid and semi-arid vegetation of the unforested parts of eastern Georgia is absent from the densely forested west, where forestation begins at sea level.

Western Georgia is distinguished by four main zones: forest (sea level to 1,900 meters/6,234 feet); subalpine (1,950–2,500 meters/6,398–8,202 feet); alpine (2,500–3,100 meters/8,202–10,170 feet); and nival (3,100 meters/10,170 feet and up). Beginning at sea level, alder and wingnut trees thrive in the swampy Colchian lowlands. In less moist areas are ample numbers of oak, chestnut, hornbeam, and liana. The famous Pitsunda pine grows in Abkhazia on the Black Sea coast. A unique grove of these trees on the Pitsunda Cape is protected as a natural monument.

Eastern Georgia is divided into six zones: semi-desert (150–600 meters/492–1,969 feet) dominated by dry steppes and sparse treegrowth; forest (600–1,900 meters/1,969–6,234 feet); subalpine (1,900–2,500 meters/6,234–8,202 feet); alpine (2,500–3,000 meters/8,202–9,843 feet); subnival (3,000–3,500 meters/9,843-11,843 feet); and nival (3,500 meters/11,843 feet and up). The lowlands and foothills are forested along the Mtkvari, Iori, and Alazani rivers, with oak, poplar, several types of willows, and occasionally mulberry. The Alazani valley forests are rich with liana. Eastern Georgia's dry valleys support wormwood and

Wildflowers bloom in great variety throughout Georgia

Russian thistle. A little higher, where the climate is more humid, bear grass steppes are dotted with pistachio, juniper, maple, and pomegranate.

Fauna

A hundred mammals, over 330 birds, 48 reptiles, 11 amphibians, and over 160 fish species have been recorded in Georgia, whose fauna combines European, Central Asian, and North African elements. There is also a large variety of invertebrates: insects, arachnids, myriapods, crustaceans, and worms. The alpine and subalpine zones are populated with two species of wild ox, Daghestanian and Caucasian, both of which are indigenous to the Caucasus.

Birds found in the alpine and forested zones include the Caucasian jackdaw, black grouse, pheasant, pigeon, woodcock, curlew, cuckoo, kingfisher, woodpecker, crow, magpie, finch, crossbill, wagtail, tomtit, nightingale, swallow, chiff chaff, and linnet. The rivers are home to trout, barbel, sazan (a type of carp), and occasionally pike and river perch.

The endangered goitered gazelles, wild boar, roe and other deer roam the low-lands of eastern Georgia. The dwarf shrew, also endangered, lives in the Tbilisi area. The Iorian plateau supports a population of partridges and pheasants; Bronze Age Greeks supposedly imported the pheasants into Europe.

The lowlands of western Georgia feature extremely diverse fauna. Mammals include the hedgehog, mole, shrew, horseshoe bat, Caucasian squirrel, and various other rodents. In the area between Gagra and Sokhumi live badger, weasel, stone marten, wildcat, grizzly bear, wild boar, wolf, jackal, fox, and lynx. Birds of this region include the pheasant, quail, large curlew, woodcock, gull, goose, duck, pochard, and cormorant. During migrations pelicans are seen, as well as storks, bitterns, herons, falcons, hawks, hen harriers, eagle owls, cuckoos, hoopoes, king-fishers, woodpeckers, martlets, starlings, orioles, western nightingales, and swallows. Among the fish found in this region are trout, Black Sea salmon, Atlantic sturgeon, pike, sea roach, vobla, Caucasian chub, Colchian barbel, and sazan.

The common and bottle-nosed dolphin and the porpoise populate the Black Sea coast, while its fish includes shark, ray, beluga, Russian and Atlantic sturgeon, Black Sea salmon, khamsa, herring, dogfish, flounder, and swordfish.

The European bison and beaver, as well as the Transcaucasian leopard, became extinct early in the 20th century, and populations of goitered gazelle, wild goat, and striped hyena have been seriously diminished. However, Georgians are now taking steps to protect rare and indigenous fauna. Game reserves have opened in Lagodekhi, Borjomi, Saguramo, Ritsa, and Kintrishi.

Facts for the Traveler

Planning Your Trip

Before Georgian independence, you could not travel from abroad to Tbilisi (or any other place in what had been a republic of the former Soviet Union from 1921 until 1991) without first going through either Moscow or Leningrad. Your trip had to be organized through Intourist, the state-run tourist organization. Freedom of movement, the flexibility of your itinerary, and your access to people were definitely circumscribed. All this, thankfully, has now changed. Georgia is a free and sovereign country moving toward full-blown capitalism. Apart from the region of Abkhazia, which at the time of writing is off-limits to travelers because of the war that ended in 1993 and the current political situation, travelers can go wherever they want and arrange to see whatever is of greatest interest to them.

While many Georgians lament that there isn't a sufficiently developed infrastructure to handle large numbers of tourists and thus grow that sector of the economy, as an intrepid adventurer you might well rejoice in this situation. What you lose in not being able to obtain the dubious charms of an Econolodge every 50 miles, you gain in unspoiled landscapes, the warmth and intimacy of the guesthouse experience, and immersion into the Caucasian reality. Functioning within this context, if you can pay the going rate you can pretty much get whatever you want. However, unless you are a very experienced traveler in the Southern Caucasus, or have many Georgian friends, or speak Georgian or, at the very least, Russian, you will definitely need an intermediary to help you get what you want.

For English-speakers, the most experienced agency specializing in travel to Georgia is Regent Holidays, which is listed on page 314. They have the most realistic appraisal of what current local conditions are and how those might strike a western traveler. If you want the authenticity of dealing more immediately with the country's current trials and tribulations, and you want to take all planning into your own hands and work directly with travel agents within Georgia, there are only two agencies worth considering at the time of this writing: Saba Kiknadze c/o Caucasus Travel, P.O. Box 160, 380008 Tbilisi, with two office locations at: 5/7 Shavteli, 380005 Tbilisi and 36 David Agmashenebeli Avenue, 380002 Tbilisi, tel. (995 32) 98 74 00 or 98 73 99, fax. (995 32) 98 73 99 or 93 11 75, e-mail: saba@comp.ge; and Rainer Kaufmann, Sak Tours Limited, 43 Tamriko Tshovelidze Street (formerly Belinski Street), 380003 Tbilisi, tel. (995 32) 98 29 66 or 99 54 29, fax. 99 91 34, e-mail: saktours@kartli.com.ge, homepage:

CAUCASUS TRAVEL'S SHORT TOURS

AREA	DURATION		PRICE (in US $) per person*			
	DAY	NIGHT	1	2	3	4
CULTURAL						
TBILISI CITY TOUR	1	0	80	42	65	45
DAVID GAREJA	1	0	135	65	75	65
MTSKHETA	1	0	105	55	72	55
GORI	0	1	115	60	75	60
VARDZIA–ABASTUMANL	2	1	275	155	185	155
TBILIS–MTSKHETA–GUDAURI–KAZBEG	2	1	290	195	220	195
GORI–KUTAISI–BATUMI	3	2	535	285	340	285
DAVID GAREJA–TELAV–LAGODEK	3	2	450	245	275	245
HORSEBACK						
BAKURIANI REGION	5	4	620	420	395	325
BAKURIANI REGION	2	1	295	205	195	170
TREKKING						
MTIULETI AND KHEVI PROVINCES	3	2	440	295	255	205
KHEVSURETI AND KHEVI PROVINCES	3	2	275	190	160	115
KARTLI PROVINCE AND BIRTVISI CANYON	2	1	210	130	105	95
MOUNTAINEERING						
HAUKHI MOUNTAINS	3	2	360	240	190	145
MT. KAZBEK	5	4	450	290	255	215
SKI-MOUNTAINEERING						
GUDAURI AREA	3	2	460	350	330	315
MT. KAZBEK	5	4	475	365	255	220

Prices include: accommodation in the best available hotels (tents if in a remote region); all meals on tours outside of Tbilisi; inland transportation; guides (English-, German-, French-, Japanese- speaking guides); English speaking certified mountain guides; admission fees to sights.

*Prices include VAT. For 1–2 persons, mode of transport is a car; for 3–4 people, mode of transport is a van.

http://ourworld.compuserve.com/homepages/erkareisen. Saba Kiknadze, who is Georgian, speaks excellent English and has built an efficiently run, service-oriented organization staffed by enthusiastic, multilingual young Georgians of the next generation, i.e. oriented toward the West. Most travel agents outside of Georgia (*see* page 313) that organize tours to the country work in conjunction with Caucasus Travel. If you want to go solo, however, you can also work directly with Caucasus Travel, either making arrangements in advance from home, or on the spot once you're in Tbilisi. They can take care of all of your needs, from getting a bus ticket to Telavi (US$15 service charge) to arranging a five-day horseback tour of the Bakuriani region (US$620 per person). At present, payments can only be made in cash, but credit cards may soon be accepted. On page 45 are some of this company's shorter tours.

Caucasus Travel has also created cultural and adventure tours for groups of ten to 20 people. These tours are usually one to two weeks long. The best times to go on most of them are late spring and early fall. "The Soul of Georgia," a 15-day tour, takes in Tbilisi, Telavi, the David-Gareja Monastery Complex, Alaverdi Cathedral, Gremi Cathedral, Mtskheta, Ananuri, Gudauri, Kazbegi, Gori, Borjomi, Vardzia, Kutaisi, and Batumi. "The Path of the Holy Assyrian Fathers", also 15 days, covers important architectural monuments in Kartli, Kakheti, Imereti, and Samtskhe (Meskheti) and Javakheti, including Gelati, Motsameta, Nikortsminda, Vardzia, Khertvisi, Sapara, Alaverdi, Nekresi, Gremi, Shuamta, and David-Gareja. "The Land of the Golden Fleece" is a 12-day cultural tour with one day of hiking, which covers the province of Svaneti (Mestia, Ushguli, Becho). "Transcaucasus Treasury," a 15-day cultural tour, travels the Silk Road from Georgia to Armenia and Azerbaijan, and back to Georgia. "Caucasus Mountain Life" is an eight-day tour with three days of hiking through the mountain villages of Tusheti. "Georgian Wildlife" is a 15-day nature tour with hiking in the mountain highlands of Kazbegi and the Lagodekhi National Park of eastern Georgia. "Caucasus Heartland" is eight days of moderate trekking through the provinces of Khevsureti, Khevi, and Mtiuleti. "Traverse the Caucasus" is 15 days of rigorous trekking through the provinces of Mtiuleti, Khevi, Khevsureti, Tusheti, and Kakheti. "The Bride of the Khevi–Mt. Kazbek" is eight days of mountaineering, including the ascent of Mount Kazbek, at 5,047 meters. Basic climbing skills are required. "Ski Adventure Gudauri–Mt. Kazbek" is an eight-day skiing program for experienced skiers. March and May are considered the best months. "The Sovereign of Svaneti–Mt. Ushba" is 12 days in Svaneti, culminating on the seventh day with an ascent to the summit of Mt. Ushba. You must be capable of climbing IV–V UIAA or French TD/D and have experience with mixed and ice routes. July and August are the most highly recommended months. "The Wine Route" is an eight-day tour of Kartli and Kakheti, taking in the main

CAUCASUS TRAVEL'S PRICE STRUCTURE

SERVICE CHARGES   PRICE (in US$)

GUESTHOUSE BOOKING	15 per booking
RESTAURANT BOOKING	10 per booking
PLANE, BUS, AND TRAIN TICKET RESERVATION	15 per leg of journey

TRANSPORTATION COSTS PER VEHICLE...
(includes fuel, unlimited mileage and driver)

MODE	BUS	MINIBUS	MINIVAN	CAR	4x4 CAR
NO. OF SEATS	40–45	20–21	7–11	3	3
HIRE PERIOD (DAYS)					
1–5	320	220	120	70	90
6–14	300	200	110	60	80
MORE THAN 14	280	180	100	55	75

TRANSFERS...
AIRPORT

TO/FROM TBILISI	250	120	80	30	—

INTER-CITY
FROM TBILISI TO:

BAKU*	420	290	190	50	—
BATUMI	320	220	120	90	—
KUTAISI	320	220	120	90	—
POTI	320	220	120	90	—
YEREVAN*	390	270	170	130	—

*add 20 percent in opposite direction

TRIPS WITH GUIDES (includes accommodations and food)...

	3/4 DAY	FULL DAY
CULTURAL		
CITY	42	59
COUNTRYSIDE	—	59

	PER DAY
TREKKING	25–70**
MOUNTAINEERING	40–120**
SKI-MOUNTAINEERING	40–120**

**according to duration and difficulty of trip

ADDITIONAL COSTS .... PER DAY

ASSISTANT	17–25

(photo tours, press trips, expeditions, etc)

PORTERS	17–25

(trekking, mountaineering, etc.)   Prices include VAT

SAK TOURS PRICE STRUCTURE

VEHICLE RENTAL (IN LARI)	UP TO 4 HOURS IN TBILISI	5–7 HOURS IN TBILISI	MORE THAN 8 HOURS IN TBILISI	A DAY OUTSIDE TBILISI	DISCOUNT (%) MORE THAN 3 DAYS	6 DAYS
VW PASSAT 3 PASSENGERS PLUS DRIVER	40	60	80	100	10	15
VW BUS 7 PASSENGERS PLUS DRIVER	60	80	100	120	10	15
OASI JEEP 8 PASSENGERS PLUS DRIVER	60	80	95	100	10	15
NIVA JEEP 3 PASSENGERS PLUS DRIVER	40	50	60	80 (100 IF IN MOUNTAINS)	10	15
OTHER PASSENGER VEHICLES, SUCH AS A LADA OR SHIGULI 3 PASSENGERS PLUS DRIVER	35	40	45	55	10	15

Trip to Erevan by VW Bus	310 lari + 62 lari VAT, plus driver's hotel (40 lari)
Trip to Baku by VW Bus	410 lari + 82 lari VAT, plus driver's hotel (40 lari)

wineries around Tbilisi and Telavi. *Rtveli* is the time of the grape harvest in Georgia, usually in September and October. Prices for the above tours range from US$150 to US$700 per person depending on the tour and number of people. English-speaking guides are provided.

Caucasus Travel can also handle individual touring, with hotel or guesthouse bookings as well as car rental with driver. On page 47 is a list of its rates.

Kiknadze is also involved with the first professional organization of mountain guides in Georgia, which has been working with the Swiss Mountain Guide School.

Georgia is now a candidate to join the International Union of Mountain Guides. Mountaineers should contact the Georgian Guide Service & Georgian State Mountain Guide School, P.O. Box 160, 380008 Tbilisi. The office address is 7 Niko Nikoladze Street, 380008 Tbilisi, tel. and fax. (995 32) 93 11 75, e-mail: guide@ ggs.com.ge.

Sak Tours is a German-Georgian joint venture. Rainer Kaufmann, who is also the owner of Rainer's Cafe and the Hotel Kartli, spends half the year in Georgia organizing and leading tours. His travel agency in Bruchsal, Germany, specializes in travel to the Caucasus: Erka Reisen, Robert-Stolz-Strasse 21, 76646 Bruchsal, Germany, tel. (49 7257) 930 390, fax. (49 7257) 930 392, e-mail: 101321.1274 @email:

Kaufmann, like Kiknadze, runs numerous group tours of one to two weeks throughout Georgia and the Caucasus, but these are geared toward German travelers who are provided with German-speaking guides. His organization, however, is very responsive to individual travelers and though his staff in Tbilisi function best in Georgian, German, and Russian, English-speaking guides can be arranged. Sak Tours also books hotels and guesthouses outside Tbilisi. A room with meals costs approximately 60 lari (about US$80) a night. Sak Tours can also arrange a rental car with driver. Most drivers only speak Georgian and Russian. Rates are shown opposite—all prices are in lari and per vehicle. Payment can only be made in cash. If you prefer to make most of your travel arrangements before arriving in Tbilisi, Erka Reisen in Germany will accept a check or wire transfer, but not credit cards.

A new travel agency, The Sustainable Tourism Centre, 14 Gribedov Street 380004, Tbilisi, tel. (995 32) 99 58 73 or 99 93 04, specializes in day trips and weekend excursions from Tbilisi.

Working through a tour company in the States or the UK will be the most organized and safest way to visit Georgia. Working directly with Caucasus Travel or Sak Tours (Erka Reisen) in advance will help you to customize your trip; but if you are traveling solo then some of the excursions that require a group of ten or more people will probably be too expensive to do on your own. Making plans once you get to Tbilisi—provided you have booked a hotel in Tbilisi beforehand—probably gives you the greatest freedom, as long as you're flexible and have time to take things as they come.

What to Bring

Given the area's climatic conditions, a thorough tour of Georgia demands clothing ranging from bathing suit to winter parka. Certainly in the alpine meadows below Mt. Kazbegi, parkas and sweaters are advised even in summer. The usual beach paraphernalia is appropriate for the Black Sea coast, especially your favorite sun-

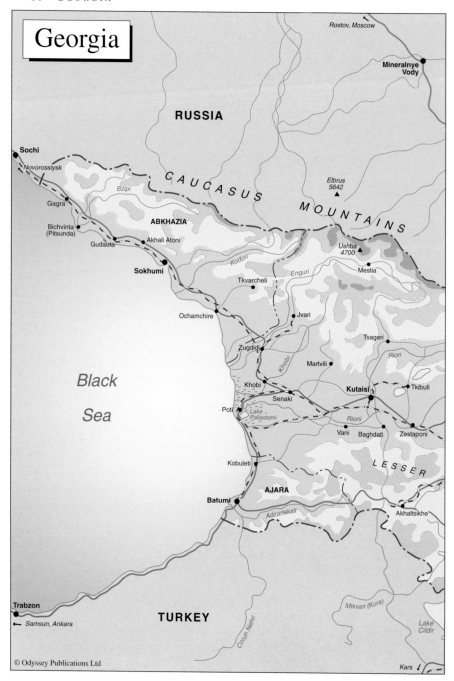

Georgia

Rostov, Moscow

Mineralnye Vody

RUSSIA

Sochi

Novorossiysk

C A U C A S U S

Elbrus
5642

Gagra

Bzipi

Bichvinta
(Pitsunda)

ABKHAZIA

M O U N T A I N S

Gudauta

Akhali Atoni

Ushba
4700

Sokhumi

Kodori

Mestia

Enguri

Tkvarcheli

Ochamchire

Jvari

Zugdidi

Tsageri

Rioni

Khobi

Martvili

Black

Sea

Khobi

Senaki

Kutaisi

Tkibuli

Poti

Lake
Paliastomi

Rioni

Vani   Baghdati   Zestaponi

Kobuleti

L E S S E R

AJARA

Batumi

Adzariskali

Akhaltsikhe

Trabzon

Mtkvari (Kura)

Samsun, Ankara

TURKEY

Coruh Nehri

Lake
Cildir

© Odyssey Publications Ltd

Kars

screens, which might be difficult to find in Georgia. The same holds true for all over-the-counter drugs. Take aspirin, antacid, calamine lotion, cold remedies, and whatever else you generally stock in your medicine cabinet. In addition, take all the toiletries you generally use—razor blades, shaving cream, toothpaste, sanitary napkins, lipstick, and perfume. Though new pharmacies have opened (*see* page 331 for a list) you might not find your usual brand. Bring toilet paper with you at all times, as the public toilets rarely have it. Laundry detergent can also be useful, although most hotels have a laundry service.

A portable iron (voltage is 220, so bring an adapter) would also be useful as the Georgians, especially in the capital, are an elegant people who take great care in the way they dress. Like the Italians, they are concerned about cutting *una bella figura*, and they judge you harshly if you look slovenly. Formal dress is rarely required but men might want to bring a jacket and tie for the theater or opera. For the same reason women should bring at least one dress which would also be appropriate if invited to a Georgian's home for dinner. In the summer women should have a sweater to cover bare shoulders when entering a church.

Lastly, do not fail to pack an assortment of appropriate gifts for the people you will inevitably meet. As Rustaveli wrote in *The Knight in the Panther's Skin,* "Everything you give away remains yours and everything you keep is lost forever." Georgians live by this code and will shower you with gifts at the first opportunity. You simply must have something with which to reciprocate. Useful items include cigarettes, lighters with company logos, key chains, buttons and badges, postcards from the West, small, illustrated guidebooks to your home city, T-shirts bearing any kind of design or writing, and crayons, coloring books, and storybooks for children.

Getting There

BY AIR

Back in the bad old days of the USSR, travelers to Georgia had to fly via Moscow or Leningrad and then grab a domestic Aeroflot flight to Tbilisi. No more! Routes and airlines are changing with some frequency in these exciting times of burgeoning entrepreneurship in Georgia and other recently independent states. One can now fly directly to Tbilisi from London, Frankfurt, Amsterdam, and Vienna, as well as from Istanbul, Tehran, and over 20 cities within the Commonwealth of Independent States (CIS).

British Airways, Swissair, Austrian Air, Turkish Airlines, Air Georgia, and Georgian Airlines service some of the cities mentioned above. If you see Internet listings or receive other data about a Georgian airline named Orbi, know that it is now defunct with some of its business absorbed by Georgian Airlines, and that many of its flights, such as Berlin–Tbilisi, Paris–Tbilisi, and Prague–Tbilisi, have been suspended. Many flights from cities of the CIS are run by relative newcomers to the world of commercial aviation: AEK, Air Zena, Fortuna, GAKO, Stavropol Airlines, Vnukovo Airlines, and numerous others formed after the Aeroflot monopoly was disassembled.

British Airways service to Tbilisi is superb, with flights leaving London on Monday, Wednesday, and Friday and returning to London on Tuesday, Thursday, and Saturday. The flight takes about five hours and the cost of a round-trip ticket is approximately US$1,500. The British Airways office in Tbilisi is in the Sheraton Metechi Palace Hotel (see page 317 for address). The telephone number is 94 07 19 or 94 07 20. Office hours are Monday to Friday, 9.30 a.m.–6 p.m. and Saturday 9 a.m.–12 noon.

Swissair flies from London to Tbilisi on Wednesdays and Saturdays, and Tbilisi to London on Thursdays and Saturdays; and Austrian Air flies in both directions on Tuesdays, Fridays, and Sundays.

Air Georgia has offices in Tbilisi at 49a Chavchavadze Avenue, tel. 29 40 53, 23 54 07 or 92 00 52. In Germany, Air Georgia has an office at Schuchard Strasse 4, 64283 Darmstadt, tel. (49 6151) 296 450 or 296 557, fax. (49 6151) 296 653. Air Georgia flies from Frankfurt to Tbilisi for US$530.

The head office of Georgian Airlines is at Tbilisi airport, tel. 94 74 47 or 94 71 80. The offices of Turkish Airlines in Tbilisi are located at 147 Agmashenebeli Avenue, tel. 95 90 22.

Travel agents such as Sak Tours and Caucasus Travel can book plane tickets for you once in Tbilisi for a service charge of ten to 20 lari. Another excellent resource for taking care of ticketing for you in Tbilisi is the tour and travel desk of the Sheraton Metechi Palace Hotel, tel. 95 73 76 or 95 42 70, ext. 180, fax. 00 11 27, ext. 132, telex: 64/21 22 48 MPHTB SU. You do not have to be a hotel guest to partake of this service. The add-on service charge cost is comparable to that of the other travel agents.

The newly remodeled Tbilisi airport is 18 kms (11 miles) east of the city center. Arrival and departure information is in Georgian and English. Russian is conspicuously absent. Bus and taxi service is available to the city center (*see* page 47 for bus and taxi information).

By Bus

A number of privately held tour companies run buses between Tbilisi and Athens, Thessaloniki, Istanbul, Trabzon, Baku, and Yerevan, as well as cities in the Ukraine and Russia, including Moscow and St. Petersburg. Travel along these routes can be very dangerous. Consult your embassy before you leave.

There are four major bus terminals in Tbilisi. The Didube Terminal and the newly privatized Okriba Didube Terminal next door are both located on Tsereteli Avenue at the Didube Bridge and metro stop. They service cities to the west and the north. The Central Bus Terminal, also called the Ortachala Terminal, at 1 Gulia Street, provides service to the east. The Rustavi Terminal, near the Marjanishvili Bridge, provides service to Rustavi and certain cities in the south. You can go abroad from all four terminals. Buses leaving from the Okriba Didube, for example, go to Moscow (two days, 50 lari), St. Petersburg (two days, 70 lari) and Vladikavkaz (six hours, ten lari). From Rustavi, tour operator Laki-Taki goes once a week to Thessaloniki, for US$80, and Ri-Tour goes daily to Istanbul for US$40. From the Central Bus Terminal, Octave goes once a week to Athens for US$110. Tour operators Aibaki, Buse, and Masmudoglu leave daily to Istanbul for US$40. Masmudoglu also runs a daily bus service to Trabzon for US$25. Also from Central, there are buses to Baku (a ten-hour trip that leaves on Tuesdays and Fridays, at 7.30 a.m. for 13 lari) and to Yerevan (a seven-hour trip that leaves twice a day, 8.15 a.m. and 9.35 a.m. for eight lari).

Note: The Central terminal's ticket and information offices are not found at street level but downstairs near the departure gates. There isn't a large arrival or departure Board and English speakers are scarce. The telephone number for information is 72 34 33. The #7 and #21 trolleys come to this terminal as does the #10 bus from the city center.

For a listing of bus routes within Georgia, as well as departure times and fares, see page 60. These timetables cannot be completely relied upon, but they do serve as a framework. The roads and buses are in very poor condition, and buses often won't leave until they are full.

BY RAIL

Trains link Tbilisi with Moscow, Kiev, Baku, and Yerevan. Between 1991 and 1995 train travel was very dangerous, with incidents of banditry and terrorism along many routes both in and outside of Georgia. This is no longer the case and you can travel reasonably safely everywhere. However, you should take the usual precautions with your belongings once on board. Traveling by train is not the fastest method of getting about, but sharing a compartment is a nice way to meet people. The schedule on the facing page lists prices from Tbilisi to selected cities. There are four classes of fare—unreserved, reserved, first class, and international—for two types of trains: regular and express.

BY SHIP

All three passenger ship ports—Poti, Batumi and Sokhumi—are on the Black Sea coast. With the conflict in Abkhazia and the blockade that has been imposed, Sokhumi is not functioning as an international port. Poti and Batumi continue to provide international connections to other ports on the Black Sea and the Mediterranean. A list of ferries operating to and from the seaport of Poti is shown on page 56. These are both cruise and container ships.

Train Fares

REGULAR TRAIN				EXPRESS TRAIN			
DESTINATION	UNRESERVED	RESERVED	FIRST CLASS	INT'L	UNRESERVED	RESERVED	FIRST CLASS	INT'L
Abasha	2.00	2.95	4.80	9.00	2.40	3.60	5.90	11.20
Akhaltsikhe	1.90	2.70	4.30	8.40	—	—	—	—
Batumi	2.25	3.10	5.10	10.60	2.70	4.15	7.05	13.20
Chiatura	1.90	2.75	4.40	8.60	—	—	—	—
Kharagauli	1.70	2.45	3.90	7.50	2.05	2.95	4.80	9.30
Khashuri	1.55	2.25	3.50	6.80	1.85	2.65	4.30	8.40
Kobuleti	2.15	3.30	5.50	10.20	2.60	4.05	6.80	12.70
Kutaisi	1.95	2.80	4.50	8.70	2.35	3.40	5.55	10.80
Lanchkhuti	2.05	3.05	5.00	9.20	2.45	3.70	6.15	11.40
Natanebi	2.10	3.20	5.30	9.80	2.55	3.90	6.55	12.20
Ozurgeti	2.15	3.30	5.50	10.20	2.60	4.05	6.80	12.70
Poti	2.05	3.10	5.10	9.40	2.50	3.80	6.30	11.70
Rioni	1.90	2.75	4.40	8.60	2.35	3.35	5.40	10.70
Sachkhere	1.95	2.86	4.60	8.80	—	—	—	—
Samtredia	2.00	2.90	4.70	8.90	2.40	3.55	5.80	11.10
Senaki	2.05	3.05	5.00	9.20	2.45	3.70	6.15	11.40
Supsa	2.10	3.15	5.20	9.60	2.55	3.85	6.40	11.90
Tkibuli	2.00	3.00	4.90	9.10	—	—	—	—
Tskaltubo	1.95	2.85	4.50	8.80	—	—	—	—
Vale	1.90	2.75	4.40	8.60	—	—	—	—
Zestaponi	1.90	2.60	4.10	8.10	2.20	3.15	5.50	10.10

All prices are in lari.

BY CAR

Driving your own car into Georgia is currently not recommended, given the condition of the roads and the scarcity of road signs in any language other than Georgian. Banditry is also on the rise in certain regions. On the bright side, fuel is no longer a problem and there are gas stations everywhere and no shortages. The long queues of the early 1990s have also disappeared. Diesel costs about 28 cents a liter, and gasoline is 35 cents a liter for regular and 42 cents a liter for super. In Georgia you drive on the right.

Travelers who drive into Georgia from Turkey cross the border at Kemalpasra into Sarpi, Georgia, on the Black Sea coast of Ajara. From Russia you could drive into Georgia along the Georgian Military Highway from Vladikavkaz. Given the current situation in Abkhazia, you cannot go from

FERRIES	COMPANY	FREQUENCY	ROUTES	OPENED
Continental	CMN	Once every two weeks	Gioia Tauro (Italy)–Piraeus (Greece) –Poti–Novorossijsk (Russia)	Feb 1996
Nautica	Sleak Sea	Once every two weeks	Imzot (Israel) –Novorossijsk (Russia)–Poti	June 1997
SHIPPING				
MSC Venener	MSC	Once a month	Gioia Tauro (Italy) –Novorossijsk (Russia)–Poti	Oct 1996
MSC Lariza	MSC	Once every two weeks	Istanbul (Turkey)– –Poti–Novorossijsk (Russia)	July 1997
Peltiner	Sealand	Once every two weeks	Ravena (Italy)– Piraeus (Greece)–Poti	July 1996
Peltiner	Sealand	Once every two weeks	Gioia (Italy)– Piraeus (Greece) –Poti	Nov 1996
Pelmarina	Sealand	Once every two weeks	Gioia (Italy)– Piraeus (Greece)–Poti	May 1997
Gevo Victor	ECS	Once every two weeks	Piraeus (Greece)–Poti	Jan 1993
Sofia	Robul Deta	Once a week	Varria (Bulgaria)–Poti	Apr 1995
SERVICE				
Sredec	Exlm TK	Once a week	Burgas (Bulgaria)–Poti	Oct 1996
Geroy Shipky	Ukrferry	Once a week	Ilyichivs'k (Ukraine)–Poti	Dec 1996
3TK–1011	Birtrans	Once every ten days	Istanbul (Turkey)–Poti	May 1997
Uranus		Once every two weeks	Rotterdam (Netherlands)–Poti	July 1997
Prestau		Once a week	Burgas (Bulgaria)–Poti –Novorossijsk (Russia)	Aug 1997
Mint Arrow	Murphy	Once every two weeks	Antwerp (Netherlands)–Poti	Sept 1997

Sochi across the border at Adlyer toward Sokhumi but you can drive in from both Azerbaijan and Armenia.

An International Driver's License is required. Georgians express their individuality and often their impatience with conformity when behind the wheel. This can be extremely dangerous. Drive defensively.

Visas

Visas can be obtained from the Embassy of Georgia, Consular Office, 1511 K Street NW, Suite 424, Washington, DC 20005, USA, tel./fax. (202) 393-6060.

These are the requirements for visa applications:
1. Completed application form (obtainable from the Consular Office). Photocopies of application forms are accepted.
2. Applicant's passport (not a photocopy).
3. A letter of invitation from a Georgian citizen or an organization based in Georgia. Invitations from foreign organizations based in Georgia should be endorsed by the Ministry of Foreign Affairs of Georgia.
   (Invariably travelers ask, What do I do if I don't know a Georgian citizen or organization? The answer is that a letter from the hotel that you've booked or a travel agent like Caucasus Travel or Sak Tours will work just fine.)
4. One passport-size photo. Photo may be either black-and-white or color.
5. A money order or certified check payable to the Consular Office of the Embassy of Georgia. Processing fees for single-entry visas are:
   a. For duration of stay up to two weeks: US$20
   b. For duration of stay up to one month: US$25
   three months: US$30
   Processing fees for multiple entry visas:
   a. For duration of stay of six months: US$90
   b. For duration of stay of one year: US$120

All fees are nonrefundable. Processing time for single-entry visas is five days and for multiple entry visas 20 days. If applying by mail you should include a prepaid, express mail self-addressed envelope, e.g. FedEx, UPS.

Important: In order to insure that your visa is processed without delay, clearly write the name of the inviting individual or organization, as well as the exact dates and the purpose of your visit. All forms must be typed or printed in ink. For questions concerning visa procedures, telephone (202) 393-6060 Monday to Friday, 10 a.m.–12.30 p.m. and 2 p.m.–4.30 p.m..

It is also possible in a crunch to obtain an urgent entry visa upon arrival at Tbilisi Airport. You should have a passport photo with you. Payment can only be made in cash.

For a complete listing of Georgian Embassies throughout the world that issue visas, see page 318.

Customs

The American Embassy has this to say about Customs. It is accurate information:
    Customs regulations are in a state of flux and are not consistently enforced. Customs forms may not be available when you arrive in Georgia, but travelers should make every effort to obtain one to avoid being charged a 10 percent tax on cash taken out of the country. You should declare all items of value on your customs form upon arrival in Georgia. If your Customs form is lost or stolen, report it to the police and obtain a certificate to show to customs officials when you depart the country. If you do not receive an original Customs form or you cannot obtain the police certificate indicating the original was lost or stolen, you may ask the American Embassy for a form letter to present to Customs. This letter often helps.
    Generally speaking, you should obtain a receipt for all items of value purchased in Georgia. All items that may appear to have historical value, such as icons, art, rugs, or antiques, must have a certificate indicating that they have no historical value. This is to protect Georgia's cultural heritage, which should be every traveler's duty. You may obtain this certificate from the Ministry of Culture, 37 Rustaveli Avenue, 3/F, Room 16, tel. 99 02 85, 93 71 33, 93 34 26, and 98 74 32.

Getting Around

INTRA-CITY

While Tbilisi is the only city in Georgia with a metro system, all cities have some form of public transport—buses, trolleys, trams, or some combination thereof. The metro, buses, and trolleys in Tbilisi operate from 6 a.m.–1 a.m.; trams 5 a.m.–2 a.m., though certain major lines continue around the clock. The metro, trolley, bus, and tram cost 20 tetri. The bus, trolley, and tram usually require exact change, as conductors are rarely present. Deposit the appropriate amount in the cashbox and pull off a ticket. In the metro, you buy a token at the booth and deposit it at the barrier. *See* page 99 for a metro map.

TAXIS

Tbilisi has recently introduced 200 bright red new Mitsubishi taxis in the city. They can be hailed, picked up at taxi stands or phoned at 008. They are metered and begin at 50 tetri with an additional 30 tetri charge with each kilometer. Pay what's on the meter. Tip by rounding the amount off to the next lari. Yellow cabs are also very reliable and can be phoned at 23 11 47. The smaller, older cabs running about the city can be identified by their small checkered pattern. Two lari should be enough to take you anywhere in the center of the city. Prices to and from the airport vary, but US$10 will certainly get you there or back.

When dealing with unmetered cabs, always agree upon the price before you get in. This is also true of cab sharing, which is very common in Tbilisi. If you just go out to the street and stick out your hand, a private motorist, keen to make a little extra money, will soon stop. If he's heading in that direction, he'll take you to your destination. He might stop to pick up people along the way. The American Embassy strongly discourages its citizens from participating in this form of taxi sharing because of fears about crime. It's a hard call. Georgians travel like this all the time.

INTER-CITY

Currently, bus and train services link the major towns of the country in a barely adequate way. You will always do best setting out from Tbilisi, the junction of all connections. You might, however, find yourself stranded at a platform or bus stop for half the day or night if you're trying to get from one smaller place to another. Before leaving Tbilisi, make sure you get the most exact route and schedule. The chart below shows distances in kilometers (and miles) from Tbilisi to many of the larger towns and vacation spots.

Tbilisi's central train station is in Vakzlis Moedani, in the Nakhalovka district northeast of town. There is a metro stop of the same name. Bus terminals are listed on page 60 and airport information on page 53.

TOWNS	ROAD	RAIL
BAKURIANI	189 km (119 miles)	187 km (116 miles)
BATUMI	387 km (240 miles)	349 km (216 miles)
BORJOMI	162 km (100 miles)	151 km (94 miles)
GAGRA	547 km (339 miles)	477 km (296 miles)
GORI	86 km (53 miles)	75 km (46.5 miles)
KOBULETI	357 km (221 miles)	325 km (201.5 miles)
KUTAISI	249 km (154 miles)	191 km (118 miles)
AKHALI ATONI	472 km (293 miles)	420 km (260 miles)
PASANAURI	88 km (54.5 miles)	————
RUSTAVI	22 km (14 miles)	29 km (18 miles)
SOKHUMI	447 km (277 miles)	404 km (250 miles)
TSKHALTUBO	260 km (161 miles)	236 km (143 miles)

BUS SCHEDULE

DESTINATION	DEPARTURE TIMES (FROM TBILISI)	BUS TERMINAL	PRICE (IN LARI)
Adigeni	12.20	Didube	7.00
Akhaltsikhe	09.00, 11.20, 14.30, 16.00, 17.30	Didube	5.00
Akhmeta	09.00, 10.30, 12.45, 14.10, 15.25, 16.45	Central	3.70
Aspinza	10.20	Didube	6.00
Bagdadi	11.20	Didube	5.00
Banza	09.00	Okriba Didube	4.00
Batumi	09.30, 12.00, 15.00	Central	7.00
Batumi	09.30, 11.00, 12.05	Didube	7.00
Borjomi	10.15, 11.20, 12.10, 13.40, 14.45, 15.50, 17.30	Didube	4.00
Chiatura	10.00, 11.00, 12.00, 14.00, 16.00	Okriba Didube	4.00
Chkoni-Martvili	09.00	Okriba Didube	4.00
Chokhatauri	10.30	Central	5.50
Dedoplistskaro	09.00, 11.00, 12.30, 13.35, 14.25, 15.55, 17.35, 18.30	Central	2.00
Gori	08.50, every 40 minutes until 18.00	Didube	2.50
Gurjaani	08.50, 10.20, every 30 minutes until 20.00	Central	2.00
Kakhi	10.40	Central	6.50
Kani	08.30	Didube	5.00
Kaspi	09.00, every 40 minutes until 18.00	Didube	1.00
Kharagauli	15.30	Didube	4.00
Khashuri	09.00, 11.00, 13.20, 14.55, 17.20, 18.05, 18.40	Didube	3.00
Khoni	11.00	Okriba Didube	4.00
Kutaisi	08.00	Central	4.00
Kutaisi	08.00, 13.00, 14.00, 15.00, 17.00, 18.00	Didube	4.00
Kutaisi	04.00, 16.00	Okriba Didube	3.00
Kvareli	09.40, 11.00, 12.00, 13.00, 14.00, 16.00, 17.30	Central	3.00
Lagodekhi	09.00, 12.30, 14.10, 15.40, 17.20, 18.05	Central	4.00
Ninotsminda	08.30	Didube	7.00
Orpiri	12.00	Okriba Didube	4.00
Ozurgeti	10.30	Central	6.00
Ozurgeti	10.00	Didube	6.00
Sachkhere	12.00, 15.00, 17.00	Didube	3.00
Senaki	10.30	Central	5.00
Senaki	10.30	Didube	5.00
Signagi	11.25, 14.55	Central	3.00
Telavi	07.20, 08.00, 09.50, every 30 minutes	Central	3.00
Tkibuli	11.00	Okriba Didube	5.00
Tskhinvali	08.15, 09.45, 11.00, 12.10, 13.30, 16.00, 17.30	Didube	3.50
Yerevan	08.15, 09.30	Central	8.10
Zestaponi	11.50, 14.45, 15.50, 17.30, 18.30	Didube	3.00
Zugdidi	15.00, 17.00	Central	6.50
Zveli Abasha	10.00	Okriba Didube	4.00

TRAIN SCHEDULE

TRAIN #	DESTINATION	DEPARTURE TIME FROM TBILISI	ARRIVAL TIME	DAYS OF DEPARTURE
37/38	BAKU	17.45	09.00	DAILY
659/660	BATUMI	19.00	07.40	DAILY
207/208	KIEV	21.40	19.51	SUN
644/663	KUTAISI	21.30	06.42	DAILY
13/14	MOSCOW	23.30	04.26	THURS
669/670	OZURGETI	21.30	10.02	DAILY
657/658	POTI	21.30	10.54	DAILY
639/640	TELAVI	16.10	00.40	MON, WED, FRI, SUN
671/672	VALE	23.20	09.10	DAILY
671/672	YEREVAN	18.00	06.00	MON, WED, FRI, SUN
601/602	ZUGDIDI	20.20	08.48	DAILY

BY BUS

Travel by public bus from city to city can be bone wearing, but it's a cheap way to see the country. Private concerns have started organizing minivans that hold about 15 people to go to different towns and villages. The bus schedule on the facing page gives an idea of what's available.

BY RAIL

Train travel is sometimes more commodious but slower than travel by bus, and the system is not as extensive as the intra-city bus and van network. Georgia has 1,500 km (932 miles) of railway. The chart on page 55 gives an idea of prices to different cities and villages. The chart above provides a schedule of trains leaving from Tbilisi for several cities, including Batumi, Zugdidi, Poti, Ozurgeti, and Kutaisi.

This 1927 Packard can still be seen driving around Kutaisi

BY CAR

At the time of writing there aren't any local or international rental car companies that can set you up with a self-drive vehicle. Georgian law, insurance, and the general difficulties for a foreigner to drive around on his or her own probably all contribute to this state of affairs. With improved infrastructure, this situation will probably change. For the moment, you can only hire a car with a driver. Sak Tours, Caucasus Travel, and the tour and travel Desk of the Sheraton Metechi Palace Hotel can arrange a car or jeep for you. *See* page 48 for Sak Tours' rates.

BY AIR

The number of plane and helicopter flights between cities has been reduced from previous levels. While there used to be daily flights to Batumi, Zugdidi, and Poti, as well as less frequent helicopter flights to Lentekhi, Mestia, Chykhareshi, and Shatili, this is no longer the case. Check with a travel agent to see what is currently available.

Climate

The climate of Georgia differs markedly from west to east. The west, including the Black Sea coast (Abkhazia and Ajara), Imereti, and Samegrelo (Mingrelia), has a

| AVERAGE TEMPERATURES (FAHRENHEIT) AND DAYS OF RAINFALL PER MONTH | | | | | | |
| SOKHUMI | | | TBISILI | | | |
MONTH	HIGH	LOW	RAIN	HIGH	LOW	RAIN
JAN	45	35	7	32	16	7
FEB	46	37	8	35	18	5
MAR	49	37	6	53	33	7
APR	57	45	5	67	43	9
MAY	68	58	5	78	51	2
JUN	77	63	3	88	58	2
JUL	82	70	1	96	64	3
AUG	81	68	1	93	65	3
SEPT	74	61	5	84	55	1
OCT	65	55	6	69	45	4
NOV	57	45	8	51	35	6
DEC	48	37	8	38	26	7

damp, subtropical climate. Eastern Georgia includes Kartli and Kakheti, which are separated from the warm winds blowing in from the Black Sea by the Likhi range (the major bridge between the mountains of the Greater and Lesser Caucasus). This results in a drier, more continental climate. In addition, the height of mountains in the eastern part of the Greater Caucasus exceeds 5,000 meters (16,400 feet). Snow caps these mountains for half the year. The above chart gives average temperatures and days of rain per month throughout the year in Sokhumi (west) and Tbilisi (east).

Medical Aid and Immunization

Westerners traveling in Georgia would do well to carry evacuation insurance before departing. Medical facilities in Georgia are not up to American and European standards. There are, however, more options now than in Soviet times thanks to privatization.

Small biplanes like this are no longer flying to the more remote regions of Georgia. Plane and helicopter travel within Georgia has been much curtailed during the current period of economic crisis.

There is a British practice in Tbilisi that every English speaker should know about: OMS Clinic (private clinic), 25 Odessa Street, Saburtalo, David Cook (Dr.), Graham Edwards (Medic), tel. 37 56 59 or 94 14 98, mobile phone 8 774 03911.

Medexpress Limited (tel. 90 or 90 01 11) is a private medical insurance firm in Tbilisi that provides medical service to individuals. Curatio (tel. 901, 93 80 61 or 90 11 11) is a private ambulance service in Tbilisi. The telephone number for the Tbilisi City Ambulance is 03 or 99 92 08. Cardio Express (tel. 009 or 95 00 00) is another private ambulance service specializing in cardiac conditions. For minor medical problems, the private medical firm Curatio claims to be ready to deal with members of the American and European communities. It is located at 123 D. Agmashenebeli Avenue, tel. 96 86 79.

Dr. Maia Sharashidze of the Cardiac Center speaks English. She can be contacted at the Cardiac Center (Emergency Cardiology Centre of the Ministry of Health of Georgia), 4 Liubliana Street (inside the Institute of Therapy in Digomi), tel. 98 86 32.

The following companies can help with medical evacuations from Georgia: Air

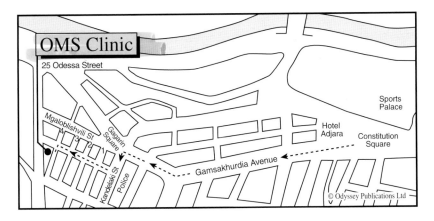

Georgia in Tbilisi, tel. 23 51 56 or 29 40 53; Trans Air Globe, tel. in Tbilisi 22 61 25, tel. in Germany (49 30) 4101 3528; SOS International, tel. in Geneva, Switzerland, (41 22) 476 161; Air Ambulance America, P.O. Box 4051, Austin, TX 78765, USA, tel. (512) 479-8000 (call collect) or (800) 222-3564 (toll free).

For American citizens with serious medical problems, contact the Consular Section of the U.S. Embassy. Embassy personnel will try to help with the logistics of treating problems. British citizens and other European nationals should contact their own embassies.

The home page of the U.S. Embassy in Tbilisi (www.sanet.ge/usis) provides health information. Like so much official information, the tone is perhaps overly admonitory and excessively cautious. Certainly the Embassy's assessment, that the two greatest health risks in Georgia come from car crashes and secondhand cigarette smoke, seems right on the money. The Embassy does recommend rabies, tetanus, polio, hepatitis A, diphtheria, and typhoid immunizations for extensive travel in the country.

For a list of pharmacies in Tbilisi, *see* page 331.

Money

From July 1, 1924, until April 5, 1993, the ruble, the currency of the USSR, was the only legal tender in the territory of Georgia. During this period Georgia, of course, was one of the republics of the Soviet Union. After the dissolution of the USSR, the Cabinet of Ministers of Georgia decided to introduce the coupon of the National Bank of Georgia as a temporary monetary unit in conjunction with the already circulating ruble. One coupon was equal to one ruble. In the fall of 1995 a new Georgian national currency was introduced: the lari, which is worth US $1.28. The lari is comprised of 100 tetri. Tetri come in coins of one, two, five, ten, 20, and 50. Lari notes come in denominations of one, two, five, ten, 20, 50, and 100. The great Georgian painter Pirosmani is on the one lari note. Queen Tamara is on the 50 lari bill.

Georgia is a cash economy. Credit cards and travelers' checks are only accepted at major hotels. There are no ATM machines. A list of the major banks that change money is on page 325; you can also change money at numerous stores and stands throughout the center of the city. You need to be careful about the rates being quoted. All hotels will also change money. Only banks and certain hotels, however, will be able to provide you with a receipt of your transaction that you might need to show at Customs upon leaving the country (see page 58). Money changed officially may be reconverted upon leaving the country, but the hit you'll take on the commission amount suggests you would do well to change reasonably small sums as you go to avoid this.

The pound sterling is quoted much less often than the deutsche mark, French franc, or the ruble, and when it is quoted, it appears significantly below its normal rate against the dollar elsewhere in the world.

The conclusion seems to be: take dollars. In past years the advice has generally been to take small denominations of currency to ensure getting your money exchanged, but this has now changed and you can feel comfortable carrying bills of higher denominations. The skittishness around US $100 bills because of the large amount of counterfeits is also a thing of the past. The new Ben Franklin design has seen to this. It is still best, however, to bring US currency printed after 1990.

For money transfers, Western Union is fairly ubiquitous throughout Tbilisi.

Photography

Kodak and to a lesser extent Fuji print films are widely available in the center of Tbilisi, slide film less so. Kodak Gold 36-exposure print film is available for 5.20 lari (100 ASA) and 6.50 lari (200 ASA). Film processing shops can be found throughout Tbilisi.

There are no special rules about what can and cannot be shot. Common sense should prevail, however, when approaching military installations, etc.

Time Zones

Georgia is eight hours ahead of New York (Eastern Standard Time) during the summer and ten hours ahead during daylight savings time. For the past few years

Georgia has not adjusted for daylight savings time for economic reasons involving the cost of electricity at peak hours.

Tipping

No set percentage for tips is universally agreed upon in Georgia. The best method is to round off your bill or fare to the next higher sum: if your restaurant bill is 93 lari give the waiter 100, if 46 lari give 50. Georgians despise nothing so much as stinginess, so whatever you give, do so with the élan of glad-handedness. Never be seen counting your tetri.

Communications

Most major hotels in Tbilisi can provide you with phone, fax and e-mail services. There is an AT&T direct access number in Georgia: 8 0288. This will connect you to an AT&T operator. This access number may not work from all phones or pay phones, but when it does work no deposit is necessary. Local calls from pay phones cost ten tetri.

The best place to deal with all your communications needs is at the Central Telephone and Telegraph Office, at 31 Rustaveli Avenue in Tbilisi. The international section is on the ground floor and staff members speak some English. The office is open 24 hours a day, seven days a week.

Georgia now has phone cards that can be purchased at the Central Telephone and Telegraph Office, but not all public phones will accept them. The cost is as follows: 50 units = 5.20 lari, 100 units = 10.40 lari, 200 units = 20.80 lari. For 50 units you can get two minutes of calling time anywhere in the world. There are no discount rates.

A more congenial way to make your phone calls is from the Wheels Irish Bar (Guinness Bar) at 16 Akhvlediani Street in Tbilisi. While having a meal or a drink you can place an order for a call and wait at your table for it to be put through. The cost for the call is between 1.64 lari and 4 lari per minute depending on where you're phoning.

With independence has come access to information, as seen by this advertisement for television stations available to residents of Tbilisi (photo by David Halford)

If you are calling direct internationally, add 8 10 before the standard country code, (1 for the U.S., 44 for the U.K., etc.)

The following are area codes for major cities in Georgia:

Adigeni	266	Lagodekhi	254
Akhaltsikhe	265	Marneuli	257
Akhmeta	249	Ozurgeti	296
Batumi	88222	Poti	293
Bolnisi	258	Senaki	213
Borjomi	267	Sighnaghi	255
Dedoplistskaro	259	Sokhumi	88122*
Dusheti	246	Tbilisi	32
Gagra	88132*	Telavi	250
Gori	270	Tianeti	248
Gurjaani	253	Tsalka	263
Kaspi	271	Tskhinvali	241
Khashuri	268	Zestaphoni	292
Khvareli	252	Zugdidi	215
Kutaisi	231	* Temporarily not in service	

Georgian Activities in the USA

The Georgian Association in the USA Inc. produces a quarterly newsletter (US$25 for an annual subscription) that is the best source of news on everything Georgian happening in the States. News excerpts are edited from articles in the Black Sea Press and Caucasus Press. The Association also organizes a number of Georgia-related events each year. For more information, contact the association: 205 West 95th Street, Suite 1C, New York, NY 10025-6310, tel. (212) 222-8951, fax. (617) 325-0593, e-mail: georgassoc@shore.net.

Those thinking about doing business in Georgia, should contact Caucasus Business Advisors, 35 Wallis Road, Chestnut Hill, MA 02167-3110, USA, tel. (617) 325-3470, fax. (617) 325-0593, e-mail: georgassoc@shore.net.

Qualified teachers who would like to teach for six weeks in the summer in Tbilisi should contact: AGSI (American Georgian Summer Institute)-Redjeb Jordania, 7 Lotus Avenue, East Hampton, NY 11937, USA, e-mail: redjeb@aol.com.

The Embassy of Georgia is the best source of information on both traveling to

Georgia, Georgia-American business opportunities, and Georgian events in the U.S. See page 319 for contact information.

For those interested in Georgian food, a new restaurant has opened in Brooklyn: Tbilisi, 811 Kings Highway, Brooklyn, NY 11223, USA, tel. (718) 382-6485.

Internet Listings

There are more than of 150 web sites relating to every aspect of Georgia, from a copy of the Constitution to the homepage of the US Embassy in Tbilisi. Many of these are linked to each other. The collated web sites provided by the state and a few individuals and businesses are particularly helpful. Start with these. They will lead you to most of the other homepages:

www.sakartvelo.com   Almost everything can be reached from this list of sites, which has been sorted into subject and includes annotations on content and timeliness. This site was created by a Georgian graduate student in the US, but a recent posting indicated he might not have the funds to continue. This would be a pity as most sites listed below can be found here, together with many charming and useful homepages by individuals.

www.parliament.ge   The website of the Georgian parliament, this site provides profiles of parliamentary committee chairpeople as well as access to important political information on the country with links to other areas, including cultural and travel advice.

www.sanet.ge   This is the state Internet provider. The Biweekly online subscriber newpaper (*Georgian Times*) can be reached here at www.sanet.ge/gtze, as can the daily bulletin provider, BGI News Agency, at www.sanet.ge.bgi.

www.geuniverse.com   This site has been provided by CIPDD (Caucasian Institute for Peace, Democracy, and Development) and contains several other online media services, including www.geuniverse.com/org/cipdd/chronicle, www.geuniverse.com/org/cipdd/digest, and www.geuniverse.com/resonance.

www.steele.com   This homepage is where you will find the Georgian Association site link (www.steele.com/georgassoc), together with a number of other Georgian sites including human rights and art. *See* also www.steele.com/georgia for travel information.

eurasianews.com/erc/caucasus.htm#georgia is a good source for news information and reports on Georgia and the area as a whole, as well as links to other sites. You can find the Georgia Profile here (successor to the Chronicle) at www.armazi.demon.co.uk/profile.html. voyager.rtd.utk.edu/~zlotchen/georgia provides another list of Georgia-related sites.

The embassies also have online information services as follows: www.steele.com/embgeorgia is the site of the Georgian Embassy in Washington, DC. travel.state.gov/georgia.html is part of the US Department of State for Consular Affairs' traveler information line. www.sanet.ge/usis is the home page for the US Embassy in Tbilisi, and includes information sites and consular sites.

The majority of search engine travel sections and online travel guides/booking services have not yet reached Georgia, but the following are quite good, and some are linked to the above: www.wtgonline.com/country/ge (World Travel Guide), www.turknet.com (Atlas Travel Magazine). www.great-adventures.com is a helpful site with links to other Georgian pages.

Health pages worth checking are: www.tripprep.com and www.cdc.gov/travel/easteurp.htm.

Most of the other interesting sites are linked to one or often many of the above. www.sakartelo.com is definitely the best place to start for any kind of subject search. Using search engines with the key word Georgia is not very productive since you will be inundated with sites on its American counterpart.

Press

Caucasus Press and Black Sea Press are daily e-mail publications that contain economic and political news about Georgia and the Caucasus. For more information, send e-mail to caucasus@access.sanet.ge and bspress@access.sanet.ge.

The *Georgian Times* is a biweekly English-language newspaper that has been published since 1993. An excellent source of news, classifieds, and other advertisements for English speakers, it is available at news kiosks for 1.30 lari. You can always find copies at Betsy's Hotel and the Sheraton Metechi Palace Hotel as well as on Georgian Airlines and British Airways flights into Tbilisi. You can read the *Georgian Times* online at: http://www.sanet.ge/gtze/. The newspaper's offices in Tbilisi are located at 6 Tsabadze Street, tel. 94 25 92, fax. 23 70 12.

Georgia Profile, a monthly news magazine, is another means for English speakers to stay abreast of what's happening in Georgia. Usually available on British Airways flights into Tbilisi, you can also subscribe by contacting Caucasus & CIS Civitas Georgica, tel. and fax. in Tbilisi 29 28 89 or e-mail: profile@armazi.demon.ac.uk.

Shopping

As a result of the devastating war in Abkhazia and the huge challenges associated with untethering the Georgian economy from years of Moscow's central planning, Georgia's economic reality has spelled serious hardships for significant numbers of the population. Georgia's intelligentsia has been particularly hard-hit and you will find many of them selling extraordinary family heirlooms at the *mshrali hidi* or Dry Bridge behind the American Embassy in Tbilisi. Jewelry, silverware, china, and paintings—often from the Russian Imperial Period—are available in some profusion. Here the term "distressed" has greater significance than price, and each shopper must deal with his or her personal moral code in these transactions.

A wide selection of antiques including weapons, furniture, crystal, jewelry, musical instruments, paintings, and prints are available at antique shops along Rustaveli Avenue. Stop in at the art gallery at 44–46 Rustaveli Avenue and at the shops Pirosmani and Patmani across the square from the Iveria Hotel; Solani Shop at 19 Rustaveli Avenue; and Salome Art Salon at 41 Vetskhli Street near the American Embassy.

Numerous small stalls along Rustaveli offer a range of books in Georgian, Russian, English, and German. The Saunje Bookshop at 28 Rustaveli Avenue still exists but with slimmer pickings than in years gone by. There is a book counter in the Telecommunications Building on Rustaveli and in the arcade at 16 Melikishvili.

The following list of traditional Georgian handicrafts and souvenirs will give you some gift ideas as you travel throughout the country:

khanjali (kinjal): the famous Georgian dagger comes with a highly decorated scabbard.

sabre: sword with curved blade in a scabbard of elaborate filigree work.

mcheduroba (chikanka): metal bas-reliefs of both historical and contemporary themes.

khantsy: winehorns, made from the horns of mountain rams and decorated with engraved niello, usually sold in pairs.

katkha: wooden goblet with a wooden ring at its stem, all of which is carved from a single piece of wood.

tasi: unusual black glazed ceramic bowls and mugs.

nabadi (burka): the traditional mountain woolen cape.

chokha: traditional Georgian jacket complete with special breast pockets designed for gun cartridges.

Svanetian and Kakhetian felt caps.

Rings, necklaces, brooches, and earrings, beaded and filigreed with non-precious stones.

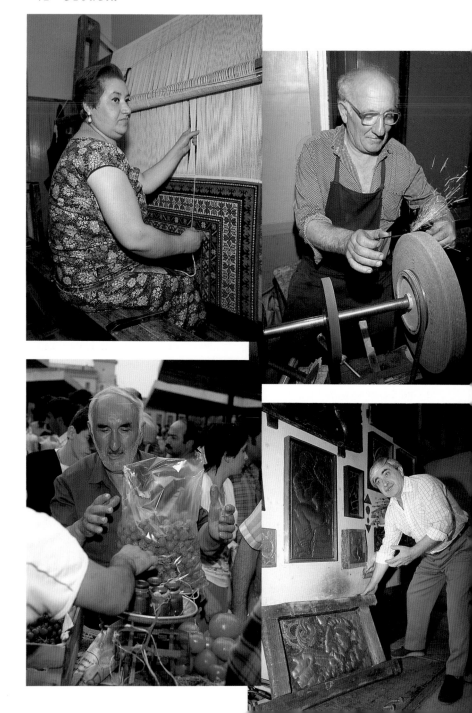

The population of Tbilisi is 1,234,600 compared with the next largest city, Kutaisi, which has a population of 240,900. Given these numbers, you can count on the fact that your greatest shopping opportunities will be in the capital. The rule of thumb in this part of the world is if you see it and want it, then buy it: this item might not surface again during the rest of your stay.

Language

The three related languages of the Georgian people—Georgian, Svan, and Mingrelo-Laz—are not part of the Indo-European, Finno-Ugric, or Semitic families but belong to the Ibero-Caucasian or Kartvelian (Southern Caucasian) language group. Although many theories link these languages to Basque and even Etruscan, most scholars derive their origins from an indigenous proto-Georgian language called Old Kartvelian. Because of various tribal migrations within Georgia and the resuling divisions, and the loss of contact due to geographic barriers, Old Kartvelian evolved along different lines. Tzanic, the ancient language spoken in Colchis, from which Megruli (Mingrelian) and Chanuri (Laz) ultimately derived, split around the 19th century BC. Classical Georgian, which eventually evolved into modern Georgian—the official language of the country—developed parallel to Tzanic until the eighth century BC, after which it followed patterns of its own. Svanuri, the language of the Svans who live in the Enguri basin of the Caucasian highlands and around the upper part of the Tskhenystskaly River, seems to have split directly from Old Kartvelian around 2000 BC.

Modern Georgian is used throughout the country, but the other languages are spoken "domestically" in their regions. Although all three languages derive from Old Kartvelian, it is interesting to note that a native of Tbilisi, for example, cannot understand the Megruli spoken by a native of Zugdidi. In addition to these three languages, there are, of course, regional dialects: in the west, the Imeruli dialect of Imereti, the Rachuli dialect of Racha, Guruli in Guria, and the Acharuli of Ajara; in the east, there are the Kartluri of Kartli, and the Kakhuri and Kiziquri of Kakheti. The mountain people communicate in Pshauri, Khevsuruli, Tushuri, Mokheuri, Mtiuluri, and Gudamakruli.

The mountainous topography of Georgia has for centuries made it a safe haven for persecuted peoples. The multiplicity of languages found has been a hallmark of the country since antiquity. According to Pliny, the Romans needed 130 interpreters to do business in this land. Strabo records that in the Black Sea coastal town of Dioscuris (Sokhumi), 70 tribes gathered daily in the market: "All speak different

Artists, artisans, and tradesmen all form part of the life of Tbilisi

languages because of the fact that by reason of their obstinacy and ferocity, they live in scattered groups and without intercourse with one another."

Georgian is a difficult language to learn. Though it shares the same basic parts of speech as most Indo-European languages, it uses distinctive word formations with morphemes, and a complex set of rules governs its verbs. Foreigners are most struck by the tongue-twisting cluster of consonants that are present with dazzling variety, e.g. Mtkvari, the Georgian name for the Kura River; *brtskinvale* meaning "brilliant," and the sentence that foreigners are often asked to pronounce for the amusement of their Georgian friends: *Baqaqi tskalshi kikinebs* (The frog is croaking in the water). If you can say this you'll probably have no trouble learning Georgian.

The Georgian alphabet probably evolved around the fifth century BC with characters possibly derived from a variety of eastern Aramaic. It is one of 14 world alphabets and consists of 33 letters. With the advent of Christianity in Georgia in the AD 300s, the alphabet underwent some changes due to Greek influence. The oldest known inscriptions in Georgian script were found in the Judaean desert in Palestine (*c.* AD 433) and at the church at Bolnisi (*c.* AD 493). The oldest known manuscript (AD 864) is from St. Catherine's Monastery on the Sinai peninsula. The durability of the Georgian language throughout the country's turbulent history is perhaps the single greatest factor in the survival of the Georgians as a people. Of the more than 70 Caucasian peoples (excluding the Armenians), only the Georgians had a written language of their own before Russian colonization in the 19th and 20th centuries.

The following is Professor Howard I. Aronson's suggestion for a workable and popular transliteration.

GEORGIAN LETTER	TRANSLITERATION	GEORGIAN LETTER	TRANSLITERATION
ა	a	ს	s
ბ	b	ტ	t
გ	g	უ	u
დ	d	ფ	p
ე	e	ქ	k
ვ	v	ღ	gh
ზ	z	ყ	q
თ	t	შ	sh
ი	i	ჩ	ch
კ	k	ც	ts
ლ	l	ძ	dz
მ	m	წ	ts
ნ	n	ჭ	ch
ო	o	ხ	kh
პ	p	ჯ	j
ჟ	zh	ჰ	h
რ	r		

A Svanetian woman stands before an 11th-century watchtower in Mestia

USEFUL GEORGIAN WORDS AND PHRASES

English will not get you very far in Georgia. You should hire an interpreter if you speak no Georgian or Russian. Georgians are very proud of their language and culture so even if you speak some Russian, using Georgian words like *gmadlobt* (thank you) and *gamarjobat* (hello) will earn you bonus points wherever you go. Georgian is pronounced the way it's written. *Survival Georgian* is a phrase book for English speakers that contains many helpful words and phrases. Copies can be purchased for US$8.95 plus US$2 postage from Patricia Hall Taniashvili, Box 1833, Surry, Maine 04684, USA, e-mail: patania@downeast.net. *The Georgian Dictionary and Phrasebook* by Nicholas Awde and Thea Khitarishvili (Curzon Press Limited, 1997) is also very useful.

BASICS FOR SURVIVAL AND MAKING FRIENDS

hello: *gamarjobat*
goodbye: *nakhvamdis*
goodnight: *dzili nebissa*
yes: *diakh, ki, ho*
no: *ara*
please: *inebet*
thank you: *gmadlobt*
 (pronounced *madlobts*)
good: *kargia*
it is bad: *tsudia*
beautiful: *lamazi*
it is hot: *tskhela*
it is cold: *tsiva*
My name is: *me mkvia*
What's your name?: *tkveni sakheli?*
How much is?: *ra ghirs?*
 (pronounced *ra rhirs*)
Formal dinner: *supra*

NUMBERS

one: *erti*
two: *ori*
three: *sami*
four: *otkhi*
five: *khuti*
six: *ekvsi*
seven: *shvidi*
eight: *rva*
nine: *tskhra*
ten: *ati*
100: *asi*
1,000: *atasi*

FINDING YOUR WAY

Where is?: *sad aris?*
How far is?: *shors aris?*
street: *kucha*
stop: *gachereba*
go: *tsadi*
turn: *moukhvie, gauxvie*
left: *martskhniv*
right: *mardzhvniv*
straight ahead: *pirdapir*
hotel: *sastumro*

church: *eklesia*
building: *shenoba*
lake: *tba*
river: *mdinare*
bridge: *khidi*

FOOD AND DRINK

wine: *ghvino*
 (pronounced *rhvino*)
water: *tskali*
bread: *puri*
tea: *chai*
coffee: *kava* or *qava*
egg: *kvertskhi*
rice: *brinji*
fruit: *khili*
vegetable: *bostneuli*
lamb: *batkani*
chicken: *katami*
beef: *khortsi*
fish: *tevzi*

Food and Drink

Georgian food is one of great subtlety and variety. Virtually unknown in the West, it combines a broad palette of ingredients and spices that share certain similarities with Mediterranean cooking but are ultimately as distinct as the songs that accompany every banquet. Freshness is the watchword in the Georgian kitchen, and given the incredible fecundity of the land, this goal is most often attained. Sauces do not mask primary ingredients as in some other cooking traditions; they highlight flavors and textures with the unexpected. Regional variations do abound, but the classic dishes, using lamb, chicken or fish, hazelnuts and walnuts, eggplant, plums, corn, pomegranates, kidney beans, coriander, scallions, hot peppers, mint, and basil, fill homes and restaurants throughout the country. While many dishes are highly seasoned, nothing is searingly hot.

Georgian hospitality reaches epic proportions, and the spirit of open-handed, huge-hearted generosity is nowhere better displayed than at the table. No matter what you do in Georgia, you will miss the essence of the place if you don't somehow manage to get invited home for dinner. (Given the great friendliness of the Georgian people, this should not be difficult.) You cannot help but be amazed by the sheer quantity of food. In Georgia the table must groan with plenty: a Georgian inextricably links abundance to his sense of self, his exuberance, his sense of community and sharing. With such a tradition, distinct courses do not exist. Heaped platters and plates and bowls vie for space amid bottles of wine, champagne, lemonade, and Borjomi mineral water. A roast suckling pig—generally carved in the kitchen rather than served whole—or the famous *mtsvadi* (shish kebab), cubes of lamb marinated in oil, vinegar, and spices and served on a skewer, or a variety of stews, might suddenly appear later in the meal. Most dishes served midway, however, merely replenish those you see from the start, so don't hold back! You can pay no greater compliment to your hosts than to stuff yourself with abandon.

One word about your hosts: Georgia has not yet embraced feminism. Your male host will remain seated at the head of the table acting as the *tamada* or toastmaster. His wife, and perhaps the daughters of the house, will cook and serve and may not have time to sit at the table during the meal.

An extensive list of the dishes in the Georgian culinary repertoire follows. Not all of these will appear at a home dinner, at a formal banquet, or even on the menu of a given restaurant, but the dedicated gourmet should be able to sample nearly everything listed over the course of a two-week stay.

adzhika: This spicy condiment hails from Abkhazia and is made from red chili peppers and herbs.

Shepherds drive their flocks through the Kakhetian Range

badrijani: Baby eggplants served whole with their skins and stuffed with a ground walnut paste seasoned with oils and spices.

basturma: Air-dried beef served in thin slices. The nearest equivalent is pastrami.

bazhi: A sauce of ground walnuts, walnut oil, water, and the combination of Georgian spices known as *khmeli-suneli*—the exact mixture of which varies with every cook.

chadi: Cornbread.

chakapuli: A stew of lamb cubes and *tkemali* (a green plum), *tarkhuna* (tarragon), and scallions.

chakhokhbili: Chicken (pheasant, if available) stew with tomato and every green vegetable available. Especially redolent of fresh coriander and lots of onion.

chanakhi: Whole tomatoes baked in a clay pot with greens and garlic, whole eggplants, chunks of lamb, and big green peppers.

chicken chkmeruli (tabaka): Chicken pressed between two clay plates and fried.

churchkhela: A candy made from boiled grape skins and walnuts, sometimes combined with raisins. Never found in restaurants, but sold in village markets or along country roads. Walnuts are strung on a thread and dipped into a hot grape mixture, then hung to solidify.

ghomi (pronounced *rhomi*): The Georgian equivalent of an Italian polenta. Crushed corn kernels to which corn-flour is added, continually stirred, and cooked for a long time. Often served with slices of *suluguni*, cheese placed in the middle of the hot corn purée to melt. A familar taste for Americans from the South.

gozinaki: A sweet of boiled honey and sugar poured over a bed of walnuts.

A fresh loaf from a bakery in Telavi

khachapuri: A cheese pie made from dough, *suluguni* cheese (resembles mozzarella), and sometimes egg. If the Georgians had emigrated to the United States in the same numbers as Italians, these cheese pies would no doubt be as familiar and beloved as pizza, which—minus the tomato sauce—they most resemble. Every housewife prepares this dish somewhat differently, and it exhibits marked regional characteristics as well. There are four types:

imeruli: Most often found in homes. Commonly baked as a round with *imeruli* cheese. Comes from Imereti.

achma: Usually baked as a square and made of many thin layers of dough, cheese, and butter, resembling lasagna. Comes from Ajara.

adjaruli: A version similar to *imeruli* except that it is served open-faced with an egg beaten into the cheese center with a fork. Also from Ajara.

enovani: Like a mille-feuille, with many thin layers of dough and *suluguni*. Found throughout Georgia but especially fine in Tbilisi.

kharcho: a meat and rice soup, highly spiced with black and cayenne peppers.

khashi: a soup of tripe and cow trotters and lots of garlic. This is eaten in the morning and is an excellent remedy for a hangover.

khinkali: Bell-shaped meat dumplings filled with ground beef, pork, lamb, and spices. Black pepper, always provided, should be sprinkled liberally. This delicacy is eaten by holding the doughy twisted end, which is not consumed. Special restaurants called *sakhinkle* specialize in *khinkali*; they rarely appear in the home. Chefs from Dusheti are considered the experts at *khinkali* preparation. A famous anecdote attesting to the addictive nature of these dumplings tells of a man who goes into a

Shepherds near Shatili in Khevsureti prepare mtsvadi (shashlik) and khinkali

sakhinkle and orders 99 *khinkali*. When asked, "Why 99 and not 100?" the man replies, "What do you think I am—a pig?"

lobio: Kidney beans baked with water in a ceramic pot and then crushed with a pestle and mixed with coriander and a spice called *umbalo* (European pennyroyal).

matsoni: Georgian yogurt.

mtsvadi (shashlik): A lamb or beef shish kebab of Caucasian rather than Georgian origin. Found on most restaurant menus, and the preferred dish for picnics in the countryside. Usually made by men, as with the preparation of a Spanish paella.

nadugi: Curd mixed with mint.

pkhali: Comes in two types, green and red. Both consist of minced spinach mixed with ground walnuts, the famous *khmeli-suneli* spices, garlic, and a little vinegar with a topping of pomegranate seeds.

puri: The bread (both round and crusty, and long and doughy) that accompanies every meal. *Dedaspuri* is long and doughy and is often featured in the paintings of Pirosmani.

satsivi: Chunks of turkey (sometimes chicken) in a sauce of corn flour, saffron, and enough ground walnuts to give a granular consistency. Always served at room temperature.

tkhemali: A spicy, tart green plum sauce. The essential accompaniment for shish kebab or any other meat.

WINE

As deeply satisfied as you'll find yourself after any Georgian repast, it ultimately would be incomplete without the magnificent red and white wines that accompany every lunch and dinner. Just as we in the West so often mistakenly called the former Soviet Union "Russia" as though the two were synonymous, we also tended to think of vodka as the alcoholic beverage that lubricated every festive occasion throughout the former empire. Nothing could be more inaccurate with respect to Georgia. Georgian life remains rooted in the Bacchic tradition, in which reverence for the grape influences everything from Christian iconography to the oral traditions embedded in toast-making. St. Nino, the Cappadocian nun who brought Christianity to Georgia in the fourth century AD, made her cross from vine branches tied with her own hair. This remains the cross of the Georgian Church.

Georgian winemaking is an ancient art. In fact, Georgia is thought to be the place where viticulture began. Hugh Johnson in his book *Vintage: The Story of Wine* has this to say: "Archaeologists accept accumulation of grape pips as evidence (of the likelihood at least) of winemaking ... the oldest pips of cultivated vines so far discovered and carbon dated—at least to the satisfaction of their finders—were found in Soviet Georgia, and belong to the period 7000–5000 BC."

Additional archaeological findings are large *kvevris*, cone-shaped clay jugs buried in the ground, which stored wine and allowed it to mature.

Georgians currently cultivate over 500 grape varieties throughout the country, and commercially produce 60 wines. These wines have won well-deserved fame throughout the world. The most famous of the Georgian grapes are Rkatsiteli, Saperavi, Mtsvane, Tsolikauri, Tsitska, Cabernet, Chinuri, Goruli-Mtsvane, Aligote, Aleksandreuli, Ojaleshi, Chkhaveri, Krakhuna, Khikhvi, and Izabella.

Most wines take their names from their place of origin. The most famous wine-growing regions in Georgia are Kakheti, Imereti, and Racha-Lechkhumi. The autonomous republic of Abkhazia also produces excellent wines, especially in the regions of Gali, Gudauta, and the city of Sokhumi. Most wines have a strength of 10–12 percent alcohol. They possess amazing purity which generally allows for huge intake and no raging hangover later. You will most likely encounter the famous wines described below. You can taste an even larger selection at a *sachashniko*, or wine-tasting shop.

Rtvelli, the grape harvest, occurs in early October. While the great wine cellars of the major vinyards have bins carefully catalogued by year, the wine labels themselves do not carry a date. Questioned about this, a friend remarked that Georgians enjoy drinking their wine, not worshipping it as though at a shrine.

VINTAGE DRY WHITE TABLE WINES

Gurjaani: Of a pale straw color, fruity bouquet, and piquant flavor, this wine is made from Rkatsiteli and Mtsvane grapes cultivated in the Gurjaani, Sighnaghi, and Sagarejo districts of Kakheti.

Manavi: Ranging in color from pale straw to straw green, this much-loved wine has a fruity aroma and

Lunch is prepared in Motsameta Monastery in Imereti

finely balanced flavor. It is made from the Mtsvane grape cultivated in Manavi, Kakheti. The author has come to associate this wine with the particularly fine ruins of an ancient fortress on the outskirts of the town.

Napareuli: This wine has a pale straw color and light fruity flavor. It is made from Rkatsiteli grapes cultivated in the Napareuli district of Kakheti.

Rkatsiteli: From Rkatsiteli grapes cultivated in Kardanakhi, Kakheti, this wine undergoes the process of fermentation in clay jars buried underground, a unique Kakhetian practice. It has a dark amber color, a rich fruity bouquet, and a very smooth taste.

Tsinandali: The pride of Georgian wines, made from Rkatsiteli and Mtsvane grapes cultivated in Telavi and Kvareli, it matures for three years in oak barrels in the cellars of the Tsinandali winery. For information concerning an excursion to this winery, see page 297.

VINTAGE DRY RED TABLE WINES

Kvareli: Made from Saperavi grapes cultivated in the Kvareli district of Kakheti, it is aged for three years in oak barrels in the Tsinandali wine cellars. In color, bouquet, and aroma, it resembles Napareuli.

Mukuzani: Probably the best of the vintage reds, this wine is made from Saperavi grapes cultivated in the Mukuzani district of Kakheti. It has received eight gold medals, four silver, and one bronze at various international competitions.

Napareuli: Made from the Saperavi grape cultivated in the Napareuli district of the left bank of the Alazani Valley in Kakheti, this full-bodied red has a superb dark pomegranate color and a heady bouquet and aroma.

SEMISWEET WHITE WINES

Akhmeta: Made from Mtsvane grapes cultivated in the Akhmeta district of Kakheti, this wine is of a greenish straw color and possesses an admirable light sweetness.

Chkhaveri: Grapes grown in the Bakhvi part of western Georgia and Abkhazia make this pale wine infused with a pinkish tint and hints of the flavor of apples.

Tetra: Rachuli-Tetra grapes are cultivated in the Ambrolauri district to make this naturally semisweet wine, which has a fruity and delicate exuberance.

SEMISWEET RED WINES

Akhasheni: Often found on the tables of Georgian homes, this wine comes from Saperavi grapes cultivated in Akhasheni of the Gurjaani district in Kakheti. This wine, along with Kindzmarauli and Khhvanchkara, is sometimes referred to as "the blood of giants."

Khvanchkara: An excellent red wine made from Alexandreuli and Mujhureteli grapes cultivated in the village of Khvanchkara in western Georgia. This wine has

Georgian wine accompanies every meal

the dubious distinction of having been Stalin's favorite; you will inevitably hear this upon its being served. Extremely popular, it has a dark ruby color with a potent aroma and bouquet.

Kindzmarauli: On par with Khvanchkara, this wine comes from Saperavi grapes cultivated on the slopes of the Caucasian mountains in the Kvareli district of Kakheti. Rich burgundy in color, it is full-bodied and sinuous.

DESSERT WINES, BRANDIES, CHAMPAGNES
Among the most famous semidry wines are Pirosmani and Barakoni; the most famous white is Tbilisuri. Among the fortified dessert wines are Kardanakhi, Anaga, Sighnaghi, Iveria, and Kolkheti. Other dessert wines include Saamo, Salkhino and Atenuri (both white and sparkling), and Sadarbazo (a sparkling red).

Georgian brandies are first-rate and equal in quality to some of the better-known Armenian cognacs. Like heroic soldiers, they receive medals denoting quality and age. The best of the best—the 40, 50, and 60 Year Jubilee brandies—are hard to come by. In descending order, however, you should seek the following:

Vardzia (25 years), *Sakartvelo* (20 years), *Tbilisi* (15–20 years), *Eniseli* (12–15 years), *OS* (12 years), *Abkhazeti* (ten years), *Kazbeki* (ten years), *Gremi* (nine years), *Vartsikhe* (6–7 years), *Egrisi* (six years), *Georgian Brandy* (3–5 years).

Georgian champagne is pleasant and refreshing, though a little too sweet if you enjoy chewing a Mumm's Extra Dry.

Chacha is the Georgian aquavit, made from undistilled alcohol produced from grape pulp in oak barrels. With 50 percent alcohol or greater, this stuff can really knock you for a loop. Georgian city dwellers often buy *chacha* directly from farmers who make large volumes of it at harvest time. Be warned, therefore, that a Georgian host may well keep his supply in a champagne bottle. If you don't hear a pop when you open a bottle, go slowly.

Borjomi is the Georgian Perrier. A sparkling water high in mineral content, stronger than San Pelligrino, less fizzy than Perrier, it is widely consumed for its curative and digestive properties. The Borjomi factories, located in a famous spa town of the same name on the banks of the Mtkvari (Kura) River in central Georgia, produce more than 300 million bottles a year from a source that has a daily yield of 500,000 liters.

Etiquette

Despite the Georgian love of wine, or perhaps because of it, it is generally considered in very bad taste to get drunk. Women are not required or indeed expected to keep pace with men's consumption. Men, however, had better have a good head for what they drain; their very manliness—and the judgment of a traveler's manliness—depends upon it.

While some of the more important toasts require drinking your glass to the bottom as a sign of respect (*bolomde* in Georgian), the traditions of the Georgian table space the drinking out over the course of the meal. Here are the rules. You cannot drink until the *tamada* (toastmaster) has made his toast and drunk. Only then, and usually in order around the table, can other revelers echo the toast and drink. Never propose a different toast unless you are given permission: that is an offense to the *tamada*. If the toast is made to you as a visitor, to America or England, to the President or the Queen, or in any way bears directly upon your presence, you must wait to drink until everyone else has gone before you. Your toast in response should be one of thanks. Occasionally you will hear the *tamada* say *Alaverdi* to someone. This means that one guest has been chosen to elaborate upon the *tamada*'s toast. All others present then drink to this same theme.

Toasting is not taken lightly in Georgia! In addition to the time-honored forms are time-honored subjects. Here, in order, are the subjects to which you will most likely be drinking: to peace (especially in the west of Georgia), to the reason for the gathering, to the hostess, to parents and ancestors, to Georgia as motherland, to friends, to the memory of those who have died (this is usually accompanied by pouring wine onto bread before you drink), to life, to children, to the *mandilosani* (in honor of women), to each guest present, sometimes individually, sometimes combined. After this the *tamada* usually allows anyone who so desires to make a toast. A closing toast is made in honor of the *tamada,* and the very last toast is to a safe journey home and to future meetings. Most Georgian homes have a large ram's or goat's horn called a *khantsi*. This will invariably be brought out at some point during the meal, filled with wine, and handed to an honored guest. Usually you must drink this to the bottom.

You can find the soul of Georgia at the seaside and the riverbanks, in the orchards and the mountains, within the sacred precincts of ancient churches and

among the crumbling ruins of fortress walls. But nowhere is it so immediately and joyously felt as at a long Georgian table where, dining with the most hospitable people in the world, you lift your glass and feel powerfully connected to human sentiments that transcend mere bonhomie.

Gaumar . . . Jos! (Cheers!)

Holidays

With the exception of Tbilisoba (last Sunday of October), which was created by the State as a holiday to celebrate all things Georgian, most authentic folk holidays are tied to the calendar of the Georgian Orthodox Church. Many are celebrated only in certain villages. Others have no fixed date. What is common to all of them, however, is that they have never been sufficiently well known to attract tourists. If you go, you will be among the first. You must act with circumspection. Do not enter a church scantily clad and unkempt. Men must be shaved. Do not take photos inside the church.

On most of these holidays, in the smaller villages a church service is followed by a meal and festivities in the central square. As a guest you will most certainly be welcome; you might want to leave before the heavy drinking takes you late into the night.

In addition to the folk and religious holidays listed below, May 26 is **Georgian Independence Day**, March 3 is **Mother's Day**, January 1 is **New Year's Day**, April 9 is **Memorial Day**.

MAJOR RELIGIOUS HOLIDAYS THROUGHOUT GEORGIA

Akhaljaroba: Respect for the Cross. May 7 in the villages of Khidistavi (province of Kartli) and the village of Akhmeta (Province of Kakheti).

Alaverdoba: On September 14 in the precincts of the Cathedral of Alaverdi in Kakheti.

Arbooba: St. George's Day. Third Sunday after Mariamoba (August 28) in the villages of Arboshi and Geri (province of Kartli).

Djvarpatiosnoba: Respect for the Cross. May 7 throughout Kartli and Kakheti.

Didbatonoba: St. George's Day. November 23 in the village of Matani (province of Kakheti).

Didgoroba: On May 7 near Digomi (Kartli) and August 15 in the Monastery of Kvatakhevi (Kartli).

Garegnoba: The day after Easter throughout the provinces of Imereti and Guria.

Iakharoba: In autumn in the village of Matani (Kakheti).

Notwithstanding Georgians' sophistication about the present, all families instill in their children a great reverence for Georgia's cultural traditions

Historical and Geographical Provinces of Georgia

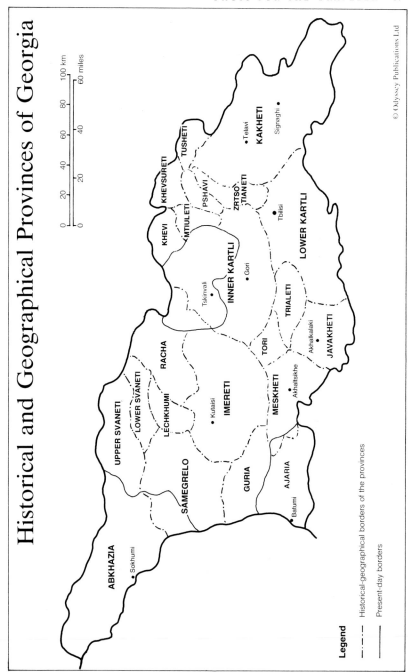

Legend

– · – · – Historical-geographical borders of the provinces

——— Present-day borders

*The appearance of the famous medieval watchtowers in Svaneti has not changed much
since they were photographed by the great mountain photographer Vittorio Sella in 1890*

Kashvetoba: The Holiday of St. George. Third Sunday of Easter in Tbilisi and many towns throughout Kartli, Kakheti, Imereti, Svaneti.

Kvirikoba: July 15 in the village of Lamiskana (Kartli), Akhmeta (Kakheti), Kviriketsminda (Racha); July 28 outside of Mestia (Svaneti).

Lavroba: Easter Monday in the village of Lavriskhevi (Kakheti).

Mtavarangelozoba: Easter Thursday in the village of Sadgavro (Imereti).

Mtavarmotzameoba: The Holiday of St. George. July 3 in Khorkheli (Kakheti).

Okanoba: Celebration of the day Iberia became Christian. The second day of Easter in Gori and generally throughout Kartli.

Tzikhegoroba: Easter Tuesday in Matani (Kakheti).

Basilididisa: The Remembrance of St. Basil the Great. January 1.

All Saint's Day: January 19.

Our Saint Mother Nino the Georgian, the Great Educator: January 27.

Ioanenatlismtzemlisa: The Birth of St. John the Baptist. June 24.

The Remembrance of Saints Peter and Paul: July 12.

Saint Mary's Day: August 28.

Saint George's Day: November 23.

Skiing

Gudauri is a ski resort built on the slopes of the Caucasus mountains as a Georgian-Austrian joint venture. The hotel and sports complex, completed in 1987, has an indoor pool, sauna, whirlpool, two indoor tennis courts, and bowling. The slopes are superb, with a vertical drop of about 1,000 meters (3,300 feet) and unbroken runs of between six and 14 km (four and nine miles). Maintenance on the lift equipment and trails in the past few years, however, has reportedly been poor. The conditions are now ideal for off-piste and heliskiers. Excursions can be arranged through Caucasus Travel and the people at the hotel at Gudauri; see page 44 for more information.

For information about the ski resort of Bakuriani *see* page 151.

Tbilisi

Tbilisi's multi-ethnic cosmopolitan tradition goes back to the time of David the Builder in the 12th century. The city's cultural life reflects this diversity: where else could you find Armenian, Russian, and Georgian theaters all within 15 minutes of each other? As you walk around the city you will be impressed by layer upon layer of cultures, peoples, historical periods, and unique monuments. This city reveals its charms slowly. In the morning, walking along the banks of the Mtkvari (Kura) River, you'll think you've grasped the essence of the city that's somewhat akin to Florence on the Arno. Later, on Rustaveli Avenue you'll come upon the Moorish-style Opera House and you'll think of the Mezquita in Cordoba. Both are correct. The city is neither entirely European nor entirely Asian. You, like so very many before you, are standing at the crossroads between those two great continents.

The capital of Georgia, Tbilisi, population 1,234,600 and 349 sq. km (135 sq. miles), is one of the most ancient cities in the Caucasus. The city is favorably situated on both banks of the Mtkvari River and is protected on three sides by mountains: to the south the Sololaki ridge and Mt. Tabori, to the east Mt. Makhata, and to the west spurs of the Trialeti range. On a clear day you can see the mighty peak of Mt. Kazbek jutting from the Greater Caucasus in the north. The sheltering mountains, such as the northeast slope of Mt. Tabori, are the source of sulfuric hot springs, and of cool breezes that blow through the valley. On the same latitude as Barcelona, Rome, and Boston, Tbilisi has a temperate climate with an average temperature of 13.2° C (56° F). Winters are relatively mild, with only a few days of snow. January is the coldest month, with an average temperature of 0.9° C (33° F). July is the hottest month, averaging 25.2° C (77° F). Autumn is the loveliest season in which to visit the city.

History

The advantages of the Mtkvari River valley as a place of habitation have been appreciated since at least the Neolithic period. Archaeologists have found burial grounds and dwellings from as early as 5000 BC throughout the city. The first documents relating to Tbilisi date from AD 400. At that time the city was controlled by the Persians, who were responsible for building the Narikala fortress along the crest of the Sololaki ridge. Impressed by the strategic advantages of this fortress and its protection of the city on the slope beneath, King Vakhtang Gorgasali of Iberia decided to move his capital here from Mtskheta in 458. Georgians regard King Vakhtang as

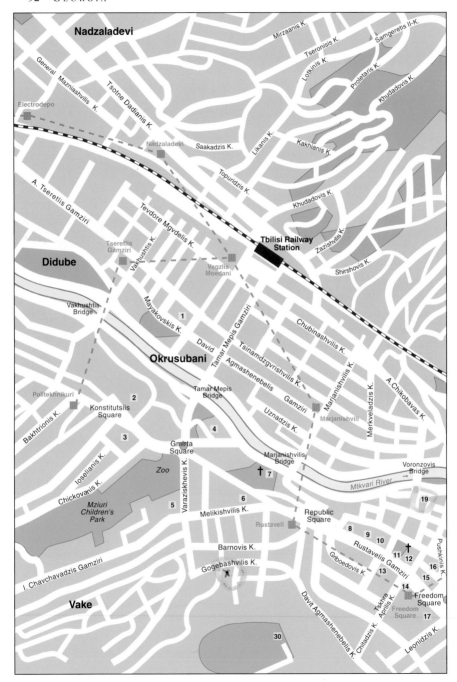

Nadzaladevi

Mirzaanis K.

Tseronisis K.

Lotkinis K.

Samgeretis II-K.

Proletaris K.

Khudadovis K.

General Mazniashvili K.

Tsotne Dadianis K.

Electrodepo

Nadzaladevi

Saakadzis K.

Likanis K.

Kakhianis K.

Topuridzis K.

A. Tseretlis Gamziri

Tevdore Mgvdelis K.

Khudadovis K.

Tbilisi Railway Station

Zazishvilis K.

Tseretlis Gamziri

Vakhushtis K.

Didube

Vagzlis Moedani

Shirshovis K.

Vakhushtis Bridge

Mayakovskis K.

1

Chubinashvili K.

David

Okrusubani

Tamar Mepis Gamziri

Tsinamdzgvrishvilis K.

Agmashenebelis

Marjanishvilis K.

Merkveladzis K.

A.Chikobavas K.

Politekhnikuri

Konstitutsiis Square

2

Tamar Mepis Bridge

Gamziri

Uznadzis K.

Marjanishvill

Bakhtrionis K.

3

4

Zoo

Gmirta Square

Marjanishvilis Bridge

Voronzovis Bridge

Ioselianis K.

Chickovanis K.

Varaziskhevis K.

† 7

Mtkvari River

19

Mziuri Children's Park

5

6

Melikishvilis K.

Rustaveli

Republic Square

8

9

10

I. Chavchavadzis Gamziri

Barnovis K.

Rustavelis Gamziri

11

12

†

Gogebashvilis K.

Griboedovis K.

13

16

15

Davit Agmashenebelis K.

14

Vake

Tskhra Aprilis K.

Freedom Square

Freedom Square

17

30

Chitadzis K.

Leonidzis K.

Pushkinis K.

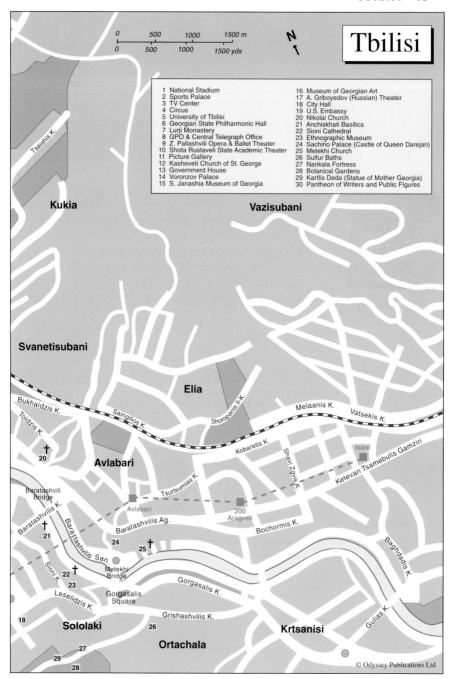

Tbilisi

1 National Stadium
2 Sports Palace
3 TV Center
4 Circus
5 University of Tbilisi
6 Georgian State Philharmonic Hall
7 Lurji Monastery
8 GPO & Central Telegraph Office
9 Z. Paliashvili Opera & Ballet Theater
10 Shota Rustaveli State Academic Theater
11 Picture Gallery
12 Kasheveti Church of St. George
13 Government House
14 Voronzov Palace
15 S. Janashia Museum of Georgia
16 Museum of Georgian Art
17 A. Griboyedov (Russian) Theater
18 City Hall
19 U.S. Embassy
20 Nikolai Church
21 Anchiskhati Basilica
22 Sioni Cathedral
23 Ethnographic Museum
24 Sachino Palace (Castle of Queen Darejan)
25 Metekhi Church
26 Sulfur Baths
27 Narikala Fortress
28 Botanical Gardens
29 Kartlis Deda (Statue of Mother Georgia)
30 Pantheon of Writers and Public Figures

Kukia

Vazisubani

Svanetisubani

Elia

Bukhaidzis K.

Toidzis K.

Saingilios K.

Shoropanis II K.

Melaanis K.

Vatsekis K.

20

Avlabari

Kobaretis K.

Shavi Zgvis K.

Isani

Ketevan Tsamebulis Gamziri

Baratashvili Bridge

Baratashvilis K.

Tsurtsumias K.

Avlabari

300 Aragveli

Baghdadis K.

21

Baratashvilis San.

Baratashvilis Ag.

Bochormis K.

24

25

22

Sioni K.

23

Metekhi Bridge

Gorgasalis K.

18

Leselidzis K.

Gorgasalis Square

Grishashvilis K.

Gulias K.

Sololaki

26

Krtsanisi

27

Ortachala

29

28

© Odyssey Publications Ltd

the city's founder, and the equestrian statue in front of the Metekhi Church honors his legacy. The name of the city, Tbilisi, is also connected to him through a legend; King Vakhtang went hunting one day and happened to shoot a pheasant. The pheasant fell wounded into a nearby spring but soon bounded out, apparently healed. Vakhtang deemed the life-giving water a good location for his new city. He founded Tbilisi near these hot sulfur springs and named the city after them. *Tbili* means "warm" in Georgian.

Vakhtang Gorgasali died in 502 before he could see the completion of his ambitious building program for the new capital. This work was continued by his son and successor, King Dachi, who built the walls around the town.

The strategic and economic advantages of Tbilisi's location were both a blessing and a curse: the town became a magnet for foreign invaders eager to reap its benefits. The city was sacked or destroyed more than 29 times in a 1,500-year period. From the Byzantine invasion of 626–627 to the complete destruction of the city in 1795 by the Persians under Agha Mohammed Khan, Tbilisi has suffered at the hands of Arabs, Mongols, Seljuk and Ottoman Turks, and numerous tribes from the North Caucasus. Yet it has always been rebuilt, a testament to the tenacity and resilience of the Georgian people.

The longest period of foreign rule began with the Arab invasion of the mid-seventh century. By the 730s, the Arabs had established the residence of their emir in Tbilisi, who resided in the precincts of the Narikala Fortress. The Arabs ruled Tbilisi for more than 400 years, until David the Builder, the great Georgian king, liberated the city in 1121. Throughout the Arab occupation, Tbilisi bore a far greater resemblance to a Moslem than a Christian city. Indeed, the vast majority of the residents were Arab and Turkish merchants, with Georgians, often refusing to submit to Arab domination, living in the countryside.

When King David the Builder (1089–1125) recaptured Tbilisi he went to great lengths to show tolerance to its Moslem population. His enlightened policy engendered great loyalty from the Moslem citizens and led to the development of Tbilisi as a cosmopolitan metropolis at the center of a trade route linking Europe and Asia. As King David's empire expanded, so did the prestige and power of his capital. By the time of his great-granddaughter, Queen Tamara (1184–1207), Tbilisi was one of the most important cities in the Middle East. Marco Polo passed through and wrote, "There is a handsome city named Teflis, around which are settlements and many fortified posts."

But the Golden Age of Georgian history, with Tbilisi at the center of events, was not to last. Forced to submit to Mongol rule, the citizens of Tbilisi paid large tributes to the Khan in exchange for peace. The city's decline continued into the 15th century with the collapse of the Byzantine Empire in 1453. Only during the

reigns of King Teimuraz II and his son Herekle II did the eastern Georgians manage to gain a significant degree of independence from Turkish control and then from the Persians. In 1762 Tbilisi became the capital of eastern Georgia.

Despite the broken promises of the Russians, the Georgian monarchy—specifically King Herekle II's heir, Giorgi XII—continued to press for Georgia to be made a Russian protectorate. Tsar Alexander went one step farther. In 1801 he abolished the Kingdom of Kartli-Kakheti and incorporated eastern Georgia into the Russian Empire. After the destruction of the city by the Persians in 1795, the way was open for the sort of planned city the Russians had in mind. They concentrated on the Garetubani area (now the site of Freedom Square and Rustaveli Avenue), laying out streets either parallel or perpendicular to the Mtkvari River. Affluent merchants and other members of the rising bourgeoisie built villas south on the hills around Sololaki and Mtatsminda. Laborers found housing in the spreading slums of Vake and Saburtalo, west of Garetubani. With the building of the Transcaucasian Railroad in the second half of the 19th century, the number of the urban proletariat swelled.

From a population of just over 200,000 in 1917, the city has grown to well over one million today with the incorporation of outlying villages like Kukiya, Chugureti, Vera, Didube, and Navtlughi. The city's subway system opened in 1966; there are now 20 stations.

The Old Town

The original settlement of Tbilisi, like other fortress towns throughout Georgia such as Kutaisi and Ujarma, developed below the walls of an elevated citadel and continued down to the river. The town and citadel were protected by fortifications. The area known today as the Old Town is also called Kala. It is the original settlement on the right bank of the Mtkvari (Kura) River that developed below the walls of the Narikala Fortress when Vakhtang Gorgasali established his capital here in the fifth century.

Today the Old Town is delineated by Pushkin and Baratashvili Streets in the north and northwest, and by the Mtkvari, the Monument to the 300 Men of Aragvi, and Mt. Tabori in the east and southeast. When David the Builder drove the Arabs out of Tbilisi in 1122, he established his residence on the high left bank of the Mtkvari in a district known as Isani or Isni, which means "fortified place." This district grew under the Arabs in the eighth and ninth centuries, and was connected across the Mtkvari to the district of Kala by a fortified bridge with watchtowers at either end. The contemporary Metekhi Bridge spans the spot where the earlier bridge stood.

Spiral staircases grace many Tbilisi courtyards

In Queen Tamara's time the residential district of Isani developed along the entire length of the plateau above the Mtkvari. Today this district is known as the Avlabari (Place around the Palace), home to Tbilisi's large Armenian population. The view of these typical Tbilisi houses rising precariously above the plateau of the left bank will leave an indelible impression.

Walking from east to west along the right bank of the river, the Church of Metekhi is the climax—after having seen these buildings on the plateau of the opposite bank. The church appears at the bend in the river, and one glimpse gives you an understanding as to why it is the symbol of the Isani Palace district.

Unlike the planned streets of 19th-century Tbilisi (to be toured later), the Old City is a wonderful maze of twisting, crooked alleys that lead to dead ends, unexpected squares, and little courtyards. It is, without doubt, the most distinctive area of Tbilisi. Explore it on foot, at your leisure, and allow chance to govern a good portion of your stroll. It is here that you will feel most strongly that extraordinary amalgam of Asia and Europe that is peculiar to Georgia.

The houses in this district are characterized by deep, elaborately carved, wooden balconies painted white, ochre, pale blue, and cinnamon. Sometimes the balconies are cantilevered from the front of the façade; sometimes they wrap around three sides. Balconies, usually taking the form of glassed-in verandas, are also found facing the inner courtyard. Exterior spiral staircases—often of metal, with the treads worn paper thin—join one story to another. Both balcony and courtyard reflect the Georgian love of company, of sharing one's life with friends and neighbors. They also bespeak a deep attachment to the outdoors and a repugnance at being shut in. Many courtyards boast large mulberry trees or a pergola of tightly woven grape vines beneath which sits a picnic table or two. Many a citizen's sense of well-being is directly linked to these spaces.

Cantilevered wooden balconies like this one in the Old Town of Tbilisi are often elaborately carved (photo by David Halford)

The Old Town has been razed and rebuilt many times during its long history. The last time was in 1795 as a result of the invasion of Agha Mohammed Khan. Most of the houses at that time were of wood, built in a step-like manner, with the roof of one house serving as the front yard for the one above: thus Agha Mohammed Khan burned the entire city. Only the stone sulfur baths and the Anchiskhati Church survived. Although the present edifices date mainly from the 19th century, they were erected upon the foundations of the older buildings and along existing streets. The basic layout therefore conforms to the pattern of streets and squares that existed in the 17th and 18th centuries.

The 19th-century homes, the prototypical "Tbilisi houses," blend centuries of Georgian traditional styles with elements of Russian classicism. Two types of houses were predominant in the city before the development of this amalgamated style: the *baniani sakhli* and the *darbazi*. The first is a low, single-story dwelling with a flat earthen roof. The second is a rectangular house with a hearth in the middle of a room, covered by a beehive type of wooden cupola, with the beams set in a dodecahedron that ends in an open smoke hole. Only one of these *darbazi* buildings remains in Tbilisi, the famous Darbazi of Porakishvili at 10 Chekhov Street. Examples of both types of dwellings can be found in the Museum of Georgian Folk

THE CITY

*L*ook—the city! It is both large and small. This perhaps constitutes its principal charm. On the one hand, it has everything you find in an octopus-city: a million inhabitants, a subway, traffic, industrial outskirts, and a climate that is not, strangely enough for such a promised land, the very best, with a certain perniciousness to the air. On the other hand, it has none of these. You turn . . .

And around the corner, this city is like a tree, a nest, a beehive, a vineyard, an étagère, a wall twined all over in ivy. It suggests a house overgrown with floors, wings, superstructures, and galleries—just as its every house is a city, in a way. Its every twig is unfinished, in the same way as a living branch that has a bud and is growing. You can't be sure the house will not have another little balcony added to it, or another stairway, or another attic on top of the attic: either you didn't notice it yesterday, or they'll build it tomorrow. And if you hail your friend from the courtyard and he answers "I'm coming!" he vanishes and reappears three times, you see him first on the left, then on the right, then on the stairway, then again on a little balcony, before he finally gets all the way down, stands before you, and shakes your hand, most probably suspecting that you don't need anything from him. And if two liters of white wine take the place of your night vision, you will surely get lost on these branches, realizing that you were supposed to climb, not that stairway, but the one that twines around it like a vine but takes you to some other window. Oh, pardon, kolbatono, I'm looking for someone else. Pardon, pardon, I'm dreaming you: these stairs don't stop short, entangling yours—they simply lead to someone else.

Andrei Bitov, A Captive of the Caucasus, 1992

Architecture and Local Lore in the Vake district (*see* page 134). The best zone of the Old Town in which to see the elaborate balconies and staircases of the 19th-century Tbilisi house is in the incline between Puris Moedani and Azizbekov Street. Just beyond Azizbekov Street is Gomi Street, where in addition to a number of interesting traditional houses are steps cut into rock that lead up to the Ateshga (Zoroastrian temple). This square stone structure, distinguished by the lancet arch marking its entrance, is said to stand on the site of a mosque built by the Turks and destroyed by Agha Mohammed Khan in 1795. Another legend has it that long before there was a mosque this was the site of a Zoroastrian temple, hence the name. Where else but in Tbilisi could you find within one neighborhood two synagogues, a mosque, an Armenian church, a Georgian cathedral, and a Zoroastrian temple?

In 1975, over 90 hectares (200 acres) of the Old Town were declared a historic zone and put under a government-sponsored archaeological and restoration program. Work done since 1982 in the northern part of the Old Town, between Leselidze and Pushkin streets, already shows the success of these efforts.

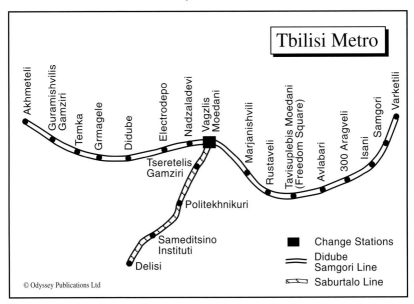

The best place to begin your tour of the Old Town is at the Metekhi Church. Alhough the church itself is located outside the precincts of Kala, it is an appropriately central point that provides an excellent vantage from which to survey the district across the river on the right bank.

THE METEKHI CHURCH OF THE VIRGIN

On the Isani promonotory at a bend in the Mtkvari (Kura) River, the Metekhi Church (1278–1289) is the focal point of Tbilisi. This rocky outcrop had strategic importance from the earliest days of the city's history; on this site in the fifth century Vakhtang Gorgasali, the city's founder, built one of the first five churches that Tbilisi possessed. Here, one of Georgia's most beloved saints, St. Shushanik, was buried after she had been tortured by her husband when she refused to convert with him to Zoroastrianism in 544. When David the Builder drove the Arabs out of Tbilisi in 1122, he moved the royal residence from the area enclosed by the walls of the Narikala Fortress to this plateau on the left bank of the Mtkvari. In this palace Queen Tamara married her second husband, the Ossetian prince David Soslan. In 1235 the Mongols destroyed the Metekhi Palace complex and cathedral. The palace was re-erected after several decades and the palace church, the present Metekhi Church, was built by Demetre II (the Self-Sacrificer) from 1278 to 1289.

Metekhi was captured and damaged during a Turkish invasion in the 17th century and reconquered and reconstructed by Herekle II in 1748. A Persian invasion of Tbilisi in 1795 brought about the final destruction of the palace. In 1819 the Tsarist regime used the site to build the infamous Metekhi jail, which housed many Russian and Georgian revolutionaries, including Maxim Gorky. The jail was torn down in 1937. In 1958, to mark the 1,500th anniversary of the founding of Tbilisi, the **equestrian statue of Vakhtang Gorgasali** was unveiled next to the church. It is the work of the sculptor Elguja Amashukeli, who also created the huge statue of Mother Georgia (*Kartlis Deda*) on the Sololaki ridge.

The Metekhi Church is a cross-cupola church. While this style was the most common throughout the Middle Ages, the Metekhi Church is somewhat anachronistic with its three projecting apses in the east façade and the four freestanding pillars supporting the cupola within. The church is made of brick and dressed stone. The restorations of the 17th, 18th, and 19th centuries mostly employed brick. A new dome was built entirely of brick at the time of Herekle's reconquest in 1748. The façade is for the most part smooth, with decorative elements concentrated around the windows of the eastern apses. Horizontal bands below the gables run around all four sides and serve as a unifying element. The north portico of the main entrance is not a later addition but was built at the same time as the rest of the church.

Having been turned into a state youth theater in the early 1970s, Metekhi is once again functioning as a church. From here there is a magnificent view of the Old Town, the Narikala Fortress, and the monumental **Statue of Mother Georgia** on the top of the Sololaki range. The wooden armature of this statue was completed

The equestrian statue of Vakhtang Gorgasali and the Metekhi Church

in 1958 and the aluminum panels were affixed in 1963. She holds a sword in one hand and a goblet of wine in the other: the sword is for the enemies of Georgia and the wine for those who come as friends. It would be hard to find a more all-inclusive symbol of the national character.

Instead of descending to cross the Metekhi Bridge at this point, continue up toward Avlabari to visit the Sachino Palace behind you.

SACHINO PALACE (CASTLE OF QUEEN DAREJAN)

The stairs on the left side of the Metekhi slope (behind the church and across the street) climb to the Avlabar Heights and the summer palace of Queen Darejan, wife of King Herekle II. The 200-year-old palace was built of stones and bricks that had been used in the earlier construction of the Avlabari fortress. All that remain today are the fortress walls and a tower encircled by a wooden balcony. The view from here of the right bank of the Mtkvari (Kura) is superb. *Sachino* in Georgian means "eminent" and refers to the lofty position of the Queen's abode. Nearby, within the precincts of Sachino, is a palace chapel constructed in 1776 and consecrated as the Church of the Transfiguration. Services are still conducted here. The interior frescoes are from the early 20th century and are not particularly distinctive.

From Sachino you can continue into Avlabari and explore this Armenian neighborhood (*see* page 116) or descend, cross the Metekhi bridge, and visit the Old Town.

GORGASALI SQUARE

Crossing the bridge to the right bank you come to Gorgasali Square. Known as far back as the 17th and 18th centuries as Maiden Square or Tsikhis Moedani, this square was the site of a bazaar that attracted traders from Russia and the Middle East.

Here camel caravans brought spices, fabrics, silk, and carpets from the East while Georgians sold their felt and woolen goods, *papakhi* (sheepskin hats), silverwork, weapons, and wine. If you're looking for one tangible spot where Europe and Asia meet in Georgia, you need go no farther than Gorgasali Square. The character of the square has changed dramatically since the construction of the embankment and the expansion of the Metekhi Bridge. Previously the area was a densely packed rabbit-warren of small stalls, where business was conducted in Georgian, Hebrew, Persian, Turkish, Armenian, and Russian. Take a moment to close your eyes, expunge the noise of traffic, and listen for the exotic mix of languages left hovering here from the days when the Sunday Bazaar meant minstrels, conjurors, bards, and the sights and sounds of every remote corner of the Caucasus and beyond.

GORGASALI STREET

With your back to the river, turn left (east) on Gorgasali Street. This street was called Vorontsov Street when it was opened in 1850, in honor of Count Mikhail Semenovich Vorontsov, the Tsar's viceroy in the Caucasus. It was completed in 1851, replacing the maze of narrower streets that distinguished the Old Town. In the center of a lawn, approximately 85 meters (280 feet) from Gorgasali Square, is Elguja Amashukeli's 1975 sculpture of the great Georgian primitive painter Niko Pirosmanashvili (1862–1918), known as Pirosmani. The artist is shown kneeling, holding a lamb in his arms. A self-taught painter who combined a celebration of everyday Georgian life with immediate access to the spiritual world that lay behind it, Pirosmani is revered in Georgia as the artist who best expressed the national psyche. The statue stands at the entrance of the Ortachala Gardens, an area Pirosmani was known to haunt as he wandered from tavern (*dukani*) to wine cellar, offering to paint a mural or sell a canvas for a meal or a bottle of wine. He died in obscurity and poverty and was not recognized until many years after his death. The work of Pirosmani can be seen at the Museum of Georgian Art. Wonderful homages to Pirosmani also line the walls of the Daryal Restaurant at 22 Rustaveli Street and give an excellent idea of what his work must have been like *in situ*. Those interested in learning more about this great painter's life should see Giorgi Shengelaya's film *Pirosmani*, which is occasionally shown in art cinemas throughout Europe and the US.

Continuing your walk east on Gorgasali Street you pass the unmistakable stone domes of the sulfur baths. You can either go into this section of the Old Town now, experience the baths and climb to the Narikala Fortress, or continue on Gorgasali to see the outlying monuments and return to the baths later.

Beyond the sulfur baths on Gorgasali Street, look across the river to see the residential houses perched on the Isani Plateau. There is one sulfur bath on the left bank, the Goglio Baths, visible from where you stand and distinguished by its domes and stained-glass windows. A ten-minute addi-

Suffice it to have a common language and every resident of Tbilisi would be glad to help you find your way

Pure Pleasure

*A*ll day long, Finot had been hinting that he had a suprise for me that evening. Now I was hardly in the mood for any festivity, but I was in Finot's hands and left all the arrangements to him. As we took our seats in his carriage I heard him instruct his coachmen to drive to the baths.

"What?" I exclaimed. "You think it would surprise me to take a bath?"

"But this is a Persian bath," he replied. "Have you ever had one?"

I had to agree that if there was any special virtue in a Persian bath I knew nothing about it, so we drove on through the dark streets, up and down such steep slopes that I expected to be thrown out at any moment. Fortunately for me, we came upon a heard of camels lying in the roadway and had to pick our way between them at a walking pace. How strange those animals seem, seen at close quarters in the dark! There was not a single light anywhere, and it took us a quarter of an hour to pass them, for not one of them would move aside.

Five minutes later we halted at the door of the baths. Finot had reserved a private room for us, and a Persian in a pointed cap led us through a gallery overhanging a precipice into a hall crowded with naked bathers. I could hardly believe my eyes! They were all women!

"Tuesday is 'Ladies' Day' here," Finot remarked. "That is why I decided to bring you this evening. When I arrange a surprise for a friend I like to make it as complete as I can."

There must have been fifty women standing, talking or resting on couches, and I noticed with a certain humiliation that our passage through their midst did not seem to perturb them in the slightest. Two or three of them (not young or pretty ones, alas!) snatched up their little towel from the spot where it lay and used it to cover their face, but the others hardly noticed us. Through the steam swirling round them they looked to me like so many frightful witches.

It would have been tactless to linger (in any case I had no desire to do so), and we followed our guide to the private rooms beyond. The first was a vestibule with three benches, where we undressed and were each given a small towel—doubtless to hide our faces with, if any women came in. Then we went over to the second room.

I confess I had to come straight out again, for I thought my lungs would burst in that hot, steamy air, but after standing in the doorway for a while I grew more accustomed to it and managed to go inside. The stark simplicity of that inner room was almost biblical. It was all of bare stone and contained three stone troughs full of water so hot that at first I could not even put my finger in the coolest of them. Finot, more experienced than I, plunged into the hottest and stayed there with every appearance of pleasure until I gradually worked my way through the other troughs and could lie beside him.

Suddenly, when I least expected it, two attendants seized me, laid me out on a wooden bench and began to crack every single joint in my body, one after the other. Though I felt no discomfort I was convinced they were all dislocated, and half expected that at any moment these silent Persians would fold me up like a towel and pop me away in a cupboard. Then one of them held me still while the other positively danced up and down my whole body. He must have weighed a hundred and twenty pounds or more, but he seemed as light as a butterfly. A great sense of freedom and well-being permeated me. All my tiredness had gone and I felt strong enough to lift a mountain.

At last I was taken back to the vestibule, where Finot was already lying at ease on one of the wooden benches that were now spread with snow-white sheets. We were offered pipes—hookahs and chibouques—and to complete our pleasure one of the attendants brought in a kind of guitar and played to us softly, so sweetly, that the pipes soon slipped from our fingers and we fell fast asleep. It was a delightful experience, and as long as I stayed in Tiflis I went to the Persian baths three or four times a week.

Alexandre Dumas, Adventures in Caucasia,
translated by A. E. Murch

tional walk on Gorgasali will bring you to the **Memorial to the 300 Men of Aragvi.** This large white and gold stela and slab was sculpted by Alexander Bakradze in 1961. The monument is a memorial to the 300 warriors of the Aragvi region who rescued King Herekle II in 1795 when he was about to be captured by Agha Mohammed Khan. When Herekle's grandson, Ioane, learned of his grandfather's imminent capture, he mustered 300 men who rode to save the king. They succeeded, but not one survived. The stela marks the spot where they fell.

Opposite the memorial to the men of Aragvi is **Machabeli's Wall,** designed by Nodar Mgalobishvili and sculpted by Teimuraz Chkonia in 1967. This monument honors another Georgian hero, David Machabeli, an actor at the royal court who distinguished himself during that same battle with the Persians. Sculpted on a 7x12-meter (23x40-foot) vertical slab is a warrior's head, his sword and shield and lines from Rustaveli's 12th-century poem, *The Knight in the Panther's Skin.* In medieval times the spot at which these two monuments now stand marked the southeastern limit of the Old Town.

Beyond this point, farther along Gorgasali Street, you come upon Merab Merabishvili's 1982 equestrian **Statue of Pyotr Bagration,** the Russian general of Georgian origin who fought against Napoleon in 1812. At 39 Gorgasali Street is the Krtsanisi restaurant. Named after the battle against the Persians in which the 300 men of Aragvi died, this restaurant serves a variety of Georgian dishes; in good weather you can eat on the veranda. A little farther on you can get a good view across the river of the unusual modern architecture which distinguishes the Central Registry Office. This white palace has sloping lines as though the stone had been poured from on high. It houses the Marriage Office as well as a number of clubs and discos.

To continue your tour of the Old Town, return to the sulfur baths just before Gorgasali Square. Here you can decide whether to have a bath and massage now or wait until after you have climbed the Sololaki ridge to visit the Narikala Fortress and the Botanical Gardens. Whatever order you choose to do things, do not miss the baths of Tbilisi.

THE SULFUR BATHS

Walk away from the river and Gorgasali Street onto Abanos Street, home to the sulfur baths and immediately recognizable by their domes. Almost all of the baths of Tbilisi are in this vicinity. The baths are, of course, an inextricable part of Tbilisi's history— responsible, according to legend, for Vakhtang Gorgasali's decision to move his capital here (*see* page 94). Rich in hydrogen sulfide, these waters have curative effects that have been commented upon by numerous travelers.

In the 12th century, according to historians, some 68 baths used these waters. By the 17th century, however, six were left. At the corner of Abanos and Akhundov streets is the oldest remaining bath: the Herekle Bath. Like all the sulfur baths in

A view of the baths toward Tbilisi's only mosque and the Narikala Fortress before the construction in 1996 of the Church of St Nicholas

Tbilisi, the baths themselves are below ground. The domes serve the bath as a cupola does a church, providing wonderful oblique illumination that adds to the near mystical experience of it all. Anyone fortunate enough to have enjoyed the pleasures of the Cagaloglu Hamami Baths in Istanbul will have an immediate sense of déjà vu, especially if you have a massage.

The massage is an absolute must. For a reasonable amount of lari, a small, wiry masseur (or masseuse) will come wearing a black *khalat* (robe), strip down to shorts, lay you down on a stone slab, thwack and rub your back, legs, and arms, stand on your back and walk up and down your spine, take off your dry skin with a horse-hair mitten, and show you to a shower. A most extraordinary balloon of soap is created from a piece of old material with which you are given a washing of delicious refinement. Lying down on the slab again you are gone over with a lighter mitten and receive another massage. Buckets of warm water are unceremoniously thrown at you to finish you off. Few pleasures in life are better.

At the end of the square, at 2 Abano Street, is the unmistakable Orbeliani Bathhouse, distinguished by its blue faience façade, lancet arches, and flanking minarets. It is the single best remaining example of Islamic architecture in Tbilisi. Also called Chreli Abano (Motley-colored Bath) and Tsisperi Abano (Blue Bath), the building dates from the second half of the 17th century, though the façade was largely redone in the 19th century.

Whether you go to the Herekle or the Orbeliani baths or both, be sure to arrange for a pot of tea after your session. As Peter the Great himself said, "Sell your white stockings if you have to, but have tea after your bath."

Other baths in the area are the 18th-century Bebutov Bath on Akhundov Street and the 17th-century Sumbatov Bath on the right bank of the Tsavkisistskali River. While you're on Akhundov Street, stop at the bakery (at number six) to see a baker at work and to try a variety of Georgian breads.

The area immediately around the baths affords some of the most interesting walking you can do in Tbilisi. Walk up Botanikuri Street to the only remaining mosque in the city. This Sunnite Mosque was built in the 19th century and serves the largely Islamic population of this neighborhood and others throughout the city. Feel free to enter. You will, of course, have to remove your shoes.

NARIKALA FORTRESS

Running along the crest of the Sololaki ridge, prominent above the Old Town, are the mighty ruins of the Narikala Fortress, also known as Shuris Tsikhe (the Rival Fortress) or the Sololaki Citadel. The first fortress on this location was built at the end of the fourth century by the Persians. Vakhtang Gorgasali moved his capital here from Mtskheta in the fifth century and erected additional fortifications to protect his new city. The foundations of the towers and the walls of both the upper and lower fortresses that we see today, however, stem from the work of the Arab lords of Tbilisi in the eighth century. The Arab Emirate of Tbilisi lasted until David the Builder reconquered the city in 1122, and the emir's palace was within the fortifications of the Narikala. Though King David moved his palace to Isani on the opposite bank of the Mtkvari River, he recognized the Narikala's strategic position over the narrowest portion of the river valley and as his primary defense against attack from the south. He, like the Mongolians, Turks, and Persians who came after him, continued to rebuild destroyed sections of the walls. Each conqueror built according to his own ideas on military fortifications. This process continued until 1827 when gunpowder stored in a section of the fortress was struck by lightning.

The subsequent explosion was of such magnitude that it is now difficult to get a clear picture of the layout of Narikala.

From Samgebro Street in the Old Town, climb up to the Fortress along Orpiri Street. Prior to 1996 the site had lacked a satisfying cohesiveness. Now, as a result of the newly constructed Church of St. Nicholas, many feel that the complex has gained in character. The church, a classic cruciform, cone and drum structure, was built upon the foundations of a 12th-century church that had been destroyed. Painstaking research went into the building of this new structure, which was completed in December 1996. Georgian experts mainly agree that it is a successful reconstruction. Westerners tend to feel that the site would have been more evocative, if not as comprehensible, had it been left alone and cite Sir Arthur Evans efforts at Knossos as the kind of aesthetic decision-making that happened here.

The money for the construction of the church was given by two private Georgian citizens, Temuri Kvaratskhelia and Roman Gventsadze. They responded to Catholicos Ilya II's call for greater devotion on the part of the people and the building of churches as the force which will save Georgia during these challenging times. The Church of St. Nicholas is just one example of new ecclesiastical construction occurring throughout the country, often in memory of a loved one killed in the war in Abkhazia.

You can walk a portion of the circuit of the fortress walls. The best preserved tower stands alone just southwest of the lower fortress. This square, roofless turret

A view of the Old Town and the ruins of the Narikala Fortress with the newly-built Church of St. Nicholas at left (photo by David Halford)

is the 16th-century Istanbul Tower, so called because during the Turkish occupation of that period it was used as a jail. The imposing Shakhtakhti Tower in the west dates from the seventh to ninth centuries. In Arab times it served as an observatory and stood next to the emir's palace.

Continuing your walk on the other side of the Narikala Fortress along Sololaki Alley you come to **Kartlis Deda**, the statue of Mother Georgia by Amashukeli that has come to be a national symbol. Continue on Amagleba Street to the Botanical Gardens.

THE CENTRAL BOTANICAL GARDENS OF THE GEORGIAN ACADEMY OF SCIENCES

These gardens are one of the most beautiful spots in all Tbilisi and a must for every traveler. Lying behind the Sololaki ridge, below the southwest side of the Narikala Fortress, the gardens were opened on March 17, 1809, on land that had served as the gardens of the Georgian kings in the 17th and 18th centuries. They were first used to grow medicinal herbs. Officially opened on May 13, 1845, the Botanical Gardens are now under the auspices of the Georgian Academy of Sciences. They cover more than 128 hectares (300 acres) and contain over 4,900 species. The flora is primarily from the Caucasus, but special sections are devoted to a wide variety of trees, plants, and flowers from other parts of the world. The rose garden boasts over 950 varieties.

LESELIDZE STREET

With Gorgasali Square once more as your point of departure, you can make further explorations of the Old Town by going up Leselidze Street. Although this street was widened and partially reconstructed in 1924, it still bears a strong resemblance to its previous self, when each turn of its 800-meter (2,624-foot) winding way revealed another caravanserai, workshop, or stall reminiscent of the old medinas of Fez or Tangiers. In the 19th century if you wanted to buy a *khanjali* (Georgian dagger), soft leather boots, or felt cloak, you didn't go to a shop on Rustaveli Avenue but rather to the stalls in Leselidze Street where merchants were so cramped for space they did most of their business out in the open.

The street mixes the mercantile with the spiritual. As well as being famous for its shops, Leselidze boasts a synagogue (at number 46), an Armenian Gregorian church, and a Georgian Orthodox church. A second smaller synagogue is nearby.

At the junction of Sioni and Leselidze streets, you can turn right, down to the precincts of one of the largest and most important buildings in this neighborhood.

The interior of a Tbilisi synagogue

SIONI CATHEDRAL

Named after Mt. Zion in Jerusalem and called Sioni by the townspeople, this cathedral is dedicated to the Assumption of the Virgin. The original church on the site was founded between 575 and 639 by Prince Guaram of Kartli. The cathedral has been destroyed, looted, and reconstructed many times. Sultan Djalal Eddin's invasion of Tbilisi in the 13th century was responsible for the destruction of the dome. The cathedral suffered further damage at the hands of Tamerlane in the 14th century, of various Persian shahs in the 16th and 17th centuries, and of the Turks in the 18th century who attempted to convert it into a mosque. The basic elements of the existing structure date to the 13th century. The addition of the southern chapel and significant restoration of the cupola took place in 1657 under the direction of Bishop Elisey Saginashvili. King Vakhtang VI carried out additional restorations of the cupola and cathedral walls in 1710. The interior frescoes are the work of the Russian artist Grigory Gagarin, who executed them between 1850 and 1860, covering the older Georgian frescoes in the process. The stone iconostasis dates to this period as well. It replaced the wooden iconostasis burned by Agha Mohammed Khan in 1795. Of the sacred objects that have survived the numerous pillages, the most important and venerated is St. Nino's cross, to the left of the altar. Tradition has it that Nino, the Apostle of Iberia who brought Christianity to Georgia in the fourth century, made this first cross from vine branches and her own hair on her way to Mtskheta. The reliquary itself was given by King Vakhtang III in the early 14th century.

Sioni is a typical example of a cross-cupola church with projecting polygonal apses in the east facade. The yellow tuff from which the cathedral was built comes from the area of Bolnisi, southwest of Tbilisi. The golden hues of the stone work to great effect in infusing the structure with warmth and welcome. Although architecturally unremarkable, Sioni is distinguished by being the seat of the Catholicos of the Georgian Orthodox Church, Ilya II, whose residence is just north of the cathedral (left of the entrance), above the rose garden. Also north of the cathedral, within the courtyard, is a three-story belltower dating from 1425. All but the ground floor of this structure was destroyed by Agha Mohammed Khan in 1795. It was restored to its present condition in 1939. Of greater architectural interest is the three-story belltower across the street from the cathedral; built in 1812, it is the oldest example of Russian classical architecture in Tbilisi.

If you're interested in taking the spiritual pulse of the Georgian people, you cannot do better than to come to Sioni. Here His Holiness Ilia II celebrates Liturgy, and the largest number of Tbilisians come to pray; wimpled, black-habited Georgian nuns attend to the rose garden of the Catholicos, and visiting church dignitaries from other parts of Georgia come to discuss church business.

Nearby at 8 Sioni Street is the building that served as the best caravanserai in Tbilisi during the 19th century. It was restored in 1984 to house the city's ethnographic museum.

GRISHASHVILI MUSEUM OF HISTORY AND ETHNOGRAPHY

The 19th-century caravanserai or inn was built on the site of a 17th-century building that served the same purpose but was destroyed by Agha Mohammed Khan during his invasion. European in exterior design, the building conforms to the Middle Eastern requirements for the interior of such a structure: a large inner courtyard with a fountain is surrounded by three tiers of galleries. The basement area, which had housed stables and warehouses, is now lined with small shops, a cafe, and a historical exhibition. The museum on the other two floors contains more than 50,000 items that represent a vast, well-displayed overview of the city's history from its founding to the present. Coins, weapons, clothing, domestic implements, portraits, furniture, carpets, tools, and musical instruments provide great insights into the daily lives of the Georgian people in general and the citizens of Tbilisi in particular.

HEREKLE II SQUARE

Continuing up Leselidze Street brings you to Freedom (formerly Lenin) Square. Standing on Sioni Street facing the cathedral, go left until Sioni becomes Herekle II Alley. This pretty pedestrian walk has a number of shops and bars. The alley leads into Herekle II Square.

At 11 Herekle II Square is a small two-story building with balcony that was the residence of the last king of Georgia, Giorgi XII, after Agha Mohammed Khan destroyed the city. It is now **The Museum of Drama, Music, and Cinema**. In the west corner of the square is **The House of Journalists**. There is a very good restaurant in the basement of this building where you would be welcome. Both Russian and Georgian cuisine are served.

Between Herekle II Square and the Right (formerly Stalin) Embankment is an obelisk erected in 1959 to mark the site of the first Georgian printing press. Founded in 1709 by King Vakhtang VI, the press was located in a palace building that was destroyed in the last Persian invasion.

Off Herekle II Square, turn onto Shavteli Street to visit Anchiskhati Basilica, the oldest ecclesiastical building still standing in Tbilisi.

ANCHISKHATI BASILICA AND BELLTOWER

Anchiskhati Basilica, at 5–7 Shavteli Alley, dates from just after the founding of Tbilisi in the fifth century, when Vakhtang Gorgasali moved his capital here from

Mtskheta. Vakhtang died in 502, and the order to build Anchiskhati is credited to his son and successor, Dachi Ujarmeli.

The church is dedicated to the Mother of God and in the sixth century was called "The Conversion of Georgi." In the 17th century it was renamed for the justly famous Anchiskhati icon, brought from the monastery of Anchi in southwestern Georgia, which was then in Turkish hands. The embossed gold setting of this icon is the work of the famous 12th-century goldsmith Beka Opizari and is a magnificent example of his artistry. The icon is now in the Treasury of the Museum of Georgian Art.

Anchiskhati is a three-naved basilica whose ground plan conforms to sixth-century norms. The middle nave runs into a horseshoe-shaped altar apse while the side naves end in right-angled side chambers. The eastern façade does not reveal the internal shape. The basilica has been rebuilt and restored many times, most thoroughly in the 17th century when the upper portions of the building and its internal columns were redone in brick. In 1958, 19th-century frescoes were removed from the walls to reveal some 17th-century work. At that time also the floor was lowered by 1.25 meters (4 feet).

Set into the surrounding western wall, which serves also as entrance to the church precincts, is a very

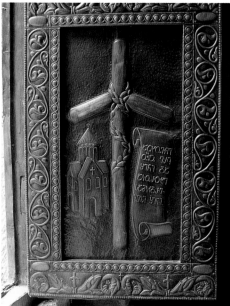

(top) An ornamental gate in Tbilisi; (bottom) modern repoussé work on the doors of the Anchiskhati Basilica depicting the Georgian Cross

unusual belltower commissioned by Catholicos Domenti in 1675. A keeled-arch passageway breaches the ground floor of the belltower. The patterned brickwork of the arch reveals the strong Islamic influence of the time. Above the passage, at the second story, is a residence, presumably for the bell ringer. The tower is crowned by a belfry made of gray-blue stone that is in marked contrast to the brick structure below.

Directly across from Anchiskhati Basilica on Shavteli Street is an Oriental Sweet Shop where you can drink excellent Turkish coffee and occasionally eat some first-rate *halvah*.

BARATASHVILI STREET

Shavteli Street runs into Baratashvili Street, which follows the original north wall of the Old Town down to the Mtkvari River. Baratashvili Street combines old and new Tbilisi; on the south side, incorporated into the remains of the city wall, are shops, cafes and houses with balconies in a variety of styles, while on the north side are apartment houses and multi-storied office blocks built in the 1950s and 1960s. Some of the older buildings near or on the wall are from the 19th century, but many more are reconstructions of period buildings that were done in 1979 under the guidance of the architect Shota Kavlashvili. Discovering ancient cellars forming a part of the

Details found on buildings throughout Tbilisi make strolling a pleasure

foundation of the walls, he utilized the space to house cafes, wine cellars and shops that evoke old Tbilisi in every respect.

At the corner of Shavteli and Baratashvili streets is the **Tbilisi State Marionette Theatre**, 26 Shavteli Street. Next door is the wonderful Mukhrantubani Restaurant—one of Tbilisi's best, with superb 19th-century decor, Georgian minstrels, and excellent food. Closer to the river are the **Museum of Children's Art** and the **Children's Toy Museum**, both at 17a Shavteli Street. In front of the Museum of Children's Art is the beloved Berikaoba sculpture by Avtandil Monselidze, unveiled in 1981. The sculpture is of *berikebi* (merrymakers) dancing in a carnival procession.

AVLABARI
This ends your tour of the Old Town. If you have the energy, however, you can continue down Baratashvili Street to the river, cross Baratashvili Bridge, and keep going up the rise toward the Avlabari. The **Statue of Nikoloz Baratashvili** (1817–1845) is at the beginning of the ascent. Sculpted by Boris Tsibadze and unveiled in 1975, the statue honors one of Georgia's most important Romantic

Architect Viktor Jorbenadze's Central Registry Office was designed to come as close to a church without being a church as the Soviet authorities would allow in 1984 when it was built (photo by David Halford)

poets, best known for poems such as *Twilight on Mtatsminda, Meditation on Mtkvari's Banks,* and *Merani,* which combine deep personal longing with patriotic fervor. Behind the statue is an open-air amphitheater that seats 400 for poetry readings and theatrical performances.

The Baratashvili Rise leads to Ketevan Tsamebulis (formerly Shaumian) Street , the major artery of the Avlabari. Here is the (Shaumian) **Armenian Theatre**, founded in 1936, where performances in Armenian can still be seen. Just beyond are the Goglio Sulfur Baths. Take your time wandering through the Armenian Quarter. You'll find a number of Armenian Gregorian churches; small, narrow winding streets leading onto neighborhoods that have the quality of small villages, and surprise views of the right bank of the city across the river.

A relatively new housing development on the southeastern outskirts of the Avlabari is home to 60,000 people. The district is called Varketili, which means "I am kind." You will discover in your wanderings throughout the city that the citizens of Tbilisi are just that.

The City Center

FREEDOM SQUARE

Standing in Tavisuplebis (Freedom) Square, you are well-positioned to begin exploring Tbilisi's center, which contains its most important contemporary political and cultural institutions. Freedom Square was called Lenin Square up until August 1990 when the oversized statue of Vladimir Ilyich was removed. The square was completed in the 1870s; part of the Russian urban renewal begun in 1848 when Viceroy Vorontsov cleared the remains of the Old City wall to expand the city into the suburb called Garetubani. The intent was to erect every building on Freedom Square in the Russian neoclassical style, but only two of these remain.

In the northeastern corner, at the beginning of Rustaveli Avenue, stands the former headquarters of the Russian Caucasian Army. Built in 1824, this example of late Russian classicism now houses various government departments.

Taking up the entire south side of the square is the former town council building, built by the German architect Peter Stern in 1880. Designed with a self-conscious historicism and a nod to the Moors, it's a fun building with a serious purpose: it houses the Tbilisi City Hall, the most important body of city government. The third story with its clock tower was added to the building in 1910–1912.

On a small lawn with a fountain in the northeastern corner of the square is a bust of Pushkin by Felix Khodorovich, unveiled in 1892.

A SOCIAL GAFFE

Vorontsóv took his place in the centre of one side of the long table, and his wife sat opposite, with the general on her right. On the prince's right sat his lady, the beautiful Orbelyáni; and on his left was a graceful, dark, redcheeked Georgian woman, glittering with jewels and incessantly smiling.

"Excellentes, chère amie!" replied Vorŏntsóv to his wife's inquiry about what news the courier had brought him. "Simon a eu de la chance!" And he began to tell aloud, so that everyone could hear, the striking news (for him alone not quite unexpected, because negotiations had long been going on) that Hadji Murád, the bravest and most famous of Shamil's officers, had come over to the Russians and would in a day or two be brought to Tiflis[Tbilisi].

Everybody—even the young aides-de-camp and officials who sat at the far ends of the table and who had been quietly laughing at something among themselves—became silent and listened.

"And you, General, have you ever met this Hadji Murád?" asked the princess of her neighbor, the carroty general with the bristly mustache, when the prince had finished speaking.

"More than once, Princess."

And the general went on to tell how Hadji Murád, after the mountaineers had captured Gergebel in 1843, had fallen upon General Pahlen's detachment and killed Colonel Zolotúkhin almost before their very eyes.

Vorontsóv listened to the general and smiled amiably, evidently pleased that the latter had joined in the conversation. But suddenly his face assumed an absent-minded and depressed expression.

The general, having started talking, had begun to tell of his second encounter with Hadji Murád.

"Why, it was he, if your Excellency will please remember," said the general, "who arranged the ambush that attacked the rescue party in the 'Biscuit' expedition."

"Where?" asked Voróntsóv, screwing up his eyes.

What the brave general spoke of as the 'rescue' was the affair in the unfortunate Dargo campaign in which a whole detachment, including Prince Voróntsóv who commanded it, would certainly have perished had it not been rescued by the arrival of fresh troops. Everyone knew that the whole Dargo campaign under Voróntsóv's command—in which the Russians lost many killed and wounded and several cannon—had been a shameful affair, and therefore if any one mentioned it in Voróntsóv's presence they did so only in the aspect in which Voróntsóv had reported it to the Tsar—as a brilliant achievement of the Russian army. But the word "rescue" plainly indicated that it was not a brilliant victory but a blunder costing many lives. Everybody understood this and some pretended not to notice the meaning of the general's words, others nervously waited to see what would follow, while a few exchanged glances, and smiled. Only the carroty general with the bristly mustache noticed nothing, and carried away by his narrative quietly replied:

"At the rescue, your Excellency."

Having started on his favorite theme, the general recounted circumstantially how Hadji Murád had so cleverly cut the detachment in two that if the rescue party had not arrived (he seemed to be particularly fond of repeating the word "rescue") not a man in the division would have escaped, because . . . He did not finish his story, for Manana Orbelyáni, having understood what was happening, interrupted him by asking if he had found comfortable quarters in Tiflis. The general, surprised, glanced at everybody all round and saw his aides-de-camp from the end of the table looking fixedly and significantly at him, and he suddenly understood! Without replying to the princess's question, he frowned, became silent, and began hurriedly swallowing the delicacy that lay on his plate, the appearance and taste of which both completely mystified him.

LeoTolstoy, Hadji Murád, translated by John Bayley

MUSEUM OF GEORGIAN ART

Continuing down Pushkin Street, at the corner of Gudiashvili Street, is the Museum of Georgian Art built between 1827 and 1834. Originally a hotel, the building next functioned as a seminary until 1905. A plaque to the left of the entrance once proclaimed that Stalin studied there from 1894 to 1898, until it was removed in 1989. The museum was founded in 1933 by bringing together other diverse collections of artworks. The permanent collection of sculpture and painting from all over the world is enriched by unique works by Georgian painters and sculptors. The treasury, which can be visited only with a guide and for an additional fee, contains an awesome display of gold and silver sculpture, jewelry, and ancient cloisonné enamel from Georgia's medieval period. A visit to this museum is a must.

The treasury is immediately opposite the main doors of the museum. Here you will see extraordinary masterpieces of Georgian repoussé work from the ninth to the 19th centuries. With the exception of the jewelry of the Georgian kings and queens, most of these objects served ecclesiastical purposes, as shown by the chalices, processional crosses, and icons that abound. The pride of the collection is the **Khakhuli Triptych**, which has been kept here since 1952. Its name comes from the Khakhuli Monastery in Tao (now in Turkey) where the tenth-century cloisonné icon of the Virgin was originally kept. Believed to be miracle-working, the icon was brought to the Monastery of Gelati by King David the Builder and given a new repoussé case with pearls, rubies, and cloisonné enamels from an earlier period. The preserved side panels of the triptych exemplify tenth-century silver-chasing techniques. All that remains of the central part of the triptych are the cloisonné hands and face of the Virgin. The background of precious metals has been lost.

The *Icon of the Saviour from Anchi* from the sixth century is the oldest extant example of Georgian icon painting; it came to the Anchiskhati Basilica in the Old Town from the Anchi Monastery in southwestern Georgia. The embossed gold setting is the work of the famous 12th-century goldsmith Beka Opizari. The *Tondo of St. Mamai Riding a Lion* is an 11th-century silver plaque with masterfully executed embossing. The Gold Pectoral Cross of Queen Tamara dates from the end of the 12th century. Set with four emeralds, six pearls, and five rubies, it is a superb example of the bejeweled splendor with which religious metalwork was decorated. The Golden Goblet of King Bagrat III and Queen Gurandukht dates from 999. Made from a single piece of gold, the chalice is embossed with figures of the Virgin, an adult Jesus, and ten saints.

Among the works in the collection of European paintings are a 14th-century triptych by the Florentine painter Bernardo Daddi, a polyptych by Paolo Veneziano, *Landscape with Waterfall* by the Dutch master Jacob van Ruisdael, and *The Procuress* by the German painter Lucas Cranach the Elder. The museum also displays Egyptian, Chinese, Japanese, and Iranian art. Noteworthy is the collection of

Woman and Children Going to Draw Water *by Pirosmani (1862–1918), from the Museum of Georgian Art in Tbilisi*

19th and 20th-century Russian masters, including Ilya Repin, Valentin Serov, Ivan Aivazovsky, and Apollinary Vasnetsov. The first and second floors also contain a significant collection of medieval Georgian stone carvings: bas-reliefs, altar screens, and fragments of carved stone.

Perhaps of greatest interest to the inveterate gallery-goer are the examples of 19th- and 20th-century Georgian paintings. Note especially the works of Gigo Gabashvili (1862–1936) and his contemporary, Mose Toidze. The work of the following three 20th-century painters is housed in separate museums: Lado Gudiashvili (1896–1980), David Kakabadze (1889–1952), and Elene Akhvlediani (1901–1976). See pages 131 and 132 for more information about these painters and the museums devoted to their lives and work.

Besides the medieval works in the treasury, the other most significant holdings in the museum are the paintings of Niko Pirosmanashvili (1862–1918). The self-taught Pirosmani was born in the small Kakhetian village of Mirzaani and became an itiner-

Fervent political activity was a feature of Tbilisi life throughout 1989 and 1990 leading up to independence in 1991. At one point there were more than 100 opposition groups.

ant sign painter, rendering scenes of the Caucasus on the walls of wine cellars and taverns. He captured the quintessential nature of everyday life in Georgia by celebrating the traditions of towns and villages in an unaffected, startlingly straightforward style. Georgian admirers of his animal paintings are equaled in number only by those who favor his historical narratives. Others prefer his portraits, and still others his scenes of feasts and celebrations. Pirosmani is revered in Georgia as the painter who best captures the national essence. Certainly, new generations of Georgians have come to define their vision of themselves through his work.

In his own time, Pirosmani was appreciated in the milieu in which he worked and lived: the owners and patrons of the shops and taverns (*duknebi*). He was never part of the artistic establishment, and his work was not considered "art" but at best a rough and quirky kind of primitivism. Only in 1912, through the efforts of painters Kirill Zdanevich and Michael Le Dentue and the poet Ilya Zdanevich, was Pirosmani's work introduced to a wider public. In time Pirosmani's genius at expressing the essential aspect of whatever he depicted—a *tsvadi* (shish kebab), a loaf of bread, a shepherd with his flock—came to be recognized. Unfortunately this recognition didn't come until after the painter's death in April 1918. He died penniless in a cold basement that had been one of his temporary abodes.

RUSTAVELI AVENUE

Leaving the museum, go back up to Freedom Square and then turn right onto Rustaveli Avenue. Running northwest and parallel to the Mtkvari river, this 1,500-meter-long (4,920-foot) avenue has been an important thoroughfare since medieval times. Named Golovinskii Avenue by Vorontsov, the Tsar's viceroy in the Caucasus, who constructed it in the 19th century, it is now named for the great 12th-century Georgian poet. Lined with plane trees, decorated with flower beds, graced by a variety of neoclassical and Renaissance revival façades, and site of the city's most important theaters and the Opera House, Rustaveli Avenue was and will no doubt again, in less stressful times, be the street of choice for Tbilisians to take their evening *passegiata*.

Here's where the young used to "check each other out," with groups of girls walking in one direction up the avenue and encountering their male counterparts coming the other way. Families shop, old men sit on the benches in the small recessed parks, children buy ice cream from street vendors. So integral to the lives of Tbilisians is the ebb and flow of movement on the avenue that most citizens couldn't conceive of not having easy access to it. A joke was told about a professor from Tbilisi who was thinking of emigrating. After his friend agreed on the wisdom of his leaving, expounding on all the problems in Georgia, the Tbilisian said, "But does that mean I wouldn't be able to stroll on Rustaveli?" The realization was, of course, enough to make him stay.

With the Tbilisi War fought right on Rustaveli Avenue in December 1991, the relationship to the avenue has changed somewhat. Now Tbilisians walk down the street saddened at those events which heralded the start of new problems in the post-Soviet era. People point to the shell of the once beautiful Tbilisi Hotel, the bullet-marked façades of various buildings, the site where the House of Georgian Artists once stood. That this Civil War took place in the heart of their world remains an astounding fact, a fact that will not be soon forgotten regardless of how quickly new construction might takes place.

The first building on your left as you look down Rustaveli with your back to Freedom Square is the **Tbilisi Department Store**, built in 1975. The store's atrium creates a passageway to the **Alexander Griboyedov (Russian) Theatre**, founded in 1845 by Vorontsov to promote Russian culture in Georgia and to make a posting to the Caucasus less of a hardship for Russian officers. Just behind the entrance to the Freedom Square subway is the **Children's Palace**. Set behind a tall fence and a lovely garden, the house was built in 1807 and served until 1917 as the residence of the Governor General of the Caucasus. Designed to conform to the official classical style of the time, the strict Doric order was altered by architect Otto Simonson, who supervised fundamental renovations and changes to the interior and the façade between 1865 and 1868. Today the palace is used as a youth center where dancing, music, and chess are taught. A very extensive **Toy Museum**, comprised mostly of dolls, is also here.

S. JANASHIA MUSEUM OF GEORGIA

Across the street from the Children's Palace is the enormous S. Janashia Museum of Georgia, built between 1923 and 1929 to house the collection of the earlier Caucasian Museum, founded in 1852. This museum covers the entire history of Georgia, providing riveting testimony to the antiquity of Georgian culture and its tenacious evolution. It is the largest single repository of Georgia's treasures, housing more than 850,000 items. The most important part of the museum's holdings is displayed in the basement in the treasury. Here you must be accompanied by a guide. Extraordinary specimens of repoussé work and jewelry from archaeological sites throughout pre-Christian Georgia will astound you with their beauty and level of artistry. Don't miss seeing the

magnificent filigreed gold pendants of horses from Akhalgori (sixth to fourth centuries BC) and the gold bowls and ornaments from Trialeti (first half of the second millennium BC). Superb finds from Vani and Algheti complete the examples of workmanship of the sixth to fourth centuries BC. Objects and jewelry from the Iberian rulers of the first century AD show the technical virtuosity of Georgian gold and silversmiths of the period. Note the necklace with the amulet jar and the amethyst ram's head from Armazis-Khevi. Precious imports of gems and silver vessels from the classical world complete the collection and demonstrate Georgia's contact with Greece and Rome.

The ground floor contains archaeological findings up to the fourth century BC. Arranged chronologically, stone artifacts from the Paleolithic period found in Georgian caves are next to cases of Neolithic and Bronze Age implements and ceramics. Noteworthy are the weapons and jewelry from the late Bronze Age (14th century BC) to the early Iron Age (13th century BC). Handicrafts and farming implements from the Kura-Araxes culture (4000–2000 BC) are represented, as well as painted and glazed pottery, household implements, weapons, and objects of precious metal from the barrows of Trialeti (1500 BC). You'll discover cases of ancient coins found in Georgia, including some from Colchis in western Georgia which date to the sixth century BC. Georgia's contacts with the Hellenistic and Roman worlds are seen in the Greek vases found in Colchis and Iberia, and from inscriptions on stone fragments: one found in Mtskheta in 1867 was sent from the Roman Emperor Vespasian in AD 75: "To King Mithradates of Iberia—Friend of Caesar and of the Romans."

The first floor covers the fourth century BC to the 13th century AD. Archaeological excavations in centers of Iberian culture such as Urbnisi, Mtskheta, Samtavro, and Bolnisi reflect Georgia's conversion to Christianity. Manuscripts, coins, weapons, glassware, ceramics, stone fragments from churches, and housewares all tell the story of Georgia's cultural development and contacts with other parts of the world. Also displayed here are photographs of important basilicas, palaces, cave dwellings, and domed churches; political and cultural maps; reproductions of frescoes, and copies of valuable works that are stored elsewhere. Though not of intrinsic value, the items, arranged chronologically for narrative purposes, provide a more complete picture of Georgia's history. The other rooms are devoted to Georgia's history from 1801 (the year of unifi-

Politics continues to be a major topic of conversation in every setting where men gather

Janashia Museum treasures: (top l.) Necklace, 2000–1500 BC, Trialeti; (top r.) clasp, third or fourth century BC, Ureki; (lower l.) ornaments for horse's harness, fourth century BC, Akhalgori; (lower r.) neck ornament, late second century AD, Armaziskhevi

cation with Russia) to the present. Portraits of important Georgian and Russian figures are interspersed with the personal possessions of kings Herekle II and Solomon II, among others. A comprehensive ethnographic display includes clothing, musical instruments, household implements, and native costumes.

RUSTAVELI AVENUE CONTINUED

Continuing down Rustaveli Avenue on the same side as the museum, make the first right and continue to 11 Gudiashvili Street where you can visit the **Lado Gudiashvili Memorial Museum**, located in the artist's former apartment and studio. More than eight rooms are chock-a-block with his paintings and graphic works. Born in Tbilisi in 1896, Gudiashvili started drawing at an early age and had his first one-man show in 1915. Four years later he went to Paris and stayed for six years, associating with Picasso, Modigliani, Léger, and Utrillo as well as Aragon, Breton,

Independence has brought advertising, as seen along Rustaveli Avenue. Note on the side of the bus how Coca-Cola is spelled in Georgian (photo by David Halford)

and Mayakovsky. Despite Gudiashvili's awareness of the artistic movements afoot in Paris, his work remained distinctively Georgian with a unique combination of lyricism and witty appreciation of the grotesque. More than any other Georgian painter, his work is deeply rooted in the fantastic—an element that comes to the fore whether he is painting a mythological scene, portrait, or animal. He returned to Georgia in 1925 and worked in a wide variety of media, contributing to numerous group and one-man shows at home and abroad until his death on July 20, 1980. He is buried in the Pantheon on Mount Mtatsminda.

Return to Rustaveli and cross the street. You will see an enormous structure with a row of arches that occupies the entire block. This is the **Government House of Georgia**. This structure was damaged during the street fighting of the civil war in 1991 and 1992 but has since been restored. Built in 1953 in the self-aggrandizing style of the period, the building houses the Georgian Parliament. The stone monument in front honors those Tbilisi citizens who perished on April 9, 1989, when their peaceful demonstration was savagely dispersed by Soviet troops.

Next to the Government House is a high school established for sons of the Georgian nobility at the beginning of the 19th century. This structure burned down completely in the Tbilisi War in 1991 and was one of the first buildings to be completely restored. The faithful reconstruction took place in two years, a wondrously short amount of time for a project like this in this part of the world. It was funded with a gift from the Russian government.

On the front lawn is a monument to Ilya Chavchavadze (1837–1907) and Akaki Tsereteli (1840–1915), the two Georgian writers of the second half of the 19th century whose works embodied the ideals of a free and democratic Georgia.

Across the street from this statue is the **Kashveti Church of St. George**. Set below street level, one used to enter through the courtyard that opens onto Jorjadze Street, but after the Tbilisi War during the restoration of the bullet-scarred façade, a new Western narthex was built which became the main entrance directly off Rustaveli. The church was designed by the German architect Leopold Bielfeld between 1904 and 1910. He used as his basic model the 11th-century domed Cathedral of Samtavisi, 60 km (37 miles) northwest of Tbilisi. Designed to accommodate services both in Georgian (upper level) and Russian (lower level), the church is distinguished by its rich ornamentation, especially the stone carving around the windows and arches. The altar was painted by Lado Gudiashvili in 1946. The name of the church comes from a legend. The daughter of a Tbilisi nobleman, finding herself pregnant, accused St. David of being the father. Answering his accusers, St. David touched the belly of the pregnant girl with his staff and asked who was the father of the child she carried. A voice inside her named the real father, after which the girl went into labor and gave birth to a stone. *Kva* means "stone" and *shva* means "gave birth." Next door to the Kashveti Church at number 11, the midway point in Rustaveli Avenue, is the **Picture Gallery**. Built between 1883 and 1885, this amalgam of Renaissance, Classical, and Baroque styles originally saw life as a Museum of Military History. It is now used for rotating art exhibitions.

Across Jorjiashvili Street is the **Hotel Tbilisi**. Built in 1915 by Gabriel Ter-Mikelov, the hotel was designed with lovely rounded corners that follow the bend of Rustaveli Avenue. It was destroyed during the Tbilisi War in 1991. An American businessman currently owns the license to restore the hotel.

Continuing on Rustaveli, you next come to the **Shota Rustaveli State Academic Theater**. Built for the Theatrical Society between 1899 and 1901 by the architects Korneli Tatishchev and Alexander Shimkevich, the elegantly decorated auditorium seats 840. In addition to a concert hall and classrooms for the Tbilisi Drama Institute, a cafe in the basement is decorated with frescoes by Lado Gudiashvili, David Kakabadze, Sergei Sudeikin, and the Polish artist Sigizmund Valishevsky. The theater is the home of the Rustaveli Theater Company, founded in 1921. It is currently under the directorship of Robert Sturua, whose productions of Shakespeare, Brecht, and Sophocles have played to rave reviews throughout the world. Sturua's *Richard III* was a huge success in London in 1980 and a decade later his production of *King Lear* garnered acclaim when it appeared at the Brooklyn Academy of Music.

If you are hungry and want an elegant meal in a romantic setting you can dine at Restaurant Rampa at 19 Rustaveli Avenue. If you just want a quick snack, go on to number 24 Rustaveli Avenue. Tsklebi (Soft Drinks) Cafe, affectionately and better known as Lagidze, after the two brothers Mitrofan and Mikhail who invented these famous carbonated flavored drinks, used to be a great favorite among citizens. Downstairs you can eat some of the best *khachapuri* (cheese pastry). Also, music lovers can meet many of the students from the **Sarajishvili Conservatory**, which is just up the hill on Griboyedov Street. Named after a famous tenor from the beginning of the 20th century, and founded in 1917, the conservatory claims such recent illustrious graduates as the great bass Paata Burchuladze and the pianists Elisso Virsaladze and Lexo Toradze. Tbilisi is a musical city: Fyodor Chaliapin began his career at the Tbilisi Opera House and Tchaikovsky began *The Sleeping Beauty*, *Iolanthe*, and *The Queen of Spades* here.

Nearby at 22 Griboyedov Street **The Tbilisi Academy of Arts** is one of the loveliest 19th-century homes left in the city. The second floor is a museum where you can see the work of recent graduates. Be particularly attentive to the examples of metal chasing, an ancient Georgian craft that is perpetuated by the Academy.

Back once more on Rustaveli, look across the street at the marvelous pseudo-Moorish **Z. Paliashvili Opera and Ballet Theatre**. The opera house on this site has been ravaged by fire. The original theater, which burned down in the 1870s, was replaced between 1880 and 1896 by a Moorish-style building designed by P. Sretter. In 1973 that building burned down, leaving only the front portico and a portion of the side walls and foyer. The 1977 rebuilding of the opera house preserved the original appearance of the building. Although the backstage area and auditorium were enlarged and modified, the changes are virtually undetectable from the street. The auditorium seats more than 1,000. The Z. Paliashvili Opera and Ballet Theatre was founded in 1851. Before 1917 primarily Russian and Italian opera companies performed here. Tbilisians were perceived as an appreciative and discerning audience and new works like Verdi's *Othello* and Tchaikovsky's *Eugene Onegin* were staged not long after their debuts. National opera began to be produced at the beginning of the 20th century. Zakharia Paliashvili, for whom the Opera House is named, is considered the father of Georgian opera and is best known for *Absalom and Eteri and Daisi*. A statue of him wearing a toga, holding a torch, and reading a score is in the adjoining garden. Sculpted by Merab Berdzenishvili, it was unveiled in 1973. The composer's grave, and that of the tenor who first sang his works (and for whom the conservatory is named, Vano Sarajishvili) are on the left side of the garden.

The last building on your right before entering the wide open space of Republic Square is the **Central Telegraph Office**. This is one of the best places in Georgia to make long-distance phone calls and send faxes.

REPUBLIC SQUARE

Rustaveli Avenue ends at Republic Square, a product of badly conceived urban renewal of the 1980s. It destroyed interesting turn-of-the-century buildings in favor of a wide-open space marred by a reviewing stand of poured concrete arches. In the center of the square stands the new equestrian statue of David the Builder which was unveiled on May 26, 1997. The statue is justifiably much criticized both for its terrible proportions and for the large amount of money the sculptor, Berdzenishvili, received to execute it.

Opposite the reviewing stand, on the east side of the square on a plateau above the Mtkvari, is the 22-story Iveria Hotel built in 1967 and designed by Otar Kalandarishvili. The hotel now houses, in overcrowded conditions, many refugee families from Abkhazia. The laundry hanging from the balconies of what was once one of Tbilisi's best hotels is a poignant statement of the high cost of independence from the Russian bear.

The left-hand side of Rustaveli continues past the Ministry of Culture, which stands in the middle of the square as an example of Tbilisi architecture victimized by urban renewal. At 52 Rustaveli Avenue, on the west side of the square, is the historically confused (but not unpleasant) building housing the **Georgian Academy of Sciences**, distinctive for its massive campanile topped by a spire. Built in 1953 and

Republic Square as seen from the top of the Iveria Hotel

faced with ochre-colored tuff, the building contains a vast number of academicians' offices. The statue of Shota Rustaveli, dating to 1937, in the northwest corner of the square is the work of Kote Merabishvili.

At this point you can go up to the park on Mount Mtatsminda (Holy Mountain) by the cable car located behind the Academy of Sciences, in a station at the end of a long arcade; or, saving your trip to the Mount for later, proceed to G. Chanturia Street which rises to the south. At number 11A is the **David Kakabadze Memorial Museum.** Located in the artist's former apartment and studio, the museum contains many of his paintings and graphic works. Born in 1889 in the village of Kukhi and raised in Kutaisi, Kakabadze possessed a strong attachment to the province of Imereti, reflected especially in his landscapes. He worked in Paris from 1920 to 1927 and absorbed many of the innovations of cubism. This attempt to meld avant-garde Western aesthetics with traditional Georgian themes perhaps best summarizes his personal vision. He died in 1952.

Also nearby at 12 Kiacheli Street is the **Elene Akhvlediani Memorial Museum.** In this artist's former studio, the museum is kept in such a way as to suggest that she will be returning at any moment. Her paintings and graphic works line the walls, as do the Georgian artifacts that inspired her. Born in 1901, Akhvlediani was raised in Telavi and Tbilisi. She attended the Tbilisi Academy of Arts and in 1922 won a scholarship to study abroad. She lived in Italy and then in Paris with the other most important Georgian painters of her era—Kakabadze and Gudiashvili—until 1927. She is best known for her scenes of Old Tbilisi and other historic sites in Georgia. She died in 1976. Her home was turned into a museum in 1978.

Rustaveli Street forks into Merab Kostava (formerly Lenin) and Melikishvili Streets. Dominating the square formed by this intersection stands the rotunda of the **Georgian State Philharmonic Hall**. Built in 1971, the auditorium here can seat 2,500. The large bronze sculpture in front of the Philharmonic unveiled in 1971 is Merab Berdzenishvili's *Muse*.

Bordering on Kostava Street not far from the Philharmonic is **Vera Park** (formerly Kirov Park). Near the park's southern gates, on Nikoladze Street, stands the 12th-century Church of the Lurdji (Blue) Monastery. Named for the tiles that once adorned its cupola, this church was drastically reconstructed in both the 17th and 19th centuries. The unusual round cupola dates from the 19th-century reconstruction. Only the lower walls and the stone ornamentation around the windows date from Queen Tamara's era.

MOUNT MTATSMINDA

There are several ways to reach Mount Mtatsminda. The cable car, behind the Academy of Sciences, opened in 1958 and is now being restored. The number five bus takes you to Sololaki, where you can catch a number six to the top. The best method, however, is the funicular railway in Chonkadze Street, which allows you to get off at midpoint to visit St. David's Church and the Pantheon of Writers and Public Figures of Georgia. It's also an experience in itself. Completed in 1905, its one of the longest and steepest funiculars in the world, with a length of 501 meters (1,653 feet) and a gradient angle of 55 degrees.

Be sure to request the funicular to stop at St. David's Church. St. David was one of the 13 Syrian Fathers who returned to Georgia in the sixth century to spread Christianity. The present-day cupola church was built between 1855 and 1859 on the site of St. David's cell and chapel, which was destroyed in medieval times. His presence here explains the other name by which Mount Mtatsminda is known: Mamadavidis Mta (Father David's Mount).

The Pantheon of Writers and Public Figures of Georgia is nearby, on a two-tiered terrace a little below the church. On the upper level you'll find the graves of the poets Nikoloz Baratashvili (1817–1845) and Galaktion Tabidze (1892–1959), the educator Yakov Gogebashvili (1840–1912), and others. The grave of the writer and Georgian patriot, Ilya Chavchavadze (1837–1907), is in the central section. His grave can be recognized by the high-relief *Grieving Motherland* set against a red marble background. Chavchavadze was canonized a saint in the Georgian Orthodox Church in 1988. The Mtatsminda cemetery was officially given the status of Pantheon in 1929, the year that marked the 100th anniversary of the death of Alexander Griboyedov, a Russian writer and diplomat murdered in Tehran. His body was brought back to Tbilisi and buried on the mountain he himself called "Tbilisi's most poetic possession." His grave is in the lower section of the cemetery in a stone grotto created in 1832 by his 16-year-old widow, Nina, daughter of the Georgian author Alexander Chavchavadze.

Continue your trip to the top of the Mount. The upper funicular station in the 115-hectare (280-acre) park (formerly named for Stalin) was built in the 1930s. The terrace offers a glorious view of Tbilisi. The terrace and the viewing platforms are especially spectacular at night when the lights of the city are spread out before you with all the city's magic and romance. A restaurant and cafe are located in the upper station. Take a moment to look at the large-scale fresco, *The Initiation of Pirosmani*, by Nikolai Ignatov, in the smaller dining room. Near the upper station is a prominent radio and television tower which soars to a height of 300 meters (985 feet). This is a convenient marker as you tour the city; it can be seen from most everywhere and indicates which way is south.

Mount Mtatsminda rises from the right bank of the Mtkvari 400 meters (1,210 feet) above the river and more than 700 meters (2,297 feet) above sea level. Getting to the top is a must for everyone who enjoys mountain vistas.

Vake and Saburtalo

These two districts in western Tbilisi were unpopulated and outside city limits in the 1920s. The university was Vake's only claim to fame, and it was not until just before World War II and into the 1960s that development took off. Vazha Pshavela and Kazbegi (formerly Pavlova) streets are the major arteries in Saburtalo. Chavchavadze and Paliashvili streets were built to open up Vake. Because Tbilisi University, numerous institutes, and other professional organizations are situated in these two posh districts, they are also home to many of the city's intelligentsia, academics, professionals, and the well-to-do. Since the distance between places of interest in these two areas is great, it is best to tour them by car or taxi.

Vake

Melikishvili Street leads into the Vake district which is defined by the junction of Melikishvili and Varazis-Khevi streets and Chavchavadze Avenue. Where Chavchavadze Avenue and Varazis-Khevi Street meet is the main building of **Tbilisi University.** Built between 1900 and 1916, this stately white building has the special charm of a neoclassical edifice in a southern clime. It houses the office of the rector of the university and a number of the humanities departments. Other buildings in Vake and Saburtalo house the 20 departments that instruct in 145 fields. Courses are conducted primarily in Georgian as well as some in Russian and English.

Opposite Chavchavadze Avenue to the north is the 2,000-hectare (4,940-acre) **Mziuri (Sunshine) Children's Rest and Amusement Park.** Stretching along the Vera valley, the park includes a 120-hectare (296-acre) zoo and a botanical garden. Nodar Dumbadze, the novelist, founded this park and is buried near the entrance.

At the end of Chavchavadze Avenue is the main entrance to **Vake Park**, which covers 226 hectares (558 acres) across the valley and up the slopes of the Trialeti Range. The waterfall that runs down the hillside emanates from a square that contains the **Tomb of the Unknown Soldier,** a World War II memorial. The **Statue of Victory,** 28 meters (92 feet) high, was unveiled in 1976. You can reach the park's Turtle Lake by cable car near the main entrance or by driving along a road that wends its way up the hill for three km (1.9 miles). The Museum of Georgian Folk Architecture and Local Lore is halfway between the entrance and the lake.

MUSEUM OF GEORGIAN FOLK ARCHITECTURE AND LOCAL LORE

Founded in 1960 and opened in 1976, this open-air museum consists of more than 70 dwellings from 10 distinct regions in Georgia and has over 7,000 artifacts. The houses are not replicas but have been moved piece by piece from their native villages. From western Georgia come the *oda sakhli* and the older-style *sajalabo*. The *sajalabo* (house for a large family) is a one-room windowless structure with an earthen floor and an open hearth in the middle. The *oda sakhli* is square, with two or three rooms and an open porch running along the width of the façade. Beautifully carved wooden pillars usually support the roof of the veranda. Other carefully designed smaller buildings in the back bespeak the care and craftsmanship that went into the daily tasks of husbandry.

From the Kartli region come excellent examples of the *darbazi* dwelling and the *baniani sakhli* (flat-roofed dwelling). You will recall that an example of the *darbazi* dwelling can still be seen in the Old Town at 10 Chekhov Street (*see* page 97). This rectangular unpartitioned dwelling is distinguished by a hearth in the middle and a smoke and light hole in the top. The beehive cupola (*gvirgvini*) that ascends to that hole is the most extraordinary feature of the dwelling. Believed to go back to a prototype from the third millennium BC, *darbazi* dwellings were described by Vitruvius in his treatise on architecture from the first century BC. The building and dome that he mentions are close enough to a *darbazi* dwelling to make us feel that the structure has developed uninterrupted in Georgia right up to its present form. The beehive dome you see here is composed of 452 beams resting on each other in concentric layers. The two main supporting pillars, called *dedabodzi* (mother pillars), are often ornately carved.

The *baniani sakhli* from the village of Khandaki is smaller, with only one pillar in the room. The smoke hole in the cupola in the *darbazi* dwelling here is substituted by a fireplace with chimney and windows. Tusheti, Khevsureti, and Svaneti offer some fine examples of the unusual watchtower dwellings that dot these constantly besieged parts of the Caucasus. Don't miss the wonderful wood carving in the interior of the Jameh mosque that comes from the village of Chikuneti in Ajara.

An 11th section of the museum has been established to house archaeological monuments such as sculpted gravestones, ancient inscriptions, and capitals. Complete basilicas from the Middle Ages are already being assembled.

If your visit to Georgia is limited to a stay in Tbilisi, touring this museum is an excellent way to grasp the great architectual distinctions that exist among the various provinces. A visit here should certainly whet your appetite for greater touring throughout the country.

Saburtalo

Saburtalo and Vake are separated by the Vera River gorge. It's reached by driving down Tamarashvili (formely Guramishvili) Street opposite Vake Park. A neighborhood consisting of research institutes and new buildings of Tbilisi University, Saburtalo and its outskirts are also a residential district of high-rise apartment buildings developed in the 1960s. For those with an interest in bee-keeping, Saburtalo is worthy of a pilgrimage. At 15 Tamarashvili Street, the **Bee-Keeping Museum**, houses a specialized collection of all the appurtenances and products related to this most ancient enterprise.

Modern architecture is not one of Georgia's strong points, but if you're keen to rest your eyes and sensibilities from the feudal wonders that abound, head off to the western part of this neighborhood and have a look at the **Building of the Ministry of Highways** on Moreti Street. Built in 1977 on a rocky slope near the Right (formerly Stalin) Embankment, the building has two towers and five horizontal blocks that work admirably on this difficult topography.

In Constitution Square you will encounter the 18-story Hotel Ajara, built in 1975. Like the Iveria, this was one of the better Intourist hotels but it now is home to refugees from the war in Abkhazia. To the east of Constitution Square is the **Palace of Sports**. Built in 1961, this arena holds 10,000.

Gmirta Moedani (The Square of Heroes) is the nexus for the major arteries of Vake and Saburtalo and the streets of the left bank that run into Station Square and the nearby Nadzaladevi district. On the southeast side of the square, standing on a hill, is the circular **Circus**. Built in 1940, the auditorium seats 2,000. From Gmirta Square continue across the Mtkvari River and along the full length of Queen Tamara Avenue (formerly Cheluskintsev Street) until you come to Tbilisi's central train depot in Station Square, from where trains run regularly to major towns throughout Georgia and beyond (*see* page 55). South of Station Square and west of Queen Tamara Avenue is Tbilisi's largest market. Food enthusiasts should not miss seeing the vast array of fruits, vegetables, meat, poultry, and unusual Caucasian spices sold in these tiny stalls.

The Left Bank

David Agmashenebeli (David the Builder) Avenue (formerly Plekhanov) runs along the left bank of the city more or less parallel to Rustaveli Avenue on the right bank. Known as Mikhailovskaya Street in the 1830s, this road linked the villages of Chugureti, Kukia, and Didube beginning in ancient times.

This zone will not be of enormous interest to first-time visitors to Tbilisi. Sports fans will want to visit **National (formerly Dynamo) Stadium**, rebuilt in 1976 and home to the enormously popular and successful Tbilisi soccer team Iberia (formerly the Dynamos). Renovation of the 1935 stadium increased the seating capacity from 35,000 to 75,000, a good thing given the city's enthusiasm for its home team.

The westernmost part of the city is called **Dighomi**. Film aficionados will want to arrange a tour of Gruzia Film Studios located here at 6 Akhmeteli Street. Such greats directors as Tengiz Abuladze, Revaz Chkeidze, Eldar and Giorgi Shengalaya, Lana Gogoberidze, Otar Ioseliani, and Alexander Rekhviashvili have all worked here.

Behind the Makhata Ridge is the **Tbilisi Sea**. This natural depression was enlarged in 1951 and uses water from the Iori River to irrigate the Samgori Steppe in the east. The reservoir is also a favorite swimming hole for Tbilisi residents.

Kartli

History

Kartli is the Georgian name for the eastern Georgian kingdom known to the classical world as Iberia. The name is derived from the powerful Georgian tribe, the Karts, who emerged in the eastern part of the country in the eighth or seventh century BC. The Georgian name of the Georgian nation is Sakartvelo (land of the Kartvel-ebi). The names of both the country and the people are derived from the principal province and the tribe that first settled there.

The Iberian or Kartlian Kingdom with its capital at Mtskheta-Armazi came into existence in approximately the sixth century BC. Iberia-Kartli maintained contact with the Greeks, Achaemenid Persia, the Seleucids, Arsacid Iran, the Pontics, and many others. In the third century BC the first king of Iberia-Kartli, Parnavazi, rose to power in Mtskheta-Armazi, establishing his dynasty over rival Iberian princes. As a result of the political organization created by Parnavazi, the differences between Georgian tribes were reduced and the tribes were gradually assimilated into the dominant Kartveli group.

In the first century BC, because of Pompey's punitive expedition into the South Caucasus, Kartli-Iberia fell under Roman domination. However, by the last decade of the first century AD Kartli-Iberia was recognized as an ally of Rome, not a vassal state required to pay taxes. In 298 the Romans and Iranians signed the Peace of Nisibis, making Kartli-Iberia a dependent state of Rome but putting an Iranian candidate, Mirian, on the throne. The orientation of Kartli-Iberia to Rome allowed for the subsequent advent of Christianity, when St. Nino arrived preaching the gospel in 328. King Mirian converted in 334, and Christianity became the state religion of Kartli-Iberia. In 588 the Byzantine emperor Maurice restored Kartli-Iberia's autonomy after having defeated the Iranians, but instead of re-establishing the monarchy he appointed a ruling prince named Guaram (588–602). Byzantium and Iran reached an agreement in 591 that split Kartli-Iberia between them: one region with the capital in Mtskheta ruled by a Byzantine appointee and the other ruled by Iran in Tbilisi. Guaram's son Stepanoz I (602–627) deserted the Byzantine camp and gave his allegiance to the Iranians, thus reuniting Kartli-Iberia. Emperor Heraclius I (610–641) sent a punitive expedition to Kartli-Iberia, captured Stepanoz I, and flayed him alive. Adarnase I of Kakheti was appointed ruler of Kartli-Iberia, and Byzantium continued to wield authority over this region until the Arab invasions twenty years later.

The Arabs captured the Kartli-Iberian capital of Tbilisi in 645. Byzantium had no intention of giving up its interests in the Caucasus, and for the next two centuries Kartli-Iberia was the prize for which the Byzantine and Arab armies constantly contended. By the end of the eighth century, local Georgian lords had wrested a degree of autonomy and ruled their individual regions as they saw fit, while the Arabs controlled the cities, including Tbilisi.

The tenth century saw the rise, in Tao, of the powerful new Bagratid prince David. Favored by the Byzantine emperor Basil II (975–1025), David was ultimately instrumental in helping Bagrat III become the first king of a united Abkhazeti and Kartli-Iberia. In 1068, however, the Seljuk Turks from Iran began incursions into Kartli, Tbilisi was captured and given to a Moslem emir. It remained in Moslem hands until the greatest of all Georgian kings, David the Builder (1089–1125), ascended the throne and recaptured the city in 1122. He made Tbilisi the capital of an expanding empire, which came to encompass all the land from the Black Sea to the Caspian and from the Caucasus south through greater Armenia. He established seats of learning and was especially generous to the monastery of Shiomgvime in Kartli.

King David's great-granddaughter, Queen Tamara (1184–1212), ruled at the height of the Georgian empire's power and was instrumental in expanding her kingdom's borders and enriching its culture. When her son Giorgi IV Lasha took over in 1212, he inherited a kingdom that was respected throughout Christendom and the Middle East.

The success was short-lived, however, with the coming of the Mongol invasions. By the end of the 15th century, Georgia was divided into three kingdoms: Kartli, Imereti, and Kakheti. The country was not to be reunited until the beginning of the 19th century when it was annexed by Russia.

Kartli Today

Today the province is divided into Shida (Inner) Kartli and Kvemo (Lower) Kartli. Kvemo Kartli comprises 6,688 sq. km (2,582 sq. miles) and has a population of 612,880. Shida Kartli now comprises 8,815 sq. km (3,403 sq. miles) and has a population of 433,000. These figures include the South Ossetian Autonomous Region within Shida Kartli. Before the Bolshevik annexation of Georgia in 1921, this region was part of Shida Kartli. Georgians explain with outrage Stalin's creation of an autonomous region for the Ossetes (descendants of the ancient Alans who speak a language related to Iranian) on Georgian territory when they had their own homeland in North Ossetia. Ossetes were relative newcomers to Georgia, having migrated to Shida Kartli during the 18th to 20th centuries. According to Georgians, at the time the Bolsheviks established the capital of the South Ossetian Autonomous Region at Tskhinvali, only two Ossetian familes lived there. In 1926, 1,152 Ossetes comprised 19.8 percent of the population. By 1989, 31,500 comprised 74.5 percent of the town's population.

On December 12, 1990, three Georgians were murdered in the center of Tskhinvali, an act which culminated in armed conflict between Ossetes and Georgians living in the region. Over the next three years, hundreds of Georgians were killed, ten thousand Georgians have been forced to leave their ancestral homes, and tens of thousands of Ossetes have likewise become refugees in the fighting. On June 24, 1992, President Eduard Shevardnadze met with Russian President Boris Yeltsin in Sochi to broker a ceasefire. In the summer of that year, a peacekeeping force of 700 Russians, 500 South Ossetes, and 33 Georgians was sent to the region.

The situation has now improved and there is hope that a lasting solution to the conflict will be found. Many Ossetes associate the origins of this conflict to Zviad Gamsakhurdia's nationalism and feel that they can work with Shevardnadze. Georgians have traditionally been very responsive to developing the Ossetian culture and economy. Whereas in North Ossetia there were no schools that provided instruction in the Ossetian language, Georgia at the beginning of the 1990–1991 academic year had 97 secondary schools where Ossetian was taught. Clearly the key to this conflict is a recognition that the Ossetian population in Georgia is a national minority, whose rights must be guaranteed like those of other minorities.

Refugees have begun returning to their homes and travelers can take buses to Tskhinvali. The region, however, is unstable, and political tensions do not show any signs of abating any time soon.

Gori and Vicinity

Eighty-six km (53 miles) west of Tbilisi, the town of Gori, population 68,924, is situated on both banks of the Mtkvari River where it meets the Liakhvi and Mejuda rivers. From Tbilisi take the M27 toward Sokhumi and bear left when the road forks approximately 35 km (21.7 miles) out of town.

The exact date of the founding of Gori is unknown. The Fortress of Gori, Goris-Tsikhe, which dominates the city and offers a superb view overlooking the Mtkvari River valley, is known to have been besieged by Pompey in 65 BC during his campaign in the South Caucasus. (Goris-Tsikhe means "Fortress on a Hill." The name of the town comes from the Georgian word for hill, goraki.) The first mention of the

A woman in the city of Akhaltsikhe displays an old portrait of Stalin

fortress occurs in a seventh-century Georgian chronicle. The existing walls and towers of the fortress date from the Middle Ages and from the Turkish and Persian occupations of the 16th and 17th centuries. Certain Islamic architectural features such as the keel arch can still be seen in the masonry.

In 1123, King David the Builder was responsible for establishing the city of Gori that developed beyond the fortress. He settled Armenian refugees here who had been fleeing north into Georgia from the Turkish and Byzantine conquerors of Armenia. Gori became an important trade center on the caravan route from Byzantium to India and China by way of Trabzon. Between the 15th and 19th centuries, possession of Gori changed hands among the Turks, Persians, and Georgians. In 1801, with the incorporation of Kartli into the Russian Empire, Gori was made a district center, which it remains. This rich agricultural region is known throughout Georgia for its apples, pears, and peaches.

Gori came to the world's attention along with Joseph Stalin: Gori is his birthplace. **Stalin's House Museum**, is in the center of a garden in the middle of Stalin Prospect, where he was born on December 21, 1879, and resided until 1883. His father, Vissarion Jugashvili, was a local shoemaker. The wooden hut where they lived is now enshrined in a Greco-Italianate pavilion built in 1939. The self-aggrandizing palazzo built in 1957 is in the same style as the pavilion; behind it is the Stalin Museum, which houses numerous photos, documents, and personal memorabilia relating to Stalin's political and military career. Particularly chilling is the rotunda on the second floor in which Stalin's death mask is displayed surrounded by red velvet.

The museum has been closed, reopened, closed again in 1989, and since reopened. The museum is very interesting, with lots of photos of Stalin, often with other leaders airbrushed out. You can get a guided tour by a respected historian who is a great admirer of Stalin; these tours are only in Russian or Georgian.

To this day Stalin is regarded by many of the older citizens of Gori as a hero, a favorite son. In Gori the first toast of an evening's drinking is always made to Stalin. Moderates in Gori feel that the museum should stay open, and that although Stalin was "bad," he is still part of history. The tourist trade that accrued to the city when Gori was a site of pilgrimage for all Soviet and East Bloc tourists has certainly fallen by the wayside.

Those interested in seeing other traces of Stalin should take a look at the Pullman parked on the grounds of the museum. This was Stalin's private railway coach, used for much of his traveling, to the Potsdam conference in 1945, for example. Perhaps the strangest sight in Gori is the oversized statue of Stalin in the center of Stalin Square. It is the only monument to him of such a size which is still standing anywhere in the world today. (Ulan Bator, the capital of Mongolia, had such a statue some years ago but friends report that it has now been removed).

Outside of Gori, Stalin is usually revered only by the Georgian equivalent of rednecks. Such people talk about him as a great military leader who saved the USSR from the Nazis, as a reformer of society who only punished criminals and "speculators," as the man who got lazy people to work and kept the prices down. The majority of Georgians, however, especially members of the intelligentsia and the new generation, are all too aware of what he represented. The Stalin question, after the subjects of Abkhazia and South Ossetia, is one of the most sensitive subjects that can be broached in Georgia. Be prepared for heated discussions.

Gori also has a small **Local History and Ethnographic Museum**, at 7 Lomauri Street. In a building within the precincts of the Catholic Church of the Dormition, the museum is open 10 a.m.–6 p.m. and primarily contains archaeological artifacts excavated from Goris-Tsikhe and environs. The museum possesses more than 85,000 objects, but because of budgetary constraints only a few rooms are open and the end result is disappointing. Gori is an excellent starting point for trips to the cave town of Uplis-Tsikhe, the Church of Didi Ateni, the Samtsevrisi and Kintsvisi Monasteries, and the spa town of Borjomi.

UPLIS-TSIKHE

The cave town of Uplis-Tsikhe is seven km (4.3 miles) southeast of Gori. Take the road that goes to Akhalkalaki, which you can pick up in Gori by following Ketskhoveli Street to Eristavi Street. Beyond the village of Uplis-Tsikhe, turn left and cross the bridge over the Mtkvari (Kura) River. You will have seen the actual site on the left bank of the river as you were driving parallel to it.

The cave city grew over a period of hundreds of years in the first millennium BC. In antiquity the city was one of the most important centers of Kartli, and in the Middle Ages it stood on an important trade route that linked Byzantium with India and China. At the height of its development in the Middle Ages, Uplis-Tsikhe was a flourishing community of over 20,000 inhabitants, primarily merchants and artisans.

The city is laid out over nine hectares (22 acres), rising from east to west up a mountain slope. The south side of the site drops steeply to the Mtkvari (Kura) River, which served as natural protection. Moats surrounding the city also acted as an obstacle to its numerous invaders. The ultimate decline of the city can be attributed to Tamerlane and the Mongol invasions of the 13th century. A series of earthquakes, and the decline of trade caused by the collapse of the Byzantine Empire, combined to weaken the city to such a degree that by the 15th century only shepherds used the caves as shelter from the elements.

Uplis-Tsikhe is the prototype of the cave monasteries that developed later at Vardzia and David-Gareja. At Uplis-Tsikhe, an entire town (streets, churches, storerooms, palaces, and residential dwellings) was carved into the soft stone of the mountainside. As the city grew, wooden structures were either added to the caves or built to stand alone. All of these dwellings have since disappeared. The caves, plus remnants of streets and city walls, have afforded archaeologists a good view of the demarcation of neighborhoods and their functions within the community.

The southern part of town was the trading center, where the stalls of the merchants and artisans' workshops were located. The small pits dotted throughout the surface of the stone slope were originally used for pagan ceremonies; later, after Christianity was introduced, they were used for food storage. All the small sidestreets joined with Central Magistrate Street, which divided the city in half. You can climb it going towards the ninth-century Three-Church Basilica at the summit.

The central part of town was the primary residential area for craftsmen and their families. West of the main street are dwellings from the late Hellenistic period. Situated at the edge of the cliff that drops dramatically to the Mtkavri below, this settlement has a number of caves carved in imitation of architectural motifs, including gabled entrances and coffered ceilings. These date back to AD 200–300.

The northwestern part of town features a medieval palace and the administrative district. Before reaching the Three-Church Basilica, turn left off the main road to the Hall of Queen Tamara. Although Tamara never lived here, this deluxe cave dwelling was an apartment for the town's rulers. Scholars speculate that the western area was reserved for the king, and the northern and southern portions housed other political leaders. Two columns, which stood here until the 19th century, separated the central room into two naves. Note the stone carving on the ceiling, designed to simulate wooden beams. Niches were carved into the wall for storage and entrances to side chambers were carved through the stone.

Above Tamara's hall is one of Uplis-Tsikhe's largest cave dwellings: the Three-Naved Cave Basilica. Now in ruins, this basilica has four columns that separated the space into three naves. The structure functioned as a religious hall in antiquity and became a Christian basilica in the sixth century. The basilica was destroyed by the Persians in the seventh century but was restored in the 12th to 13th centuries and converted into a residence and bakery.

The Three-Church Basilica, near the end of the uncovered main street, dates to the ninth to tenth centuries and functioned until the 15th century when the last of the clergy were killed. Their graves were discovered in the church in 1986. The walls were covered with tenth-century frescoes which were plastered over in the 19th century during the Russification campaign against the Georgian Orthodox Church.

Along the perimeter of the town's eastern portion you can still see sections of the old defensive walls dating to 920, which remained intact until the 15th century.

Returning to the southeastern section, leave through the secret tunnel that extends for 45 meters (147.6 feet) through the rock, emerging at the riverbank.

Uplis-Tsikhe is one of those eerie places that confirm so eloquently the Old Testament injunction against vanity. Looking over all the burrows in the soft stone and feeling the wind erode the structures even as you stand there, you can't help but be spooked by all this troglodytic ambition and what remains of it.

THE CHURCH OF ATENI SIONI (DIDI ATENI)

From Uplis-Tsikhe, return toward Gori on Eristavi Street. After approximately seven km (4.3 miles), turn left beyond the bridge in the village of Khidistavi and head toward Kvemo-Boshuri. The Church of Ateni Sioni is seven km from Khidistavi through the fertile Tana gorge, where lush garden plots, vineyards, and grape arbors will make you think you are in Arcadia. The region produces a superb white wine called Atenuri. Unfortunately, it doesn't travel well; it's best to drink it while there.

The church is beautifully situated on the plateau of a cliff above the Tana River and the village of Didi Ateni. Your approach from the road on foot is under a wonderful pergola of grape vines.

Built in the first half of the seventh century, this tetraconch structure with corner rooms is a close copy of the Jvari Church at Mtskheta built in 586–604 (see page 161). The degree of emulation can be seen in the absence of niches beside the polygonal conch on the western façade. This feature is also missing at Jvari, but whereas in Jvari the western façade is not the most easily seen, at Ateni it's the principal one. Through an inscription, we know the name of the architect: Thodosa.

The ninth to tenth-century Three-Church Basilica in Uplis-Tsikhe

A relief of a herd of stags on the west façade of the Church of Ateni Sioni in Kartli

Built of the local sandstone, the church colors vary from gray, white, light green, to pink to deep red. This stone tends to darken with age, and it is interesting to compare the red lower tiers of the western façade with the lighter hues of the 16th-century renovation of the cupola and other portions of the walls. The façades on all sides contain an assortment of reliefs. Given what appears to be their random arrangement, they are believed to date from a period later than the construction of the church, or to have been moved from their original position on the façade during the 16th-century restoration. Although many of these reliefs are somewhat crudely rendered, others reflect a lovely fusion of early Georgian folk art and Sassanid Iranian influence.

On the west façade is a well-carved portrait of a hunter wearing the headdress of a Sassanid Iranian who has just shot an arrow at a herd of stags. The stags themselves are not nearly as well carved as the horseman. Wrought in low relief in the tympanum above the northern entrance is a beautifully carved portrayal of two stags drinking from a stream. Scholars disagree about the iconographic significance, but it probably has to do with the theme of redemption through baptism.

On the front of the polygonal apse of the eastern façade is a relief of Christ. To the right is a patron holding a model of the church.

The interior of the church reveals a harmony of design that is lacking in the façade because of the random placement of the reliefs. The unity of the interior is achieved by the strict proportions of the alternating conches and niches as well as the overall plan in the cycle of wall paintings.

The frescoes are a high point in Georgian wall painting, dating from the second half of the 11th century. Although some have been defaced or destroyed, one can still gain an overall impression of this school of painting from what remains.

In the apse vault is a portrayal of the Virgin and Child flanked by the archangels Michael and Gabriel. Above, across the arch of the bema, are Christ Pantocrator in the medallion along with John the Baptist, the prophet Zacharias, and David and Aaron.

In the northern apse are scenes of the Baptism, the Crucifixion, the Transfiguration, the Raising of Lazarus, and the Resurrection. The southern apse shows the Prophecy to Joachim and Anna, the Birth of Mary, the Visit to the Temple, the Prophecy to Mary, the Visitation, the Dream of Joseph, the Birth of Christ, and the Death of Mary. Note particularly the delicate rendering of Joseph's repose and the free flight of the angel above him. The Georgian Asomtavruli characters between them relate what is happening.

The uppermost register of the west conch shows the Last Judgment. Below are shown prophets and martyrs, including the prophets Habakkuk and Ezekiel, and St. Nino. On the north side of the west conch, in the lower register, are portraits of patrons and kings, including King Giorgi II and Bagrat IV.

KINTSVISI

Return to the M27 and continue west toward Khashuri. Take the left-hand turnoff toward Kareli and drive to the center of the town (approximately three km/two miles) until you come to a T-junction at the central square. Turn right and then immediately left onto Ninth of April Street, and follow this street until you come to a roundabout. Take the second right and head out of town. After three km (two miles) is a turnoff on the right for the Church of Samtsevrisi, which is one km (0.62 mile) farther. Save this for your return and continue another six km (3.7 miles) to the left-hand turnoff for the monastery of Kintsvisi. The monastery, another 3.5 km (two miles) up the hill, is visible through the dense forest. This entire area stretching into the Shida Kartli plains belonged to the noble Panaskerteli family, which came here from Tao in the 14th century after fighting and losing to the Turks. Zaza Panaskerteli-Tsitsishvili is responsible for building the western extension to the Church of St. Nicholas in the 14th century. He was also the author of Georgia's first medical treatise, which lists various medicines for specific illnesses.

Fresco of an angel in the Church of St. Nicholas in the Kintsvisi Monastery

THE CHURCH OF ST. NICHOLAS

Sequestered on a hillside above the Dzama River valley, this cruciform domed Church dates to the beginning of the 13th century. Similar in design to the Church of Timotes-Ubani, the Church of St. Nicholas is also made of brick, a technique not common in Georgia at the time. With the exception of the two niches on the east façade and the small architectural models of churches that adorn the tops of the gables, the exterior is devoid of decoration.

The western narthex was added in the 14th century. Access is provided by three tall arches, above which is a gallery. Annexes were also built in the north and south. Of greatest interest is the superb fresco cycle that adorns the interior and dates to the time of construction. These frescoes are among the very best that have survived from this epoch. Expressive, elegant, and monumental, the images are set against an intense and unifying blue background.

The cross in the dome of the cupola is a treatment unique to Georgia. Between the twelve windows in the drum are prophets and saints, with the four Evangelists within the medallions of the pendentives. In the eastern apse is the traditional iconographic treatment of the Virgin and Child surrounded by angels.

In the north and south cross-arms are scenes from the life of Jesus. The arrangement of the pictorial registers is unusual. The expected strict ordering of zones is interrupted by the oversized figure of the seated angel. This tendency arose at the end of the 12th century and signaled a greater degree of fluency and freedom in pictorial representation. The angel, separated by the windows from the scene of the middle zone, actually belongs to the depiction of the Mourning at the Grave of Christ. (This angel is much revered throughout Georgia; a recently painted icon of this angel now adorns a pillar in Sveti-tskhoveli in Mtskheta.)

Above the middle zone is the Entry into Jerusalem. The first register contains portraits of rulers of Georgia: King Giorgi III, Queen Tamara, and her son Giorgi IV Lasha. Across from them along the first register of the south wall is the patron of this church, Anton Gnohistavisdze, head of Christian ideology and history under Queen Tamara. He is seen here presenting a model of the church to St. Nicholas. With our knowledge of these historical personages, these frescoes have been dated to the years 1207–1213.

In the western narthex are frescoes from the 14th century, including what is thought to be a portrait of Zaza Panaskerteli made by his son.

Also in the grounds of the monastery precincts are two small hall churches and the remains of the monastery buildings. South of the grounds, a path leads to a wonderful picnic area, in the forest by a glistening stream.

SAMTSEVRISI

Return the way you came to the turnoff for Samtsevrisi (approximately nine km/15.6 miles). Turn left onto the dirt road and follow it one km (0.62 miles), through a tiny village, until you see the small centralized dome church of Samtsevrisi on a hill rising gently from the expansive Mtkvari River plain. The church lies on the right bank of the river.

Built in the first half of the seventh century, this church is of the "free-cross" type, in which a horseshoe-shaped apse is contained within a cruciform ground plan, that is maintained both in the interior and exterior. Samtsevrisi is a triumph of balanced proportions and is distinctive for the quality of its masonry, evident in its evenly hued stone walls. The two rows of squinches that allow for the transition from the square bay to the round cupola are a structural feat. Seriously damaged in an earthquake in 1940, the church was recently restored.

South of the church is a small brick mausoleum from the 16th century belonging to the Tsitsishvili family. This is doubtless the same family whose feudal residence was part of the ruins of the large 16th-century fortress 1,000 meters (3,280 feet) to the west on another small hill overlooking the Mtkvari River.

TSROMI, CHURCH OF THE REDEEMER

From the village of Agara on the M27 west of Kareli continue west on the highway until you come to the village of Gomi. Turn left at the police station eight km (five miles) beyond Gomi, cross the Mtkvari River, pass through the village of Khtisi, and proceed east parallel to the Mtkvari for six km (3.7 miles).

Famous as the oldest ecclesiastical building in Georgia with four free-standing pilasters supporting the dome, this early predecessor of the cruciform domed church can be dated to approximately 630. From an inscription we know that the patron of the church was Stepanoz II of Kartli, son of the ruler Adarnese who is featured in a relief on the façade of Jvari.

The architect of Tsromi managed to build a massive edifice that, despite its size, in no way betrayed his search for a harmony of line and totality of parts. The deep-set triangular niches of the east façade are particularly noteworthy. By flanking the central window of the altar apse, the architect succeeded in lightening the mass while increasing the dignity of the structure.

Earthquakes (the last one in 1940) have reduced the cupola and the majority of the vaulting to ruins, but it is still possible to see the majesty of this church and to understand the innovative solutions that came to serve as a model for domed cruciform structures well beyond Georgia's borders.

BORJOMI

Continuing on the M27 from Gori, proceed to Khashuri (46 km/28.5 miles) and turn left at the junction with the A308 going southwest. Borjomi is 29 km (18 miles) from Khashuri and 160 km (99 miles) from Tbilisi.

Situated in the beautiful Borjomi Gorge between the Vakhani and Trialeti ridges, Borjomi (population 17,000) is the largest mountain spa in Georgia. Famous for its curative mineral waters, mountain air, favorable climate, and dense forests, the town is home to numerous sanatoria where many Georgians return every year for the 24-day cure. Georgians swear by the healing effects of the water and believe that the regimen followed here in the summer is the only way to prepare adequately for the next season's round of parties that will inevitably exact a high price on their livers.

Borjomi was, in fact, called the Caucasian Vichy. Its waters became widely known when the daughter of the Russian Commmander-in-Chief of the Caucasus, Yevgeni Golovin, was cured of her gynaecological problems through treatment. The spa was further developed by Prince Mikhail Vorontsov, who replaced General Golovin in 1841. Tsar Alexander II, visiting the spa in 1871, found it sufficiently beautiful to make Borjomi and its environs a gift to Grand Duke Mikhail, son of Tsar Nicolas I.

Today Borjomi has a daily yield of 500,000 liters (130,000 gallons) of water. The numerous big bottling plants in town annually produce more than 300 million bottles of water, which are sold throughout the Commonwealth of Independent States and abroad. New Yorkers will have no trouble finding endless supplies of this elixir in Russian stores concentrated in Brooklyn's Brighton Beach neighborhood.

Borjomi is 800 meters (2,625 feet) above sea level. The Mtkvari runs through town, and you must cross to the right bank from the A308 to reach the town's historic center. Cross the bridge (four km/2.5 miles from the town line) and take

Ninth of April Street (formerly Lenin Street, which ran into Orjonikidze Street), past the train station to the entrance of Mineral Park. On the way you'll pass some wonderful 19th-century houses distinctive for their elaborate wooden carvings and range of architectural styles. They certainly convey the flavor of the Russian-created spa town. The building at 48 Ninth of April Street, formerly home of the Persian consul and now the Firuze Sanatorium, is a superb medley of Moorish, Georgian, and Armenian ornamentation. Mineral Park is one of three in which many of the mineral springs are located; you can taste the waters for a few tetri paid to an attendant handing out glasses from a small kiosk. The kiosk is constructed around one of the springs, which was enclosed with stone and covered by a glass dome in the 19th century. A large restaurant is nearby.

From a small station in the park you can take a cable car up to the 136-hectare (336-acre) Sadgeri Arboretum. Lying 1,000 meters (3,300 feet) above sea level, this wide plateau is home to a wonderful forest with ancient trees. Here too are the ruins of the Sadgeri Fortress, where a famous Georgian general of the 17th century, Giorgi Saakadze, once stayed with his army. The cable car runs from 9 a.m. to 8 p.m. daily except Monday.

The Borjomi Gorge, covering 143 sq. km (55 sq. miles), has been designated a National Reserve. With 450 varieties of plants, the region can lay claim to some of the most exquisite natural beauty to be found in Georgia.

Bakuriani was the most famous downhill skiing complex in Georgia. At 1,829 meters (6,000 feet) above sea level in a protected hollow, Bakuriani had been likened to Davos in Switzerland or Squaw Valley in the U.S. for its climate and conditions. Unfortunately, it is now in a terrible state of disrepair due to a lack of funds. The heaviest snowfall is in December and it lasts through March. One run begins 2,500 meters (8,202 feet) up Mount Imerlebis. Worthwhile excursions from Bakuriani include a hike to the summit of Mt. Tskhra-Tskharo (2,711 meters/8,844 feet), and to Lake Tabatskuri (2,000 meters/6,562 feet), one of the most beautiful alpine lakes in Georgia.

You can get to Bakuriani by train (37 km/23 miles from the Borjomi station), by car (27 km/16.7 miles on the twisting road that is to your left, two km/1.2 miles past the town line of Borjomi), or on foot in the summer from the Sadgeri Plateau. The drive allows you to visit other health resorts between Borjomi and Bakuriani. Of greatest interest would be a stop at Tsagveri (1,020–1,050 meters/3,346–3,445 feet) to visit the famous Timotes-Ubani Monastery; follow the road that runs east along the Gujaretistskali River. Built at the end of the 12th century, this brick church is stylistically closest to the Church of St. Nicholas at Kintsvisi. Like Kintsvisi, it contains excellent frescoes.

SAMTAVISI

Returning to Tbilisi on the M27 from Gori, you'll come to the village of Igoeti. Turn left at the sign for Samtavisi and go another one km (0.62 mile). Alternatively, you can come here as a short day trip from Tbilisi, since the church is only 40 km (24.9 miles) west of Mtskheta, also on the M27.

Park in front of the defensive wall encircling the monastery. Within are the 11th-century church, remains of the bishop's palace dating from the same time as the cathedral, and a 17th-century belltower.

The Samtavisi Church is of extraordinary artistic merit. An inscription on the east façade, documented in the 19th century but missing today, dated the construction of the church to 1030 and named the founder as Bishop Illarion of Samtavisi. He is also thought to have been the architect. Another inscription in the east façade states that the church was finished by a Bishop John in 1168. The church originally had ambulatories in the north, south, and west, but these were removed. The west façade was restored in the 15th century after the cupola drum collapsed upon it as a result of the destruction of Tamerlane's invasion. The restoration of the cupola drum dates from the 15th century as well. The defensive walls were restored in the 15th and 17th centuries. The church also shows some signs of 19th-century refurbishing.

SAMTAVISI CHURCH

Like its contemporary Samtavro, in Mtskheta, Samtavisi Church is a cruciform domed church most remarkable for the high quality of the sculptural design on its façades. As with the cathedral at Sveti-tskhoveli, blind arcading is used to great advantage to emphasize the verticality of the structure. One's eye is seduced into following these arcades to their conclusion beneath the gable of the tall transepts, after which the progression to the drum and cone becomes inevitable. The whole structure displays an elegance, balance, and harmony that have been retained despite renovations.

The most significant feature of the church is the beautifully carved ornamentation of the east façade. The workmanship represents the pinnacle of Georgian stone-carving, and many of the designs served as models for other churches. Deep triangular niches flank the altar apse window. They are adorned with a fan carving within and bordered by repeating stone rods that serve as a unifying element throughout the façade as they travel to outline the blind arcading. Intricately carved floral and vegetal designs surround the windows and make up the body of the large cross above the altar window and the two diamond moldings below it. Elegantly carved Asomtavruli characters form three inscriptions around the cross. Reliefs of bunches of grapes, pomegranates, and a lone griffin supply added dynamism to the elements. The effect is further augmented by the use of different color stone to highlight certain sculptural elements, such as the green bosses in the center of the diamonds.

The ground plan is a simple and straightforward cruciform with no surprises. The cupola is supported by four freestanding pillars. (The eastern pillars do, however, join the apse wall toward the top.) Mural fragments from the 17th century decorate the altar.

Bolnisi and Dmanisi

A fascinating day trip from Tbilisi into the southwestern region of Kvemo Kartli (Lower Kartli, which also comprises the historic province of Trialeti) could include visits to the famous fifth-century three-aisled Basilica of Sioni in Bolnisi and the ninth-century fortified city of Dmanisi. A second day trip to the Trialeti region (to which today's Tetri-Tskaro region belongs) could be made to the churches at Samshvilde and Pitareti.

TO BOLNISI AND DMANISI
Leave Tbilisi on Rustaveli Avenue, heading south toward Marneuli. After ten km (6.2 miles) the road splits: left to Erevan and right to Kumajri in Armenia. Take the A304 toward Kumajri by way of Marneuli. Marneuli is 39 km (24 miles) from Tbilisi. This part of Georgia has a large Azeri population, and many of the villages are Moslem. After approximately 54 km (33.5 miles) you can see the beginning of the Trialeti Range. The city of Bolnisi is 63 km (39 miles) from Tbilisi. A sign marks the lefthand turnoff to the Church of Sioni seven km (4.3 miles) away.

Three km (1.9 miles) along this road you'll pass on your right the shell of the sixth-century triple-church basilica of Kvemo-Bolnisi. This is not your main destination. Influenced by its conterpart Sioni Bolnisi, the central nave of this church, in keeping with the new style, was larger and taller than the side naves that flanked it.

THE SIONI CHURCH AT BOLNISI
On the left bank of the Poladauri River, the Sioni Church is an outstanding example of one of the earliest stages of Georgian ecclesiastical architecture. The basilica form is a legacy from the classical world that flourished in Georgia. The Sioni Church is a three-aisled basilica that dates from the late fifth century. An inscription over the north portal gives us the exact period: 478–493. The inscription, in

the Georgian form of writing known as Asomtavruli, which developed contemporaneously, reads, "With the help of the Holy Trinity, the building of this Church was begun in the 20th year of King Peroz and completed 15 years later. Whosoever bows down here, God will pardon, and whosoever prays here for David, Bishop of the Church, him also will God pardon. Amen." This is the earliest example of writing in Georgian ever found in Georgia. (Earlier inscriptions dating to the early fifth century have been found in the Georgian Monastery in Palestine.) The inscription at Bolnisi is a copy. The original is in the Janashia Museum of Georgia in Tbilisi.

The church conforms to the classic floor plan of a three-aisled basilica with the exception of the chapel in the northeast corner, which was added in the eighth century. North and south galleries are on both sides of the basilica. The north gallery probably served as a side altar, and the southern apse was most likely used as a baptistry. The primary entrances to the church are from the north and south; this greatly diminishes the effect that would have been created by the longitudinal orientation typical of basilicas. The western entrance dates only from the 17th century. The power of an east-west axis is also mitigated by the fact that the five interior pillars serve most fully as supports for the roof, creating an emphasis on the vertical, and not to delineate the side aisles, which barely exist.

Of greatest interest is the mixture of pagan and Christian symbols and motifs found in the sculptural ornamentation on imposts, capitals, and the bases of pillars. Lions, bulls, plants, and geometric patterns are often next to or incorporated into images of the cross and Christ. You can find a particularly wonderful example of this in the baptistry to the right of the altar. On the front of the capital a pagan bull's head has been transformed into a Christian symbol by the presence of a cross. The baptistry is open only on Saturdays and Sundays.

The varied colors add tremendously to the venerability of the façade: green and golden tuff of evenly hewn stones intermingle in a patchwork of a hundred shades. The brick work of the upper portion of the east façade dates to a 17th-century restoration.

The belltower was built in 1678–1688 by the Bishop of Bolnisi.

THE CHURCH OF TSUHRUGHASHENI

If you look east from the village of Kvemo-Bolnisi you can see the Church of Tsuhrughasheni on the slope of a hill. Standing two km (1.2 miles) away on the other side of the Poladauri River, this 13th-century cruciform domed church has excellent ornamental carving on the drum and east and west façades. In a terrible state of disrepair, it is currently being restored. The view of the river and the Trialeti Range from the church's position on the summit of the hill is first-rate.

DMANISI

Returning to Bolnisi and the A304, continue southwest for another 21 km (13 miles) until you come to a T-junction. Take the road to the right, which heads to the modern village of Dmanisi. Bear left toward Kumajri for another five km (three miles) to Patara Dmanisi. Turn right at the sign indicating the fortress city of Dmanisi.

Similar to Gremi insofar as it is a fortress town on an elevated site, Dmanisi is both older and much larger than its Kakhetian counterpart. Towns in Georgia developed with the rise of feudalism, and Dmanisi dates to the ninth century. The site encompasses 13 hectares (32 acres) enclosed by fortress walls. An entire city of residential buildings, baths, artisans' workshops, caravanserais, and public buildings once flourished here, of which only a small portion was excavated by archaeologists in 1936, again in 1960, and in the years following.

Located above the Mashavera and Pinosauri rivers, the city was also on the main transit route between Georgia and Armenia. The Armenian border is only 20 km (12.4 miles) away. Fueled by trade, crafts—especially metalwork—and tariffs, the city thrived in the 13th century. Tamerlane's invasions of the 14th century ended its glory days, and by the 17th century there was no longer anyone living in Dmanisi.

Of greatest interest are the three-church basilica dating to the sixth century and the remains of the royal palace at the southwest summit of the site.

The **Sioni Basilica** follows the classic three-church basilica plan, with the exception of the narthex, which was added to the west by Giorgi Lasha, son of Queen Tamara, between 1213 and 1222. The sculptural ornamentation and reliefs are beautifully executed. The stone of the façade is a mixture of rose and green tuff and basalt. The church was reconsecrated in 1988, and the bishop of the Dmanisi region conducts services every Saturday and Sunday. The belltower and smaller church on the site date to the 13th century.

Ascending to the ruins on the summit, be sure to visit the baths, one of which is named after Queen Tamara. These stone cupolas, of a design akin to the ones still functioning in Tbilisi, date from the 13th to 14th centuries. The view from the summit of the Mashavera River and the Javakheti Range of the Little Caucasus is magnificent.

In the region of Tetri-Tskaro are two architectural monuments that are well worth seeing. It would be pushing it to try to see them on the same day that you go to Bolnisi and Dmanisi, but it is possible. Whether you go from Tbilisi or on your way back from Bolnisi, you want to make your way to the village of Tetri-Tskaro. (From Tbilisi take the turnoff at Koda. From Bolnisi, turn at Marneuli.)

SAMSHVILDE

In Tetri-Tskaro, at the junction of the roads to Tsalka and Gudarekhi, go left toward Tsalka and the Tetri-Tskaro bazaar. After one km (0.62 miles) turn and go along a dirt road for three km (1.9 miles) to Samshvilde.

This ancient village dates to the first century BC and was continuously inhabited until the 18th century. The church is three km (1.9 miles) above the village.

The church of Samshvilde is a centralized domed structure built between 759 and 777. It bears marked similarities to the church at Tsromi in its ground plan and conception. Four freestanding pillars supported the dome, of which only the eastern part remains. The yellow sandstone blocks were skillfully hewn and laid. Both the material and method of construction were unusual for the eighth and ninth centuries, when tuff, boulders, and rubble were more commonly used.

PITARETI

Arriving in Tetri-Tskaro town square from Marneuli, turn left and continue over the bridge above the railroad tracks. You'll be driving through the magnificent pastures and forested slopes of the Khrami massif, an ancient mountain system famous for the wealth of homeopathic herbs that grow here; the church at Pitareti is on one of the many plateaus of this massif. The rolling hills are of exceptional beauty and you won't find a better spot for hiking, a picnic, or both. The asphalt road to Pitareti is serpentine. After approximately 37 km (23 miles), beyond the 2,000-meters (6,562-feet) mountain pass, the road begins to run parallel to the Khrami River. After 48 km (29.7 miles) you'll see a bridge over the river to your left. Cross it and continue for approximately another five km (three miles) to Pitareti.

The beauty of this 13th-century cruciform domed church is heightened by its isolation on a protected plateau deep within the mountain forests, its rich ornamental carving, and the beautiful and variegated shades of the stone.

An inscription on the south portico states that Pitareti was constructed between 1213 and 1222 by Kavtar Kajibaisdze, a court official of King Giorgi IV Lasha, son of Queen Tamara. Given the inaccessibility of Pitareti and other contemporary churches such as Betania and Ikorta, it is believed that Pitareti functioned more as a court chapel for a feudal lord and his family, rather than as a cathedral for the people.

The ground plan stems from the tradition established at Samtavro and Samtavisi in the 11th century. A shortening of the east-west axis emphasizes the square outline. The vertical orientation is celebrated through the taller drum, which soars to the sky.

The architect displayed amazing virtuosity in his sculptural ornamentation of the east façade. Cross, gables, window frames, medallions, and the insides of niches all show an imaginative use of animal, vegetal, and human motifs that work to create a unified whole. Eschewing the use of blind arcading, the architect achieved a powerful aesthetic through the contrast between smooth surfaces and elaborate decorative carving.

As is characteristic of Georgian churches of this time, the entrance is in the south. It is the only entrance. The church is surrounded by a double wall built in the late Middle Ages. The two-story entrance tower dates from 1696.

Another site of interest in this region is the church of Manglisi. This is one of the few 11th-century churches whose cupola drum has survived in its original form. Some fresco fragments have also survived.

TRIALETI

On the road from Tsalka to Bediani, the excavations at Trialeti have unearthed more than 200 funerary objects, including weapons, goblets, artwork, and jewelry from the Bronze Age. These are now housed in the Janashia Museum in Tbilisi.

Along the
Georgian Military Highway

The Georgian Military Highway runs north from Tbilisi through the Greater Caucasus Mountains to Vladikavkaz (Orjonikidze) 207 km (128 miles) away. It is the main artery connecting Georgia to Russia, a route that has served as an important trade link between Europe and Asia from early times. Strabo (63 BC–AD 21) mentions the dangerous mountainous route in his *Geography*, and Pliny (AD 23–79) describes how the Romans erected the Caucasian Gates (Porta Caucasia) in the Darial Gorge. At the height of Georgia's power in the 12th century the route was of significant strategic importance both militarily and economically, and new towns grew up along it. Moslem incursions from the 13th to the 17th centuries weakened the country and the possibility of contact with the north until Herekle II, King of eastern Georgia, initiated the negotiations with Russia that ultimately led to Georgian-Russian unification in 1801. Recognizing the need for a more efficient means of communication, Alexander I appointed General Alexei Yermolov (1772–1861) commander of the Russian forces in the Caucasus, to be responsible for building a new road. Work in the Darial Gorge alone lasted five years, and in 1817 the entire route was finished. General Yermolov was heralded at the time as the builder of the Russian Simplon. The name of the Georgian Military Highway originates in its 19th-century military associations and not from anything bellicose in the post-revolutionary era.

As the major route through the Greater Caucasus, the highway crosses important historical provinces and is the jumping-off place to others. Leaving the Mtkvari and Aragvi river valleys in Kartli, the road goes through the present Dusheti region (specifically, historic Mtiuleti) before crossing the Jvari Pass (Krestovy Pereval or Cross Pass; the highest point at 2,379 meters/7,805 feet) into Khevi and the town of Kazbegi. From there the road continues for another 17 km (10.5 miles) to the bridge over the Tergi (Terek) River known as Eshmakis Khidi (Devil's Bridge), which marks the boundary between Georgia and North Ossetia in Russia.

After leaving Tbilisi, roads branch northwest off the highway into the historic provinces of Ertso-Tianeti, Pshavi, and Khevsureti. (The isolated province of Tusheti lies considerably east of the highway.) As with the mountain region of Svaneti, the more remote provinces of Khevsureti and Khevi are of particular interest to climbers, nature lovers, and aspiring ethnographers. The Military Highway is sufficiently well traveled that you're unlikely to see many vestiges of authentic folk practices in its immediate environs, unless you happen to come upon a village having a holiday. If

The confluence of the Aragvi and Mtkvari rivers, as seen from the Jvari Monastery

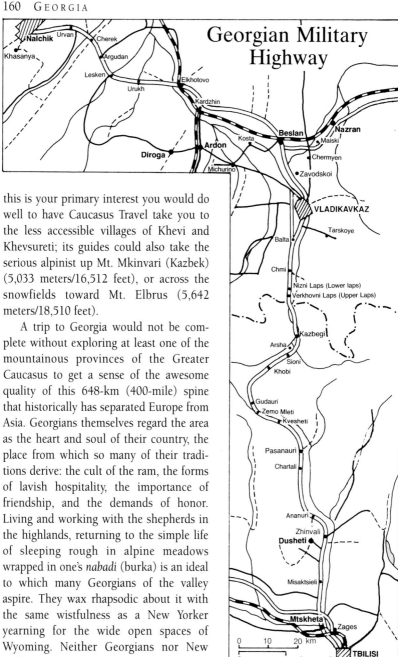

Georgian Military Highway

this is your primary interest you would do well to have Caucasus Travel take you to the less accessible villages of Khevi and Khevsureti; its guides could also take the serious alpinist up Mt. Mkinvari (Kazbek) (5,033 meters/16,512 feet), or across the snowfields toward Mt. Elbrus (5,642 meters/18,510 feet).

A trip to Georgia would not be complete without exploring at least one of the mountainous provinces of the Greater Caucasus to get a sense of the awesome quality of this 648-km (400-mile) spine that historically has separated Europe from Asia. Georgians themselves regard the area as the heart and soul of their country, the place from which so many of their traditions derive: the cult of the ram, the forms of lavish hospitality, the importance of friendship, and the demands of honor. Living and working with the shepherds in the highlands, returning to the simple life of sleeping rough in alpine meadows wrapped in one's *nabadi* (burka) is an ideal to which many Georgians of the valley aspire. They wax rhapsodic about it with the same wistfulness as a New Yorker yearning for the wide open spaces of Wyoming. Neither Georgians nor New Yorkers have much of a chance of implementing the dream. Alexander Kazbegi (1848–1893), the famous 19th-century Georgian writer who eventually did take up the pastoral life, depicts in his numerous stories the ethos of the tribesmen of these mountains. Other writers and artists whose experience of this world have come through traveling along the Georgian Military Highway include Pushkin, Lermontov, Chekhov, Tolstoy, Tchaikovsky, Mayakovsky, and Gorky. You will have no difficulty understanding their enthusiasm.

The following sights, towns, and villages are what can be seen with a minimum of effort either along the highway or on a nearby connecting road. Any car with trustworthy brakes will be able to cover the entire length of the highway without difficulty. The highway was completely asphalted, although recent reports state that it is now potholed and covered in places in landslide debris. The most difficult driving is the series of switchbacks you'll encounter beginning at the village of Kvemo Mleti (112 km/69.4 miles from Tbilisi) until you're over the Jvari Pass.

Jvari Monastery

Eighteen km (11 miles) north of Tbilisi (seven km/4.3 miles) off the M27, exit on the right for the Church of Jvari (586–604). Situated on a cliff above the point at which the Aragvi and Mtkvari (Kura) rivers meet and providing a magnificent vantage where you can see Mtskheta and the Cathedral of Sveti-tskhoveli, the Jvari Monastery is the culmination of a number of artistic and architectural aspirations in early Christian Georgian architecture. Distinguished by its harmonious proportions, clean lines, and superior masonry, Jvari seems to grow organically out of the landscape, providing a marvelous silhouette against the sky.

> At that place, where
> The streams, Aragvi and Kura,
> Embracing as two sisters,
> Flow together with a roar,
> There was a monastery.

—Lermontov, *Mtsyri*

A ninth-century chronicle, *The Conversion of Kartli*, tells that St. Nino, who brought Christianity to eastern Georgia in the fourth century, had a cross built on this site. The Cross of Mtskheta was a symbol of the victory of Christianity over heathen gods and became a place of pilgrimage throughout Georgia and beyond. In the second half of

Jvari Church

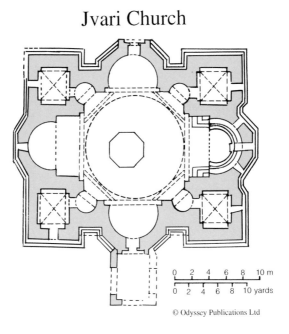

```
0   2   4   6   8   10 m
0   2   4   6   8   10 yards
```

© Odyssey Publications Ltd

the sixth century, Prince Guaram, ruler of Kartli, built a small church north of the cross; the small **Jvari (Cross) Church** is now in ruins. A larger church was erected by Guaram's son, Stepanoz I, with his brother Demetre and Stepanoz's successor, Adarnese. This church included the cross. Its stone foundations can be seen today in the center of the existing structure.

The church suffered some damage during an Arab attack in the tenth century but is generally well preserved. Portraits of the founders in the form of figured-relief panels are found on the eastern façade: Christ with Stepanoz I in the middle panel, Demetre and Adarnese in the left and right panels, respectively. Above them are the archangels Michael and Gabriel. A relief on the south side, crowned by a gable, also shows Christ and Stepanoz. The transference to an external wall of the Byzantine mosaic apse depicting the founder of the church and Christ is a unique feature of Jvari. Also noteworthy is the relief in the tympanum above the south entry, the door through which you enter the church: a cross within a medallion is carried by two angels. This Exaltation of the Cross is a major theme of Georgian sculpture in the Middle Ages, and the quality of the carving represents a high point of the early feudal period.

The Jvari church is a tetraconch (four-apsed) with a slightly elongated east-west axis. The deep niches between the four semicircular conches lead to corner rooms. The southwestern conch, the only one with an external entrance, was, according to

DIVINITY

*T*he most inaccessible peaks seem to have been chosen, both by the monk and the soldier; and strong battlements, now tumbling from their giddy heights, and monastic walls still well preserved, crowning a conical hill that shoots up into the very blue of heaven, make the approach to Mtskheta one of thrilling interest. It is not solely because they are lofty, that they are ruins, or that their history dates back to times when man had strange ideas of religion, and were endeavoring to modify idolatry and unite it with Christianity; or were so wedded to the one, it was impossible at once to shake off its influence while they erected new temples, and bowed down to worship the unknown God;—it is not solely because such associations cling round those ancient structures and hallow them, making them sacred landmarks in the history of civilization;—it is not that they stand there as almost the sole records of a people long since passed away, and who erected them as durable monuments, and did not dream of decay and change;—it is not solely the imagination which, influenced by the history of these great wrecks, gathers about them a halo of storied associations, and clothes them with a time-sanctified majesty and beauty no modern fabrics claim; but all these combined, that give them a power over the beholder which he cannot surmount and which he can never forget. The huge crack in the gigantic wall, which stands on the edge of that near cliff, shows that convulsion of the earth has taken place, and that the deep ravine below is yet to receive those huge rocks which have for so many ages defied the storm, and you pause for a moment, as though you would wait to see it reel on its solid base and plunge into the fearful depths; while you shudder when you think of the crash and the shock, and pass timidly by it lest it occur in an evil hour. Besides all this, the light which gathers on these summits—the first golden hue of morning and the last of evening—fails not to impress the devout with the idea that God thus shows His special regard for them.

George Leighton Ditson, Circassia, 1850

an inscription, designed to be used only by women. The broad and open octagon of the central room is crowned by a cupola that rises from the supporting walls by means of three tiers of squinches. The well-proportioned interior of this church evokes tranquility, harmony, and a mysterious spiritual grandeur, no doubt reinforced by the absence of mosaic or other decoration, although the eastern apse was originally covered in mosaic. These same qualities inform the exterior. Its uniformly dressed stone blocks and the careful balance of the four façades forming the arms of the cross are an extraordinary achievement, especially in the face of the technical difficulties of the site's steep western slope. The architect's success make this a paragon that influenced subsequent ecclesiastical buildings throughout Georgia. The Russians closed Jvari as a church in 1811. It served as a historic monument until January 7, 1988, when amidst much jubilation it was once again consecrated.

Jvari church is an absolute must-see because of its historical importance and the beauty of its location. This can be the first stop of your journey along the Military Highway or a day trip from Tbilisi, combining a visit to Mtskheta and Zedazeni fortress and monastery.

Mtskheta

This ancient and important town is 20 km (12.4 miles) north of Tbilisi (five km/three miles off the main road) at the confluence of the Mtkvari and Aragvi rivers. It was the capital of the eastern Georgian kingdom of Iberia from the third century BC through the fifth century AD when King Vakhtang Gorgasali moved his court to Tbilisi. During that time Mtskheta was an important trading center. Because of its location, goods moved along the roads that ran parallel to its two rivers: east and west beside the Mtkvari (Kura) and north and south beside the Aragvi.

The site was also an important cultural and religious center. The popular belief is that the town is named after Mtskhetos, son of Kartlos, the eponymous ancestor of the Georgian people who is said to be buried on a slope of Mt. Kartli on the right bank of the Mtkvari overlooking the town. More probable is that the town's name derived from one of the proto-Georgian tribes that settled in the region: the Meskhi. The Armazis-tsikhe acropolis, built on Bagineti Hill in the late fourth century BC, is described by Pliny (who calls it the "Fortress of Armasicum") as the center of a powerful Iberian civilization where the god Armaz, along with a pantheon of other idols imported from the Hittites, was worshiped. Close contact was maintained with the Hellenistic and Roman worlds. Georgia's conversion to Christianity occurred at Mtskheta with King Mirian's in 337 AD. He ordered the pagan temples destroyed and churches built, specifically the precursors to the Sveti-tskhoveli cathedral and

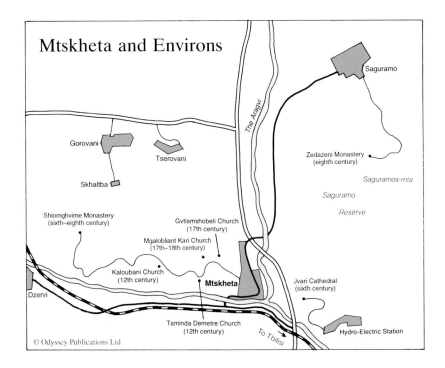

Mtskheta and Environs

Saguramo

The Aragvi

Gorovani

Tserovani

Zedazeni Monastery
(eighth century)

Skhaltba

Saguramos-mta

Saguramo

Shiomghvime Monastery
(sixth–eighth century)

Gvtismshobeli Church
(17th century)

Reserve

Mgalobliant Kari Church
(17th–18th century)

Kaloubani Church
(12th century)

Mtskheta

Jvari Cathedral
(sixth century)

Dzervi

Tsminda Demetre Church
(12th century)

To Tbilisi

Hydro-Electric Station

© Odyssey Publications Ltd

Samtavro monastery. Even with Vakhtang Gorgasali's move to Tbilisi, Mtskheta remained the residence of the Georgian Catholicos, head of the Georgian Orthodox Church, until the 12th century. The cathedrals built during that time are judged among the finest in Georgia. In recognition of the importance of Mtskheta as a historical treasure, the entire city has been made a state historical site.

SVETI-TSKHOVELI

One of the most sacred places in all of Georgia, the Cathedral of Sveti-tskhoveli (1010–1029) is located in the center of Mtskheta and contains the grave of Sidonia, who was said to have been buried holding Christ's robe. Called the Church of the Life-Giving Pillar, the legend accounts for the cathedral's name: in the first century AD a Georgian Jew from Mtskheta named Elias converted to Christianity and was in Jerusalem when Jesus was crucified. Elias bought Jesus' robe from a Roman soldier at Golgotha and brought it back to Georgia. Returning to his native city, he was met by his sister Sidonia who upon touching the robe immediately died from the emotions engendered by such a sacred object. The robe could not be removed from her grasp, so she was buried with it. Later, from her grave grew an enormous Lebanese cedar. In the fourth century, when King Mirian decided to build the first Christian church in Georgia, he chose Sidonia's grave as the site. Ordering the cedar chopped down, he had seven columns made from it for the church's foundation. The seventh column, however, had magical properties and rose by itself into the air. It returned to earth only after St. Nino of Cappadocia, credited with bringing Christianity to the Georgians, prayed the whole night. It was further said that from the magical seventh column a sacred liquid flowed that cured people of all diseases. In Georgian *sveti* means "column" and *tskhoveli* means "life-giving," hence the name of the cathedral. An icon portraying this event can be seen on the second column on the right-hand side as you enter. Reproduced widely throughout Georgia, it shows Sidonia with an angel lifting the column into heaven. St. Nino is in the foreground; King Mirian and his wife, Queen Nana, are to the right and left.

The present cathedral, with certain features from later periods, dates from the 11th century and is the third building on the site. The first, of which only traces remain, was a wooden structure built by King Mirian in the 330s. That is the church of the legend. A second church was built by Vakhtang Gorgasali in the fifth century.

Sveti-tskhoveli

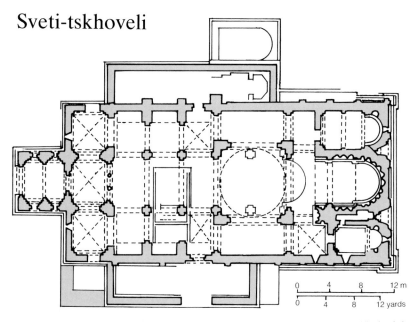

0   4   8   12 m
0   4   8   12 yards

© Odyssey Publications Ltd

The main gate to the cathedral of Sveti-tskhoveli in Mtshketa

This was a three-aisled basilica, similar to the Sioni Church in Bolnisi, with a polygonal apse and three aisles of roughly the same width. Excavations conducted between 1968 and 1972 revealed portions of the original stone foundations of the walls and some fifth-century piers within the 11th-century columns.

By the beginning of the 11th century, the fifth-century basilica was in such bad repair that the then-Catholicos of Georgia, Melkhisedek, commissioned the great architect Arsukidze to build a new cathedral. Arsukidze incorporated elements of Vakhtang Gorgasali's church, specifically by adding height to the existing pillars, extending the east-west axis by moving the altar apse farther east, and adding a porch (narthex) in the west. His creation is a masterpiece of the early Georgian Renaissance. Along with such important cathedrals as that of Bagrat III in Kutaisi and Alaverdi in Kakheti, it demonstrates the degree of technical and artistic achievement required to construct centralized domed structures of such grand and noble proportions.

Legend has it that the success of Sveti-tskhoveli brought Arsukidze a bitter reward: a minister of the king who had also been Arsukidze's patron and teacher was so outraged by how far his pupil had surpassed him that he had the architect's right hand cut off. A relief high up on the northern façade of a right hand holding a bevel—symbol of the stonemason—attests to this story. An inscription reads: "The Hand of Arsukidze, slave of God, may forgiveness be his." An inscription on the east façade further attests to the fact that Arsukidze did not live to see his masterpiece finished (in 1029): "This holy church was built by the hand of Thy wretched servant, Arsukidze. May your soul rest in peace, O Master."

Other aspects of the façade are of great interest. Two bulls' heads are incorporated into the east façade from the fifth-century church, testimony to the wonderful mix of pagan and Christian iconography in that early period. (The two bulls' heads on the front gate as you enter the cathedral complex are reproductions.) The beautiful carved blind arcading on all sides is unaltered from the 11th century. The subtle use of different colored stones is highly successful. The basic stone is a sandy yellow with trimmings, while around the apse window a red stone is used. The green stone used in the drum of the cupola is from the 17th century.

The cathedral suffered serious damage from an earthquake in 1283 and from a Mongol invasion under Tamerlane at the beginning of the 15th century. The last king able to reign over both east and west Georgia, Alexandre I (1412–1443), was responsible for restoring the cathedral, imposing special taxes that replenished a treasury depleted by years of war. He repaired the cupola drum, the columns that had been dismantled, and the galleries of the western interior. In 1656 the cupola and roof were again restored. New frescoes in the interior were also painted in the 17th century, but the 19th-century Russian policy of whitewashing the interior of Georgian churches was enforced here as well. The defensive walls surrounding the cathedral complex date for the most part from the 18th century and were built by Herekle II. Archaeological excavations around the west gate, however, have revealed an original structure. Because of the creativity of design, it is thought to have been built by Arsukidze. In front a founder's inscription on the second story names Catholicos Melkhisedek.

As you enter the cathedral, on your right is a stone baptismal font dating from the fourth century. It is thought to have been the font used for the baptism of King Mirian and Queen Nana. It was once covered in gold, but this was taken by Tamerlane when he sacked the cathedral. Immediately behind the font is a reproduction of the relief of Arsukidze's right hand and bevel found on the north façade. Proceeding toward the altar down the south (right hand) aisle, you'll see a small stone church. This is a symbolic copy of the Chapel of Christ's Sepulchre in Jerusalem. Built between the end of the 13th and the beginning of the 14th centuries, it was erected here to mark Sveti-tskhoveli as the second most sacred place in the world (after the church in Jerusalem), thanks to Christ's robe.

In front of the stone chapel, the most westerly structure aligned with the columns between the aisle and the nave marks Sidonia's grave. Remains of the magical life-giving pillar are also here. It was built in the 17th century. Scenes of the lives of King Mirian and Queen Nana, and portraits of the first Christian Emperor, Constantine, and his mother Helene, were painted by G. Guldzhavarschvili at that time. Traces of the foundations of the fourth-century church have been found here.

The second structure aligned with the columns of the southern aisle was also built in the 17th century as the throne for the Catholicos Diasamidze. It no longer serves this function, as current tradition requires a throne for the Georgian patriarch to be in the center of the church. Next to this structure are remains of the foundation of the fifth-century church built by Vakhtang Gorgasali. The large Jesus figure in the altar was painted by Russian artists in the 19th century. The majority of the icons here date to the 20th century. Some are copies of older icons and frescoes from other churches throughout Georgia.

Sveti-tskhoveli was not only the site of the coronation of the Georgian kings but also served as their burial place. Ten are known to have been buried here, although only three tombs have been found, all before the altar. The tomb of King Vakhtang Gorgasali can be identified by the small candle fortress standing before it. He was called Gorgasali by his Persian enemies because he wore a wolf's head on his helmet when going into battle. A man of large stature and enormous physical strength, he founded the city of Tbilisi.

King Herekle II's tomb is identifiable by the sword and shield upon it. He ruled in the 18th century and is responsible for placing eastern Georgia under Russian protection in 1783. His son, Giorgi XII, was Georgia's last king. Reigning only two years, he died in 1800, after which Georgia was annexed to Russia. His gray marble tomb is next to his father's. Also in front of the altar are tombs of various members of the Bagrationi royal family.

On the wall of the southern transept of the cathedral is a large fresco depicting an old Eastern calendar with signs of the zodiac. The date of this fresco is not clear, and art historians are currently trying to determine both the period and the full meaning.

A visit to Sveti-tskhoveli should not be rushed. As much can be appreciated from strolling around the grounds of the complex, looking at Jvari—standing like a dedicated sentinel on its hill—and discovering new forms and images within the carvings of the façade as from a tour of the interior. You will probably find yourself wanting to return for another visit. Marriages take place in the cathedral on Saturdays. The services on Sunday are accompanied by a superb choir.

SAMTAVRO MONASTERY COMPLEX

Located in the northwestern corner of Mtskheta on Stalin Street, only a five-minute drive from Sveti-tskhoveli, the Samtavro complex comprises four edifices. The first, to the right as you enter the enclosure, is the tiny fourth-century Church of Samtavro. Erected on a site where St. Nino frequently prayed, this chapel has been restored many times, most recently in the 20th century. The frescoes, painted in the Russian style, are from the 19th century. The main building of the complex is the great Church of Samtavro, built in the 11th century. In the northwest is a handsome three-story belltower built not earlier than the 13th century. It is distinguished by a cylindrical open-arcaded belfry that sits elegantly on the two cubic stories below. In the southwestern part of the complex are buildings that have functioned both as a nunnery and as the main theological seminary of the Georgian Orthodox Church.

The name Samtavro in Georgian means the place of the ruler "Mtavari" and refers to the belief that the original fourth-century church was erected by King Mirian in his garden to honor St. Nino of Cappadocia, who brought Christianity to Georgia. St. Nino was wont to pray in the king's garden and was responsible for baptizing King Mirian's wife Nana. The king himself was converted while hunting. When everything suddenly went dark, he called upon his pagan gods to help him, to no avail. But when he prayed to St. Nino's God, the light was restored. He subsequently baptized all the people of Mtskheta and declared Christianity the state religion.

THE MAIN CHURCH OF SAMTAVRO

This 11th-century church is dedicated to St. Nino and called The Redeemer. Built in the first half of the 11th century on the site of the fourth-century wooden church erected by King Mirian, Samtavro is a central domed building with its cupola resting on projections of the walls of the altar apse and two freestanding piers. Although built on a straightforward plan that does not evoke the triumphant quality of Sveti-tshkoveli, Samtavro is nonetheless an impressive example of the architectural progress made in the 11th century, particularly in the decorative treatment of the façades. The elaborate stone carving of the north and south façades is of an especially high degree of artistry and imagination. This is not the case with the decorative work on the cupola, which collapsed in an earthquake in the 13th century, and was reconstructed during the 13th to 15th centuries without the same skill. On top of the clean lines of the dressed stone of the walls, the drum looks a bit shabby, like a stove-pipe hat that has seen better days. Projecting from the north and south sides are annexes that are contemporary with the rest of the building. The western portico is of a later date. The long chamber forming a part of the northern annex is from an earlier period, probably the eighth or ninth century.

The interior of the church was covered in frescoes, which were whitewashed during the 19th century by the Russians. Some fragments dating from the 15th to 17th centuries can still be seen in the apse and cupola drum. Thirteen windows in the cupola drum provide lovely illumination. Note the decorated star vaulting of the southern portion of the roof. In the west of the church (to the left as you enter) are the graves of King Mirian and Queen Nana. The sepulchers themselves are from the 19th century. The royal couple chose to be buried here rather than at Sveti-tskhoveli because they desired their simple piety to be reflected by these humble surroundings. The nunnery was also founded here in their honor.

Getting to Ananuri

Continue north along the M27 (left turn after leaving Mtskheta). After 4.5 km (2.8 miles), note on the right a white obelisk in the village of Tsitsamouri. This marks the spot where the great Georgian writer and patriot Ilya Chavchavadze (1837–1907) was assassinated by Georgian radicals who feared that his social reforms would reduce class tensions and delay the revolution. A little farther on is a right-hand turnoff for the village of Saguramo (seven km/4.3 miles from the highway). The village boasts Chavchavadze's home, which has been converted into a museum and is wonderfully evocative of Georgian literary life at the end of the 19th century. Saguramo can serve as a jumping-off place for Zedazeni Monastery, but since it is southeast of the village, better to visit it on a day-trip out of Tbilisi or Mtskheta.

Twenty-seven km (16.7 miles) from Tbilisi, the road forks, with the M27 veering left toward Sokhumi (434 km/269 miles), and the A301 (the Georgian Military Highway) continuing straight in the direction of Vladikavkaz (formerly Ordjonikidze), 168 km (104 miles) away. From this fork, Pasanauri is 58 km (36 miles) away and Kazbegi is 124 km (77 miles). Actual kilometer posts use this fork as zero point, but since our odometer started at zero in Tbilisi we shall continue to use that as our reference.

Just before the Zhinvali dam, a right-hand turnoff goes to **Barisakho** (52 km/32 miles). This is the road to Shatili, another 49 km (30 miles) from Barisakho, and the best destination to choose for a journey into Khevsureti (*see* page 158).

Ananuri

Ananuri is a superb fortress complex dating from the 16th and 17th centuries and located along the Georgian Military Highway in the Arkalas Canyon of the Aragvi River valley, just beyond the Zhinvali reservoir (69 km/42.8 miles). It is a spectacular example of the architecture of the period. With its crenellated walls, drum and cone cupolas, and defensive towers seen against the surrounding forested mountains, it is among the most memorable monuments along the entire stretch of your

A PROUD BOAST

I was making south for the Kura valley, which divides the northern, Greater Caucasus from the Lesser, and nurtures the veteran capitals of Mtskheta and Tbilisi. As the last hills dropped behind me, I escaped the noon sun in a huge bare corpse of a church, enclosed by a castle in the foothills. It was empty and desanctified. A single brazier guttered before its frescoed Christ, and the muralled saints seemed to occupy their pillars apologetically, like denizens of a forgotten felicity.

A fierce-eyed Georgian youth burst in on me as I studied them. He tugged my elbow and talked in rapid, urgent tones. But I knew no Georgian. As this dawned on him, he grew frantic with frustration. His eyes bulged and threatened, his hands flew in a furious sign-language. He started to shout. But I could only stare back at him in doltish helplessness.

He could contain himself no longer. "Leeverepul-too-Tbilisi-tree!" he screamed. He plucked out a knife, sank on his haunches and feverishly inscribed something in the stone floor. It was a cup.

I stared at it. A chalice. Was he a member of some mystical sect? I became as maddened as him. I tried Russian, English, French, school-boy German, but nothing worked.

For a minute he went on shouting and gesturing in despair. Then he enclosed his head in his hands for a mammoth feat of recall, and suddenly yelled: "World Cup!" He positively danced in front of me. "Liverpool—two! Tbilisi—three!" Then he pummeled the floor to indicate the return match in Georgia. "Tbilisi—three! Liverpool—nought! Nought!"

I showed polite rejoicing at this news—all Georgia must have raged with it for months.

Colin Thubron, Where Nights Are Longest

*The isolated medieval fortress village of Shatili lies along the route of a planned road
from Grozny in Chechnya along the Argun River into Georgia*

journey. It certainly stands as testimony to the life of the warring dukes (*eristavis*) of
that feudal period, conjuring up deeds of chivalry and treachery.

The dukes of the Aragvi were, in fact, very violent, having committed many
bloody deeds. They built this complex to control the main road and as a sanctuary
during their frequent fights with rival dukes. Ananuri was their residence at the end
of the 17th century. The fortress was restored in the 18th century and was in use
until the beginning of the 19th century.

The complex consists of two fortresses, an upper and a lower. The lower citadel
is not well-preserved. Portions of an east-west fortress wall and a small one-naved
church on the east side called Mkurnali (Doctor) remain. The Mkurnali church
dates from the middle of the 16th century.

Within the fortress walls of the upper citadel are a small cupola church from the
first half of the 17th century, a large cupola church built in 1689, a tower in the
north Caucasian style, towers belonging to the encircling ramparts, water cisterns,
and a small 17th-century belltower.

The Khevsureti and Tusheti-style tower is the oldest building in the ensemble
but still has not been positively dated. It has four floors, small embrasures on each
wall, and a distinctive pyramidical roof that is an important feature in the overall
impression the ensemble conveys.

The magnificent fortress complex of Ananuri along the Georgian Military Highway

THE LARGE CUPOLA CHURCH GHVTISMSHOBELI (MOTHER OF GOD)

Built by the architect Kaikhossro Bakhsarashvili for the son of the Aragvi Duke Bardzem, this 17th-century church is an example of the centralized dome style developed during the tenth and 11th centuries.

Entrances to the church are in the south and north. The altar apse with small chapels on either side is in the east. The interior of the church was frescoed but the majority of this work was destroyed by fire in the 18th century. The fragments are on the south wall are the best preserved.

The exterior carving decorating the façade is among the best from this period and is certainly the most distinctive feature of the church. Most notable is the large cross on the south façade, entwined with grape vines. Charming reliefs of various animals—tigers and sheep—add to the composition, conveying the image of the tree of life. Archangels support the grape vines from below while the cross itself sits atop a serpent, symbolizing the triumph of Christianity over evil.

The iconography is another wonderful example of the Georgians' sacred relationship with the grape. Remember that when St. Nino entered Georgia, she made a cross from grape vines and tied it with her hair. Certainly the stone carvers at Ananuri had not forgotten.

THE SMALLER CHURCH

The centralized cupola church in the western part of the ensemble is older than Ghvtismshobeli. Built of brick in the first half of the 17th century, it is entered through a portico in the south. Of greatest interest is the stone baldaquin erected by the widow of the Duke Edishera, who died prematurely in 1674 without giving her a child.

You can walk along the battlements and climb to the top of the large rectangular tower where people lived. The view of the Aragvi River and the surrounding mountains is well worth the climb.

Zemo (Upper) Mleti

Zemo Mleti (115 km/71 miles) is generally considered the demarcation line between the warm southern world that the name Georgia evokes and the cold, harsh mountain world of the northern Caucasus. The village sits at an altitude of 1,556 meters (5,105 feet), and here begins a 640-meter (2,100-foot) ascent to Gudauri that necessitates negotiating six great hairpin bends. The road, built between 1857 and 1861, runs along the cliffs overlooking the left bank of the Aragvi. Frequent lookout points are positioned along the route, and the views are glorious. The first, marked by a statue of Mayakovsky, provides a dizzying perspective on the switchbacks just driven and a wonderful panorama of the Lomisi Range.

Before you begin the ascent you should stop at the roadside Mleti Bazaar. Fill your bottles with excellent spring water from the cliffs and buy *churchkela* (grape and walnut candy) and *tklapi* (a sweet made from grape skins that looks like shoe-leather but is tart and tasty) from the vendors. Also consider purchasing a Khevis hat (*pokhokhi*) made from tufts of uncarded sheep fleece.

Gudauri and Jvari Pass

At 2,196 meters (7,205 feet) Gudauri is the highest village on the highway and the last village on the south side of the Greater Caucasus (123 km/76 miles). Here are alpine meadows of yellow rhododendron, and mountain vistas whose slopes seem to show white outcrops of stone that upon closer inspection reveal themselves to be flocks of sheep grazing in the most inaccessible locales. Gudauri is now famous for skiing (*see* page 90).

Jvari Pass (Krestovy Pereval or Cross Pass) at 127 km (79 miles) is the highest point of the Georgian Military Highway at 2,395 meters (7,858 feet). An obelisk marks the altitude but the pass gets its name from a cross of red stone 500 meters to the right installed by General Alexei Yermolov in 1824 to replace one originally placed there by King David the Builder. The views are magnificent, and the air is of a purity that will make city dwellers weep.

After the pass you leave the historical province of Mtiuleti (600 sq. km/ 225 sq. miles, with a winter population of 7,600) and enter Khevi (1,081 sq. km/470 sq. miles, winter population 6,700). On the descent, after passing through two tunnels, you pick up the Tergi (Terek) River which parallels the road. Eerie basalt, granite, and slate formations lend a primordial quality to the landscape.

At the juncture of four valleys, the village of **Khobi** (148 km/92 miles) sits at an altitude of 1,932 meters (6,339 feet). The road continues toward the village of Sioni along the side of Mt. Kabardzhin (3,155 meters/10,351 feet).

Kazbegi and Vicinity

Under Mt. Kabardzhin along the road is the village of Sioni (148 km/92 miles). Of greatest interest is a late ninth- and early tenth-century three-aisled basilica, visible from the road. In front of the church, perched at the edge of the hill, a stone watchtower dates from the end of the Middle Ages.

Medieval watchtowers guard over passes throughout the province of Khevi

INSECURE RULE OF RUSSIA IN THE CAUCASUS

Surely we may expect that the day is not far distant, when these interesting countries will be thrown open to the enterprise of those nations, who have lent the aid of their money and their arms to depose that power which has so long and so arbitrarily opposed a barrier to the progress of enlightenment and free institutions among the nations. May we not expect that the gallant inhabitants of the Caucasus will be declared independent, and their beautiful country become the magnet of attraction to all the tourists of Europe? What a field will then be open to the lover of the picturesque, the mineralogist, the botanist, the geologist, and those interested in the history of nations, in the study of the legendary ballads and traditions of the most interesting, and perhaps most ancient, of all the races of the world!

It was impossible to look on that glorious scene, now pictured before us on the broad arch of heaven,—that mountain barrier, the fabled home of our race, against which the waves of Russian ambition have for more than a quarter of a century chafed and raged in vain,—without feeling an enthusiasm, a glow of mingled wonder and admiration, for the heroism of the gallant inhabitants, who, while the indolent Turk and the Persian submitted to the encroachments of their powerful neighbour,—nay, trembled at the very name of the mighty despot of the north,—alone had the courage to arrest his progress. Gladly, indeed, would Russia have pursued her usual policy in the Caucasus, and which had so well succeeded with more civilized nations—and followed the advice given by the oracle at Delphos to Philip of Macedon: "If thou wouldst conquer the Greeks, fight with silver spears." Gladly indeed, would she have paved with her gold a way through the Caucasus to the long-coveted districts of Central Asia. Happily for the success of the present war, there was one virtuous race still left in Asia—one brave people that loved their country and their independence better than the gold of the stranger; who preferred their mountain home, their simple habits, and liberty, to all the splendour and luxury the tempter had to offer them.

Captain Spencer Turkey, Russia, the Black Sea, and Circassia, 1854

The three-aisled basilica at Sioni possesses a most evocative belltower; some scholars date it to the early Middle Ages, others to the 16th century

The village of **Arsha** (151 km/96 miles) is the gateway east to the mountains and valleys of Khevi for walks toward the village of Sno, or by car to the Khevsur village of Juta (*see* page 182). Across the river from Arsha is the village of Pansheti, with splendid fortress ruins and a perfectly preserved 17th-century watchtower.

Kazbegi (155 km/96 miles), the principal town of Khevi, with a population of 6,000, is located on the banks of the Tergi (Terek) River at an altitude of 1,850 meters (6,070 feet). Formerly known as Stepantsminda after a monk named Stephen who constructed a monastery here, the town's present name derives from a 19th-century princely family, Kazi Bek, who controlled the territory. Kazbegi is also the birthplace of the great 19th-century Georgian writer Alexander Kazbegi (1848–1893). His statue (unveiled in 1960) holds the place of honor in the central square beside the river. His house (Kazbegi House Museum) is a short distance farther along Stalin Street. Formerly the Ethnographic Museum, it is now devoted solely to the life and work of the writer. His grave is on the grounds. Next to the house is the family church, Mtavarangelosi (the Archangel), now the town church, having been reconsecrated in 1989. Behind Kazbegi's house is the new Ethnographic Museum containing artifacts from Khevi and outlying regions. Both museums are open daily 9 a.m.–1 p.m. and 2 a.m.–6 p.m. For fervent alpinists, Kazbegi also boasts a small museum of alpinism at 24 Vazha Pshavela Street named after the great climber Kazalikashvili. Neighbors have the key and will open the door for you.

The hotel in Kazbegi serves the best food in town. But recent travelers state the hotel is now closed. It is best to check before you go. The view from the hotel is extraordinary: the twin peaks of Mt. Mkinvari (Kazbek) (5,033 meters/16,512 feet) when visible through their veil of clouds, and the 14th-century cupola church of Tsminda Sameba (The Holy Trinity) with its belltower perched on an outcropping 2,170 meters (7,119 feet) up the mountain above the village of Gergeti. Make sure to request a room facing the river.

Kazbegi is the quintessential alpine village, providing the comforts of civilization that mountaineers expect from a base camp, while exuding a kind of civic confirmation of your prejudice that more exciting things are happening elsewhere, namely in the mountain peaks, grottoes, and ice fields a mere day's hike away. How can it be otherwise when you consider all the legends and religious beliefs associated with Mt. Mkinvari and the region? One legend has it that Amirani (the Georgian Prometheus) was chained in a cave on Mt. Mkinvari as punishment for giving mortals the gift of fire. The anchorite tradition, spread and elaborated by the numerous hermits who have chosen these austere mountains as their retreat, holds that a palace of ice sits on the summit of Mt. Mkinvari and contains the tomb of Christ, the tent of Abraham, the manger where Jesus was born, and untold riches. Only the pure in spirit could see these things and return alive. Whatever the state of their souls, Messrs. Freshfield, Tucker, and Moore of the London Alpine Club managed a southeast ascent in June 1868. They were followed by the great female Russian alpinist Maria Preobrazhenskaya who, beginning in 1900, made the ascent nine times.

Qualified guides can take you on excursions to the Gergeti glacier, the foothills of Mt. Mkinvari, and possibly even the cave of Betlemi (4,100 meters/13,451 feet up the side of Mkinvari) that is mentioned in ancient Georgian chronicles as a place where treasures are hidden.

Continuing from Kazbegi north along the Georgian Military Highway, you cross the Tergi River and proceed approximately two km (1.2 miles) to the beginning of the famous **Darial Gorge**, a 15-km (9.3-mile) gash in the earth that is somber and oneiric.

Just before the village of Gveleti, the road crosses the Tergi again over the Gveleti Bridge (164 km/101 miles). Off to the left on an elevated bank across the river are the ruins of **Tamara's Castle** (169 km/105 miles). Thought to have been built in the 12th century by King David the Builder (1089–1125), more legend than fact is attached to this structure. The Queen Tamara supposed to have lived here has nothing to do with Georgia's beloved Queen Tamara (1184–1213), King David the

The Belltower and Church of the Holy Trinity on the slopes of Mt Mkinvari (Kazbek)

Builder's great-granddaughter. This Queen Tamara was an evil temptress who, upon getting handsome travelers into her bed, spent but one night of pleasure with them before having them beheaded and thrown into the river.

The road continues over the *Eshmalis Khidi* (Devil's Bridge), which is the border between Georgia and North Ossetia (172 km/107 miles). It also marks the end of the Darial Gorge. It was in this general vicinity that the Caucasian Gates (Porta Caucasia) mentioned by Pliny were supposedly constructed. The name Darial itself comes from the old Persian Dar-y-Alan (Gate of the Alans) for this was the beginning of the territory of the ancient Alans, descendants of the Sarmates and ancestors of the present-day Ossetes. Because this is the border, the area is crawling with Russian soldiers, and at the time of writing tension is high.

Excursions from Kazbegi

The village of **Gergeti** is just across the river from Kazbegi on the slope of Mt. Mkinvari (Kazbek). Farther up the mountain at 2,170 meters (7,119 feet) is the Church of **Tsminda Sameba** (The Holy Trinity). This 14th-century church is the only cross-cupola church in Khevi. The belltower dates from the same period. Visible only in clear weather, both church and belltower are revered landmarks of the region. Springing almost autochthonously from their rocky outcrop they stand in that great natural vastness as a symbol of the tenacity of faith. A jeep with an excellent driver could get you there in half an hour. The walk, though rigorous, is more gratifying and takes between three and four hours.

Of the places along the Military Highway mentioned above, walks to Sioni and Pansheti, from Arsha to Sno, and through portions of the Darial Gorge are all rewarding.

JUTA

A spectacular day trip into the eastern valleys and mountains of Khevi is to Juta, the only Khevsur village on Khevi territory. The village is, in fact, very near the border between Khevi and Khevsureti, a border that is defined by the massifs Rochka and Jaoki. If you're looking to get away from it all, the pleasure of this trip is guaranteed. If you're searching for the untampered-with spirit of the Caucasus, for the rhythms of a pastoral way of life, and expanses of nature as unsullied as on the day God created the Earth, then by all means make your way to Juta. Take food for a picnic as nothing is available for sale in the village.

GETTING THERE

In good weather this trip can be made in a car, although a jeep is advisable. Take the A301 south out of Kazbegi for 4.5 km (2.8 miles) to the village of Arshkhoti.

(above) Shepherds tend their flocks in Khevi

(right) Tbilisi friends don Khevsur attire in Juta, the only Khevsur village in Khevi

Make a left onto an asphalt road and follow it for 2.5 km (1.5 miles) to the village of Sno. You'll pass some monumental stone sculptures in a field. They are contemporary, the work of a local sculptor Merab Piranishvili. When your odometer shows eight km (five miles), bear right off the asphalt and continue two km (1.2 miles) across the Artckhmo River. (From Sno to Juta, you're traveling due east.) The road branches after another one km (0.6 miles). Bear right through the village into the Jutistskali canyon for another 1.5 km (one mile) or until you've found a good place to drive across the river of the same name. There isn't any bridge. This canyon is home to masses of vultures that line the cliff face or circle hideously above the river. Continue east along the opposite bank to the 16-km (9.9-mile) point, where you will see a shrine at the confluence of two rivers. From there, continue bearing left for another four km (2.5 miles) to reach Juta.

Juta is a village of 20 Khevsur families living in terraced houses on a hillside. Each house has its own small vegetable plot, haystack (depending on the season), and brick walls of dried excrement for burning as fuel in winter. While it is unlikely that you'll see the traditional Khevsur dress worn except during a holiday or wedding, families might be willing to show you their folk attire if the matter is handled with discretion. The clothes are made of thick wool naturally dyed, ornamented with beads, coins—some minted in Tsarist days—and elaborate handstitched embroidery. The women's headdress is called *satauro*. The scarf around the headdress is the *mandili*. The main dress is the *kaba*. The coat on top of the dress is the *katibi*. The men's shirt is the *perangi*. Walks above the village into the mountains are delightful and the ideal place to spread out your picnic.

Svaneti

This mountainous region in the northwestern part of Georgia is made up of two parts, Upper and Lower Svaneti. Upper (Zemo) Svaneti encompasses an area of 3,044 sq. km (1,175 sq. miles) and has a population of 14,600. Lower (Kvemo) Svaneti covers 1,344 sq. km (519 sq. miles) and has a population of 11,400. A total of 45,000 Svans live throughout Georgia.

Svaneti's terrain makes it one of the most remote and inaccessible regions of Georgia. The first car arrived in Mestia, the administrative center of Upper Svaneti, only in 1935 with the widening of the cart track from Zugdidi. The road was built with dynamite and shovels, and Svans joke that they would like to give a prize to Nobel (the inventor of dynamite). That same year, the first plane landed in Mestia. In November 1975, Georgian communications specialists completed the Kutaisi-Mestia radio relay line, allowing for the first television transmission from Moscow and Tbilisi. Despite the advent of cars, television, and helicopter and plane service, Svaneti retains a pristine medieval quality, with villages and back streets that look as though they were constructed as sets for the Caucasian version of *The Return of Martin Guerre*. This sense of time warp, combined with the grandeur of the natural setting, makes a trip to Svaneti well worth the effort no matter how difficult it may be to get there.

The Svans are indigenous Georgians and speak their own language. *Svanuri* belongs to the Southern Caucasian language group known as Kartvelian. Svanuri broke away from the original proto-Georgian tongue to develop on lines of its own in the 19th century BC. It has no alphabet and is mostly spoken at home and socially. Georgian is taught at school and used officially. Most people speak and understand Russian with varying degrees of fluency, but in this remote region, one wonders if it won't go the way of Italian in Rhodes. English will get you absolutely nowhere here.

The harsh climate and mountainous landscape of the region are the principal

The village of Ushguli in Svaneti is a place where time has stopped

SVANETIAN SPLENDOR

M ountaineers, as a rule, see Suanetia after mid-
summer. In June among the blossoms, and again
in October when the beeches, the wild fruit-trees and
the azaleas turn red, and the birches golden against the
fresh autumn snows, the brilliancy of the landscape
must be marvellous. Suanetia is a country for travelers
and artists as much as for mountain climbers. Space,
variety, sunniness—these are the constant and characteristic qualities of Suanetian scenery. The great
mountain basin is broken by no heights that approach
the snow-line. The glens are divided only by long
grassy or forested ridges. Their gentle undulating crests
furnish the most effective contrast to the icy clefts and
rigid cliffs of Shkara and Ushba. From the beauty of
flowers and forests close at hand, the eye is carried
through soft gradations of distance to the pure glaciers
which hang down like silver stairs from the snowy
chain. The atmosphere has none of that sharpness of
definition we associate with the Alps in summer. It more
resembles that of the West Coast of Scotland or the
English Lakes. The afternoon breezes from the Black
Sea bring up showers and vapours to colour the atmosphere, to soften the mountain outlines and magnify
their bulk. The north wind from the steppe suffuses the

sky with an impalpable haze through which the great peaks glimmer like golden pillars of the dawn. To the natural beauties, the snowy peaks, the flowers and forests of the Suanetian landscape, man has added something. It is a land where every man's house is his castle. The meadows and the cultivated valleys are strewn with high white towers. In one spot a single tower stands isolated, in another they cluster in groups of fifty to eighty. Every hamlet has as many towers as the cities of Tuscany in the Middle Ages. Nothing so fantastic as these family fortresses can be seen elsewhere outside San Gimignano or the frame of an Old Master.

Mestia alone boasts seventy towers, each 40 to 80 feet high; Ushkul over fifty, and two black castles besides. The houses to which the towers are attached are quadrangular blocks, slate-roofed, without chimneys, and with narrow slits, closed by wooden shutters, for windows. Sometimes they have no windows at all, the light penetrating only through the interstices in the unmortared wall, while the smoke escapes through the roof. Torches made of birch-bark are used at night: a wooden passage, capable of being cut down in case of necessity, leads to the first floor of the tower of refuge.

Douglas W. Freshfield
The Exploration of the Caucasus, 1896

factors behind the Svanetian character. They are a proud, laconic people who find virtue in a certain austerity and stoicism. Vendettas and blood feuds between certain families and villages exist to the present day. Hunters and alpinists are the most respected members of the community. Although perhaps not as immediately gregarious as Georgians from other regions, the Svans are in no way remiss in the practice of traditional Georgian hospitality. At the time of writing, however, Svanetian hospitality has been sorely tested by the number of refugees who were forced to flee there from Abkhazia. The financial constraints that many Georgians are now feeling because of the war in Abkhazia and the state of the economy requires travelers to be circumspect in their exchanges with people. Because of the elevation of the region, wine is not served as frequently as a potent vodka made at home from yeast. As in other parts of Georgia, you'll come to know your hosts best during the drinking of toasts: a Svan who wears the traditional felt cap will never take it off except to drink the third toast of the night to St. George, whom some here revere above Christ. Before taking your leave you might hear the last toast of the night couched in the following terms: "I drink to your safe journey, and may every person on your road greet you as a mother and father."

Lower Svaneti's administrative center is in the town of Lentekhi, at an elevation of 800 meters (2,625 feet). Although the entire province possesses spots of great natural beauty, Lower Svaneti is not a place where a traveler without an inexhaustible amount of time should bother going. There are very few of the famous Svanetian towers in this region, and the Lower Svans themselves refer to the Upper Svans as *Gvidam Svan*, their version of "the Real McCoy."

Upper Svaneti is most famous for its 11th-century watchtowers and superb mountains. Among the tallest are Mt. Ushba (4,700 meters/15,420 feet), Mt. Tetnuldi (5,007 meters/16,427 feet), and Mt. Shkhara (5,068 meters/16,627 feet); at least ten mountains in the region are higher than Mont Blanc. Alpinists are the most frequent visitors here, and Upper Svaneti has produced some of the most famous climbers in Georgia. Mikheil Khergiani, known as the Lion of the Rock, was considered the first citizen of Mestia. After his death as a result of a climbing accident in the Dolomites in 1969, his house in Mestia was turned into a museum. (By the way, Mikheil's father Beknu climbed Mt. Elbrus in 1943 and the took down the Nazi flag that Hitler's Edelweiss Corps had planted there when they advanced upon the Caucasus.)

Upper Svaneti has an eight-month winter, with the lowest temperature -32° C (-26° F) and an average of -15° C (5° F). Snow can reach two meters (6.5 feet). In summer the average temperature is 25° C (77° F) during the day and 7–10° C (45°–50° F) at night. June is the beginning of the season and a wonderful time to go. Indeed, most touring and climbing is done in summer; the ferocious winters feature often impassable roads and frequent avalanches. You'll note small bird-house-like structures along many mountain roadsides. These memorials mark the spot where someone was killed in an accident. Inside the small stand is a picture of the victim along with glasses and a bottle of wine. Friends or relatives passing that way stop when so moved to drink in memory of their loved one.

The reverence for tradition and continuity has its physical manifestation in the medieval watchtowers and the family plots of land that dominate the villages and environs and contribute to the tenor and tempo of this virtually feudal way of life. The towers were constructed primarily as a defense against the invading Northern Caucasian tribes, the Kabardians and Balkars. More than 200 towers are found in Mestia alone, the last having been built in the 19th century. Potatoes and beans are the staple agricultural product, and entire families can often be seen bent double over hoes. Most fruit, with the exception of citrus, also grow here. Stock-breeding is also an essential occupation, and the alpine and subalpine belts provide rich pasture lands primarily for cattle.

Upper Svaneti itself is subdivided into two regions by the Bal mountain range. The people of the Upper Bal have never known a ruler; they have a reputation as one of the proudest and most independent peoples in Georgia. This region is said to serve as the sanctuary for many important icons from the central districts of

Shepherds near Ushguli (left) and Kazbegi (right)

Georgia, supposedly brought here to protect them from the Moslem forces that have invaded Georgia many times throughout her history. The people of the Upper Bal remain tight-lipped on this subject.

Getting to Mestia

At the time of writing, helicopter and plane service from Tbilisi and Kutaisi to Mestia has been suspended. A public bus leaves Zugdidi three times a day and arrives five to six hours later. If you're driving from Tbilisi, take the M27 through Kutaisi to Zugdidi. Proceed east through the town and turn right (north) just beyond the bridge over the railroad tracks, onto the road to Jvari. Jvari forms the border between Samegrelo and Svaneti. Proceed to Mestia, stopping for a break at what is nearly the halfway point, Khaishi, where you can get a sweet, watery beer at the local bar in the central square. The trip from Zugdidi to Mestia (136 km/ 84 miles) will take four and a half hours. The road is asphalt but rough, winding as it follows the turns of the rushing Enguri River. The road can climb abruptly and is extremely narrow in places. Over-confident Georgians come zipping toward you while you watch your outside wheels hug the edge of the precipice. Mistakes can be fatal. Don't be shy about using your horn.

Mestia has 3,700 inhabitants and stands 1,470 meters (4,823 feet) above sea level. Lying on the banks of two rivers, the Enguri and the Mulakhi, the town is reminiscent of an Austrian village where the peaks of the surrounding snowcapped mountains seem so deceptively close that a short stroll could bring you to the top. The Enguri is connected to the legend of the Golden Fleece and Jason's journey to Colchis to obtain it. Svanetian practitioners still exist who know a gold-prospecting technique described by Strabo as early as the first century AD. The technique entails putting a sheep fleece into the river to trap the flecks of gold being carried down from the mountains. It is believed that just such a fleece, covered in gold, was brought down from these mountains, along archaeologically proven trade routes, as an offering to the Colchian King Aeetes in his palace along the Phasis River.

HISTORICAL AND ETHNOGRAPHIC MUSEUM

Located in the *seti* (downtown) area of Mestia in the 11th-century Church of St. George, this two-room museum contains a superb collection of medieval icons, fine examples of metal-chasing (repoussé) work, and processional crosses from Svaneti and other parts of Georgia. The Svanetian iconographic tradition places particular emphasis on the life and deeds of St. George, sometimes to the extent of providing unusual interpretations of church canon. One repoussé work (first part of the 11th

century) shows Christ, flanked by St. John and St. Mariam (Mary) dressed in the clothing of St. George. Another repoussé work of the same period shows St. George spearing the Emperor Diocletian rather than the usual dragon; this iconographic treatment, however, is found in many places in Georgia. The technical virtuosity of metal-chasing throughout the medieval period in Georgia is extraordinary (*see* page 40). The Svanetian school is perhaps most notable for the amazing depth of the raised images.

Perhaps the single most important work in the collection is the Icon of the Forty Martyrs. This 11th-century icon is not Svanetian but most probably belongs to the central Georgian school of painting. The painting (oil on canvas over wood) depicts the martyrdom by drowning of 40 warriors near Sebastia (Asia Minor) in AD 320. The composition is remarkable for the harmonious rendering of 40 individualized figures within the confined two-dimensional space of the canvas. The mastery of composition, together with a distinctiveness of portraiture usually associated with the European Renaissance, makes this one of the most beloved and frequently reproduced works throughout Georgia. The church of St. George was converted into this museum in 1936–1937, but there is a new larger museum under construction on the south bank of the Enguri.

Repoussé work portraying St. George from the Historical Museum in Mestia

HOUSE MUSEUM OF MIKHEIL KHERGIANI

Of greatest interest to climbers, this museum houses the personal possessions of Mikheil Khergiani, the famous Svanetian alpinist who was killed in a climbing accident in the Dolomites in 1969. The museum is located in the western part of town in the Larami district.

A short walk from the house is the 13th-century Church of Matskhvrish (Saviour), where fresco fragments of Adam and Eve (copies of which are in the historical museum) are still visible on the façade. A unique feature of Svanetian churches is that their façades are more often painted than carved.

SVANETIAN WATCHTOWERS

All of Mestia's watchtowers remain in private hands; ownership has been passed from generation to generation. One, near the Church of St. George, has been converted into a museum. The towers are made of granite and slate, often with wooden roofs. They're usually 28 meters (92 feet) high, a measurement derived from a building formula in which the height is equal to the combined width of the four sides of the base. It generally took four years to build a tower. The strength of these

The medieval watchtowers in Ushguli have survived many avalanches

towers is still a source of wonder, having withstood many avalanches. Laboratory analyses of the mortar have still not yielded an exact formula, but it is thought that egg yolk was used as a binding agent. The towers were built for defensive reasons but also symbolized the strength and standing of a family within the community.

The towers usually have four floors. The first is used for storing fodder for livestock; the second as a sacred area in which are piled the bones of all the animals the family ever killed—these animals are regarded as holy because they were given by God. The third and fourth floors were used as defensive positions from which enemies were repelled. In times of peace, such as today, the top two floors also serve as a kind of natural refrigerator: even on the hottest day the absence of all but the narrowest embrasure keeps the room dark and cool. The walls of the top floor act as a coping for the entire tower, creating three machicolations on each side from which all sorts of things could have been hurled with great effect upon an advancing enemy.

Day Trips

USHGULI

Lying 47 km (29 miles) east of Mestia, Ushguli at 2,200 meters (7,218 feet) is the highest continuously inhabited village in Europe. The mountain scenery alone is worth the trip, but the more than 20 medieval watchtowers rising throughout the village beneath the majesty of Mt. Shkhara provide testimony to the unique rigors of life here.

From Mestia, go east on the road that runs above the south bank of the Enguri River. After 14 km (8.7 miles), just before crossing the Ugveri Pass (1,700 meters/5,599 feet) there is an excellent view of the twin peaks of Mt. Ushba. The cross at the 28-km (17.4-mile) point along the road is the spot from which the procession for the holiday of Kvirikoba (July 28) begins. There is a two-km (1.2-mile) walk to the church of Kvirike at the top of the hill. From the village of Kala the ten or so km (six miles) on to Ushguli wind below dangerous mountains of slate. Falling pieces are frequent, as witnessed by the striated chunks that litter the road. Best not to stop here, regardless of the temptation to get out and photograph the Enguri roaring through the gorge below.

Ushguli is comprised of four settlements: Murkmeli, Zhibiani, Chazhashi, and Chvibiani. All were built with defense foremost in mind. **Murkmeli** is the first settlement you come to on the road. Proceed to **Zhibiani**, which is home to the Ethnographic Museum.

Protected on two sides by rivers and secured on the third by a fortress, Zhibiani

MTSYRI

A long a narrow path that led
　Down to the shore, above her head
A jug held high, the Georgian lass
Her way slowly making. As
I watched, a slippery stone betrayed
Her cautious foot: she stumbled, swayed,
Laughed at herself and haltingly
Walked on . . . Her clothes were poor, but she
Had pushed her veil back, and the rays
Of sun had gold shades on her face
And bosom traced; a warmth, a glow
Came from her lips and cheeks, and so
Deep and bewitching was her eye,
So full of love's sweet mystery,
Its secrets, that my heart and mind
Were set aflame, and I turned blind
To all about me . . . Nothing now
Can I at all recall save how
I watched her slowly walk away . . .
Up in the hills two huts of clay
Like two fond mates perched side by side;
Glued to the rock they were and hid
In part by haze . . . Smoke curled up o'er
A low flat roof . . . I saw a door
Glide open, then as softly shut . . .
You not know how I suffered, but
'Tis better so, 'tis for the best—
With me those simple scenes will rest,
With me, this will I not deny,
I want my memories to die.

Mikhail Lermontov

The 12th-century La Maria Church in Ushguli with Mt. Shkhara in the background

is a textbook example of a fortified village from early feudal times. Legend has it that the two towers above this village were the winter and summer residences of the famous Georgian Queen Tamara who reigned from 1184 to 1212. Archaeologists are excavating in the church just below the winter residence (located on the lower of the two hills) to see whether there is any truth to the folk belief that this might be Queen Tamara's grave—one of no less than eight sites thus identified.

The **Ethnographic Museum** is in a tower located in the center of the settlement. Special permission must be arranged in Mestia to visit the museum, which has first-rate examples of medieval repoussé work, icons, and processional crosses from churches in this region and other parts of Georgia.

The 12th-century **La Maria Church** complex on a rise at the edge of the settlement provides one of the best views of Mt. Shkhara. The church complex, mostly in ruins, is also connected with the murder in the late 19th century of a lord named Puta Dadeshkeliani from the Lower Bal, who wanted to rule over the people of Ushguli and environs. The people agreed to a meeting with him in front of the church. There the entire town helped pull a cord attached to the trigger of a rifle, thus dividing equally the responsibility for killing the man who sought to rule over people who had never had a ruler.

BECHO

The village of Becho is 1.9 km (11.8 miles) west of Mestia. Driving from Mestia, turn right just before the bridge that crosses the Dolra River. On the road parallel to the river are some of the best spots to take photos of Mt. Ushba.

(Above) Ushba from Mesik at dawn. Freshfield wrote about this 1890 photo by Vittorio Sella in The Exploration of the Caucasus.

(Left) Poets of many nations have written about the intriguing beauty of Georgian women.

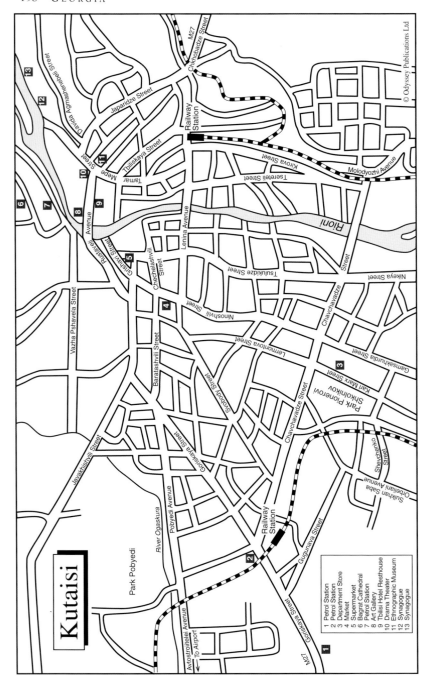

© Odyssey Publications Ltd

Kutaisi

1 Petrol Station
2 Petrol Station
3 Department Store
4 Market
5 Supermarket
6 Bagrat Cathedral
7 Petrol Station
8 Art Gallery
9 Tbilisi Hotel Resthouse
10 Drama Theater
11 Ethnographic Museum
12 Synagogue
13 Synagogue

Imereti

Imereti encompasses an area of 6,365 sq. km (2,458 sq. miles) and has a population of 772,251. Separated from Kartli by the Likhi Range, Imereti is the first western province you'll enter driving toward the coast from Tbilisi.

Imeretians have the reputation for being great talkers and jokers, who emphasize their effusive outpourings with an abundance of hand gestures and facial expressions. A fellow named Chichikia is the hero of all their jokes and tales, and they use him to make fun of others and themselves. They consider themselves the most hospitable and polite of Georgians. They also are known to be the most temperamental.

The history of Imereti is linked to the larger picture of the combined western provinces and throughout history portions of its territory belonged to both Abkhazia and Samegrelo. In the sixth century BC it was the heart of the Kingdom of Colchis. The history of this province is perhaps most conveniently understood by looking at the fate of its capital, Kutaisi.

Kutaisi

Kutaisi has a population of 234,870. The town is located 236 km (146 miles) west of Tbilisi on the M27. The road leaves the Mtkvari River valley after the village of Khashuri and climbs across the Surami Pass, the historic border between east and west Georgia. Kutaisi is the capital of Imereti and the second largest city in Georgia, lying on both sides of the Rioni River. The archaeological remains in the Gora or Ukimerioni area on the hill overlooking the right bank date from the sixth and fifth centuries BC. Some scholars are of the belief, however, that in the late Bronze Age (1300 BC) Kutaisi was the capital of King Aeetes, who possessed the Golden Fleece and whose daughter was Medea. They hold that Jason and his Argonauts came here in search of the Fleece, since the Rioni (known in the ancient world as the Phasis) is navigable down to the Black Sea. It was precisely its enviable position that allowed it to flourish as an important trade center on the caravan route from Greece to India.

Kutaisi is known to have existed as early as the seventh century BC as a town in the Greek colony of Miletus. In the third century BC Apollonius of Rhodes mentions Kutaisium/Kutaia as the capital of the Kingdom of Colchis. Byzantine sources of the mid-sixth century AD refer to the town as one of the most important fortresses in the Kingdom of Lazica, which succeeded the Romans in the region (AD 200–400). During the early sixth century when all of Imereti was a battlefield for the Emperor Justinian and his Persian adversaries, the massive fortifications above the right bank of the Rioni were constructed. The town itself spread out beneath the citadel and across the river where markets, caravanserais, and quays for merchant ships sprang up. In the eighth century, after the Arabs had captured Tbilisi, Kutaisi became the capital when King Archil established himself there. King Leon I of Abkhazia was also responsible for the growth and recovery of the city at this time.

Kutaisi became the capital of all Georgia in 978 when Bagrat III united the country and installed here his political and administrative center. It remained the capital until 1122 when David the Builder conquered the Emirate of Tbilisi and transferred his capital there. The period between the reigns of Bagrat III and Queen Tamara was the Golden Age of the city, when the most significant building projects were successfully completed: Bagrat's Cathedral, the Gelati Monastery, and the Monastery of Motsameta.

With the removal of the capital of Georgia to Tbilisi, Kutaisi remained the capital of western Georgia until the 19th century. The town was spared invasion by the Mongols during the 13th and 14th centuries but suffered from Turkish attack in 1510 when it was nearly burned to the ground. The Kutaisi Fortress (the Ukimerioni) was seized again by the Turks in 1666. Russian ambassadors in the middle of the 17th century reported the fortress and the Cathedral of Bagrat still standing, but in 1692 the Cathedral, the palace complex, and the fortress were destroyed by Turkish troops. Only in 1770 were the Turks dislodged from the town, when King Solomon I of Imereti led a combined Russian and Imeretian force to seize the city. In 1804 King Solomon II signed an act of allegiance to Russia and abdicated his throne in 1810. With that, Imereti joined Russia and Kutaisi became the residence of the governor.

Note: When visiting Kutaisi many foreign travelers decide to stay in the spa town of **Tskhaltubo**, only 12 km (seven miles) to the northwest of Kutaisi, and connected to it by a short extension of the M27. The town is wonderful if you want to "take the waters," but a little sleepy if you don't. At the time of writing the Hotel Tskhaltubo is closed. Many travelers have commented favorably on a fabulous guest house near the Bagrat Cathedral that can be booked by Caucasus Travel.

THE CATHEDRAL OF KING BAGRAT (MOTHER OF GOD CHURCH)

Bagrat's Cathedral is at the end of Kazbegi Street, on a hill above the right bank of the Rioni River. Turn left from David and Constantine Mkheidze Street onto Pshavela Street and then right onto Kazbegi Street. Alternatively, you can park below near the bus station on Mkheidze Street and walk up a staircase through what were once the courts and gardens of the cathedral and palace.

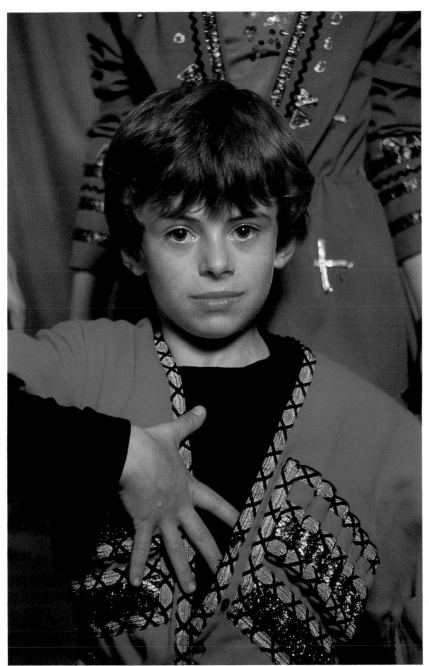

The young soloist of a Georgian dance troupe in Kutaisi

Bagrat Cathedral

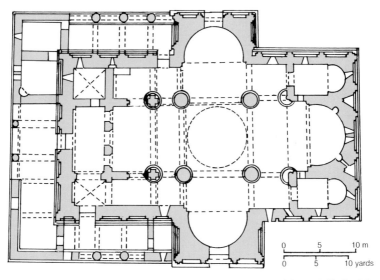

© Odyssey Publications Ltd

The cathedral was commissioned by the first king of a unified Georgia, Bagrat III. An inscription on the north wall gives us the exact date of completion: "When the floor was finished it was chronicon 223" (1003). The date is the oldest remaining example of Arabic numerals in Georgia. Intending to symbolize his unification of Georgia, Bagrat invested much of his personal prestige in the building of the cathedral. According to a chronicle of the time, at the cathedral's consecration, Bagrat "assembled the neighboring rulers, the patriarchs and archbishops, the abbots of all the monasteries, and all the notables from the lower and higher parts of his realm and from all other kingdoms." Even in its present ruined state, you cannot but feel the grandeur and nobility of the structure and the sense of power and wonder that must have attended that consecration ceremony.

Like the Church of Oshki (now in Turkey) with which it is frequently compared, the Cathedral of Bagrat is a triconch with protruding sidearms to form the cross. The cupola was supported by four detached octagonal columns and the drum raised high above. With the windows in the conches, a light-filled open space was created. The extended western arm was separated into three aisles and furnished with galleries for the king's family. A three-story tower was added to the left side of the west façade; this probably served as the king's quarters or as the residence of the local archbishop. Somewhat after the completion of the cathedral, but still in the first half of the 11th century, a portico with open arches was added to the southwest side. A little later this concept was repeated in front of the entryways on the west and south sides. Only ruins of the south portico remain today. These later embellishments were marked by elaborate, deeply incised stone carving on the capital and base of the pillars, the pillared entrances, and selected door and window frames. Mythical animals, human faces, and sometimes human faces on animal bodies predominate here, usually intertwined with rich leaf motifs. The technique is reminiscent of Romanesque capitals. This type of carving and iconography is in contrast to the overall conception of the stonemasonry of the cathedral, which utilizes more of the subdued classicism usually associated with Kumurdo. In such a concept, harmony of intent is expressed by the symmetrical disposition of the blind arcading, and the slender gables and windows.

Russian ambassadors who visited the church in the middle of the 17th century reported that the interior was covered with mosaics. Remnants of the design of the floor—broad circles interspersed with inlays of black, white, and red—are still visible at the eastern end of the building. The cathedral was sacked and destroyed by the Turks in 1691. Since 1951 Georgian restorers have been working on the site. East of the cathedral on a ridge overlooking the city is the palace complex; archaeological work commenced here in 1985.

THE KUTAISI STATE MUSEUM OF HISTORY AND ETHNOGRAPHY

The collection features armor, weapons and domestic implements, musical instruments, clothing, and money spanning a long period of west Georgian history. Of greatest interest are the icons, jewelry, coins, and illuminated manuscripts that you can see by special request in the Treasury (Okros Fondi). Many of these pieces come from the Gelati Monastery and date from the 12th to 15th centuries. Other works are from Bagrat Cathedral. The collection is strong in metal-chasing from Svaneti and coins and artifacts from Colchis. Some of these date back to the second millennium BC.

GEORGIAN ART GALLERY

The permanent collection contains Russian and Georgian works primarily of the 19th and 20th centuries. Of greatest interest are the three paintings by Niko Pirosmani. The ground floor is devoted to rotating exhibitions.

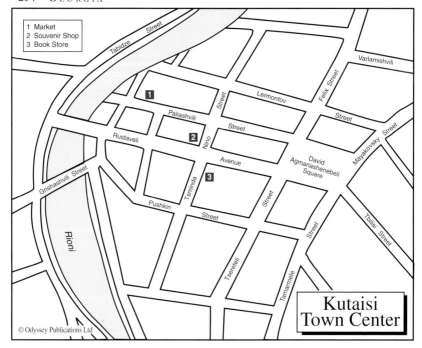

1 Market
2 Souvenir Shop
3 Book Store

Kutaisi
Town Center

© Odyssey Publications Ltd

TSULUKIDZE GARDEN

On the left bank of the Rioni, bounded by Tsulukidze and Chechelashvili Streets, this park served as the garden of King Alexander of Imereti (1639–1660). The buildings of the royal palace stood here, but only one foundation has survived. It now holds the modern building of the Tourist Club. On this spot once stood the famous Okros Chardakhi (Golden Tent). Built in the seventeenth century and reconstructed in the 1830s, it was used for receiving ambassadors and marking great ceremonial occasions. Note the large plane tree in the garden. The Imeretian kings are supposed to have conducted trials and executions beneath it. From this garden a cable car can take you to Besiki Park and its small zoo. Tsulukidze, by the way, was a Georgian revolutionary (1876–1905).

SYNAGOGUES

The main street running through the Jewish quarter used to be called Shaumyan Street; the name has now been changed to Boris Gaponov Street after the man who translated Rustaveli's *The Knight in the Panther's Skin* into Hebrew. There are three synagogues along this street. The two major ones are at number 49 and number 12, built in 1834–1835 and 1887, respectively. Before the massive emigration of Jews from Georgia to Israel over the past ten years, Jews accounted for two percent of the population of Kutaisi. Now their number is somewhat less. The houses in this district are arranged close to each other up the hill in a warm and intimate sense of community that speaks of deep neighborly interest and absolutely no secrets. Ask any Jew here and you will learn that Jews have always lived very happily in Georgia, and that their presence here dates to the time of the first diaspora. Anti-Semitism is virtually unknown in Georgia.

MTSVANE KVAVILA

Located above the Jewish quarter but still on the left bank of the Rioni is a 17th-century tower in good condition, and some churches dating from the 17th–20th centuries. In 1956 the cemetery, below the Church of the Green Flower, was organized as a pantheon of famous Georgians. Balletomanes will be particularly interested to visit the grave of Meliton Balanchivadze (1862–1937), the father of George Balanchine. His grave can be recognized by the piano keyboard carved into the rock of the headstone.

SATAPLIA NATURE RESERVE

Located six km (four miles) southwest of Kutaisi, this 500-hectare (1,250-acre) reserve is one of the few remaining pristine areas where you can still see a portion of the ancient Colchian forests. The name Sataplia means "honey-bearing" and refers to the vast number of beehives in the hills nearby. In the same area are numerous karst caves, one of which is over 600 meters (1,968 feet) long. The first cave in this huge complex was discovered in 1925 and was opened to visitors in 1929. Spelunkers may be put off by the guided tours, but for those who like to be led to their stalactites and stalagmites the descent is most worthwhile. Paleolithic tools have been discovered in one of the caves. The reserve gained particular prominence in 1933 when Petre Chabukiani unearthed traces of dinosaurs. On one exposed rock surface, 252 fossilized prints of seven different kinds of dinosaurs are visible.

Gelati Monastery

Leave Kutaisi from the northwest by David Agmashenebeli (the Builder) Street, which becomes Gelati Street, and proceed along this road for seven km (four miles). A sign beyond the village of Gelati marks the right-hand turnoff.

Beautifully situated on a forest-covered hill high above the Tskhaltsitela River, the Gelati Monastery complex consists of the main church (Cathedral of the Virgin), the Church of St. George (east of the main church), the Church of St. Nicholas (west of the main church), the Belltower, the Academy Building (west

The Cathedral of the Virgin Mary in the Gelati Monastery (eastern view)

of the Church of St. Nicholas), the South Entrance and the Chapel containing the tomb of King David Agmashenebeli.

The monastery was founded in 1106 by King David the Builder (1089–1125) at a time when Kutaisi was the capital of a united Georgia and Tbilisi was still an Arab emirate. King David built the monastery out of gratitude to God for his early victories against the Seljuk Turks. He also wanted to found a new Athos or new Jerusalem to serve as a center of Christendom as he consolidated power and expanded his empire.

Gelati, therefore, was intended as both a royal monastery and an academy. David brought famous theologians trained in philosophy such as Arsen Ikaltoeli and Ioane Petritsi to teach at the academy. Both had been professors at the Mangana Academy in Constantinople but were ousted on account of their Neoplatonist philosophies. They did, however, organize the Academy at Gelati along the lines of Mangana. The curriculum consisted of geometry, arithmetic, astronomy, music, rhetoric, grammar, philosophy, Greek, and Latin. Petritsi, the first director of Gelati, returned to his homeland after also working for a long period in the Georgian Monastery of Bachkovo at Petritsoni in Bulgaria. He translated numerous philosophical works from Greek into Georgian and is widely credited with the development of philosophy in his country. So great was the influence of the Academy at Gelati that it eclipsed the Georgian centers at Athos, the Holy Cross in Jerusalem, and Petritsoni in Bulgaria.

The plastic arts also were by no means neglected at Gelati. The school of painters at the monastery was the most important one of the time in the entire country. Manuscript illumination was practiced, as were gold and silver forging, which reached a high degree of artistry. The artists of the monastery produced the sumptuous gold, silver, and enamel frame for the Khakhuli Triptych, now in the Treasury of the Museum of Georgian Art. From King Demetre I, David's son, to all subsequent Georgian kings, each considered it his duty to lavish riches upon the monastery in the form of land, manuscripts, icons, and money. This tribute continued until the monastery's gradual decline in the 14th century. The Turks looted and burned Gelati in 1510. In 1759 the monastery was sacked and burned again, this time by the Lezgians (a northern Caucasian tribe). Despite the efforts at preservation and rebuilding by the Imeretian kings throughout these years, many important works of art were lost and the buildings severely damaged. Gelati never regained its former significance. In 1922, after Georgia had been annexed to Russia by the Bolsheviks (in 1921), the monks living in Gelati were dispersed. Only in 1988 was the monastery once more revived with the reconsecration of the Cathedral of the Virgin and the Church of St. George.

Though the two smaller churches of St. George and St Nicholas were built in the 13th century, two centuries after the main Cathedral of the Virgin, the entire monastery ensemble shows a unity in its configuration and a harmony in the building materials used.

THE CATHEDRAL OF THE VIRGIN
David the Builder did not live to see the completion of the cathedral (1125), begun as the centerpiece of the monastery complex in 1106. Finished and consecrated to the Virgin Mary by David's son Demetre I in 1125, the central-domed cruciform

church is built of pale yellow and gray limestone upon which a minimum of decorative embellishment has been carved. Blind arcading and molding on door and window frames are present, but restrained, on every side of the façade. The narthex in the west and the chapel in the south were added in the 12th and 13th centuries; the addition in the north dates from the 13th and 14th centuries. These structures replaced an ambulatory that had originally been designed to wrap around three sides but was never executed. The additions provide another level in the visual ascent to the drum and cupola, which imparts an increased dynamism to the structure. This mobility is enhanced by the steep pitch of the roofs and the decorative gables. The projecting polygonal apses in the east are reminiscent of certain churches on the Black Sea Coast, such as the one at Bichvinta, which is atypical of the flat eastern façade marking Georgian churches. Given the restrained aspects of exterior decoration here, it seems not unreasonable to surmise that special emphasis on interior decoration was always intended.

As is common in 11th-century churches in Georgia, the cupola sits on the ends of the walls of the apse in the east and on freestanding massive piers, quadrangles covered in frescoes, in the west. The windows in the drum and large windows in the choir gallery as well as in the west, north, and south walls illuminate the space, creating admirable conditions in which to view what are among the best-preserved frescoes in all Georgia.

The dominant feature of the interior is the broad altar bay with its mosaic vault of the Virgin and Child flanked by the archangels Michael on the left and Gabriel on the right. This mosaic dates from the 1130s and is the oldest remaining wall art in the cathedral. More than 2.5 million stones of over 1,500 different colors were used to execute it. The style is largely Byzantine, with certain Georgian characteristics in the linear depiction. It was probably done by local artists who studied in Constantinople. Other works covering the walls date from the 13th to 18th centuries and reflect the fortunes of the church and the royal and ecclesiastical directives as to when and in what manner sections were to be restored or repainted.

In the eastern part of the south chapel are frescoes that date from 1291–1293 and depict King David VI Narin in both royal attire and monk's robes. This chapel served as his mausoleum and contains fresco fragments from the 14th century.

In the narthex (west portico) are wall paintings from the first half of the 12th century. They depict the third and fourth Ecumenical Councils, which met in the fifth century, and are interesting for the stylistic insights they provide and as documentation of church history and politics. The councils were critical in a dispute among various church factions in the Caucasus at the time depicted.

In the north chapel of the main church are frescoes from the 17th century combining the life of Christ with Georgian historical personages. The lower register of the south wall has portraits of King Giorgi of Imereti with his family. The upper register portrays the Annunciation, the Birth of Jesus, the Entry into Jerusalem, and the Crucifixion. On the north wall are, among other scenes, the Raising of Lazarus and the Last Judgment.

Perhaps of greatest interest is the portrait of King David the Builder on the eastern portion of the north wall in the main church. David, crowned, is depicted as founder, holding the church in his hands. This is one of the most beloved images in Georgia. It is the only surviving portrait of this great Georgian king. To the left of David is the Catholicos of western Georgia, Evdemon Chkhetidze. Continuing from right to left are: King Bagrat III of Imereti, Queen Helene, their son King Giorgi II, Prince Bagrat, and Queen Rusudan. Slightly above is the depiction of Emperor Constantine and his mother Helena. The cross in their midst iconographically establishes his preeminence as the archetypal Christian ruler. These frescoes are from the 16th century.

Christ Pantocrator fills the dome of the cupola, and the four Evangelists occupy the four spandrels beneath. In the drum, standing between the windows, are 16 prophets and kings of the Old Testament. The murals in the dome date from the 17th century and are signed by an artist named Tevdore.

The core cubic structure supporting the octagonal belfry may well date from the 12th century; the belfry itself was added in the late 13th century.

THE CHURCH OF ST. GEORGE

Located to the east of the main church, this mid 13th-century church is a simplified miniature of its larger neighbor in conception and design. Of architectural interest here are the two short pilasters with capitals in the west that support the cupola. In marked contrast to the larger quadrangular ones found in the cathedral, these, in conjunction with the low arcades, suggest initially the characteristics of a basilica rather than the domed cruciform structure we expect at this period. Their presence here, and consequently the overall design of the interior, is very unusual and bespeaks a retrograde transitional style.

This church was burned by the Turks in 1510 along with the main church. All frescoes date from the 16th and 17th centuries. New Testament scenes are combined with scenes from the life of St. George and historical figures, *tavadi* or princes, of western Georgia. These have recently been restored and are beautifully alive, with a subtle Oriental delicacy. Of great interest is the Persian style of dress worn by the princes. This reflects the political realities of the time in which Sassanid Iran dominated and certain obeisance had to be paid. A portrait from the 16th century of King Bagrat III is on the south wall.

(overleaf) Frescoes of the Nativity and the Annunciation, from the
Cathedral of the Virgin at the Gelati Monastery

THE CHURCH OF ST. NICHOLAS

West of the main church, between it and the roofless ruin of the Academy building, this two-story 13th-century structure is an architecturally peculiar element within the monastery complex. The lower level of arcades seems to function almost as a gate from the Academy to the main church and may have been a symbolic but necessary transition point at which students could change their focus from worldly to spiritual concerns. The upper-level cruciform structure is reached by an outside stone staircase on the northside.

THE HALL OF THE ACADEMY

West of the Church of St. Nicholas, this building, along with the cathedral, is the oldest structure in the complex, begun in 1106. Within, the low stone benches along the sides are still visible, as are the niches for books and the stone pedestal for the master. The portico at the entrance was added later, in the 13th to 14th centuries. Some scholars believe that the positioning of the Academy with a long north-south axis was a means of emphasizing its secular function and thereby distinguishing it from the holy status of the church with its elongated east-west longitudinal axis.

KING DAVID'S GATE

The entire monastery complex was surrounded by a high stone wall. David the Builder himself asked, as a sign of humility, to be buried in the entranceway of the southern gatehouse so that those who entered would walk over his tomb. The stone slab has an inscription in Georgian: "This is my place for all eternity. I own only this now." The structure over King David's grave dates from the 12th century. The gate of the entrance was made in 1063 in the city of Ganja, in present-day Azerbaijan. Demetre I brought it as a trophy from a war fought there in 1129. Only one half of the gate remains and an inscription in Arabic states the circumstances of its arrival in Gelati. The lost half had an identical inscription in Georgian.

Motsameta Monastery

Six km (3.7 miles) northwest of Kutaisi is the village of Motsameta. Turn right onto the road across from the police control booth and continue for another three km (1.8 miles). Park at the railroad station. Cross the tracks on foot and walk up the path to the monastery.

As you walk to the monastery, you'll see strips of colored cloth tied to the myrtle bushes and fig and pomegranate trees that flank the lane. These are votive offerings, placed there in hopes that a prayer might be granted.

Situated dizzily high above the ravine of the Tskhaltsitela River, the monastery offers awe-inspiring views of the river and the surrounding countryside from any number of buildings and points on the grounds. Extremely isolated and seldom visited by tourists, this place will give you an unadulterated taste of the monastic life. The caretaker has a magnificent harlequin Great Dane named Lady that roams the grounds.

The church itself is on a site on which there had been a church and village since the fourth century. The name Motsameta is derived from the Georgian word for martyrdom. Two brothers, David and Constantine Mkheidze, were lords of this region in the eighth century. Sometime between 720 and 730, succumbing to a superior Arab force, they were captured and tortured for refusing to convert to Islam. They were thrown into the Rioni River with stones tied around their necks and their bodies washed up on the riverbank below the monastery. They were buried as martyrs in the crypt of the church, which was also destroyed by the Arabs at the time of the brothers' death.

In the 11th century, King Bagrat III built a monastery on the foundations of the destroyed eighth-century church in honor of the two brothers, now national heroes and saints in the Georgian Orthodox Church. Their tomb rests on two carved lions at the top of a side altar in the church. The lions are connected with the legend of David and Constantine Mkheidze, for it is believed that they appeared to bring the bodies of the brothers up from the river to the church. Believers also hold that if you walk three times through the small passage beneath the saints' tomb without touching the walls, your prayers will be answered.

In 1923, the Cheka (the Soviet secret police) came into the church, seized the bones of the two saints and put them in the museum in Kutaisi. After protests by a local teacher, the relics were returned, but the once-perfect skeletons were hopelessly jumbled. The Father Superior of the Monastery relates that the Cheka agents who took the bones all suffered terrible fates: one was killed by his son, one went insane, and the third died of tuberculosis. The church was once completely covered in frescoes, but a fire set in 1923 destroyed everything except some fragments in the cupola. The bell tower also dates from the 11th century.

Geguti Palace

Located 12 km (7.4 miles) south of Kutaisi in the plains of the Rioni River valley, the ruins of the palace at Geguti are one of the most important historical examples of Georgian secular architecture extant. (Take Nikea Street out of Kutaisi and turn left just beyond the Venezia Restaurant.) This site is archaeologically fascinating.

THE APPARITION

*A*vt'handil let his horse pasture while he roasted the meat. He saw six horsemen coming towards him. He said: "They look like brigands; else what good is to be found? No other human being has ever been here."

He took his bow and arrow in his hand, and went gaily towards them. Two bearded men were leading their beardless brother; his head was wounded, his heart had swooned from loss of blood; they wept and grieved; alas! his spirit was almost fled.

He called out: "Brothers, who are ye? I took you for brigands."

They replied: "Be calm, help us and put out the fire; if thou canst not help us, add grief to our grief, and make it complete; weep with us who need pity, scratch thy cheeks too."

Avt'handil approached; he spoke to the men with the grieved hearts. They told him their story, speaking with tears: "We are three brothers, for this we shed bitter tears; we have a large fortified town in the region of Cathay.

"We heard of good hunting ground, we went forth to the chase, countless soldiers accompanied us, we dismounted on the bank of a stream; the hunting pleased us, for a month we went not away; we killed wild beasts without measure in the plain, on the mountain and on the ridge.

"We three brothers shamed the archers with us, so we three vied still with one another; 'I kill best, I am better than thou,' thus each pushed his claim with words; we could not manifest the truth, we wrangled, we strove with one another.

"Today we sent away the soldiers loaded with stags' hides. We said among ourselves: 'Let us judge truly who of us is mightier with his arm.' We remained alone, we were private, we killed in our own sight, we shot not before onlookers.

"We had three armor-bearers with us; we ordered the soldiers to go away, mistrusting naught; we hunted over plain, through wood and den, we slaughtered the wild beast, and not even a bird flew up.

"Suddenly there appeared a knight, morose and gloomy of visage, seated on a black horse, black as Merani; his head and form were clad in a tiger's skin with the fur outside, and beauty such as his has ne'er been seen by man before.

"We gazed upon his rays, we scarce could support the brightness, we said: 'He is a sun on the earth; we cannot say in heaven.' We wished to seize him, we were venturesome and tried; this is the cause of our sighs, moans, weeping.

"I, the eldest man, earnestly begged my younger brother to give me this man to fight, my next brother praised his horse, this one only asked leave to conquer him. We granted him this as his due. As we went towards him he came forward unchanged, calmly and in beauty.

"Ruby mixed with crystal beautified the pale roses of his cheeks. His tender thoughts towards us turned to wrath, he explained nothing, neither did he let us go, he showed not any consideration for us at all, with his whip he ripened us who had spoken tartly to him.

"We gave him over to our youngest brother, we elders kept back, he seized upon him: 'Stand!' Thus he spake to him with his tongue. The knight held no sword in his hand, so we moved away; he struck him on the head with his whip, we saw the blood flow indeed.

"With a stroke of his whip he cleft his head thus, like a corpse he became lifeless, like earth he was brought to earth; thus he was humbled, leveled with the ground, him who had been audacious to him. Before our eyes he went away, bold, severe, and haughty.

"He turned not back again; he went away quietly and without haste. Lo! There he rides—look! like the sun and moon." The weeping ones joylessly showed him far off to Avt'handil; there only appeared his black steed carrying along that sun.

Shota Rustaveli, The Knight in the Panther's Skin,
translated by Marjory Scott Wardrop

The first building on the site of Geguti was a hunting lodge with a large fireplace, built in the eighth century. At that time the plains were covered in oak, and Geguti was the summer residence of the Georgian kings. It is said to have been the favorite residence of David the Builder (1089–1125), Demetre I (1125–1156), Giorgi III (1156–1184), and Queen Tamara (1184–1213). The additions to the original hunting lodge—the great central domed hall and wings—are from the tenth century. Side rooms serving as storage areas and private chambers were added in the 12th and 13th centuries under the initial impetus of Giorgi III.

Covering an area of 2,000 sq. meters (2,400 sq. yards), the palace stands atop a plinth 2.5 meters (8.2 feet) high. Running throughout the plinth was a heating system. The walls are of brick faced with dressed stone. The basic rectangular outline of the structure is relieved by rounded towers that project from the corners and the middle of each side. The official entrance to the palace is from the north. A staircase ran between two projecting walls into the central domed hall. The vestibule leading into the hall led past a bathhouse to the right and domestic quarters to the left. These rooms form the northern arm of the basic cruciform structure formed around the central cupola hall. The southern arm is almost twice as deep as the northern, western, and eastern ones. It contained the bedchamber of the king on the right and his treasury on the left. Beyond the walls in the south is an aisleless church that probably dates to the 12th or 13th century.

The central cupola was 14 meters (46 feet) in diameter. Only the southern vaulted portion remains. The weight of this dome was supported by enormous squinches; only the southern ones remain. The western rooms were added during the 12th and 13th centuries and were originally two stories high. The second floor was reached by an enclosed stone staircase. The eastern portion of the structure houses the original hunting lodge with massive fireplace. On two floors, it was probably built by King Archil when he lived in Kutaisi. He was obviously not overly concerned with his cholesterol level, for the huge fireplace was there to roast the game that he killed during the hunt. You can almost smell the stag turning on the spit. The palace was destroyed by the Turks in the 17th century. It was not made accessible to the public until the initial excavations of 1937 and the additional work done in 1953–1956.

Given the cruciform ground plan, the parallels with ecclesiastical architecture of the period are easily drawn. Because so few secular buildings of this scale remain, Geguti is of major architectural significance. But it has also given us insight into the lives of the Georgian kings. As a result of archaeological and preservation work carried out in the 1950s, we know that the walls of Geguti, like royal palaces elsewhere, were covered with frescoes and the windows had panes of glass. Medieval sources refer to the battle scenes depicted in these frescoes, as well as the lavish furnishings: tapestries, oil lamps, and furniture fitted with gold and silver.

Vani

Leave Kutaisi on the M27 going southwest to Samtredia (33 km/20.4 miles). From Samtredia go south on the small road toward Chokhatauri. After approximately six km (3.7 miles) turn left (west) toward Vani, which is 18 km (11.7 miles) away. To ensure that you can visit, call the museum in advance: 99 55 05.

Vari is situated in a valley of the Sulori River (a tributary of the Rioni) on a small hill southeast of the administrative center of the same name. It is an archaeological site of the greatest importance. First excavated in the 1890s by the Academician Ekvtime Taqaishvili, the site yielded archaeological evidence attesting to the fact that Vani was a major center from 700 to 100 BC before being completely destroyed by enemies. From 600 to 400 BC, Vani was the most important economic center of Colchis. Some have suggested that Vani is the city of Leukothea mentioned by Strabo; others believe that it is Aea, the capital of King Aeetes who possessed the Golden Fleece.

Still visible at the site are the ruins of the city gate and defensive walls, which date back to 300–100 BC, a stepped altar on the hilltop, the ruins of a round temple on the central terrace, and a rectangular temple near the city gate. Only a portion of the site has been uncovered, and excavations are still underway. Current work is being led by the director of the Georgian Archaeological Institute, Professor Otar D. Lordkipanidze.

Recently the Georgian Academy of Sciences under the direction of Dr. Lordkipanidze has begun an archaeological field program at Vani. Participants receive training in the excavation of fortress walls and temple structures dating from the second and first centuries BC. The program runs from July 12 to August 2 and costs US$900 per person. This includes food, accommodation, and tours. Interested parties should contact: Georgian Academy of Sciences, Institute of Archaeology, Tbilisi State University, 14 Uznadze Street, Tbilisi 38002, Georgia, tel. (995 32) 96 99 56, fax. (995 32) 96 67 68. In the United States, contact: Ms. Judith Elliott, 102 Woodside Avenue, Metuchen, NJ 08840, tel. (732) 549-3322, fax. (732) 205-9737, e-mail: elliott@aesop.rutgers.edu.

The Georgian Academy of Sciences also accommodates people who want to make one- or two-week tours of archaeological and medieval sites during the months of May, June, August, September, and October. Assuming double occupancy, costs run to approximately US $60 per person per day. For more information about these tours, contact: Dimitri Akhvlediani and Nino Berdznishvili, 14 Kalandarishvili Street, Tbilisi 38002, Georgia, tel. (995 32) 95 14 14, fax. (995 32) 96 67 68.

Much of the magnificent gold and silver jewelry, toreutics, sculpture, pottery, and coins that have been found at Vani are in the Treasury of the Museum of Georgian Art in Tbilisi. Other artifacts are in the Archaeological Museum in Vani.

The material is riveting. The Hellenistic and Oriental influences that combine with the native artistic traditions of the region form a unique style that illuminates the splendor of the Colchian culture, one known by only a small number of cognoscenti.

Racha

North of Imereti, the historic province of Racha contains an area of 2,468 sq. km (953 sq. miles) and has a winter population of 30,000. Rachans have a reputation for being particularly proud and fierce, as well as for producing some of the best chefs in all Georgia. Racha itself is most famous for the magnificent and important 11th-century St. Nicholas Church in the village of Nikortsminda.

Nikortsminda

From Kutaisi, go northeast on the road to Tkibuli for 36 km (22 miles) and then continue north on the road to Ambrolauri for another 40 km (25 miles) to Nikortsminda. Given the winding road, you should plan this as a full-day trip; given the nature of the stone carving on the façade of the church, be sure to take a pair of binoculars.

THE CHURCH OF ST. NICHOLAS

Built at the beginning of the 11th century during the reign of King Bagrat III, the Church of St. Nicholas is, in its way, as important a monument as many of its more accessible contemporaries such as Bagrat's Cathedral in Kutaisi, Alaverdi in Kakheti, or Sveti-tskhoveli in Kartli. In ground-plan conception, it bears greatest resemblance to the six-apsed domed church of Kumurdo in Javakheti, built just 16 years earlier. As in Kumurdo, the multi-apsed plan of the interior is camouflaged by the cruciform shape of the exterior. The transitional solution created by the incorporation of the tenth-century paradigm of the six-apsed centralized structure into the 11th-century innovation of the cross shape is unique to Kumurdo and Nikortsminda.

Dissimilarities certainly exist between the two structures; for example in the radial projection of the north and south pairs of apses in Nikortsminda and the existence of closed rooms in the south and west instead of the ambulatory at Kumurdo. The greatest difference, however, is found in the façades. Nikortsminda is most famous for the quality, lavishness, plasticity, and organization of the carving on its façade, which ranks among the best examples of this kind of carving anywhere in Georgia during the Middle Ages. Kumurdo, on the other hand, is notable for the absence of elaborate decoration.

The detractors of Nikortsminda hold that in its overall harmony and proportions and in its aspiration toward some kind of soaring sublimity, it falls short of the ideal realized at Sveti-tskhoveli, the Cathedral of Bagrat, and Alaverdi. Critics point to the awkwardness of the porticoes in the west and south walls, built in the first half of the 11th century, slightly later than the church. The broad and massive drum of the cupola is also considered a drawback, as is the irregularity of the arches and windows under the gable of the south façade. (Blind arcading is symmetrical elsewhere.) Despite these objections, most observers will agree that the quality of the stone carving and the nature of the reliefs are extraordinary. We are lucky that they also happen to be in an excellent state of preservation.

The main theme of the carvings is the glory of Christ and His return on Judgment Day. The following scenes are found under the gables and in the tympana over the portals. Under the gable of the south façade, set off between two windows surrounded by elaborately carved rosettes, is either the Ascension of Christ or His return on Judgment Day. He is surrounded by four angels, two of whom hold trumpets. The tympanum relief above the south portal is of the Exaltation of the Cross. Above the west door in the tympanum is a scene of Christ between the mounted warrior saints Theodore and George. St. George, on Christ's left, is striking down the Roman Emperor Diocletian, whose persecution of Christians led to St. George's death in AD 303. The inscription in the frame over this scene, in the Georgian Asomtavruli alphabet, refers to King Bagrat III and his son Giorgi I.

Under the east gable is a scene of the Transfiguration of Christ set off by an ornamental frame. On either side are St. Theodore and St. George, both on horseback. On the west side, beneath the gable, is Christ enthroned, with right hand raised and left hand holding a book. Where mounted saints were located on the east façade, there are two tiny windows elaborated with rosettes. In the tympanum above the north portal are two archangels crossing standards.

The relief under the gable on the north side has disappeared. The interesting emphasis on the mounted warrior-saint in the overall composition seems to speak especially to the fierce spirit of the people of this mountainous province. In execution, the reliefs under the gables and those in the tympanum are quite different. The former have an almost archaic, static quality but a great vividness, the latter a much greater plasticity and dynamism.

Bird, animal, and floral motifs predominate elsewhere. The birds and animals are largely fantastic creatures such as griffins and winged horses and lions. They reveal the loving integration of folk and pagan themes into the Christian iconography. Their presence is most notable in the band around the drum: of the 48 originally carved, only 29 remain.

A restoration of the church occurred in 1534, and the frescoes of the interior date from the 16th and 17th centuries; they were originally commissioned by a local feudal lord named Tsulukidze and probably executed by painters from the Gelati monastery. The belltower is from the late 19th century.

Along the Black Sea Coast

The history of western Georgia often unfolded along very different lines from that of the eastern part of the country. Separated from each other by the Likhi Range, the major bridge between the mountains of the Greater and Lesser Caucasus, geographic location often proved tantamount to destiny as both parts of Georgia saw wave after wave of invaders from near and far. As you drive from Tbilisi toward the Black Sea Coast, you enter the western part of the country once you have crossed the Surami Pass and arrived at Imereti.

The four historical provinces covered in this chapter share many similarities, not the least of which are their coastal position on the Black Sea, the beneficence of a subtropical climate, their early contact with the classical world through Greek and Roman colonizers and soldiers, and the devastation suffered at the hands of the Ottoman Turks over a 300-year period. As great as the similarities, however, are the differences. The history of each province is extremely complicated. Over a 3,000-year period many boundaries shifted and kingdoms changed.

Before the war in Abkhazia (*see* below), the best way to get a grasp of the beauties and complex histories of these provinces was to follow the Caucasian Coastal Highway from Gagra to Batumi, stopping at the places of interest along the way. While the quantity of architectural wonders of the coastal provinces does not nearly compare with that of the east, the climate and natural beauty more than make up for it. With the current status of the Abkhazian-controlled territories, however, this itinerary will be impossible for the foreseeable future.

Abkhazia (Abkhazeti)

Located in northwestern Georgia, the Abkhazian Autonomous Republic covers an area of 8,700 sq. km (3,359 sq. miles) and has a population of 535,634. The borders of the republic are delineated by the Black Sea in the west and southwest, the Greater Caucasus Mountains in the north, the Psou River in the northwest, and the lower reaches of the Enguri along with the Svanetian-Abkhazian Mountains in the east. Mountains and foothills cover 74 percent of the territory of Abkhazia; the highest peaks are Dombai Ulgen (4,046 meters/13,274 feet), Psish (3,790 meters/12,434 feet), Ertsakhvu (3,910 meters/12,828 feet), and Guandra, (3,985 meters/13,074 feet). The mountain passes connect Abkhazia with villages of the Stavropolsky region in the northern Caucasus. The balance of the landscape is lowlands stretching to the Black Sea Coast.

The climate ranges from humid subtropical on the coast to extremely alpine, with temperatures on the highest peaks falling to below 0° C (32° F) even in July–August when it is 25° C (77° F) in Sokhumi. In winter the temperature exceeds 7° C (42° F) on the coast and can fall as low as -19° C (-2° F) in the upper elevations. Travelers will benefit from the approximately 215 sunny days in the year.

Tea, tobacco, and citrus grow along the coast. There is an abundance of fruit-bearing trees like apple, pear, and persimmon, and forest covers 55 percent of the territory. Excellent honey comes from higher up in the mountains.

The origins of the Abkhazian people are unclear. The language is part of the North Caucasian language group, and scholarly opinion favors the notion that the indigenous people are related to the Heniochi tribe, a proto-Georgian group. Pliny in the first century AD and Arrian in the second century mention the Apsily and the Abazghi tribes of this region. Many Georgian scholars hold that the Abkhazians and Georgians were the two aboriginal peoples who lived in this region but that in the 17th to 19th centuries the Abkhazians mixed with the Adige, a North Caucasian people, thus losing their orientation to Georgian culture.

Western Georgia has known many rulers. In the first century BC after the Colchian Kingdom had weakened, the territory now defined as Abkhazia was con-quered by the ruler of Pontus, Mithridates VI Eupator. In 65 BC the Romans defeated him and ruled the coastal regions until the fourth century AD. From the first century AD the Romans had to contend with the Kingdom of Lazica. The Laz, a Georgian tribe that had settled in the territory of ancient Colchis, were a power to be reckoned with until the sixth century. In the sixth century the region suffered the attentions of both the Byzantines and Sassanid Iran. In the eighth century

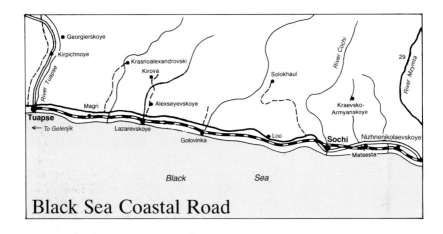

Black Sea Coastal Road

Abkhazia became independent under the military leadership of Leon I, who became ruler. His successor, Leon II, managed to unite all of western Georgia under him and establish his capital in Kutaisi (in present-day Imereti). In 978, with the death of King Feodosy the Blind, Abkhazia joined eastern Georgia under Bagrat III, ruling from Kutaisi.

In 1578, Abkhazia fell to the Ottoman Empire, which began three centuries of Turkish subjugation in which the Christian Abkhazians were forcibly converted to Islam and many Georgians were sold as slaves. During this period mountain tribes of the northern Caucasus came down into Abkhazia. Throughout the 18th century Abkhazia, reunited with eastern Georgia, made many attempts to free itself from the Turkish yoke. It was not, however, until 1810, when the Prince of Abkhazia received Russian protection that there was any relief. In the 1840s and 1860s, many Abkhazians emigrated to Turkey to join their coreligionists. Others who had participated in a peasant rebellion in 1866 were forcibly deported. Abkhazia was annexed to the Russian Empire in 1864. As a result of the emigration of Abkhazians to Turkey, new migrations of Svans, Rachans, and Russians, as well Armenians and Greeks from Turkey, occurred. On April 3, 1921, Abkhazia became a Soviet Autonomous Republic headed by Nestor Lakoba.

As an autonomous republic within the internationally recognized borders of Georgia, this region, along with all other regions that formed the country of Georgia, became independent from the USSR on April 9, 1991, by a unanimous vote of the Georgian parliament. Abkhazia's status as an autonomous republic within Georgia has never changed except as challenged by Abkhazian separatists led by Vladislav Ardzinba, who in conjunction with the Supreme Soviet of the Abkhazian

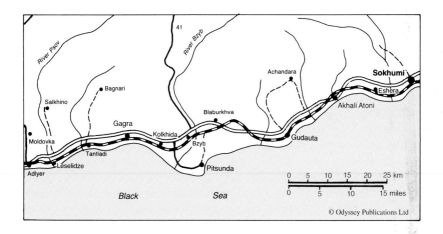

ASSR announced on August 25, 1990, in contravention of the rules of procedure, secession from Georgia. From this date until July 1992, the Supreme Soviet and its Presidium embarked on illegal legislative activities that placed everything from the banks and customs services to the police and the armed forces stationed in the territory of Abkhazia under its jurisdiction.

In August 1992, Defense Minister Tengiz Kitovani was sent to free hostages taken by Gamsakhurdia and sequestered in Abkhazia. He was also ordered to secure railroads and highways that had been under frequent terrorist attack. Kitovani, perhaps exceeding his authority, led his troops into Sokhumi, the capital of Abkhazia, and captured the parliament. Ardzinba and his government fled to Gudauta to lead a resistance. A September 3 ceasefire, negotiated by the Russians, was violated by the Abkhazians when they, aided by militant Muslims from the Northern Caucasus, mercenaries from the CIS, and Russian troops either led by rogue commanders or under the conservative majority challenging Boris Yeltsin at that time, captured Gagra. This force drove the Georgians back and took control of all of Abkhazia north of the Gumista river. Many were killed in the offensive, and Gagra itself was damaged by shelling. The fighting over the next nine months was intense, and more than 140,000 Georgian refugees were forced to flee their homes in Abkhazia. The Georgian government leveled claims of a concerted campaign by the Abkhazians of "ethnic cleansing" against Georgians.

In July 1993, a peace process was initiated by a Georgian-Russian-Abkhaz Commission. On August 14, the anniversary of the start of the war, troops began their withdrawals. The Georgian government requested that the Security Council of the UN send peacekeeping forces into the region. On September 16, Abkhazian separatist forces launched a surprise attack in the Ochamchire region, followed by a major assault on Sokhumi. Abkhazian-renewed hostilities clearly coincided with the final removal of Georgian armaments from the war zone in accordance with the July 27 ceasefire agreement and in flagrant violation of that agreement. Georgian unpreparedness plus renewed hostilities by pro-Gamsakhurdia troops in west Georgia prevented concerted opposition. The seige of Sokhumi lasted 12 days. President Shevardnadze was present in the city throughout the fight, vowing to die rather than let the city fall into Abkhazian hands. When at last the city fell, and he was forced to board the last plane out, he said, "May I be forgiven by my contemporaries and posterity." He openly blamed Russia for engineering a ceasefire that left Sokhumi unprotected. On the last day of the seige he sent Boris Yeltsin a telegram saying Georgia would join the CIS if the assault were stopped, clearly indicating his conviction that the aggression was planned "in the General Staff of the Russian Army." With ethnic Abkhazians constituting only a 17.8 percent minority within the region, a big brother from somewhere would certainly have been needed to outperform the Georgians with troops, weaponry, and planes that the Abkhazians on their own clearly could not have had. On September 27, 1993, Sokhumi fell and with it the Georgians lost all of Abkhazia.

Unfortunately, Abkhazia is a dangerous place at the moment. The aid workers, United Nations observers, diplomats and assorted specialists going across the Rukhi Bridge over the Enguri River, the one border crossing from Georgia to Abkhazia, tend to wear helmets and flak jackets when they make the journey. There is still a tremendous number of land mines along the Enguri, in the Gali Region, and in the Gumista River Valley. Given the current political situation the region is completely off limits to travelers.

Sokhumi, Gagra, and Bichvinta have all been ravaged by the war. Of the 70,000 Abkhazians living in Abkhazia, 10,000 of them were killed in the war. No country, not even Russia, recognizes Abkhazian independence, and there is a CIS-sanctioned economic blockade in force. Despite this, you can find in the markets of Sokhumi everything you can find in Tbilisi and at the same prices. Corruption on the part of the Russian peacekeeping forces and the Russian navy is clearly not a foreign concept.

The Black Sea Coast as a tourist destination was a huge boon to the Georgian economy. The loss of Abkhazia has, of course, had dire consequences. It also represented one-twelfth of Georgia's territory and caused more than 250,000 refugees to flee their homes.

The Abkhazians are isolated. There is a small amount of Russian tourism to Bichvinta but not enough to have any serious economic impact. Through the bribing of border guards there is some small trade back and forth between Georgia and Abkhazia across the Enguri River, and between Abkhazia and Russia across the Psou River.

The future is uncertain. It is unlikely that Georgia can formulate guarantees for Abkhazians as a minority within Georgia that will sufficiently persuade Abkhazian separatists to become part of a federation with Georgia. Georgia would probably not accept the formation of a confederation because this would acknowledge agreement to a change of Georgia's borders and its territorial integrity. Will Abkhazia fall under the Russian umbrella? This is, of course, anathema to the Georgians, and many Abkhazians are justifiably afraid of this option too, fearing a loss of rights whatever the autonomous status that might be guaranteed. The recently formed, self-proclaimed Confederation of North Caucasian Mountain Peoples established by the Chechens has made its capital in Sokhumi. This confederation, which has Islam as its unifying force, regards Abkhazia as a key region to its success and growth because of the access to ports along the Black Sea.

The brutality of the war, the charges of ethnic cleansing that have been leveled against both sides, and the presence of Abkhazians, Russians, Chechens, and other

Northern Caucasian peoples in what had been property owned by Georgians, do not bespeak a simple solution.

Despite the above, the decision has been made to leave in all of the information about Abkhazia from the first edition of this book, for a possible future time when travelers will be able to visit Georgia and include, without hindrance, the splendors of this region in their itineraries.

Gagra

Although the border between Georgia and the Russian republic is the Psou River just after the village of Leselidze, our itinerary begins at Gagra, 34 km (21 miles) south of it. The route is along the M27 from Gagra going south to Batumi, stopping at places of interest on the coast and inland along the way.

Gagra, 94 km (58 miles) northwest of Sokhumi along the M27, is a charming coastal resort situated below thick forests running up the foothills of the Gagra Mountains. Some peaks tower as high as 2,750 meters (9,022 feet). It is the warmest spot on the coast, with the sea ranging in temperature from 16°–23° C (61°–73° F) from May until November. Roses flourish in January and February. In the mountains, however, the alpine meadows are covered with snow for eight months of the year.

Gagra has an ancient history. In the first century AD, the Romans built a fortress, Nitica, to protect the territory from pirates. In the fourth and fifth centuries the Abaata Fortress was built by the local Abazghi tribe. The ruins can be visited in the center of town on Gagarina Square. Between the tenth and the 13th centuries, Gagra served as a transit point for trade between Kiev, Russia, and the rest of Georgia. In the 14th century the town was a Genoese colony. The first reference to the name Gagra on a map is on the one made by Pietro Visconti in 1308, where the town appears as Kakara. In the 16th century Gagra, along with all the towns and villages along the Black Sea Coast, fell into the hands of the Turks, who continued to rule on and off for more than 300 years.

In 1830, the region was taken by the Russians. To defend against raids by northern Caucasian tribes, they built a stone watchtower in 1841 in the Zhoekvara Gorge. Called the Marlinsky Tower, it is in the northeast part of town on Oktabraskaya Street. In the 1890s, the Russians constructed the Novorossiyk–Batumi Highway intersecting Gagra, allowing for its development. In 1901, Prince Alexander Oldenburgsky, who was married to a niece of Tsar Nicholas II, began to develop the town as a resort, hoping to turn it into a Caucasian Nice. (Although there's no topless bathing and an absence of luxury boutiques, the perch of some of the houses in the hills overlooking the sea might remind you of the Côte d'Azur.) The palace the prince built for himself in 1907 is now the Chaika (Seagull) Holiday Hotel, which is on fourth of March Street.

While Oldenburgsky's plans for a resort were not originally a great success because of the malaria that flourished in the region, Gagra had been before the war one of the most popular vacation spots on the coast for Georgians. The town had over 30 sanatoria, and many private homes offered an informal bed-and-breakfast arrangement. A lovely seaside park stretches for three km (two miles) and covers 14 hectares (35 acres). Many subtropical plants and trees grow in the park and shade the avenues throughout the town. The palms and eucalyptus are especially wonderful, a first-rate anomaly to confound preconceived notions about places that had once been a part of the USSR being one large frozen taiga.

A number of sites of architectural interest merit a visit: Marlinsky Tower (1841) is in the northeast part of town on Oktabraskaya Street; Gagra Church (sixth century) is on Gagarina Square in the center of town; the Abaata Fortress (fourth to fifth centuries) is also on Gagarina Square in the center of town.

Bichvinta (Pitsunda)

This village is on a promontory of the Black Sea Coast, 14 km (8.7 miles) southeast of Gagra on the M27, and another 13 km (eight miles) southeast after the turnoff at the village of Alakhadze. The road immediately into town is called the Monks' Avenue; the local monks planted the trees there as a penance.

Bichvinta means "pine grove" in Georgian. Pitsunda, as the town is known in Russian, comes from the Greek word for pine (*pitus*). In whatever language, the name refers to one of this resort's most distinctive features: the world's largest single grove of a unique species of indigenous pine (*Pinues pithysa*). The grove stretches along the shingle and sand beach for seven km (4.3 miles) and is a superb place to put down your towel, smell the pine needles, and get out of the sun. The beach season lasts from May until the end of October. The town itself has a harbor from which you can take boat trips to other spots along the coast. All in all, with its beach, large number of sunny days, flower and tree-lined paths, and tenth-century church, Bichvinta was one of the most sought-after resort towns on the coast.

Greeks from Miletus first established a settlement here in 300 BC, calling it Pitiunt. Between 105 and 90 BC the town was conquered by Mithradates VI, King of Pontus, who ruled it until he was ousted by the Romans in 65 BC. The town was completely destroyed by Heniochi pirates before the Romans made it a garrison in the second century AD. In AD 55 St. Andrew and Simon the Canaanite came to

Bichvinta, bringing Christianity to the coast. Their visit predates St. Nino's missionary work by some 272 years, but it was not until the sixth century that Justinian I finally converted the Abkhazian populace to Christianity. In 551 he ordered built in Bichvinta a three-aisled Byzantine-style cathedral dedicated to St. Sophia. (Foundation walls and floor mosaics of this church have been excavated to the southwest of the tenth-century Mother of God Church.) During Byzantine domination of the region, Bichvinta was made a diocese, thus establishing the city as one of the centers of Christianity in the Caucasus. At the beginning of the ninth century the Abkhazian church cut its ties with Byzantium and put itself under the jurisdiction of the Catholicos (Primate) in Mtskheta. This shift of allegiance is reflected in the architecture of the period, in which classic forms borrowed from Constantinople are integrated with or sometimes replaced by elements of the Georgian style. Bichvinta remained the seat of the Abkhazian patriarchs for almost 100 years. With subsequent Turkish dominance, Bichvinta lost its former importance. In 1882 Bichvinta came under the jurisdiction and authority of the Akhali Atoni (Novy Afon) Monastery.

THE CHURCH OF THE MOTHER OF GOD
Located in the center of town, within a walled close, this church, built in the late tenth century and restored in 1869, is the most important monument from the time of the Abkhazian Kingdom. It is a cruciform cupola structure with an elongated east-west axis. In the west are two pairs of detached columns. Two of these columns, along with pendentives in the east, support the cupola drum whose 12 narrow windows illuminate the interior. The interior is generous and well-proportioned, with excellent acoustics. In 1972 an East German firm built an organ with 4,000 pipes for the church. In the west is a narthex with a gallery above it. Fresco fragments remain in the narthex, but everything else was whitewashed in the 19th century. The eastern façade shows three semicircular apses, the central one most defined by its great width. The masonry of the walls reveals the Byzantine method of alternate layers of stone and brick.

Lake Ritsa

Driving southeast on the M27, just beyond the turnoff to Bichvinta is the village of Bzyb. A left-hand turnoff from Bzyb leads onto the A309, also known as the Ritsa Avenue. Here, there's an excellent four-columned domed church of the tenth century, particularly noteworthy for the quality of the ornamentaion on the arches of the windows. This turnoff is marked by a sign to Ritsa, which is 41 km (25.4 miles)

NOSTALGIA

*E*very summer from earliest childhood I had spent several months at my grandfather's house in the village. And always when I was up there in the mountains, I felt homesick—not so much for home itself as for the city. How I longed to return to the city and inhale once again that particularly city smell of dust fused with the odor of gasoline and rubber. I find it difficult to understand now, but in those days I would gaze nostalgically in the direction of the setting sun, comforted by the knowledge that our city lay there to the west, just beyond the soft and rounded contours of the mountain. And all the while I would be counting the days till the end of vacation.

Then, when we would finally return home to the city, I remember the extraordinary lightness in my legs as I took my first joyful steps on the asphalt pavement. At the time, I attributed this sensation to the smoothness of the paved city streets, but it was probably due more than anything else to my endless walks along mountain paths, to the fresh air of the mountains, and to the simple and nutritious food we ate in the village.

Nowadays, no matter where I am, I never feel a trace of that eager and joyous longing for the city. On the contrary, I have begun to miss my grandfather's house more and more. Perhaps this is because I can no longer return to it: the old people have passed away and all their children have moved to the city, or at least closer to it. But in those years when the house still belonged to our family I was always too busy to spend much time there. It was as if I were keeping it in reserve, to be visited sometime in the future. And now that there's no one there to visit, I cannot help feeling deprived, as if I have somehow been cut off from my roots.

Even though I seldom visited my grandfather's house, it helped me from afar by its very existence. The smoke from its hearth, the generous shade of its trees—everything about it made me bolder and more self-confident. I was almost invulnerable because a part of my life, my roots, lived and thrived in the mountains. And when a man is aware of his roots and has some sense of continuity in his life, he can direct it more wisely and generously.

Fazil Iskander, The Goatibex Constellation, *translated by Helen Berlingame* away. The road, which runs parallel to the Bzyb River and later one of its tributaries, the Geggi River, goes through some of the most magnificent forests and gorgeous natural settings in Georgia. At the two-km (one-mile) point, above the road a beautiful waterfall cascades down the smooth limestone cliff. A legend relates: "Once upon a time a beautiful maiden named Amra ('Sun' in Abkhazian) was herding goats on the mountain. Suddenly an evil water nymph of the Bzyb River, stung by Amra's beauty, attacked her and tried to throw her off the cliff. Amra began to cry. Hearing her sobs, Amra's beloved Adgur came running and chased the nymph away. Amra, however, was so shaken by the experience that her tears still flow from the rocks."

At the 13-km (eight-mile) point is **Blue Lake** (Adzia-vitsva in Abkhazian), 100 meters (328 feet) above sea level in a karst crater fed by underground springs. The water is, in fact, a deep blue. The lake is 200 sq. meters (2,200 sq. feet) in area and 15 meters (49 feet) deep, reaching a maximum depth of 25 meters (82 feet). The water is cold, never rising above 7°–12° C (45°–54° F). Beyond the lake, the road runs along the gorge of the Geggi River. The surrounding mountains are covered in forests of box and yew. Here the yellow waters of the Geggi and the blue of the Upshara River flow side by side along the gorge, barely mixing.

The road continues in zigzags up through the Upsharsky Canyon until reaching Lake Ritsa, 950 meters (3,117 feet) above sea level. The sight, though initially marred by the parking lot and tourist facility in front of the approach, is superb, especially once you've taken one of the paths around the lake into the woods. The lake is flanked by densely forested mountains: Pshegishkha (2,222 meters/7,290 feet) in the west and southwest, Atsetuka (2,542 meters/8,340 feet) and Agapsta (3,263 meters/10,705 feet) in the north, and the spurs of the Rikhva Range in the east and south. The area of the lake is 1.27 sq. km (0.49 sq. miles) and it has a depth of approximately 130 meters (426.5 feet). Its maximum length is 2,500 meters (8,202 feet); the width ranges from 275 meters (902 feet) to 870 meters (2,854 feet).

The water is cold, never rising above 15°C (59°F). Boat excursions can be arranged at the tourist facility or at one of the docks. The tourist facility has a cafeteria and restaurant, but if ever there was a time to pack a picnic, this is it.

Gudauta

Fifty km (31 miles) southeast of Gagra and 44 km (27 miles) northwest of Sokhumi on the M27, Gudauta is a splendid resort town situated on a slightly raised plateau overlooking a small bay of the Black Sea. Its sandy beach on the eastern portion of the shore is one of the best along the entire Abkhazian coast. The excellent subtropical climate is responsible for the citrus, tea, and tobacco production that flourishes here.

Archaeologists have discovered prehistoric sites in Gudauta, as well as first-century AD remains of the Abazghi tribe, the forefathers of the Abkhazians. In the 13th and 14th centuries, Italian merchants turned Gudauta into a trading center, calling it **Cavo di Busco** or "palm harbor." The present name comes from the Gudou River that passes through the town.

Five km (three miles) due north on the ring road that goes to Achandara is the village of **Likhny**. This village is an important part of Abkhazian history. Until 1863 it served as the seat of the Abkhazian rulers, the Shervashidze Princes. An important architectural complex here consists of the ruins of the Shervashidzes' palace, a tenth–11th-century cruciform-cupola church akin to the Mother of God church at Bichvinta, and a belltower. Particularly noteworthy are the surviving 14th-century frescoes in the church which are a supreme example of the artistry of western Georgian fresco painting. A depiction of the comet of 1066 with a notation of the exact date has provided an additional clue to the age of the structure. While in Likhny don't miss seeing the Lime of Truth, a tree hundreds of years old under which Abkhazian nobility traditionally dispensed justice. The local market of this village is alive with a panoply of distinctive colors, sounds, and smells. From Likhny, proceed north on the ring road to Duripsh and Achandara. These two villages are home to many of the 100-year-old Abkhazians who are part of a famous choir of centenarians (*see* page 236).

Akhali Atoni (Novy Afon)

Located 70 km (43.4 miles) southeast of Gagra and 24 km (14.9 miles) northwest of Sokhumi, Akhali Atoni is a resort on the Black Sea Coast nestled under the lush Iveriis Hill (350 meters/1,148 feet). The Psyrtskha River flows nearby, and the salubrious subtropical climate produces not only a bathing season of six or seven months but an abundance of olives, citrus, almonds, and grapes.

The site has been inhabited from the earliest times and traces of many peoples are evident on the southern slope of the Iveriis Hill. In the late sixth century the hilltop citadel, Anacopia, became the seat of the Byzantine rulers of Abkhazia. Also on the hilltop are the ruins of walls, towers, and a church of the seventh to eighth centuries from what had been the largest fortress on the eastern coast of the Black Sea. The church, restored in the 11th to 12th centuries, contains interesting tombs with Byzantine designs. In 756, when Leon I became king of an independent duchy of Abkhazia, he chose Anacopia as his capital.

The name Akhali Atoni (Novy Afon or New Athos) comes from the monastery built on Atonis Hill in 1875. Monks from the former Russian monastery Hagios

Panteleimon (Hagios Rossikon) of Mt. Athos, Greece, received land from Tsar Alexander III in 1874 for the project. Their New Athos consisted of a Byzantine-style, five-domed cathedral with a belltower dedicated to the Martyr Pentilemon, built in 1900 on the donated monastery grounds consisting of 14,400 hectares (36,000 acres). The donation was part of a Tsarist government program to create monasteries in Abkhazia to strengthen its influence on the Black Sea Coast. Originally inhabited by 720 monks, Akhali Atoni became one of the richest monasteries in Russia. After the revolution the monks' lands were nationalized as the Abkhazia Collective Farm. Many of the buildings are used today as sanatoria, and the cathedral was turned into a museum, which you can visit.

Also in the precincts of the monastery is the ninth–tenth century Church of Simon the Canaanite, built on the ruins of a fourth-century church and restored in 1882. This cruciform-domed church is in keeping with western Georgian churches of the period and served as a mausoleum for clerical dignitaries. It is dedicated to Simon the Canaanite, the apostle who came here in AD 55 with Saint Andrew and is revered as having brought Christianity to Abkhazia. For those who want to get the full flavor of the minestrone of peoples and interests that have passed through here, go down to the grounds of the Primorski (Seaside) Sanatorium to see a 13th-century Genoese tower.

The Akhali Atoni Caves (also called the Iveriis or Anakopia Karst Caves), 16 Chanba Street, are a major tourist attraction of Akhali Atoni and a must for all those fascinated by stalagmites and stalactites. These caves were discovered in 1961 and opened to the public in 1975. Visitors descend by a miniature electric train to the cave complex, which covers 40,000 sq. meters (144,000 sq. feet). Nine large cave halls measure up to 100 meters (328 feet) long and 40–60 meters (131–197 feet) high. You go in a guided tour from one to the other by means of paths and bridges to the strains of piped-in music. Take a sweater, as the temperature below ground is 12° C (53° F). The tour lasts an hour and a half.

Sokhumi

Sokhumi, with a population of 111,700 as of the beginning of 1993, is the capital of the Abkhazian Autonomous Republic and will most likely serve as your base for travels in the region. It is linked to other towns along the Black Sea Coast in Abkhazia by the excellent M27 highway, which also links it to Zugdidi in Samegrelo (105 km/65 miles), Kutaisi in Imereti (208 km/129 miles) and Tbilisi in Kartli, the capital of Georgia (444 km/275 miles). Regular flights to Sokhumi used to leave from most major cities and Comet hydrofoils used to ply the coast back and forth,

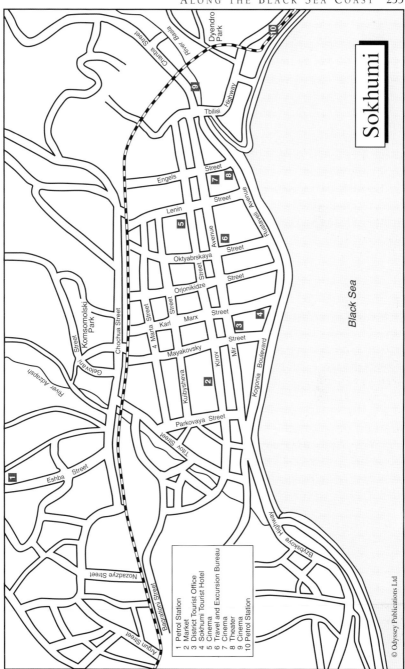

Sokhumi

Black Sea

Dyendro Park

River Besla

Oltanba Street

Tbilisi Highway

9

Engels Street

7 8

Lenin Street

5

Oktyabrskaya Street

Rustaveli Avenue

Avenue

6

Street

Orjonikidze Street

Street

Komsomolski Park

Geloveni Street

Chochua Street

Street

4 Marta Street

Karl Marx Street

Street

3 4

Street

Mayakovsky

Kirov

Mir

Kogonia Boulevard

River Adzapsh

2

Kuibysheva Street

Parkovaya Street

Titov Street

1

Eshba Street

Bagration Street

Nozadzye Street

Bzybskoye Highway

Argun Street

1 Petrol Station
2 Market
3 District Tourist Office
4 Sokhumi Tourist Hotel
5 Cinema
6 Travel and Excursion Bureau
7 Cinema
8 Theater
9 Cinema
10 Petrol Station

© Odyssey Publications Ltd

stopping at Batumi, Poti, Sokhumi, Gagra, and, in Russia, Adler and Sochi. Cruise ships also used to put in at Sokhumi. Many originated in Odessa and stopped in Sokhumi before going on to Batumi.

Sokhumi is between the broad Bay of Sokhumi and the Sokhumi Hill (201 meters/659 feet), with the Basla (Besletka) River running through it. It's a large but green and congenial resort town with a superb climate. Lying in the same latitude as Nice, it has a mean annual temperature of 15° C (50° F) and approximately 220 sunny days a year. You're certain to enjoy the sea breezes and sunshine between April and November.

Legend has it that the city was founded by Castor and Pollux, the Dioscuri, twin sons of Zeus and Leda and among the heroes who sailed with Jason to Colchis in search of the Golden Fleece. The archaeological record shows that a trading colony called Dioscuris was established here by Greeks from Miletus in the fifth century BC. The ruins of an acropolis and other dwellings from the ancient city now lie underwater in the bay. Archaeological investigations continue to bring new artifacts to light, some of which can be seen in the Abkhazian State Museum. Scuba divers keen to explore this Georgian Atlantis would do best to contact the Georgian Academy of Sciences (*see* page 217). The town, although destroyed in pre-Christian times by the Heniochi tribe, was continuously inhabited through the first century AD when the Romans established a fortified military camp here. Known as Sebastopolis to the Romans and Tschumi to the Georgians, the town in subsequent years was attacked and conquered by Byzantines, Arabs, and Georgians. Modifications to the fortress were carried out by each successive group. The Turks took control in 1578 and ruled for over 200 years.

In the 18th century the Abkhazians attempted to throw off Turkish domination and many assaults were launched against the fortress which the Turks called Su-Khum-Kale (Water-Sand Fortress). Not until the Russians took over Abkhazia in 1810 were the Turks dislodged. In 1877, the Turks reconquered Sokhumi but were again defeated by the Russians and forced to leave the city during the Russo-Turkish War of 1877–78. The present city with its broad, tree-lined avenues attracts tourists mainly because of the superb subtropical climate, and not because of the monuments of its rich and varied history, few of which remain.

Sokhumi Fortress (also called Dioscurias Fortress) was built in the second century BC on the ruins of the city of Dioscuria. It is at the end of Rustaveli Avenue on the sea. It was rebuilt many times, but only the remains of one defensive tower are visible. Even that has been partially incorporated into the Restaurant Dioscurias, which stands on the site. While the remains themselves are not terribly impressive, the view from the restaurant is. Here is the best place to sit and ruminate on the course of empire, on the ambitions of the Greek colonizers whose vestiges are now lapped by the waves.

SIGHTS OF SOKHUMI

The Fortress of King Bagrat is located on a mountain in the southeastern part of the city. Offering a magnificent view of the city and bay, this ivy-covered ruin was constructed by either King Bagrat III (975–1014) or Bagrat IV (1027–1072). Drive up Gory Bagrat Street, which branches off Tscheljuskin Street and rises 600 meters (1,969 feet) to the top. The trip past little villas perched on the hillside evokes the early days of the French Riviera when painters like Léger, Cocteau, and Chagall could hole up for next to nothing to paint. You can't help but feel all the same potential for creation here.

The Bridge over the Basla (the Besledski Most or the Venetian Bridge), six km (3.7 miles) to the northeast of the city along Chanba Street was constructed in the tenth–12th centuries and is a masterpiece of medieval bridge construction. It is 13 meters (42.6 feet) long and varies in width from five to seven meters (16.4 to 23 feet). It can still sustain a weight of eight tons. It is unclear whether the bridge was built by Venetians—hence one of its names—or by locals. A trip here would be most easily justified by aficionados of engineering history.

The Abkhazian State Museum exhibits paleolithic and neolithic finds as well as some very interesting paleontological remains. If you read Russian, many of the historical displays with ethnographic materials will help your understanding of the history of western Georgia. The prize of the collection is a marble stela of a woman and two children, found underwater in 1953 near the Old Dioscuris and probably dating back to the second half of the fifth century BC. Some think it might have come to Colchis as an import from Athens; others hold that it is Colchian.

The Botanical Gardens of the Academy of Sciences of Georgia were founded in 1840 by General Rajewski, a friend of Pushkin's. Destroyed by the Turks in 1878 and restored in 1894, the gardens comprise five hectares (12 acres) with four ponds for water plants such as the Giant Amazon Water Lily. They contain more than 4,000 subtropical plant specimens. A wonderful spot for a leisurely stroll.

The Forest Park of the Sokhumi Mountains is in the northeast part of the city on the slopes of the mountain rising 210 meters (689 feet) above the bay. This 32-hectare (79-acre) park was built by Akadi Ivanovich Geladze, the First Secretary of Abkhazia from 1941 to 1951. A cable car, an ornamental staircase, and a road flanked by oleander and magnolia all lead to a platform from which you can get unquestionably the best view of the city. A radio broadcast tower is nearby, and on the platform itself is Amza (Moon) Restaurant. This spot is Sokhumi's answer to Piazzale Michelangelo in Florence.

The **Monkey Colony** is on the slopes of Mt. Trapetskaya. This institute was founded in 1927 under the auspices of the USSR Academy of Sciences. The entire institute is now home to more than 7,000 monkeys.

The **Abkhazian Dramatic Theater**, corner of Engels Street and Rustaveli Avenue was built in 1952 and is now the home of the Abkhazian National Theater Company, founded in 1929. Both Georgian and Abkhazian troupes used to perform here, and earphones were available for hearing the performances translated into Russian. Try to hear a performance by Nartaa, the Abkhazian choir whose members are between the ages of 70 and 130. They, and other choirs made up of Abkhazians over 100 years old, are phenomenal and mustn't be missed. They can also be seen at the Summer Theater in the square off Kirov Street. If no performance is listed, you might try going to the outdoor café across from the national theater. This is a favorite hangout of the Georgian *mokhutsi* (old people) and someone might be able to tell you where they will be gathering informally for a night of drink and song. If no choir of old Abkhazians is performing—and you feel that a trip to the region would be incomplete without hearing and seeing this amazing phenomenon—you could make a special trip to the small villages of Otkhara, Khuap, Duripsh, and Achandara that are home to many of them. These are northeast of Gudauta and Likhny.

Mokvi

Six km (3.7 miles) southwest of Sokhumi on the M27 is the village of Kelasuri. Make a left turn off the M27 onto an asphalted road that runs parallel to the Kelasuri River and continue for another six km (3.7 miles). Here you will see the first fragments of **The Great Wall of Abkhazia** first mentioned in the writings of Procopius of Caesarea, a Byzantine historian of the sixth century. It was built to protect the region from incursions by the northern tribes, but it is not known who ordered the construction. The wall runs 160 km (99 miles) from the sea to the interior, largely along the bank of the Kelasuri, which was the ancient trade route linking Abkhazia and the Northern Caucasus. Fragments of varying lengths, widths, and heights can be seen all along the way, with as many pieces incorporated into the homes of the peasants of the neighborhood as are still standing.

Nineteen km (11.8 miles) from Sokhumi along the M27 on the bank of the Kodori River is **Dranda**. The cathedral of this village, one km (0.6 miles) on the road from the central square, is an important example of ninth-century western Georgian architecture. Long believed to be a central-domed structure of the Jvari type, its ground plan is significantly different from its illustrious predecessor. The absence of the four deep conches surrounding the central cupola room, the presence of a western narthex and three apses in the east, and its brick and stone construction with no bas-relief decoration on the façade all work to render Dranda more a creative fusion of Byzantine and central Georgian models than a pure Jvari type. The church was restored by monks from Akhali Atoni in 1871 but was badly damaged by the Turks in 1877 and 1878. Restored again in 1886, it was consecrated the Uspensko-Dransky Monastery.

The drive from Dranda to Mokvi on the M27 is through an impressive array of tea plantations. Tea grows in Georgia in Abkhazia, Samegrelo, Guria, Imereti, and Ajara. It's harvested from April to November. The large sacks tied to workers' waists or lying in the field hold 20 kilos. Each worker can harvest between 40 and 70 kilos a day. Don't be bashful about pulling over to the side of the road and walking into a plantation to watch how the tea is harvested. You'll be welcome.

Forty km (24.8 miles) from Sokhumi and 13 km (eight miles) before Ochamchire is the village of **Arady**. Turn left off the M27 before crossing the Mokva River and immediately left again when the new road branches. Follow this road for eight km (five miles) to the village of Mokvi. Turn right after the transformer station, continue 500 meters (1,640 feet) across the bridge over the Dvab River, and continue another 500 meters (1,640 feet) to **Mokvi Cathedral.** Set at the confluence of the Mokva and Dvab rivers in a beautiful compound planted with magnolia, cypress, pine, and cedar, Mokvi Cathedral was founded by the west Georgian King Leon III (957–967) in the middle of his reign as the seat of the archbishop.

The construction of the cathedral and the establishment of the Mokvi diocese of western Georgia was King Leon's response to certain political, as well as religious, needs. It signaled his break with Byzantium, the consolidation of his state, and the first steps toward a rapprochement with eastern Georgia that culminated in the submission of the Abkhazian Catholicos to the authority of the Catholicos in Mtskheta. This unification of the western and eastern Georgian churches did not diminish the importance of Mokvi, which remained a religious and cultural center throughout the feudal period.

Mokvi Cathedral is a five-aisled, central-domed structure.whose exterior simplicity and interior harmony distill a quiet shimmering solemnity throughout the space. The cupola is supported by four freestanding piers. Three ambulatories with galleries above run along the north, west, and south sides. Three apses are in the east, the middle one having been decorated with mosaics in conformity with the Byzantine tradition. The interior is particularly well illuminated by numerous windows in the chapels and galleries as well as 12 in the cupola drum. During the reign of David the Builder (1089–1125), the interior walls were decorated with frescoes which remained intact until the end of the 18th century. In the first half of the 19th century, however, the cathedral fell into disrepair. It was not until Prince Mikhail

Shervashidze, who was born in Mokvi, began restoration in the 1840s that it functioned once again as a church. The Prince was buried here in 1865. A belltower standing in the complex finishes the ensemble. Mokvi Cathedral is a stunning architectural and historical monument situated in an isolated and beautiful spot.

Ochamchire

Fifty-three km (32.8 miles) southeast of Sokhumi along the M27 is Ochamchire, and probably the last town along the Black Sea Coast that you'll visit while in Abkhazia. After Ochamchire, the M27 goes inland to Zugdidi, the capital of Samegrelo, crossing the Enguri River, the natural boundary between Abkhazia and Samegrelo. Ochamchire is one of the major agricultural centers of Abkhazia, with tea, tobacco, and citrus leading the list of products. It's a sleepy town without great interest to the traveler, reminiscent of a place like Fuengirola on the Costa del Sol before the building boom. Small, brightly painted homes line the road, each with a lovely garden and many with a profusion of colossal roses. Thirteen km (eight miles) from Ochamchire on a bad road to the village of Agu-Bedia is the Cathedral of Bedia, built in the tenth century by King Bagrat III.

Samegrelo

The province of Samegrelo (Mingrelia or Megrelia in Russian) covers an area of 5,394 sq. km (2,083 sq. miles) and has a population of 490,000. It is the home of the Mingrelians, a tribe of Georgian people who speak Megruli, one of the languages that belong to the southern Caucasian language group known as Kartvelian. Some travelers consider them the most beautiful people of the Caucasus. You will be able to decide for yourself, for they can often be distinguished by their blond hair and blue eyes, a rarity among Georgians as a whole. Their province occupies the largest part of historical Colchis, the land to which Jason and his Argonauts sailed in search of the Golden Fleece in the late Bronze Age (13th century BC). Colchis is the name by which this land was known to the ancient Greeks and to the indigenous Georgian tribes who lived there. The Kartlians of eastern Georgia called this region Egrisi.

The boundaries as well as the names of this region have changed many times throughout history, reflecting both the fortunes of the foreign conquerors who coveted the territory as an important trade route to India and the aspirations of local peoples and princes for hegemony. In the pre-Christian era, Colchis encompassed present-day Abkhazia, Guria, and Ajara. By the sixth century BC it was a powerful kingdom whose political center was at the Rioni River. The silver coins they minted, called *kolkhuri tetri,* circulated widely. The kingdom broke up through successive bouts of expansionism by Persians, Greeks, and Romans. In the second century AD the region was dominated by Laz kings and became known to the Byazantine world as the Kingdom of Lazica. (The Laz are a Georgian people from just north of the mouth of the Chorokhi River, who appeared in western Georgia in the second half of the first century BC). The capital of this kingdom was Tsikhe Goji (today's Nakalakevi; *see* page 243).

By the sixth century the Kingdom of Lazica had weakened, and Byzantine and Persian jockeying for the region came to a head in 512 with a war that continued for 20 years and turned all of western Georgia into a battlefield. Only at the end of the eighth century was the Abkhazian King Leon II able to liberate western Georgia from Byzantium's influence. By the 12th century a united east and west Georgia was the strongest state in the Middle East. This united Georgia consisted of many *saeristavoebi* or duchies. The duchy of Odishi, comprising much of present-day Samegrelo, lay between the Tekhury River to the southeast and the Kodory River to the northwest. The *eristavi* or duke of this region was Bedian Dadiani, the patriarch of a dynastic family that had ruled in the region since at least 1046 and continued to do so for more than 700 years.

In the 1460s, the Turkish threat began to plague Georgia. For the next 400 years, although ostensibly independent, Odishi had to pay large tributes to the Turks in money and slaves. Sometime in the 1550s the duchy of Odishi became an independent principality and a Dadiani descendant took the title of sovereign. Although Odishi reached the apogee of its power in the 17th century under the reign of Levan Dadiani II, it was not until 1774, with the help of the Russians, that the Turks were expelled and all subservience to them ended.

In 1804, the principality of Mingrelia came under Russia's protection and the reigning Prince Grigol Dadiani became a vassal of Alexander I. The relationship between the reigning Dadianis and the Tsar continued until 1857, when the Russian government abolished the Mingrelian Principality. That made Princess Katherine Dadiani (née Chavchavadze, the daughter of the Georgian poet Alexander Chavchavadze; sister of Nina who was married to the Russian writer Alexander Griboyedov), "the last Queen of Samegrelo." Although she went to St. Petersburg to appeal the decision of Alexander II, it was to no avail and the territory was united with Russia in 1867. In 1921, the region became a part of the Soviet Union along with the rest of Georgia. It is now, of course, part of independent Georgia.

The present boundaries of the Samegrelo province are the Enguri River in the north separating it from Abkhazia, the village of Jvari in the northeast separating it from Svaneti, the village of Abasha in the east separating it from Imereti, the Maltakva River in the south separating it from Guria, and of course the Black Sea in the west. The region excels in the production of tea, paper, citrus, and wine. Large-scale cultivation of tea began in 1928 with the allocation of 1,500 hectares (3,075 acres) of land for a tea plantation. Today tea plantations cover over 20,000 hectares (50,000 acres), which represents one third of the acreage of tea plantations in Georgia. The annual harvest of tea in 1989 was 140,943 tons, which fell to an annual harvest of 2,545 tons in 1996. Tea had made many Mingrelians rich, but as you travel through the countryside the once impressive homes and private plots are showing the same wear and tear as the entire country as a result of the war in Abkhazia.

Rukhi

This large fortress is the first monument to greet you as you enter Samegrelo, since it stands on the left bank of the Enguri River as you cross over from Abkhazia on the M27. It was built by Levan Dadiani II in 1636, and withstood every siege for nearly 100 years. Finally, the Turks managed to breach its defenses and capture it in 1725. In 1769, the Turks fled the forts at Rukhi and Anaklia at the mouth of the Enguri when the Russians came to Georgia's aid under the leadership of General Totleben. The fortress occupies 5,000 sq. meters (18,000 sq. feet) and has walls three to four meters (10–13 feet) thick and seven to eight meters (23–26 feet) high. Its four towers (12–14 meters/39–46 feet high) still stand. From the upper portion of the fort you have an excellent view of the Enguri Gorge.

Zugdidi

Zugdidi, population 51,700 and 110 meters (361 feet) above sea level, is the administrative center of Samegrelo. Located in the northern section of the Colchian depression only 30 km (18.6 miles) from the Black Sea, Zugdidi has a lush subtropical climate with palm trees growing in profusion. Coming from Kutaisi or points farther east, you'll feel you've entered another land and the heady, scented, warm air will caress your soul. Zugdidi is a natural jumping-off place for driving to Mestia in Svaneti, up to Sokhumi in Abkhazia, or down to Batumi in Ajara. In the 17th century the city became the residence of the Dadiani family, which had ruled Samegrelo since the 12th century, when it was known as Odishi. The city's fortunes were wrapped up with those of the Dadianis and the region as a whole. As a result of the war in Abkhazia, the city has 60,000–70,000 refugees, a situation that is

A young boy harvests tea on a plantation in Samegrelo

trying the patience of the populace. As the city closest to the border crossing with Abkhazia, it is the place in Georgia that feels the effects of the conflict most continually. Travelers should not walk alone through the city at night.

The Historical and Ethnographic Museum is at the end of David the Builder Street. Past the large stadium is the Dadiani Palace, which was converted into a museum in 1921. This wonderfully eccentric amalgam of neo-Gothic castle and Venetian palazzo dates to the 17th century and was extended in the 19th. The collection contains many items of archaeological and ethnographic interest, including an excellent collection of antique coins from Rome, Byzantium, and Georgia. The greatest treasures are the gold and silver coins from ancient Colchis. A valuable collection of manuscripts, pagan statues, agricultural implements, weapons, native dress, and applied arts from Georgia and other parts of the world can also be seen. Studying reproductions of fresco fragments and photographs of surrounding churches with their accompanying texts (in Russian) will help to put some of your later journeying into context.

The most interesting aspect of the collection relates to the Dadiani family itself. Princess Salome Dadiani, daughter of David Dadiani (the last ruler of Mingrelia) and his wife Katherine Chavchavadze, married Achille Charles Louis Napoleon Murat, the grandson of Napoleon's sister Caroline and his Marshal Joachim Murat. When the couple decided to move to their estate near Zugdidi they took with them some personal effects of Napoleon including the Emperor's death mask, one of three cast in bronze from the plaster-of-paris model made on the day of his death in 1821. The mask is on view as well as his bookcase, armchairs, and his portrait. Princess Caroline Dadiani's brother, Andria, born in 1850, seems also to have had an interesting life. A great chess master, he traveled extensively to tournaments and published a book on his moves. Exhibits of some of his personal effects, as well as those

The death mask of Napoleon in the Dadiani Palace in Zugdidi

of other family members, are on view. Chess has long been a game at which the Georgians particularly excel: Zugdidi's own Nona Gaprindashvili, the world chess champion among women, is also honored in the museum. The building itself is lovely: be sure to see the magnificent 100-year-old giant magnolia in the museum's garden as well as the intricately carved wooden ceiling above the second-floor veranda. The latter supposedly dates from the 17th century. Unfortunately, at the time of writing the museum is closed, but it will certainly reopen once greater prosperity has returned to the country.

On the grounds of the palace are a small family church built in 1838 and the shell of a second palace that was destroyed in 1854.

In the park adjoining the grounds of the Dadiani Palace are the 26-hectare (64-acre) **Botanical Gardens**. Established in 1840 by Katherine Chavchavadze Dadiani, the collection now numbers over 1,000 plant species. It is a branch of the Tbilisi Botanical Gardens of the Georgian Academy of Sciences and is a most fragrant and calm spot for a postprandial perambulation. Outside the gardens to the right of the entrance is an outdoor cafe that serves excellent Turkish coffee.

Khobi

Twenty-seven km (16.7 miles) southeast of Zugdidi on the M27 is the village of Khobi. The road takes you through the Colchian lowlands, a flat fertile plain that stretches as far as the eye can see. At the 28.7-km point (17.8-mile), just beyond the bridge over the Khobi River, turn left and continue approximately five km (three miles) to the ruins of the Khobi Monastery. Legend has it that it was founded in AD 554. The monastery complex houses a cathedral built at the end of the 13th century that features frescoes and inscriptions from the 13th, 14th, and 17th centuries. A belltower and defensive walls from the late Middle Ages can be found here as well as the ruins of an 18th- and 19th-century palace. The cathedral was the ancestral church of the Dadianis and is distinctive in the way that its exterior gives no indication of the cruciform plan of the interior. Return to the M27 the way you came.

From Khobi another 12 km (7.4 miles) on the M27 brings you to Senaki (previously called Tskhakaya). Continue 18 km (11 miles) northeast on the road to the village of Gegechkori and you'll come across the **Nakalakevi Fortress** on the slopes of a hill. This was the capital of Lazica-Egrisi between the fourth and eighth centuries. The stone walls (one meter/3.3 feet thick by three to four meters/9.8–13 feet high) enclose an area of 20 hectares (50 acres). Within this enclosure are the ruins of churches of the fourth and fifth centuries and remains of a palace and a bathhouse. From the west side of the fortress a secret tunnel led to the river, a feature common in almost all fortified Georgian structures. Archaeologists are still at work on this site.

Poti

Poti is 32 km (19.8 miles) from Khobi via a small but decent road that joins the A305 after 17 km (10.5 miles), or 33 km (20.4 miles) along the A305 directly from Senaki. The approach to the town is along a beautiful tree-lined way (the Poti Highway) that welcomes you majestically, a stretch of road that will, in fact, make you feel as though you're proceeding up the endless drive of a huge chateau. There's no French *comte* at the end but instead the Rioni River. Crossing it brings you into Poti, a town whose name evolved from the Mingrelian name for the Rioni River and the town at its mouth, Pati. Some scholars believe that the ancient Greeks, hearing the local name Pati, Hellenized it for the sake of pronunciation to Phasis. Others hold that Phasis is a word indigenous to the region. Additionally, our name for that delectable fowl, the pheasant, derives from Phasis. The Greeks, having found these birds in great numbers at the mouth of the Phasis River, took them back to Europe and called them *phasianoi*, after the place where they'd been found.

The Greek association with Poti and the Rioni does not end here. In the 13th century BC, Jason and his Argonauts set off from Iolcos (Volos) in northern Thessaly in search of the Golden Fleece. They sailed across the Aegean Sea, through the Dardanelles (Hellespont) into the Sea of Marmara, and then up the Bosporus into the Black Sea (Euxine). Jason entered the Colchian realm of King Aeetes by rowing into the mouth of the Phasis River and hiding his ship, *Argo*, upriver. Apollonius of Rhodes (third century BC) wrote in his *Argonautica* that the palace of King Aeetes was on the north shore of the river whereas the Golden Fleece itself was in a sacred oak on the opposite bank. No one knows for sure where the palace stood, but both Poti and Kutaisi claim to be built over King Aeetes' capital, Aea. Some scholars believe that Aea refers to King Aeetes' entire realm; others still seek clues through excavation of sites like Vani (*see* page 217). In 1984 Tim Severin, the Irish explorer, recreated Jason's voyage in a replica of the *Argo* and proved that the journey was physically possible. His observations in Svaneti of gold-sifting techniques with sheep fleeces in the Enguri River gave further corroboration of the historical reality behind the myth.

A farmer cycles home along Poti Avenue

Indeed, throughout Georgia the Golden Fleece, Jason and the Argonauts, King Aeetes and his daughter Medea are known to every schoolchild not as the stuff of legend but as an important part of the country's cultural patrimony. Many Georgian women are named Medea. As we all know, Jason managed to obtain the Golden Fleece with Medea's help. After falling in love, the two sailed back to Iolcus where, with Medea's help, Jason took revenge against Pelias. The story ends badly, however: in Corinth, Jason divorced Medea and married Glauce, the daughter of Creon. To exact revenge on Jason, Medea sent a magic robe to Glauce as a wedding gift. The magic ointment on the robe burned Glauce and Creon to death. Travelers should perhaps heed the legend as a cautionary tale about trifling with the affections of Georgian women.

Poti, though the most important commercial port in Georgia, does not have much to offer the traveler. You can, however, make arrangements to board ferries here that go to Bulgaria, Greece, Israel, Italy, the Netherlands, Russia, Turkey, and Ukraine (*see* page 56 for more information). In the Central Square is a statue of the Mother of Colchis and one of the oldest theaters in Georgia. The commercial port is bustling and you can take a hydrofoil to Batumi or other towns along the coast. Alas, as far as Jason and his crew go, the only reference to them is the Argo Cafe which is housed in a mosaic ship modeled after Jason's 50-oared galley. It sits beached in Nikoladze Square. (Those interested in the contact between classical Greek civilization and Colchis will be impressed by a trip to the archaeological site of **Vani**, which should be done as a day trip out of Kutaisi (*see* page 217).

Continuing south along the A305 toward Kobuleti, the road runs for approximately 18 km (11 miles) parallel to the Colchian Nature Reserve and the magnificent Lake Paliastomi. This zone is a protected sanctuary for birds and wildlife. It ends at Supsa where the Gurian Range begins. (For more infomation on the current importance of Supsa as the site of a new oil terminal *see* page 249.) The province of Guria itself begins on the other side of the Maltakva River. Though Gigoleti is the first Gurian village, it is actually inhabited by a sect of Russian Protestants. Guria occupies 2,032 sq. km (785 sq. miles) and has a population of 158,000. Guria is the place to visit if you have a taste for politics. The Gurians have a great reputation for excelling at the Great Game. Indeed, the current president of Georgia, Eduard Shevardnadze, is a Gurian from the village of Mamati. Gurians are well known for speaking their minds and defending their views. If you speak Georgian or Russian, you can be assured of scintillating conversation at any bar or restaurant where Gurian villagers have gathered. Guria ends at the Chorokhi River where the Ajaran province begins.

Ajara

Founded on July 16, 1921, approximately five months after the Bolsheviks annexed Georgia, the province of Ajara covers an area of 3,000 sq. km (1,158 sq. miles). It has a population of 379,000, many of whom are Georgians of the Moslem faith. Lenin used the religious issue as the reason for creating this autonomous country. It was an interesting tactic coming from the head of an atheistic government and exemplifies the policy of divide and rule that the Bolsheviks exercised in Georgia.

Located in the southwest part of the country, Ajara is covered with the mountain ranges and foothills of the Lesser Caucasus, which protect the Ajaran coast from cold fronts coming in from the north and east. In the west the coast along the Black Sea is a strip of lowland that is topographically a continuation of the Colchian depression. In the south the republic shares a border with Turkey. With the explosion of trade with Turkey, the little Georgian border town of Sarpi is seeing a lot of activity as a continuous stream of Georgians and Turks cross back and forth. Some Georgians also go to visit relatives who live in a fairly large region south of the Chorokhi River, which belonged to Georgia before Lenin's deal with Ataturk that gave the land to Turkey. The Turkish province of Tao has many Georgian speakers and historic monuments—most notably the churches at Oshki, Oltisi, Ishkhani, and Parkhali. (If you count all the provinces now in Turkey that had at one time in history belonged to Georgia—Lazika, Tao, Klarjeti, Shavsheti, Kola, Artaani, Chrdili, Erusheti, Speri, Tortomi, Parkhali— the total area would be 34,000 sq. km/13,125 sq. miles.)

The climate of Ajara along the coast is humid and subtropical with an average temperature of 4°–6° C (38°–43° F) in January, and 20°–23° C (68°–74° F) in July. The foothills have a similar climate, but average temperatures are a few degrees cooler. The region is famous for the amount of rain it receives: 2,400–2,800 mm (94–109 inches) annually along the coast and in the foothills facing the sea.

The province is known for citrus and tea production as well as its oil refinery located in Batumi. Despite the number of rainy days, tourism has always been big here. Batumi, Kobuleti, Tsikhisdziri, and Makhindzhauri are important resorts for Georgians.

Ajara was one of the first regions in all Georgia to receive Christianity, largely through the missionary work of Andrew the First-Called in the first century. Throughout the feudal period Ajara had a thriving agricultural-based society with the land divided amongst small *khevi* or communities consisting of hamlets in the various gorges of the tributaries of the Ajaristskali River. This feudal society reached a high degree of culture in many of the arts, but was almost entirely destroyed when the region was invaded by the Turks for the first time in the 1080s and again in the 1570s. Turkish occupation lasted until the 19th century, and very little remains of the pre-Turk period. Despite the efforts of the Turks, however, the Ajars clung to Christianity until the end of the 18th century, by which time the relentless persecution of Christians caused the populace ultimately to leave for other parts of Georgia or convert.

During the Russo-Turkish War (1877–1878) Ajara joined Russia. In 1918 the Turks, taking advantage of Russian disillusionment with the First World War, marched once more into Ajara and seized Batumi. In that turbulent year a Georgian independent state was established, and only an agreement with the German Empire checked Turkish expansion. However, within a week of Germany losing the war and signing an armistice, 15,000 British troops marched into Batumi. They stayed less than two years. Reevaluating their position toward the Bolsheviks, the British pulled out of the South Caucasus completely, evacuating their last troops from Batumi on July 9, 1920. Ajara, along with the rest of Georgia, was annexed by the Bolsheviks in 1921. It now, of course, belongs to independent Georgia. Unlike South Ossetia and Abkhazia, this autonomous republic, under the iron leadership of Aslan Abashidze, has remained relatively peaceful and prosperous throughout the tumultuous years in the immediate post-Soviet period. By adopting a conciliatory strategy both with Gamsakhurdia when he was in power and later with Shevardnadze, Abashidze has managed to retain a good deal of control over Ajara's affairs, both economic and political.

Only five km (three miles) south of the Chorokhi River and 33 km (20.4 miles) north of Batumi, **Kobuleti** is the second largest town and health resort in Ajara. It is also the site of one of the oldest towns in Georgia, settled as early as the fifth century BC. The Italian missionary Archangelo Lamberti, who visited Georgia in the 17th century, is credited as the first person to mention the town. The beach here is among the best along the entire coast, with a stretch of black sand approximately 80 meters (262 feet) wide that slopes gently into the sea. A line of coniferous trees runs parallel to the sea, providing much needed shade on a hot day.

Kobuleti boasts a former Intourist hotel, the Kolkheti, superbly positioned right on the sea front. The views from the balconies are magnificent. The hotel itself, though grand by Georgian standards and certainly among the most comfortable you'll find, is lacking in charm. Nonetheless, if you're keen to take a break from touring and want nothing more than some time on the beach, Kobuleti is probably your best bet for a few days' rest.

Continuing south along the A305 to Batumi, the road climbs and winds up and down some steep hills that will remind you of the Corniche on the Côte d'Azur. Some little and not so little villas nestle on the hillsides with stupendous views. Cap Ferrat it's not, but when the Georgian economy picks up—watch out. Two places are worth a stop on the way to Batumi. **Tsikhisdziri** has the remains of a Byzantine fortress called Petra, constructed in the sixth century AD. The Georgian name means "fortress foundation," and its position on the cape is most evocative. Tsikhisdziri also has some of the most important citrus plantations in the entire country. The next village on the coast, just 18 km (11 miles) from Batumi, is **Chakvi**. This was the first place in Georgia where tea was cultivated. The Chakvi Tea-Growing State Farm has tours, and you can see how tea, citrus, bamboo, and tung tree plantations work. An excellent restaurant in the vicinity is Makhindzhauri in the village of the same name.

Batumi

Batumi, with a population of 137,700, is the capital of the Ajara Autonomous Republic. Only 20 km (12.4 miles) from the Georgian-Turkish border, it is also the most important port and resort on the southern portion of the Black Sea Coast. The Georgian name, Bat-om-i, comes from the first settlement's location on the left bank of the Bat River. Batumi was an important port from which the Romans set out to trade with other cities along the coast. In the fourth century the region was under the control of the Kingdom of Lazica, and in the sixth and seventh centuries it was a battlefield for the imperial aspirations of the Byzantines and Persians. Batumi's history largely mirrors that of Ajara as a whole: a flowering during the Middle Ages followed by devastation in the major Turkish invasion of the 16th century. The subsequent battle between Turks and Georgians for possession of Batumi continued on and off until the 19th century. Under Turkish domination, the city diminished in size and importance; by the beginning of the 19th century, Batumi had been reduced to a small Asiatic village of approximately 2,000 inhabitants.

As a result of the Russo-Turkish War of 1877–1878, Batumi became part of the Russian Empire and began to flourish again both as a city and a port. Between 1878 and 1886 it operated as a free port. In 1918, during the civil war in Russia, the Turks occupied Batumi again but were soon forced to withdraw. In that same year English troops occupied the city while the British tried to decide their policy in the South Caucasus. They left in July 1920. Only eight months later Noe Zhordania and his Menshevik government sailed into exile from Batumi, and the 11th Red Army conquered Georgia.

Modern Batumi is a city of parks with subtropical vegetation, broad beachfront, high-rise tourist hotels, shady avenues, an old town and market section, a sprinkling of 19th-century merchants' mansions, and a commercial port.

Unfortunately, with the economic challenges that Georgia is now facing, many of the gardens, parks, and fountains are not being tended as they once were. There is no city center proper: of the three main squares, Freedom Square (formerly Lenin

Square) serves primarily administrative functions. Except for a functioning mosque at 6 Chkalov Street, the old town bears few architectural signs of its Turkish past. The city plays an important part in the Georgian economy, refining and then forwarding the oil coming from Baku. (As early as the beginning of the century the Baku oil pipeline was extended to reach Batumi.). With the rapid development of Caspian oil by multinational companies, the pipeline between Baku and Batumi (or Suspa in Guria) is viewed as one of the more important potential sources of new revenue for Georgia. Unfortunately, the Baku-Batumi pipeline has been closed since 1988, and work is currently under way to restore it or replace it in order to handle this Caspian oil. Georgia sees the importance of this industry and plans to build an oil terminal off Supsa (Guria) which will have a storage capacity of 1.6 million barrels. There are also discussions with the Azerbaijan International Operating Company to build a new pipeline for later oil that will run through Tbilisi and on to the Turkish port of Ceyhan on the Mediterranean Sea. This later oil may average as much as 700,000 barrels per day and would be a windfall for Georgia in terms of transit fees and jobs. The city is also the center of an important agricultural region where tea and citrus reign.

The city has a former Intourist hotel overlooking the sea at 11 Ninoshvili Street that is now largely filled with refugees from the war in Abkhazia. Discounting the pollution that affects the entire Black Sea and makes swimming inadvisable, you can still have a pleasant beach holiday here. Paddle boats can be rented from vendors on the beach, as can chaises longues and umbrellas. The beach consists entirely of stones, so wear thongs. Toward the south part of the Primorsky Park are seven clay tennis courts.

SIGHTS OF BATUMI

Founded in 1966 by the Institute for Maritime Economy and Oceanography, the **Aquarium** gives you the chance to get acquainted with the principal fish and types of fauna found in the Black Sea. A wealth of information is also available on the Institute's work.

Batumi's answer to San Diego's Sea World, the **Dolphinarium** opened in 1974. Three times a day from May to November you can see the dolphins put through their paces, demonstrating their amazing capacity to help man in his exploration of the oceans. Each performance lasts half an hour.

Located at the end of Rustaveli Street, **The Young People's Park** was founded in 1881 and comprises 18 hectares (45 acres). Beside a lake, the park is home to many varieties of local trees and plants.

Situated in a nice old residential neighborhood, the small **Museum of Ajara** is only for those people obsessed with seeing everything a city has to offer. The

Modern Batumi is a city of parks and fountains

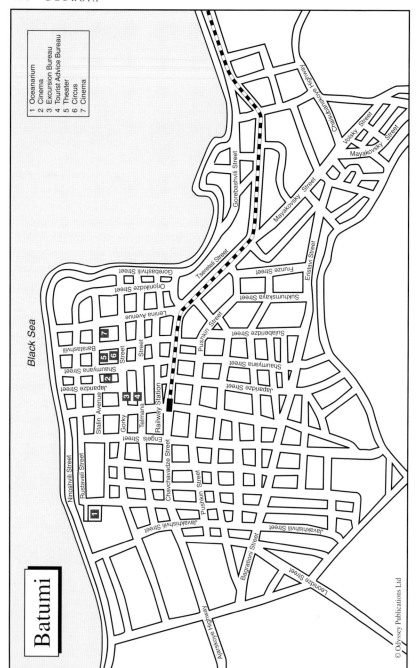

Batumi

Black Sea

1 Oceanarium
2 Cinema
3 Excursion Bureau
4 Tourist Advice Bureau
5 Theater
6 Circus
7 Cinema

exhibits give information about the natural history of the region and display weapons, tools, and native costumes. If you go, don't miss the tuna that weighed in at 516 kilograms (1,138 pounds).

The **Farmer's Market** at Market Square (formerly Kolkhoznaya) inhabits a hall larger than a football field, where 400–500 vendors sell a colorful assortment of spices, fruits, vegetables, and flowers, as well as meat, poultry, fish, and cheeses. If you're used to shopping at Harrod's, you might be a little put off, but if packaging isn't everything then you'll have no problem tasting and enjoying a remarkable assortment of produce. This is a great place to people watch. Don't leave without trying, with your coffee, as many as possible of the sweets that abound in amazing variety.

The **Octopus Café** is in the seaside park. This mosaic sculpture of an octopus by the famous

Batumi has an extensive beachfront

and fabulously wealthy Georgian sculptor Zurab Tzereteli (known as the first Georgian millionaire) houses a little café which serves light meals, coffee, and soft drinks. This is a good place to head if you're spending the day on the beach.

COFFEE

Batumi is known for making the best coffee in Georgia. This is probably due to the Turkish occupations. The best place to drink coffee is the outdoor cafe on Gogebashvili Street, just in front of the fishing port and next to the Second World War monument. You can't miss all the red and white umbrellas and the old sailors who stand around all day swapping stories and drinking cup after cup. The faces of these men are invariably fascinating. You can also get great cups of coffee at the cafe at 14 Gogebashvili Street. Also try the Oriental Sweet Shop at the southeast corner

A family enjoys khachapuri at a seaside café in Batumi

of Rustaveli and the former Lenin street. The elaborate stucco work of the interior alone is worth a visit.

Day Trips

The Botanical Gardens of the Academy of Sciences of Georgia are nine km (5.6 miles) out of town heading north. There's parking only on the lower level, but it's best to take a taxi and get off at the upper level another two km (1.2 miles) up the road. Using the entrance there allows you to walk downhill through the 113 hectares (279 acres) of gardens rather than uphill. It makes a big difference. The #101 bus from the train station goes to the lower entrance (as does the train). Get off at the last stop. Green Cape is the name given to this beautiful spot overlooking the sea by Professor Delfonse when he started cultivating subtropical plants in Chakvi in 1882. Professor Andrei Krasnov was much interested in the work being done in Chakvi and founded the Botanical Gardens in 1912. There are over 2,114 species of flowers and plants here. Between 1913 and 1917 the Australian department alone planted 52 kinds of eucalyptus. This is a glorious place and should not be missed. A little shop sells soft drinks and snacks near the upper entrance, but this would be a great place to enjoy a picnic.

The interior of the tenth-century Mokvi Cathedral

Meskheti and Javakheti

Located in southern Georgia, the area encompassed by these two historic provinces has gone by several names. To add to the confusion, both the borders and the possession of these two provinces have changed many times throughout a long and violent history, reflecting Georgia's fortunes as a conqueror in the South Caucasus or as the victim of foreign aggression. The area now known as Meskheti was called Samtskhe throughout most of its history. Both Samtskhe and Javakheti belonged to a larger principality called Samtskhe-Saatabago. At one point Samtskhe-Saatabago included Ajara, a portion of present-day Turkey and Armenia, and Samtskhe and Javakheti. In the ninth and tenth centuries this southern region of Georgia was the most highly developed both culturally and economically.

From this area the move toward Georgian unification was furthered when David III, the powerful ruler of a region of Tao, supported the young Bagrat III. Bagrat was the son and heir of Gurgen Bagrationi who ruled a large portion of Tao. Bagrat was also the heir of King Theodosi of Abkhazia (west Georgia) since his mother was the king's sister. At that time both Kartli and Inner Kartli, which essentially comprised all of eastern and southern Georgia, were under the rule of King Theodosi. Inheriting lands from his father Gurgen, his uncle King Theodosi, and David of Tao allowed Bagrat III to begin the process of unification. He became King of Inner Kartli in 975 and of western Georgia in 978. In 1001 he lost to the Byzantine Emperor Basil I the region of Tao previously ruled by David III. In 1008, however, when Bagrat's father Gurgen died, Bagrat inherited his father's portion of Tao Klarjeti. The name for a united Georgia, Sakartvelo, dates from this period.

Although the southern region of Georgia was frequently a battlefield, especially as a result of the periodic invasions of the Seljuk Turks from Iran in the 1060s, the territory became the center of Georgian culture and power at the beginning of the 12th century. This was the time of the Georgian renaissance when, under the rule of David the Builder (Aghmashenebeli in Georgian), the Turks were driven out of Kvemo Kartli, Tbilisi, and Tao, and the Georgian kingdom was extended into parts of present-day Turkey and Armenia as far south as the Araks River.

Georgia's beloved Queen Tamara (reigned 1184–1212) consolidated the gains of her great-grandfather, David the Builder, by keeping the Seljuk Turks out of Georgia and establishing tribute-paying states at the borders of her newly expanded territory. She chose the province of Javakheti to establish Vardzia, the most important monastery and at the time the primary center of culture in all Georgia. Located in a region that had known no end of invaders, a region through which ran the major

HEART TO HEART

*L*ove is tender, a hard thing to be known. True love is something apart from lust, and cannot be likened thereto; it is one thing; lust is quite another thing, and between them lies a broad boundary; in no way do thou mingle them—hear my saying!

The lover must be constant, not lewd, impure and faithless; when he is far from his beloved he must heave sigh upon sigh; his heart must be fixed on one from whom he endures wrath or sorrow if need be. I hate heartless love—embracing, kissing, loud smacking of the lips.

Lovers, call not this thing love: when any longs for one today and another tomorrow, bearing parting's pain. Such base sport is like mere boyish trifling; the good lover is he who suffers a world's woe.

There is a noblest love; it does not show, but hides its woes; the lover thinks of it when he is alone, and always seeks solitude; his fainting, dying, burning, flaming, all are from afar; he must face the wrath of his beloved, and he must be fearful of her.

He must betray his secret to none, he must not basely groan and put his beloved to shame; in naught should he manifest his love, nowhere must he reveal it; for her sake he looks upon sorrow as joy, for her sake he would willingly be burned.

How can the sane trust him who noises his love abroad, and what shall it profit to do this? He makes her suffer, and he himself suffers. How should he glorify her if he shame her with words? What need is there for man to cause pain to the heart of his beloved!

I wonder why men show that they love the beloved. Why shame they her whom they love, her who slays herself for them, who is covered with wounds? If they love her not, why do they not manifest to her feelings of hatred? Why do they disgrace what they hate? But an evil man loves an evil word more than his soul or his heart.

Shota Rustaveli, The Knight in the Panther's Skin,
translated by Marjory Scott Wardrop

trade route to the Middle East, her choice was a statement to her people—and to the world at large. That the monastery of Vardzia is a cave complex hewn out of stone and designed to be impregnable was also not a coincidence.

During the time of the Georgian renaissance, Samtskhe also gained a claim to fame: Queen Tamara's bard, the man now regarded as the national poet of Georgia, Shota Rustaveli, author of *The Knight in the Panther's Skin* (*vepkhvis tqaosani*) hailed from the village (not the town) of Rustavi, located in Samtskhe.

Georgian power proved no match for the Mongols who invaded in the 13th century, fragmenting the three kingdoms of Georgia into semi-independent principalities and playing the nobles of those principalities against the Georgian throne. The Georgian who rose highest under the Mongols' divide and rule strategy of patronage was Sargis Jakeli, the Duke of Samtskhe and once a chancellor of the Georgian King Ulu David, a grandson of Queen Tamara. In 1266 the Mongol Khan officially granted Samtskhe special protection and the region prospered, attracting peasants from other regions of Georgia, especially Kartli, who were feeling the weight of the Mongol yoke.

In the 14th century George V (the Brilliant) again joined Samtskhe to the Georgian Kingdom, but with the invasion of Tamerlane at the end of the 14th century, Georgia once more began fragmenting into separate duchies and kingdoms. By the 1460s there were four: the kingdoms of Kakheti, Imereti, and Kartli were divided by the Bagrationi, and the Principality of Samtskhe-Saatabago was ruled by the Jakeli family. The continual invasions of the Turks whittled away at the territory encompassed by Samtskhe-Saatabago until all that essentially remained was the area now known as Meskheti and Javakheti. With the Ottoman Empire as its neighbor, this southernmost province of Georgia became a Christian outpost whose independence was constantly threatened by the Turks, who continued to seize territory. In 1624 Beka III (of the Jakeli family and lord of the diminished territory of Samtskhe) found it politically expedient to convert to Islam. That decision began the Islamization of the territory. Vast numbers of Georgians migrated away from the area while others converted and intermarried with the ever-growing number of Turks who came to settle.

After the Russo-Turkish War of 1828–1829, Meskheti, defined in this period as the provinces of Samtskhe and Javakheti, joined the Russian Empire. Many Moslems were exiled to Turkey, and their land was given to Armenians from Turkey who had helped the Russians during the war. Many of the remaining Moslems spoke Georgian. However, the Russians instituted a policy of discrimination against them and the Moslems' relationship with their Georgian and Armenian neighbors deteriorated. The result of the discriminatory practices was not the desired assimilation that the Russians hoped for, but rather a stronger sense of Islamic identity.

All of this has important political ramifications on the current scene, and the problem known as the "Meskhetian question." Before Stalin deported these Meskhetian Moslems to Uzbekistan, Georgian was spoken in only 14 villages. The rest spoke Turkish. In exile, the few who spoke Georgian forgot the language. Their native villages are now inhabited by Georgians from the provinces of Racha and Lechkhumi. Meskheti is now densely populated, and the 1,000 Turks who did feel themselves Georgian have been repatriated to a western province. The Georgians have been opposed to repatriating the more than 150,000 Meskhetian Moslems from Uzbekistan because these people did not regard themselves as culturally Georgian but as Turks and, even more importantly, because some leaders of this group have been active in promoting the creation of an autonomous republic or district on the southern border of Georgia. Given the recent history of ethnic conflict in South Ossetia and Abkhazia this option is frightening to the Georgians who already have been living in the region for two generations.

In June 1989, as a result of a suspected Soviet-organized provocation in the form of a market quarrel, the Uzbek government demanded that the Meskhetian Moslems be expelled from Uzbekistan. This demand was met two days later and the Meskhets then demanded their right to return to Georgia. Georgia interpreted this situation as Soviet punishment for Georgia's movement toward independence. Georgia recognized the Meskhets' right of repatriation and in the ensuing years has repatriated some Meskhets to inner regions of Georgia. Others have remained in Azerbaijan and the North Caucasus and are insisting on the formation of an autonomous entity along Georgia's southern border.

Meskheti (Samtskhe) covers 1,081 sq. km (420 sq. miles) and has a population of 92,000. Javakheti covers 3,261 sq. km (1,258 sq. miles) and has a population of 107,000. Both share a southern border with Turkey and until 1989 were regarded as sensitive military zones where it was extremely difficult, even for Georgians, to get the necessary permission to visit. This, thankfully, is no longer the case.

Javakheti has within its territory the elegant church of Kumurdo and the extraordinary cave monastery of Vardzia. Javakheti is one of the coldest regions in Georgia, with high mountain plateaus of over 2,000 meters (6,560 feet) and many lakes of volcanic origin. It is the home of many Armenians who asked to be settled there after the Russo-Turkish War of 1828–1829. Meskheti (Samtskhe) possesses the early 14th-century monasteries of Sapara and Zarzma.

Getting to Vardzia and Sights Along the Way

Vardzia can be reached from Batumi only by four-wheel drive by traveling east on the A306 toward Akhaltsikhe (245 km/153 miles), continuing past Aspindza (32

km/20 miles from Akhaltsikhe), and following the Mtkvari (Kura) as it goes south and then west to Vardzia (60 km/38 miles).

If you're traveling from Tbilisi take the M27 west to Khashuri (131 km/85 miles) before turning left (southeast) onto the A308 to Akhaltsikhe (76 km/47 miles). From there the route to Vardzia is the same as above. Note that the A308 goes through the lovely spa town of Borjomi (a hop, skip, and jump from the ski resort and nature reserve of Bakuriani). For information on this spot, *see* page 150.

Making Vardzia a day trip from either Batumi or Tbilisi is pretty grueling and would take more than six hours traveling nonstop. You could set off from Gori, but that's only 86 km (55 miles) out of the 199 km from Tbilisi. Your best bet, if you can swing it, is to stay in Akhaltsikhe. Akhaltsikhe is the administrative center of the region and also the most central jumping-off place for Vardzia, Sapara, and Zarzma. You used to be able to stay at Hotel Vardzia, directly opposite the site of the Cave Monastery, but this is now closed.

A friend has recently written that an excellent alternative to this hotel is to stay at the Abastumani Observatory: "From Akhaltsikhe, turn left away from Tbilisi, and after a fifteen-minute drive turn right up a dirt road; after an hour you come to the Abastumani Observatory. The accomodation is spartan, as the rooms were used to house astronomers and staff working at the observatory in Soviet times. There are only a few toilets, and only cold water to wash with. The food, though, is excellent. The observatory is situated high up amongst steep alpine hills covered with trees, rare plants, and medicinal herbs. At night you can view the heavens through a telescope with an astronomer. It's a very beautiful place and as close as you will get to Vardzia for the night. Any other arrangement at the moment would leave you too tired and too little time to enjoy the monumental site of Vardzia."

FORTRESS OF KHERTVISI
At 46 km (28.5 miles) from Akhaltsikhe, situated on a cliff above the confluence of the Javakheta Mtkvari and the Artaani Mtkvari, is one of the oldest fortresses in Georgia. If you're an admirer of T.E. Lawrence, you'll certainly feel a powerful connection with him here. The pleasure that he must have felt upon visiting in Palestine and Syria the long-neglected fortresses that were the subject of his undergraduate thesis on Crusader castles cannot have been too different from the feelings that Khertvisi evokes.

The exact date of the foundation is unknown, but the fortress was certainly standing in the tenth century. Rebuilt several times, it originally consisted of an inner fortress at the very top of the cliff. The defensive capability of its thick high walls was increased by four towers. At a later date the area of the fortress was increased. Two secret passages from the eastern wall lead toward the Javakheta Mtkvari. One was for

The road to Vardzia often runs parallel to the Mtkvari River's southward course through an austere and haunting landscape

water, the other for communication with the outside. The two main towers in the east and west within the walls date from the time of Queen Tamara (1184–1212). Inside the walls are the ruins of a church, as well as living and storage buildings. An inscription in the church dates it back to 985. Another inscription above the fortress entrance dates the Khertvisi tower and a portion of the walls to 1354–1356.

The history of the Khertvisi Fortress and town is also connected with the history of Samstkhe-Saatabago. The fortress was seized by the Turks in 1578. Briefly recaptured by Georgia's Giorgi Saakadze, it was again lost to the Turks and from 1638 became one of the most important cities of the Ottoman Empire's *pashalik*, an administrative unit of the territory. By the time Samtskhe was returned to Georgia after the Russo-Turkish War, the fortress had lost its military significance. It now lies in ruins, although scaffolding attests to ongoing restoration work.

LAKE TSUNDA AND VICINITY

Fifty-four km (33 miles) from Akhaltsikhe (12 km/7.5 miles from Vardzia) is Lake Tsunda on the right bank of the Artaani Mtkvari. Not far from the lake, on a small cliff, is a wonderfully ornamented hall-type church dating from the 12th century, built by Ichkit Gurghenisdze. Especially note the 13th-century carving over the entrance arch. A famous town existed here as early as the fourth century BC. A citadel on the site served as an administrative and religious center in the fifth century AD but lost importance in the ninth and tenth centuries, when the fortified town of Tmogvi became preeminent.

One km (0.6 miles) from Lake Tsunda are the fortress and the ruins of the fortified town of **Tmogvi**. Look across the river to one of the peaks of the Erusheti Mountains and you can see the remains of the fort. Built in the tenth and 11th centuries, it later served as administrative center for the Georgian provincial governor. Below the fortress on the cliff wall are many monks' caves. Lower down on both banks of the river are two bridges and several palaces. This is the site of the town of Tmogvi, which was destroyed by earthquakes in 1089 and 1283.

Three km (two miles) from Tmogvi on your left and up the hillside is the monastery of **Vanis Kvabebi**. A sign marks the path (approximately an hour's walk) to the many-tiered cave complex carved out of the rock face. Begun in the eighth century, Vanis Kvabebi was a women's monastery, whereas Vardzia was for men. Among the structures of the complex are cells, storerooms, hall churches, stair tunnels, a water system with ceramic pipes, defensive walls, and a small domed church restored in the 1180s by Ichkit Gurghenisdze. On the highest tier the little domed church is covered in stucco upon which inscriptions and drawings have been made, all dating from the second half of the 15th century. One of the inscriptions is two lines from Shota Rustaveli's epic poem *The Knight in the Panther's Skin*. This is the oldest existing record of the poem. Vanis Kvabebi had belonged to Ichkit Gurghenisdze, but by the end of the 12th century, like Vardzia, it had already become a monastery belonging to the crown.

Vardzia

Three km upstream from Vanis Kvabebi is Vardzia. Lying 3,300 meters (10,200 feet) above sea level, Vardzia is a complex of man-made cave dwellings above the Mtkvari (Kura) River that extends over 500 meters. The caves are carved out of the soft tuff. Out of an original 3,000 caves that existed during the time of Queen Tamara, 650 remained after the earthquake of 1456. At present 550 dwellings have been discovered. In places, as many as 19 tiers of the complex extend to a height of 105 meters (340 feet). The tiers run east to west. The depth of the caves ranges from 45 to 60 meters (150–200 feet), all hollowed out north to south.

Vardzia represents the apex of cave architecture. It is the culmination of a tradition that began in its secular expression at Uplistikhe in Kartli in the sixth or fifth century BC and continued at David-Gareja in Kakheti as a religious community in the seventh to ninth centuries AD. It was established by King Giorgi III (1156–84) as a strategic stronghold in the region against the territorial ambitions of the Turkish Sultanate, but he did not live to see its completion. The work was continued by his daughter Tamara (1184–1212), who used the caves to create a monastery and a center of Georgian culture.

One legend relates how Vardzia got its name. King Giorgi went hunting with his court and took with him his little daughter Tamara. In the thrill of the hunt, Tamara became separated from the hunters and lost her way in the caves. Searching for her, the hunters cried, "Where are you, Tamara?" And she replied, *Aq var, dzia* ("Here I am, uncle").

The Vardzia ensemble actually consists of two parts: Vardzia and the earlier tenth-century rock village of

The 12th-century cave monastery of Vardzia

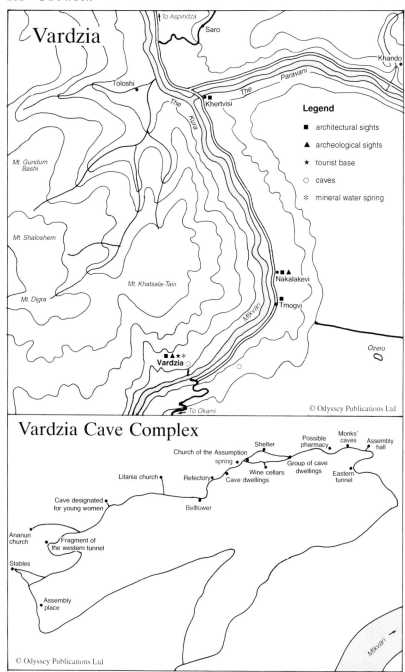

Vardzia

To Aspindza
Saro
Khando
Paravani
The
Toloshi
Khertvisi
The
Kura
Mt. Gundum
Bashi
Mt. Shaloshem
Mt. Khatsala-Tavi
Mt. Digra
Mtkvari
Nakalakevi
Tmogvi
Ozero
Vardzia
To Okami

Legend

■ architectural sights
▲ archeological sights
★ tourist base
○ caves
✳ mineral water spring

© Odyssey Publications Ltd

Vardzia Cave Complex

Monks' caves
Assembly hall
Possible pharmacy
Shelter
Church of the Assumption
spring
Group of cave dwellings
Eastern tunnel
Litania church
Refectory
Wine cellars
Cave dwellings
Cave designated for young women
Belltower
Ananuri church
Fragment of the western tunnel
Stables
Assembly place
Mtkvari

© Odyssey Publications Ltd

Ananauri. The two areas are joined by the belltower of the Vardzia Monastery. Ananauri extends over a vast area to the west; Vardzia for 0.5 km (0.3 mile) to the east. The Ananauri area is, in fact, outside the normal tourist paths, so you have to make a special effort to see the tenth-century cliff church here.

At an earlier time a distinction was made between the two zones, but now they are both known as Vardzia and only the tenth-century cliff church retains the name Ananauri. Of interest especially are its 16th-century frescoes; although badly damaged in places, their color is remarkably well preserved. Over the entrance to the church are frescoes depicting the Descent of the Holy Ghost, the Annunciation, the Deesis, St. Ivlita, and an unknown founder. Inside, in the conch of the altar on the east wall is a scene of the Virgin and Child with Archangels. Beneath that scene is the Lamentation. Scenes depicted in the northern part of the vault are the Crucifixion, the Resurrection, and the Ascension with the Transfiguration beneath.

In the terraces above and below the belltower of Vardzia are various remains that linked the eastern and western areas, such as tunnels, steps, a water supply, and an irrigation canal. All attest to the gradual absorption of the Ananauri territory into the Vardzia Monastery.

Your tour through Vardzia is from west to east. There are local guides who will meet you at the car park, but none of them speak English. You would do well to bring a flashlight. Ascending the path you pass numerous cave dwellings (sometimes with individual churches), meeting halls, refectories, a bakery, wine cellars (distinguished by the pitchers sunk into the ground), terraces, and steps that were enclosed by tunnels no longer extant.

In the western portion of Vardzia, throughout its 13 tiers, are 40 rock houses in various states of preservation, totaling 165 rooms. In the eastern part of Vardzia, comprising eight tiers, 79 rock houses have been discovered, totaling 242 rooms. Worth seeing are the two-story rock houses and storage rooms. Wine cellars are a particularly interesting feature; their sheer number attests to the economic importance of the grape to the monastery.

Your walk through the various dwellings of Vardzia takes you first to the belltower, built of dressed stone in the 13th century to replace cave dwellings destroyed in the earthquake of 1283. Originally two-storied, the belfry has not survived. This is a magnificent spot from which to survey the whole complex and the countryside all around. It is extraordinary to think that Turkey is only about ten km (6.2 miles) away and to watch the Mtkvari rushing below you to cross the border. From here you can also see the portico of two arches that marks the entrance to the Church of the Assumption, the centerpiece of the whole complex. The earthquake of 1283 also destroyed the original two-arched portico, which was rebuilt at the same time the belltower was constructed.

CHURCH OF THE ASSUMPTION

With Giorgi III's death in 1184, Queen Tamara began the second phase of construction of the Vardzia Monastery. The large hall Church of the Assumption was carved out of the cliff and decorated under the supervision of a duke of Kartli, Rati Surameli. The church and the interior frescoes date from 1184–1186.

The frescoes on the north wall are of the greatest interest. On the western portion of the north wall, under the arch, is a portrait of Rati Surameli, the donor. The inscription beside his name, though badly damaged, has recently been interpreted: "Mother of God, . . . accept the offering of your servant Rati, *eristavi* of Kartalinia, who has zealously decorated this holy church to your glory." On the eastern portion of the north wall, also under an arch, are portraits of a young Queen Tamara holding a model of a church and of her father Giorgi III. The inscriptions to the right of these portraits read, "Tsar of Tsars of all the East, Giorgi, son of Dmitri, Tsar of Tsars" and "Tsar of Tsars of all the East, Tamara, daughter of Giorgi; God grant her a long life." Commissioned by Rati Surameli, these frescoes were created by the talented artist Giorgi. His initials G and I are worked into the floral ornamentation of the conch, under the Virgin. Only three other portraits of Queen Tamara exist in Georgia: in the cupola churches of Betania and Kintsvisi, and in the cave church of Bertubani in the David-Gareja Monastery. In these three portraits she is wearing a wimple—the sign of a married woman. In the Vardzia portrait she is not. This is extremely helpful in the dating of this work, signifying that it was completed before her marriage in 1186.

In addition to the portraits of historic personages, Giorgi and his assistants painted numerous religious themes. Most powerful in its monumentality is the Virgin and Child in the conch of the altar. Below the conch, in the apse, are portraits of the 12 Church Fathers with unfurled scrolls. Scenes in both the upper and lower parts of the vault include the Annunciation, the Nativity, the Transfiguration, the Raising of Lazarus, the Entry into Jerusalem, the Last Supper, and the Washing of Feet. The Crucifixion is on the south wall, and the Descent into Hell is in the west, over the doors of the entrance. Portraits of saints adorn the pilasters, the transverse arches, and the window embrasures.

The frescoes in Vardzia are a high point of the Georgian school, for they are a remarkable stylistic achievement in the rendering of individual personality, in the elegance of pose and gesture, and in a harmonious balance of color and composition within the larger spatial context. The work bespeaks a comfortable mastery over secular and religious themes which, when combined as they are here, suggests a humanism that was not to come to Italy for another 300 years.

There are two ways to leave the Church of the Assumption: with candles through a tunnel in the north wall, or the way you came in, proceeding east. If you

A fresco of Queen Tamara and her father Giorgi III from the Church of the Assumption at Vardzia

choose the latter you can take some time to study the frescoes in the entrance gallery or antechurch. On the north wall, arranged on three registers, is the Last Judgment. On the west wall: Abraham's Bosom. On the western part of the vault: scenes from the Life of St. Stephen. In the center of the vault: Angels Bearing a Medallion with Cross.

In exploring the rest of the eastern portion of the complex, bear in mind that originally the complex was not so open to observation. As a result of earthquakes and foreign invasion, much of the cliff face has collapsed, exposing all the caves and portions of stairs and balconies. As conceived, the complex was a honeycomb of interconnected facilities virtually invisible to a traveler or invader in the gorge below.

THIRD AND FOURTH PHASES

Building at Vardzia didn't stop after the construction of the Church of the Assumption. A third phase, consisting of defensive works and complex irrigation systems, occurred between its completion and the Battle of Basiani in 1202. The Battle of Basiani pitted the Georgian forces that assembled at Vardzia against the 400,000-strong Moslem forces. The Georgians were victorious, and to celebrate this success Tamara gave the monastery many gifts. Throughout the 13th century many of the Georgian victories against the encroaching Moslems were attributed to the wonder-working icon "The Virgin of Vardzia," and Vardzia became famous throughout Christendom as an outpost of faith on the Islamic frontier. The earthquake of 1283 badly damaged Vardzia, after which began a fourth stage of construction in which the belltower was constructed and the portico of the Church of the Assumption was rebuilt.

In the 15th and 16th centuries, Vardzia's fortified monastery defended Georgia against the increasingly aggressive incursions by both Turks and Persians. It was a repository for works of art and a sanctuary for the threatened local Georgian population. In 1551, King Luarsab I of Kartli met a Persian force led by Shah Tahmasp, and fighting took place in the caves themselves. The Georgians were defeated and Shah Tahmasp looted the monastery. According to the historian Hassan Beq Rumlu, the chronicler of the Persian Safavid dynasty, Shah Tahmasp "seized incredible wealth and innumerable possessions." During the 300-year Turkish occupation of Javakheti, Vardzia became the campground of Turkish shepherds.

When leaving the complex, exit by the long tunnel that was the main entrance to the monastery in the easternmost section. The wide, even steps and curving, gradual descent are a testament to the construction capabilities of the monks and the plan of the master builder, the unknown architect of Vardzia.

Sapara Monastery

Leave Akhaltsikhe by the road that runs south to Akhalkalaki. Approximately one km (0.6 miles) from the center of town, take the second right after Ketshoveli Street onto a dirt road, where you will see the sign for the monastery. Continuing on this dirt road, bear left past the military base, then climb for three km (two miles) through wonderful wild poppy fields. Bear left at the fork. The drive to the monastery is along a twisting, steep dirt road, but an ordinary vehicle will make it. At the 10-km (6.2-mile) point from town is a wonderful view of the monastery nestled in the forested mountains high above the gorge. It is clear that defense was much in the founders' minds: the complex is accessible only by one road and can be seen from only a few select perspectives. Another two-km (1.2-mile) drive brings you to the monastery.

The monastery complex consists of numerous buildings. The most striking is the domed Church of St. Saba, built in the late 13th and early 14th centuries. The belltower and the ruins of the palace also date from that period. The oldest structure is the aisleless church attached to the main Church of St. Saba in the southwest. This hall church is dedicated to the Assumption of the Mother of God. The façade is decorated with finely carved reliefs. Note the head of a bull on the top left side of the entrance from the porch. Legend has it that at the time of the building of the church a bull helped to haul stones from the mountain to the site. Just as the work was finished the bull was killed and eaten by a bear. The builder commemorated the helpful bull by placing its effigy as the last stone set in the completed church.

The interior of the church was completely frescoed, but these were plastered over in the 19th century. All that remain are fragments in the altar and in the western portion of the church that date from the first half of the 14th century. In the west is also a second tier that was designed for use by the chorus, an architectural feature very rare in hall-type churches. Fragments of an altar screen (first half of the 11th century) from this church are on view at the Museum of Georgian Art in Tbilisi. The subjects on the screen, treated in a most expressive and delicate sculptural relief, are the Annunciation, the Meeting of Mary and Elizabeth, and the Presentation at the Temple.

The main church in the monastery complex is dedicated to St. Saba. Its history is inextricably tied to the Jakeli family and the special fate of Samtskhe Province at the end of the 13th century. This was the period during which Georgia was under the Mongol yoke; however, Samtskhe flourished as an independent duchy precisely because of the good relations with the Mongol Khan of its ruler, Sargis I. The Jakelis were responsible for the growth of monastery construction throughout the province. The story behind the Church of St. Saba is a delicious example of the incongruities between *la vita passiva* and *la vita attiva*, at least when one tries to exchange one for the other. In his old age, at the end of the 13th century, Sargis I relinquished power to his son Beka, cropped his hair, took vows as a monk, and changed his name to Saba. His son Beka decided to build a church in Sapara in honor of St. Saba and did so while his father was still alive.

The Church of St. Saba, from the turn of the 14th century, along with the church at the monastery of Zarzma, is among Georgia's best ecclesiastical structures built in this time period. An inscription over the western portico tells us that the architect was Parezasdze. While he chose the central-cupola style church, popular since the first half of the 11th century, he eschewed the excessive decoration of the façade that earmarked the end of the 12th and beginning of the 13th centuries, as well as many of the decorative motifs from the tenth and 11th centuries. The result gives flatness and austerity to the façades. Ornamentation is largely reserved for window and door frames (the western portico in spite of its nearness to the mountain is treated more elaborately). Certainly the level of craftsmanship is high, as seen in the cleanly hewn blocks of reddish stone.

The proportions of the church, however, are markedly different from the projectile sense of ascension we find in the churches of Pitareti and Betania of the early 13th century. The drum of St. Saba is lower and wider, creating a greater sense of mass and height in the structural body. A unique feature of this 16-sided drum is that eight real windows alternate on the facets with eight false ones. This technique, which is of dubious merit when one tries to view the marvelous interior frescoes, originated in Sapara and later became popular in churches throughout Georgia. The architect also made an interesting choice in the site of the church. It stands above a precipice, making it impossible to view the eastern façade from anywhere except farther down the slope or from the other side of the gorge. The position of the eastern side necessitated supporting walls to strengthen it. Originally Parezasdze seems to have wanted entrances on the remaining three sides, but at some point the southern entrance was sealed, leaving access today only through the western and northern sides.

The frescoes of the interior of the church are among the best preserved in Georgia. The eight windows of the drum and a single window in each arm of the cross create a kind of light preferred more by the mystic than the art historian, but viewing is possible. A central chandelier is lit for services—the best time to be there. These frescoes, primarily from the first half of the 14th century, show stylistic qualities assimilated from the "Palaeologus" Byzantine school. An Ascension is in the cupola. The drum features eight prophets with unrolled scrolls. Especially powerful are the frescoes in the southern arm of the church: the Bereavement (Mourning) for Christ, in which Mary's extended arms and the bowed bodies of the apostles have a dynamism and expressivity that surpass in quality some of the more static renderings. Of greatest historic value, and indeed exhibiting a distinctive individuality in each face, are the portraits of the Jakeli family in the lower register of the southern wall. Bowing before an image of the patron saint of the church, St. Saba, are (in order from the viewer's left to right) Sargis I, his son Beka I (1308), and Beka's sons Sargis II (1308–1334) and Kvarkvare (1334–1345).

To see other monuments on the monastery grounds, climb the slope up to the belltower in the west. The two-storied belltower dates from the same period as the Church of St. Saba. The first story served as a tomb for the Lasuridze family and portraits of family members are painted on the walls inside. The second story is an arched belfry.

Sapara was the residence of the Jakelis, as well as a monastery founded by them. Of the many buildings that once stood here as part of the secular complex, only the first floor of the stone palace has survived. Not much is known about the other buildings, now in ruins.

Sapara was captured by the Turks in the 16th century, and ultimately the monastery fell into disuse. The Church of St. Saba was reconsecrated only at the end of 1989, and the monastery is once more flourishing under the direction of Father Sergi. A distinguished monk with a luxuriant black beard and enlightened eyes, he might well invite you to partake of lunch with him and his novices in their refectory next to the church. A small *mtsvadior* (shish kebab stand) is also sometimes open at the entrance to the monastery complex.

Zarzma Monastery

From Akhaltsikhe, take the A306 west in the direction of Batumi. Zarzma is just beyond the town of Adigeni, approximately 30 km (18.5 miles) from Akhaltsikhe. The road follows the Potshovi River. After two km (1.2 miles) it splits. The left-hand branch goes off to Vale, the last village before the Turkish border, and the right-hand branch continues toward Batumi. Take the right-hand branch. Eleven km (6.8

Madonna and Child in the Church of the Transfiguration, Zarzma Monastery

miles) from Akhaltsikhe, the Potshovi River forks; one branch flows into Turkey and the Kvabliani River runs through Georgia. The crops on either side of the road are mostly potatoes. Apple groves are also plentiful. In the village of Adigeni, keep to the north side of the river, but at the 29-km (18-mile) point, where the road breaks, go left across the river and continue to Zarzma, which is visible on the slopes of the forested mountain.

The origin of the Zarzma Monastery is attributed to a famous monk of the sixth and seventh centuries, Serapion Zarzmeli. In an important biography of Georgian literature, *The Life of Serapion Zarzmeli*, dating to early feudal times, it is written that the ruler of this region, Georgi Chorchaneli, helped Serapion establish the monastery. The text adds that the church was the centerpiece of the monastery complex and the architect was Garbaneli. Today buildings from Serapion's time do not remain, although a tenth-century inscription from a building of that period has been incorporated into the archstone above the northern entrance of a chapel connected to the existing belltower. The main church was ordered built by Beka I in the early 14th century.

CHURCH OF THE TRANSFIGURATION (ZARZMA)

A classic central-cupola structure; access is from the south or west. The placement of a portico along the entire length of the south façade is unusual for medieval cupola churches and may be a survivor from an earlier structure.

At the end of construction in the 16th century, the interior of the church had been completely covered in frescoes. These suffered badly during the Turkish occupation; with few exceptions the work seen today is the result of heavy restoration by the Russians at the end of the 19th century. A Russian inscription on the western façade attests to this. Significant repainting has changed the basic character of the work despite the professionalism that aspired to achieve conformity with certain aspects of the "Palaeologus" Byzantine style. In accordance with monumental painting of the period, the portraits of many historical personages are depicted throughout. Here they occupy the entire lower register of the murals. The southern wall features portraits of the Jakeli family, the Dukes of Samtskhe: Sargis I, his son Beka, and Beka's sons Sargis II and Kvarkvare. You will recall the same family in a mural scene at Sapara. On the opposite (northern) wall is a scene of King Bagrat III (1510–1565), once ruler of Samtskhe, standing before Father Serapion. Behind King Bagrat is Georgi Chorchaneli, the ruler of this region, associated with helping Serapion establish the monastery in the sixth to seventh centuries. To the right of this group is a portrait of the Catholicos Evfimy before Christ. The other three full-length figures are an Arab and a Kurd (about whom nothing is known), and the Gurian Prince, Simon Gurieli.

The interior of the Church of the Transfiguration in Zarzma Monastery

The façade, as in Sapara, is flat, devoid of elaborate decoration. What ornamentation exists, primarily geometrical and floral, is concentrated around window frames and doors. The cupola has 12 sides with false windows alternating on each facet with real ones. The belltower, at the southwest of the church, is of approximately the same period. Originally built into the wall of the complex, the first floor served as an arched gate until it was walled up in 1577 by the order of the ruler Parsman Khurtsisdze, and became the chapel of St. John the Evangelist. The second-story belfry is topped by a pyramid-shaped cupola that rests on an octagonal tower. The tower itself is most unusual in that each facet contains an arch.

Four other churches are part of the monastery complex. One is connected to the Church of the Transfiguration from the east; another is to the north. These two hall churches were restored in the early 20th century. To the south are the ruins of two small churches, possibly built by the same architect who built the main church.

The Museum of Georgian Art in Tbilisi is home to the great icon of the Transfiguration (886), which comes from Zarzma.

Kumurdo

KUMURDO CHURCH

Leaving Akhaltsikhe on the A306, go southeast 71 km (44 miles) to Akhalkalaki. Akhalkalaki is itself a town from the Middle Ages, but it was completely destroyed when Alp Arslan led the Seljuk Turks in an invasion of the province in 1066. The present city is the capital of Javakheti. The medieval church of Kumurdo stands on a cliff plateau 12 km (7.4 miles) southwest of the capital.

Erected by the master builder Sakotzari on the orders of Bishop Ioane in 964, the church is a high point of Georgian medieval architecture. Unusual in the specificity of its inscriptions, we know that the foundation stone was laid in 964 in the time of King Leon and the *eristavi* Zviad. The inscription giving the date and the builder's name is above the southern entrance in the ancient Georgian writing, Asomtavruli.

The interesting ground plan of the church is masked by an exterior that suggests the standard cruciform domed church. Opening, however, onto the hexagonal space beneath the cupola are five deep apses. The two on the south and north sides are parallel to each other whereas the deepest apse, the altar of the east side, is flanked by the sacristy and deacon's chamber. In the second quarter of the 11th century, during the time of Bagrat IV, an ambulatory was built in the west side, which continued in a wraparound in the south and north, changing the original appearance. The arches leading into this area were later walled in. The east-west axis of the church is divided into three aisles by two rows of pillars. The cupola was supported by squinches rising from six slender polygonal pillars protruding from the walls at the points of the hexagon. The cupola collapsed, however, sometime after a major renovation of the church in the 16th century. The collapse, caused perhaps by an earthquake, destroyed the western section.

The tenth century is notable for the fact that sculpture began to be incorporated into the interior design. On the eastern squinches of Kumurdo, relief portraits can be seen. One is of Queen Gurandukht, the mother of King Bagrat III, and the other is of a man thought to be either King Gurgen of Kartli-Iberia, Bagrat's father, or King Leon, Gurandukht's brother. Fine relief work is also found on the exterior: the angel, bull, eagle, and lion, symbols of the four Evangelists, are found in the frame of the eastern main window.

Kumurdo is distinguished by a very high level of workmanship, particularly visible in the precision of the masonry, where rows of dressed stone have been meticulously chosen and wine-colored blocks strategically placed. Together with the tall, lightly ornamented niches of the exterior, the masonry adds to the sublime harmony and noble simplicity of the structure.

Kakheti

Lying in the easternmost part of Georgia, the province of Kakheti has an area of 11,340 sq. km (4,378 sq. miles) and a winter population of 442,296. The Gombori Range divides Inner and Outer Kakheti. The former comprises the fertile Alazani River valley, and the latter the Iori Plateau. In the 150-km (93-mile) stretch of the Alazani Valley, the climate and soil conspire to make the grape king. In the Iori Plateau where a dry steppe climate predominates, corn and wheat thrive.

Kakheti is one of the provinces richest in historic monuments. Of more than 5,000 architectural monuments in Georgia under the protection of the State, only Kartli can rival it in sheer number. Three days at least are needed to get more than a very truncated perspective on the wealth of history here. Certainly its proximity to Tbilisi, the terrain of the Iori Plateau and Alazani Valley, and the quality of the roads make travel here considerably easier than in some of the more remote, mountainous parts of the country.

The People and Their Wine

Kakheti is justly renowned as the most important wine-growing region of Georgia. Every village produces its own kind of wine; villagers speak eloquently about the advantages of their soil over that of their neighbors and why true connoisseurs favor their wine above all others. Throughout the region you can knock on any door for directions and find yourself five seconds later with a glass of wine in hand and an invitation to stay the afternoon to drink and eat. If you're not careful your touring could be seriously impeded by this superabundance of hospitality. If you're an oenophile, however, why worry? Many of the homegrown wines you'll stumble on will rival more famous labels like Tsinandali, Akhmeta, and Napareuli. (For a more detailed description of wines and their regions, *see* page 81 under Food and Drink.) Wine connoisseurs also have an opportunity for more formal tastings at the Tsinandali Winery, ten km (six miles) west of Telavi.

The best time to visit Kakheti is during *rtveli*, the harvest season at the beginning of October. The autumn colors are magnificent, and every village celebrates the bounty of its vineyards by decorating balconies with bunches of grapes and filling every basket and bucket until they're brimming over. The fields and roads are alive with this grand agricultural enterprise, and the songs and the scents are unforgettable. In many a yard you'll be offered a taste from a ladle just emerging from deep inside a *kvevri*, the large clay amphora buried underground in which Kakhetian wine ferments.

Women sell their homemade churckhela, *the famous Georgian grape and walnut sweet, on the road to Gurjaani (photo by David Halford)*

Kakhetians are more circumspect than, for example, the garrulous Imeretians. Like the wise husbandmen they are, Kakhetians tend to keep their own counsel and look on the foolishness of the world with great bemusement. Kakheti is one of the regions in Georgia that suffered most harshly from foreign invaders, and many older Kakhetians still wear the famous felt cap as a link with and a reminder of the past. The felt cap—just like the Svanetian variety—was worn at all times so that a metal helmet could be thrown atop it at a moment's notice, allowing a man to defend his village.

The arrangement of the villages throughout the region was also designed with defense foremost in mind: houses backed up against one another, with one family's terrace serving as another's roof, and so on up a hill. This allowed defenders to retreat through the maze of interconnected houses should they start losing the fray. Longitudinally, it is often difficult to determine where one village ends and another begins. This is as much due to the incredible wealth of the land, where every square meter is utilized by someone, as it is to a deliberate plan of safety in numbers.

History

Kakheti formed a part of Kartli-Iberia until the second half of the eighth century when it was governed as a separate duchy. Before that, beginning in the fifth century, it was one of the seven principalities ruled by appointees of the king of Kartli-Iberia. In the second half of the sixth century, after the death of King Vakhtang Gorgasali in 502, much of eastern Georgia was ruled by Iran. The monarchs of Kartli-Iberia were constrained to wield what influence they could from their fortress at Ujarma in Kakheti. In 575, however, with the death of King Bakur III, the Persians abolished the monarchy with the wholehearted approval of the Georgian nobility, who hoped to gain power by the absence of a strong king. This is precisely what occurred, and until the Arab invasions of the seventh century, the nobles who governed Kakheti on behalf of the king gained larger territories, which they oversaw as independent fiefdoms.

In the seventh century, when Kartli fell under direct Arab domination, Kakheti managed to remain autonomous under the rule of the Donauri family. At the beginning of the 11th century, one Kvirike III crowned himself king. Ruled by a succession of strong local princes and the occasional king, Kakheti remained autonomous until 1105, when David the Builder conquered the region and incorporated it into a united Georgian kingdom. Until then the Kakhetian principality had resisted the efforts of the Bagratid family of kings, who had sought from the ninth through the early 11th century to annex it to their kingdom in western Kartli. As a result of David the Builder's campaign in Kakheti and elsewhere, his heirs ruled over a much enlarged Georgia. The monarchy held sway over Kakheti until the Mongol invasions of the 13th century, at which time it fell, along with the rest of eastern Georgia, under the rule of the Mongol Khan and his appointees.

Throughout the 14th century Kakheti shared a history with Kartli, experiencing the benefits of a resurgence of the Georgian monarchy under Giorgi V (1314–1346) and the devastation and terror of Tamerlane's invasion in 1386. Fratricidal conflicts by the heirs of Aleksandre I, the last king of a united Georgia (1412–1442), splintered the Georgian kingdom once again. Aleksandre's son, Giorgi VIII, having lost Kartli in a power struggle with Bagrat VI in 1465, escaped to Kakheti to form a new kingdom. His son continued to rule this new kingdom from 1476 to 1511 as Aleksandre II.

Georgia's economic decline during the 16th century did not affect Kakheti which, because of its proximity to the silk route to Astrakhan, was able to participate in trade of more international dimensions. During this period Jewish, Armenian, and Persian colonies sprang up in Kakheti and enlarged the market towns. These years also saw the growth of towns like Gremi and Telavi.

When the Turks and the Persians signed the Peace of Amasa in 1555, regions of Georgia were divided between the two powers. Kakheti fell under the rule of the Safavids of Persia. Despite continual attempts to free themselves from Persian domination, Kakhetian kings ruled only by the grace of Isfahan until the Russian annexation of Georgia 245 years later.

Kakheti's desire to ally with Russia considerably predated the actual annexation. During the reign of King Levan I of Kakheti (1520–1574), initial efforts were made to interest the Tsar of Russia to aid a Christian kingdom suffering under Moslem rule. These efforts were continued by Levan's son, Aleksandre II of Kakheti, who received envoys from Moscow at Gremi and later managed to exchange ambassadors with Tsar Fedor Ivanovich. Nothing more substantial occurred, however, and when Shah Abbas I (1587–1629) took power as ruler of Iran, a period of devastation for Kakheti began—which the Russians did nothing to alleviate. Shah Abbas I was interested in establishing greater Iranian hegemony over the Southern Caucasus and was therefore determined to defeat the Turks to fulfill his ambition. To this end he pressed the Georgian kings to join him on his campaigns. Aleksandre II marched with Shah Abbas against the Turks, leaving his son Giorgi to rule. Facing a Turkish threat, Giorgi found it expedient to ally himself with the Russians.

The resulting story is a microcosm of the complexity of Georgian politics of the period, a story that led to disastrous consequences for Kakheti. Aleksandre returned to Kakheti in 1605 with his son Konstantin, who had been raised a Moslem in the court of Shah Abbas. Soon after their return Konstantin, acting on the shah's orders, murdered both his father and older brother Giorgi and crowned himself king. Kakhetian nobles, led by Queen Ketevan, one of Aleksandre's daughters-in-law, revolted against Konstantin, who was killed in battle. Ketevan's son, Teimuraz I (1606–1664), was made king. Shah Abbas thought it politically expedient to recognize Teimuraz, but at the first opportunity he invaded Georgia again and in 1616, drove Teimuraz from the throne. Shah Abbas replaced him with a grandson of Aleksandre II, Iese Khan, who had been raised as a Moslem. In 1616 the Kakhetians rebelled against the Moslem king. Shah Abbas exacted a savage retribution, invading Kakheti and killing between 60,000 and 70,000 peasants. More than 100,000 Kakhetians were deported to Iran, the majority to a region called Fereidan near Isfahan. Though now Moslem, to this day bread is still baked in the shape of a cross in the region. Many of the villages are named after places in Kakheti.

As a result of Shah Abbas' policy, the population of Kakheti declined by two thirds and whole towns like Gremi ceased to exist. Though Teimuraz, exiled in

Imereti, requested aid from the Russians to march against the Persians, he managed to regain his throne only as a result of the guerrilla war waged by the powerful Georgian soldier Giorgi Saakadze in 1625. Unwilling to face further rebellion by the Georgians and fearful of Russian intervention in the region, Shah Abbas recognized Teimuraz as king. Despite this capitulation and the death of Shah Abbas in 1629, Iranian influence in Kakheti remained strong until the beginning of the 18th century, when the Turks dominated the region.

The Turks put Teimuraz II (1733–1744) on the throne of Kakheti. He succeeded his brother, King Konstantin, who was murdered for trying to throw off Turkish domination. Teimuraz II did just that when he allied himself with Nadir Shah, the ambitious new ruler of Iran. A combined Georgian-Iranian force drove out the Turks, and Teimuraz II ruled in Kakheti as an Iranian governor. His son, Herekle, served under Nadir Shah during his Indian campaign. This fact should be remembered when you see the portrait of a turbaned Herekle in the Historical and Ethnographical Museum in Telavi (*see* page 295). As a result of loyal service to the shah, Teimuraz II was made King of Kartli (1744–1762) and his son Herekle was named King of Kakheti (1744–1762).

When Nadir Shah was murdered in 1747, the father-and-son kings of Kartli and Kakheti set about filling the void created by the absence of a strong Iranian ruler. In this they largely succeeded, and when Teimuraz died, Herekle II became king of a united Kartli-Kakheti (1762–1798). Known as *patara kakhi* ("the little Kakhetian"), Herekle forged a kingdom that actively redressed many of the economic and social problems that had plagued eastern Georgia under Iranian hegemony. Commercial ties to Russia increased.

In Kakheti, Telavi and Sighnaghi grew as market centers. Herekle realized that the safety of his kingdom from Turkish, Iranian, and Daghestani incursions could best be obtained by an alliance with Catherine the Great. Despite repeated promises from Catherine and repeated disappointments suffered by the Georgians, Herekle signed the Treaty of Georgievsk on July 24, 1783, placing Kartli-Kakheti under Russian protection. A copy of this document is in Herekle's summer palace in Telavi; the original is held in the Institute of Manuscripts in Tbilisi.

Russian troops were garrisoned in Tbilisi, but at the outbreak of the Russo-Turkish War in 1787, Catherine withdrew her soldiers and Herekle was forced to face an invading Iranian force in 1795. The Iranians, under Shah Agha Mohammed Khan, captured and burned Tbilisi, and Herekle fled to Kakheti. He died there in 1798. Herekle's son, Giorgi XII (1798–1800), had no choice but to continue to press the Russians for protection. On December 18, 1800, Catherine's son, now Tsar Paul, annexed Kartli-Kakheti to Russia. Under the terms of the Treaty of Georgievsk, the continuation of the Georgian crown was guaranteed to Herekle and his heirs.

Giorgi XII died at the beginning of 1801, just before the arrival of Russian troops in Tbilisi. Tsar Paul's son, Alexander I, simply abolished the Georgian-Bagratid monarchy and incorporated the Kingdom of Kartli-Kakheti into the Russian Empire.

Touring the Province

Allow yourself at least three days to discover the richness of Kakheti. A fourth should be added if you'd like to visit the nature reserve of Lagodekhi in the easternmost part of the province. A stop at the ancient fortress town of Sighnaghi could be made en route to Lagodekhi. The first excursion into Kakheti can be be done as a day trip from Tbilisi. This would include sites in outer Kakheti: Ninotsminda and David-Gareja. The second and third itineraries are best handled as two day trips from Telavi.

Ninotsminda–David-Gareja

Leaving Tbilisi by the airport road, pick up the A302 east toward Telavi. (The border between Kartli and Kakheti is the village of Sartichala.) The village of Ninotsminda is 47 km (29 miles) from Tbilisi on the A302. The cathedral complex is situated off to the left, above the main road through the village. Take the second left turn upon entering the village and climb the dirt road for approximately 100 meters (328 feet).

THE CATHEDRAL OF NINOTSMINDA

Though the cathedral itself (AD 575) is largely in ruins, this is a profoundly impressive site, with extremely well preserved defensive walls surrounding the complex and a belltower that reveals a decidedly Safavid-Persian influence.

The walls themselves were built in the 16th–17th centuries to protect the villagers from the continual Persian incursions. The masonry is superb, and the beehive machicolations are most distinctive. The protruding towers that flank the southern entrance add to the site's powerful effect on the imagination.

The importance of this structure cannot be overestimated, given that it predates Jvari in Mtskheta. The first major church with a centralized plan, it served as a model for the transition to the mature Jvari-style tetraconch. What remains today is the eastern apse and a small portion of the western wall. In the conch over the altar can be seen 16th-century fresco fragments of the Virgin with Child surrounded by angels. The upper arches, squinches, and a portion of the drum restored in the tenth century can be seen in the east.

Ninotsminda has the outline of a tetraconch, with corner niches surrounding the octagonal central room that was originally covered with vaulting. In the tenth to 11th centuries the structure of the vaulting was altered. Pilasters were adjoined to the ends of the conch walls, and a drummed cupola was raised with the help of squinches. Additional restoration occurred in 1671 with construction of the brick portico in front of the entrance in the west. Further restoration was done on the cupola drum by Archbishop Savva Tushishvili in 1774. At that time he also enlarged the archbishop's residence connected to the belltower in the northeast section of the complex.

The cathedral was destroyed by earthquakes in 1824 and in 1848. The sophistication of the design and construction of Ninotsminda in conjunction with its great age cannot fail to move any admirer of Georgian architecture, especially in light of its function as precursor to so many other glorious structures.

THE BELLTOWER OF NINOTSMINDA

Built during the reign of King Levan I (1520–1574) and with his direct patronage, this belltower also had a residential function served by the three stories below the polygonal belfry. Each floor is distinct as to floor plan and vaulting. All have fireplaces. Floors two and three also have alcoves. The use of brick, particularly in the decoration of the façade by staggered placement and differentiation of surface, bespeaks the Persian influence on the belltower's conception. The aura of the Orient is heightened by the pointed arch over the entrance and repeated on the

A view of the eastern apse of the Cathedral of Ninotsminda surrounded by its defensive walls (photo by David Halford)

entablatures beneath the cross reliefs and throughout the belfry. Few monuments in Kakheti better encapsulate in their architectonic elements the complicated political situation in the region during this period.

It is possible to climb to the top of the belfry, and the view will justify your exertions. The colored scraps of cloth on the window bars are tied there as votive offerings.

The cathedral complex is usually locked, so apply at the house across the road to get in. The villagers use the complex as a place for holidays, festivals, and weddings. You stand the best chance of coming upon an event on Sunday. June 27 is a religious festival honoring St. Nino, for whom the church is named.

Getting to a higher point above the cathedral complex is also worth the effort and can be achieved by either driving or walking on the only road that leads up the hill behind the north wall. The view of the cathedral, the tower, and the Iori tableland stretching south to Azerbaijan is both beautiful and instructive in comprehending the geopolitical realities that have beset this sorely tried region for so many years. South is also the direction in which you will next be heading as you drive to the monastery of David-Gareja, located between Ninotsminda and one of Georgia's southern borders.

David-Gareja

Although this isolated group of monasteries is somewhat tricky to reach, their location, architectural uniqueness, history, and important frescoes will amply reward your efforts. From Ninotsminda continue east on the main road through the village until you arrive in the town of Sagarejo. On its eastern outskirts, a sign on your left indicates Giorgitsminda one km (0.6 miles) away. Do not turn, but continue straight and turn right onto the asphalt road that runs past the large factory at the corner. This factory is now home to Chalice Wines, a Georgian-American joint venture. Follow this road for two km (1.2 miles) until you arrive at a T-junction. (It's 41 km/25.4 miles from David-Gareja to here.) Turn left onto a dirt road and continue to an overturned railroad car where you can turn right. Follow this road over the bridge that spans the Iori River and bear left onto the road to the village of Udabno, 22 km (13.6 miles) away. (Do not take the road to Krasnogorsk eight km/five miles away.) So far you've been traveling through a region of vineyards and plots of mulberry trees. The unremitting flatness of the landscape is lacking in charm. Much of the area was forest until the 16th century, when the Turks systematically leveled it as a means of better controlling the territory. It is perhaps that sad patrimony that the region evokes.

Once you head toward Udabno you're in a steppe zone with yellow fields of rape. Continue through the new village of Udabno (created to resettle Svans who

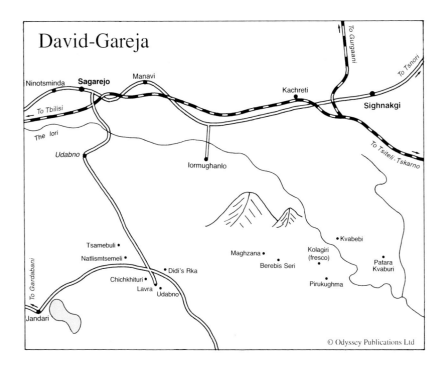

David-Gareja

To Gurgaani

To Tsnori

Ninotsminda   **Sagarejo**   Manavi

Kachreti

To Tbilisi

Sighnakgi

The Iori

Udabno

Iormughanlo

To Tsiteli · Tskarno

Tsamebuli •

• Kvabebi

Natlismtsemeli •

Maghzana •

Kolagiri (fresco) •

Berebis Seri •

• Patara Kvaburi

• Didi's Rka

Chichkhituri •

Lavra •

Udabno

Pirukughma •

To Gardabani

Jandari

© Odyssey Publications Ltd

lost their homes in an avalanche) and press on to the southeast. The landscape here is savannah-like, with a decidedly eerie barrenness occasionally interrupted by patches of salt lakes and clumps of juniper. As you get closer to the semidesert slopes of the Gareja hills and the monastery complex, the topography turns lunar and you can understand why a monk looking to chastise the flesh and hone the spirit would have chosen such a place. Watchtowers stand camouflaged among the basalt outcroppings of distant hills, created as an early-warning system against the Turkish and Persian hordes. When your odometer reads 41 km (25.4 miles), you should be able to turn left off the main asphalt road onto a dirt track that leads to David-Gareja 1.5 km (0.9 miles) farther. A sign marks the turnoff, and a watch-tower soon becomes visible to the right on the rise of a hill. You're now in one of the easternmost outposts of Christendom. From here it is no more than four km (2.5 miles) to the border with Azerbaijan. (David-Gareja can also be reached from Tbilisi via Rustavi.)

David-Gareja is actually the overall name for 12 monasteries in the immediate area: Kolagiri, Pirukughma, Patara Kvaburi, Kvavbebi, Lavra, Udabno, Maghazana, Berebis Seri, Chichkhituri, Dodo's Rqa, Natlismtsemeli, and Tsamebuli. (A 13th monastery, Bertubani, is now on Azerbaijani soil. It is particularly noteworthy for its frescoes from the beginning of the 13th century, especially those depicting Queen Tamara and her son Giorgi IV Lasha.) Apart from the parent monastery of Lavra—and to a certain extent the monastery of Udabno—the others are extremely difficult to get to; some are accessible only on foot and are of limited interest because of their ruined state. Natlismtsemeli, 12 km (7.4 miles) northwest of Lavra, is said to have a portrait of David the Builder. If you're one of those people who has to cover all the bases, the map on page 283 will be of some help, but you would do best to try to find a guide among the workers at Lavra. To take in a reasonable number of caves will take a minimum of three hours, round-trip from Lavra. Dress code is important here, since the monastery is now home to an ever increasing number of monks. They particularly ask that men wear trousers and women wear skirts or trousers and no shoulder-revealing tops.

The original monastery was founded in the sixth century by David, one of the 13 Syrian Fathers, who settled in a natural cave on the slopes of the Gareja hills. This was the spot around which the monastery of Lavra developed. Disciples of David joined him to carve out additional caves from the soft sandstone, and so the complex flourished. Two of David's disciples, Dodo and Lukiane, went on to found Dodo's Rqa and Natlismtsemeli. These two ascetics are buried in the Church of Peristsvaleba on the first level of Lavra. The church dates from the ninth century and was founded by Ilarion Kartveli, who greatly contributed to the monastery's growth in other ways as well.

Precedents for cave complexes such as David-Gareja can be found in Uplitstikhe outside of Gori in the secular vein, and throughout Syria and Cappadocia in the ecclesiastical context. It is widely believed that the so-called Syrian Fathers—Georgians who studied a mode of asceticism in the Middle East and brought it home—were responsible for the growth of cave architecture. It certainly flourished in Georgia, as single caves hewn out of cliff faces grew into a community of caves interlinked by passages and internal staircases, sustained by terrace gardens and sophisticated water-gathering systems. Thus did David-Gareja, Zedazeni in Kartli, and the great cave complex of Vardzia in Javakheti evolve.

In the 11th century the monastery was partially destroyed by an invasion of the Seljuk Turks. During David the Builder's reign (1089–1125), the monastery's development began anew. During the reign of David's son, Demetre I, it received considerable royal patronage. This patronage, in conjunction with Georgia's newly acquired power in the Middle East, allowed for a period of prosperity that lasted until the Mongol invasion in the 13th century. The 12th century saw the construction of the monasteries of Udabno, Bertubani, and Chichkhituri, as well as the enlargement and reorganization of the older ones.

The Monastery of David-Gareja is once again a working religious community

Under Father Superior Onopre Garejeli, the David-Gareja complex became the most important center of culture and education throughout east Georgia. A distinct school of manuscript illumination and fresco painting also developed here during the 12th century.

The monastery of Udabno is considered the center at which this school began, but the apogee of the style can be seen in the frescoes at the monastery of Bertubani. What makes the frescoes at David-Gareja special is their break with Byzantine canonic themes, which are replaced here for the first time with treatments of local religious themes, specifically, the life of David Gareja, the Georgian saint and founder of the monastery. (For further information on the frescoes at Udabno, *see* page 288).

The Mongol invasion of the 13th century effectively destroyed life at the monastery. Treasures were carried off, manuscripts burned, frescoes defaced. A century later a monastic community was reestablished here and restoration work undertaken. But Tamerlane's invasion in the 14th century reversed these efforts. This cycle—rebuilding followed by invasions—lasted throughout the 15th century. Unfortunately, the forces of ruin triumphed during this phase particularly, and it is to this date that scholars ascribe the end of the Gareja school of fresco painting. In 1615, the Safavid Persians led by Shah Abbas killed the monks at David-Gareja and destroyed all remaining works of art and manuscripts.

Not until the end of the 17th century was there any attempt to revive the monastery, when King Teimuraz (1605–1664) bestowed his royal patronage upon it. Invasions throughout the 18th century and the rise of the town and secular education in the 19th century effectively impeded the growth of David-Gareja. From the second half of the 19th century up to the 1920s, only a few monks lived there. Only in 1988 was work allowed to begin once more to make David-Gareja the thriving community it once was. Archaeologists, art restorers, and Georgian Orthodox monks work shoulder to shoulder to raise from the ravages of predatory invaders and indifferent time the mysterious glory of this complex.

THE MONASTERY OF LAVRA

The monastery is open every day from morning to evening. Water is a problem in this clime, so you probably should bring a canteen filled in Sagarejo. The water from the fountain at the car park will make you sick. A monk or an archaeologist might be willing to act as guide as a kindness. This can be arranged only on an impromptu basis and on the spot. In summer you should try to attend the huge festival, Garejoba, begun in 1975, which is celebrated at Lavra on the second Sunday of May.

Climbing to the main entrance of Lavra, be sure to note the channels cleverly carved into the smooth sandstone to allow water to funnel into a collecting basin at the bottom. Also note the small steps carved into the stone to facilitate access to the water-gathering system. The large stone portal through which you enter the monastery was erected by Onopre Machutadze, who was appointed Father Superior in 1690. Once inside you can better see the multi-tiered structure of the monastery and appreciate the sophistication of the builders who so cleverly camouflaged the full extent of the complex within the contours of the stony slopes.

The caves sunk into the hillside to the southeast (left as you enter) are the basis of the complex from which everything else grew. It was here in the sixth century that David chose a natural cave in which to live and worship. Other caves were carved out of the soft sandstone by his disciples, and feature churches like those found in Syria and Cappadocia: caverns with a kind of barrel vaulting. Certain caves reveal an interesting construction consisting of staggered rows of brick covered in stucco. Many of the monks' quarters here also contain small meditation chambers carved out of the wall. Following an early Christian ascetic tradition, the monks would shut themselves in these rooms no larger than holes without food for days at a time.

The monastery grew up the side of the cliff face and then across the lower level to the west, before climbing south again as higher levels were created to accommodate the increasing number of monks who flocked here. On the first level in the northwest you can visit the Church of Peristsvaleba (the Transfiguration). This ninth-century church features a 14th-century iconostasis and the tombs of Dodo and Lukian.

As you climb higher toward the south, skirting the central courtyard, you come upon two caves that functioned as a bakery and a refectory. The bakery is distinguished by two holes in the roof (one allowing light to enter, the other for smoke to depart). Much of this area still has not been excavated. Looking out over the central courtyard to the terraces joining the east and west sections, you can see a lot of the new planting that has occurred here, the continuation of a 1,300-year tradition of terraced plots.

Continuing to the upper yard, you can visit the 16th-century tower of Aleksandre II, King of Kakheti, who came here for extended periods of prayer. Though badly defaced by graffiti, his room at the top of the stairs reveals, through the eastern style of the interior decorative carving, the strong influence that Persia had over this region at the time.

Leaving the complex through the back gate of the upper yard, you can climb the steep slope of the hill behind the monastery to drink at the only spring in the area. Inside the first large cave, only five minutes away, is the spring called David's Tears, where the first hermits found water. It was consecrated as a holy place sometime between the 11th and 13th centuries. The water is clean and cold, a good place to stop before setting off for the longer, more difficult hike to Udabno.

THE MONASTERY OF UDABNO

The monastery is a difficult, one-hour hike from Lavra. It is one km (0.6 miles) up to the top of the mountain. A guide would be advisable if you can find someone to go with you. From the upper level at Lavra, take the path that winds right around the cave of the spring and up to the top of the mountain. Be careful as you walk through the tall grass—there are many snakes in this area. The same is true of any walk you might take in the fields in the immediate vicinity of the monastery complex. The view of Lavra from the top of the mountain is stupendous.

It is not, however, the sole justification for making the effort to visit Udabno. This cave monastery was home to one of the most important schools of monumental painting in Georgia from the ninth to 13th centuries. Some of the fruits of that school have survived, and fragments from the late tenth and early 11th centuries can be seen in and around the monastery's refectory and main church. These extraordinary wall paintings reveal both a distinctive Georgian style and a national hagiography of great importance.

On the north wall of the main church are fragments of a large cycle of wall paintings devoted to the life of David Gareja. Taking up the middle register of three rows of paintings, the cycle probably extended onto the destroyed south wall as well. The loving portrayal of animals, specifically the deer to the right of David and Lukian, suggests the sensibility extolled at this school. The deers' presence refers to a legend about the time that Lukian and David were wandering here with nothing. Lukian asked, "How will we survive?" David replied, "God will provide." Immediately, deer arrived and gave them milk.

Below, on the north wall in the lower register, can be seen local Kakhetian princes, doubtless connected with the patronage of the monastery and this church. The conch of the apse shows a Madonna and Child with angels. The Last Judgment on the east wall is the oldest wall painting of this subject that exists in Georgia.

The refectory is decorated with scenes from both the Old and New Testaments, including the Hospitality of Abraham and the Last Supper. The recessed apse in the east wall contains a painting of the Deesis. Also included throughout the refectory are saints who comprised the 13 Syrian Fathers, one of whom, the younger Simeon of Aleppo, is known to have been the spiritual father of St. David. St. David himself is also depicted here.

The monasteries of Lavra and Udabno are well worth the trip into this austere part of Kakheti, topographically so unlike the rich vineyards of the Alazani plain. They're akin to the cave monastery of Vardzia in feeling, though smaller in dimensions. The ability to wander through the depth of space as well as the multiple tiers makes you feel as though you have penetrated some of the mystery here that the longitudinal emphasis of Vardzia somehow denies. Lavra, nestled and hidden between those two sharp and clean diagonal slopes, an ensemble for the painter or photographer, just can't be beat. It's best to return by the road on which you came.

The Road to Telavi

Leaving Tbilisi east on the A302, you have two ways to get to Telavi. The first is to continue on the A302 as far as Bakurtsikhe before bearing left on the road to Telavi. The total distance is approximately 150 km (93 miles): 102 km (63 miles) to Bakurtsikhe and 45 km (28 miles) from there to Telavi. This route is longer by 54 km (34 miles) than your second option, but it is usually faster, the road is definitely better, and you have the possibility to incorporate interesting stops. At Gurjaani, you can visit the unique double-domed church of **Kvelatsminda** (eighth century), and, by taking a short detour of nine km (5.5 miles) before **Bakurtsikhe**, you can see the famous fortified town of Sighnaghi with its 29 towers along the city wall.

The second, more scenic, and less traveled way is over the Gombori Range in the direction of the village of Gombori. (At the time of writing this road is said to be impassable.) The turnoff for this village is 27 km (16.7 miles) from Tbilisi on the

Shepherds drive their flocks to grazing on the Kakhetian Range

A302. The distance to Gombori is 33 km (20.4 miles). This route takes you past the ruins of the famous fortified town of Ujarma that flourished between AD 500 and 1000. The road itself was an important trade route, with many caravanserais along it, which flourished until the 12th century. The ruins of custom houses and watchtowers can be seen by the road and in the hills. Continuing on this road in the direction of Khevsurtsopeli brings you to the ruins of the architecturally important tenth-century site of the six-apsed domed church of **Bochorma**. (To get to the church, bear left at the 56-km/34.7-mile point from Tbilisi where the road forks right to Gombori and left to Khevsurtsopeli. Continue one km/0.6 miles past the bridge that spans the Iori River and then turn right onto the dirt road that climbs through the forested hills. Even with a jeep you'll probably only be able to manage about one km—the road is horrible. From here it is approximately a one-hour climb up the hill).

The distance from Gombori to Telavi is 33 km (20 miles), and the route allows you to stop at the three churches of Dzveli (Old) Shuamta (from the fifth through seventh centuries) and the 16th-century monastery complex of Akhali (New) Shuamta. The turnoff to this site is 57 km (35 miles) from Gombori and 11 km (6.8 miles) from Telavi. The turnoff is clearly marked. Another two-km (1.2-mile) drive brings you to Akhali Shuamta. Three km (1.8 miles) farther is Dzveli Shuamta. Shuamta in Georgian means "between the mountains," and the isolated position of these two monasteries, nestled in the densely forested hills of the Gombori range, explains the name.

Dzveli Shuamta

Three churches stand on the grounds of Dzveli Shuamta, situated in a tight group at the northern end of a clearing in the woods, high above the Alazani River valley. Telavi can be seen in the distance. Dzveli Shuamta was a favorite place of pilgrimage throughout the Middle Ages until the founding of Akhali Shuamta in the 16th century.

THE BASILICA

The southernmost structure (the nearest one as you come through the gates) is the oldest church in the complex. Probably founded by one of the 13 Syrian Fathers in the sixth century, it is an excellent example of a triple-church basilica, a style that marks one of the earliest stages in the development of religious architecture in Georgia.

In keeping with this style, the church has three parallel naves, the central one being both the largest and highest. An unusual feature is that the height of the southern and northern lateral naves is the same as the joining western nave, each nave is crowned with barrel vaulting. The altar, raised on two steps, is set deeply into the eastern apse and separated from the central nave by an altar screen. This alabaster screen is a rare intact example. From fragments we know that these were usually richly carved with a high level of artistry. The large stone archbishop's throne in the eastern niche is also noteworthy.

The interior of the church was primarily illuminated by the three entrances into the lateral naves. Additionally, the southern and northern naves feature windows in the east wall and the central nave receives light from two high-set windows in its south wall. The end effect is a shimmering phantasmagorical half-light out of which one feels one of the Syrian founding fathers might well spring in full vestments, intoning prayers.

As was the usual practice in Kakheti, the unadorned exterior is made from even levels of fieldstone. The monks are believed to have been responsible for devising a powerful mortar that used egg yolks as the binding agent, which partially accounts for the durability of these walls. The roof is made from terracotta tiles which, with the white and yellow of the stone and the surrounding green forest, contribute to the subtle palette that infuses this quiet, dignified corner of the world.

Immediately to the north of the basilica is a tetraconch cupola church from the first quarter of the seventh century. Stylistically this belongs to the tradition embodied by the Jvari Church of Mtskheta. The elongation in the east-west axis is a result of the bema of the eastern altar, which is absent from the transverse apses. The cupola rests on walls and is supported by squinches. The central space is lit by a window in the altar and four windows in the cupola drum, as well as the two entrances. The altar is raised on three steps and is distinguished by a stone throne in the middle of the space. The inner walls contain traces of frescoes that were probably executed in the 11th and 12th centuries. A cross can be discerned in the vault of the cupola.

The exterior configuration of the church is in keeping with this architectural style: each three-faceted apse is flanked by tall niches. The walls are made of large fieldstones and the corners are finished with interlocking hewn stones. Given the close proximity of this church to the basilica, one feels that it could have been literally spawned by its elder.

To the southeast, only a couple of steps away, is another tetraconch church, a simplified miniature of its neighbor, which was probably built at the same time, by the same architect, possibly the Father Superior of the monastery. His motivation might have been the need to create a place for solitary worship. A crypt was built in the north end.

The tetraconch plan of this church features five-faceted apses that are slightly elongated along the east-west axis. The scale does not allow for corner rooms, but cylindrical niches serve to meet the artistic needs of the plan. The interior walls, illuminated by four cupola windows and an altar window, have been plastered over leaving no traces of frescoes.

The proximity of the churches and the quality of the sacred grove in which they stand suggest not only a close-knit architectural ensemble but a monastic community whose shared passion for this particular location must have helped in its path toward spiritual union.

Akhali Shuamta

Three km (1.8 miles) before Dzveli Shuamta is Akhali Shuamta. More than 1,000 years separate the two monasteries. Akhali Shuamta possesses a large central-cupola cathedral and belltower, both commissioned by King Levan (1520–1574) and his wife Tinatin in the second quarter of the 16th century. An interesting legend is attached to its founding. When Levan was King of Kakheti he married Tinatin, the daughter of Mamia Gurieli, the ruler of Guria. As a child Tinatin had a dream that she was traveling to her wedding. While resting, she saw a white dogwood tree. A clergyman told her to build the Church of the Birth of the Virgin there. Later, when she went to Kakheti as Levan's bride, she saw a white dogwood near Shuamta that resembled the one in her dream. Soon thereafter she began to build the Akhali Shuamta there. The monastery is once more functioning as a working monastic community.

THE CHURCH OF THE NATIVITY OF THEOTOKOS

Built of brick and covered in the 19th century with stucco, this church, with its elongated east-west axis, conforms to the plan of the cruciform, central cupola-style cathedral. The cupola is tall and well-proportioned, and supported by two free-standing pillars in the west. The interior is well illuminated by eight long, narrow windows piercing the cupola's drum. Additional light enters through the three entrances, a high window on each wall, and two extra windows in the north and south. This is a boon to the traveler as some of the frescoes are well-preserved and of great artistic and historical merit. They were commissioned by Queen Tinatin, who allowed herself to be immortalized by a portrait of her with her husband Levan and her son Alexander on the southern portion of the west wall. Other frescoes that remain are the large Ascension on the west wall, and the Mourning at the Grave and Washing of the Feet on the north wall.

The height and elongated dimensions of this church are uncharacteristic of the period and the soaring movement more Gothic in style. This association is reinforced by the division of the interior space into narrow lengths that lead one toward the space to be found in the lofty caverns of the extremely tall cupola.

Tinatin and Levan had two sons: Alexander and Vakhtang. Apparently Levan was not the faithful husband we all might have wished, prompting Tinatin to move into the belltower to the southeast of the church and retire from the world. She asked her sons not to bury her with Levan but in the Church of the Nativity of Theotokos in Shuamta, which is where she lies to this day in a tomb to the north of the altar.

THE BELLTOWER

Built at the same time as the church, the square belltower has four stories. The first floor features a large reception hall with a decorated dome. The second floor is cozier, with a narrower central section and wide niches in the wall. The third floor consists of small rooms that lead onto the balconies on three sides. An internal staircase goes from here to the six-faceted, dome-covered belfry. Special permission, difficult to come by, is needed to go inside the tower.

Akhali Shuamta served an important political purpose. In 1604, it was chosen as the site where King Aleksandre II of Kakheti met with the delegation sent by Tsar Boris Godunov to discuss providing Russain aid to their fellow Christians struggling against the Moslem threat.

Telavi

Lying on the northern slope of the Tsiv-Gombori range above the Alazani River valley, Telavi has a population of 28,000. Telavi was the capital of the kingdom of Kakheti three times, once in the 11th century, in the 17th century after Gremi had been destroyed by Shah Abbas, and yet again in the 18th century. The city is currently the administrative and cultural center of Kakheti.

Rich in gardens and streets lined with oak, walnut, plane, and mulberry trees, Telavi clearly retains the pleasures of a small city while at the same time offering those to be found in the nearby forests of the Gombori. Telavi's sheer staying power through 20 centuries of shifting fortunes has bred an impressive equilibrium in its citizens. They are people who take a leisurely and dignified long view of things. *Sic transit gloria mundi*, they seem to say, with the full knowledge that this is so. There is good Kakhetian wine on the table and even better friends to drink it with. Why worry? Acknowledging that the status of his city was not what it once was, one Telavian was heard telling the following joke: "What happened to the Kakhetian living in the States who tried to phone home to Telavi?" Answer: "The operator connected him to Tel Aviv."

Telavi is the best base from which to make your excursions through Kakheti. It also happens to be the only town in the entire province with a former Intourist hotel, though at the time of writing it is temporarily closed.

Known since the first century AD as a trade center on a caravan route from the Middle East to Western Europe, Telavi first appeared on a second-century Greek map under its original name, Telaiba. The town was thriving in the fifth century,

A contemporary statue in Telavi celebrating the grape harvest

and by the 11th it had become the capital. Telavi's importance certainly diminished as the power center of Georgia shifted back and forth between Tbilisi and Kutaisi. From the 16th century until its destruction by Shah Abbas in 1615, Gremi was the capital of the Kakhetian Kingdom.

Telavi rose to prominence again in the middle of the 17th century, when Herekle II became King of Kakheti. The palace and castle walls in the center of the city were built during his reign. When he united Kartli and Kakheti in 1762, he moved the capital to Tbilisi and turned the palace in Telavi into his summer residence. Herekle fought in more than 100 battles and was wounded more than 80 times. His last battle, which he lost to the Persian Khan, took place when he was 75. Forced to flee Tbilisi, he returned to Telavi where he died at the age of 78 in 1798, having served as king for 54 years.

Herekle's palace is the centerpiece of Telavi. In front of the castle gates is Merab Merabishvili's equestrian statue of Herekle, visible when you first enter the town on the road from Tbilisi. Nearby is a famous 800-year-old plane tree, measuring 40 meters (131 feet) high and 11.4 meters (37.4 feet) around the base.

On the grounds surrounded by Herekle's crenellated walls (rebuilt in the 19th century) are the lion's share of the town's interesting sites.

THE HISTORICAL AND ETHNOGRAPHIC MUSEUM

Probably the best museum of its kind in Georgia outside of Tbilisi, the museum displays its treasures chronologically to give a view of Kakhetian history, from Bronze and Iron age tools to folk costumes still worn at the beginning of the 20th century. In between are models of churches throughout the region, reproductions of frescoes, books and manuscripts printed in Georgian on the country's first press (c. 1709), 16th-century arms and armor, the 16th-century silverware of King Aleksandre II, and a painting of Herekle II wearing a turban. This last item was presented to the king by the Persian ruler Nadir Shah, with whom he campaigned in India. Although a lifelong Christian, Herekle wore a turban during his time of service with Nadir Shah, an excellent example of the bend-but-don't-break school of diplomacy. A wonderful legend is attached to Herekle's soldiering with Nadir Shah, supposedly the reason for the Persian's gratitude and the gift. When Herekle was with Nadir Shah's army in India they came upon a small stone post with a sign reading, "Anyone who steps beyond this point will be punished by God." The army stopped in its tracks and wouldn't budge until Herekle deployed one of his elephants to pull up the post. He then placed it on the animal's back, and continued the march. Thus the army never stepped beyond the dreaded post.

ART GALLERY

On the palace grounds, occupying a handful of rooms, is a small, eclectic collection of Georgian, Russian, Dutch, and Italian paintings of the 17th to 19th centuries. A rather fine Aivazovsky makes stopping in worthwhile.

HEREKLE'S PALACE

Built in the mid-18th century, the palace reflects a Persian architectural style with stained-glass panels and low doorways that required anyone entering to bow in deference or bang his head. The plan consists of five corner rooms and one large hall where guests were received. The palace was restored in 1983 to mark the 200th anniversary of the signing of the Treaty of Georgievsk that made Kartli-Kakheti a Russian protectorate. The treaty displayed inside the palace is a copy.

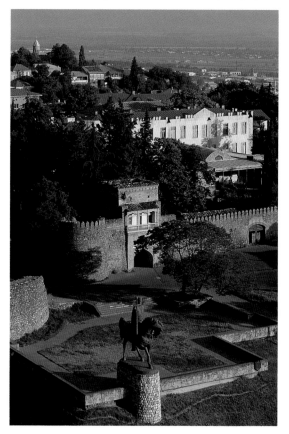

The original is in the Institute of Manuscripts in Tbilisi. Take a few moments to sit pasha-style on the balcony. You can literally smell the roses, for there is a lovely rose garden in front of the palace.

Additional monuments within the castle enclosure are the royal church of Herekle, built in 1758, an 17th–18th-century basilica, ruins of the king's baths from the 11th century, and a pantheon of famous Kakhetians' graves. The grounds are beautifully landscaped and it's a pleasure to stroll behind the fortress walls under the shade of the trees, especially on a hot summer's day.

The equestrian statue of Herekle II before his castle in the center of Telavi

Tsinandali

Ten km (6.2 miles) southeast of Telavi on the road that joins the A302 back to
Tbilisi is the village of Tsinandali. Here (to the right of the main road—a large parking area marks the spot) is the estate of the 19th-century poet, public figure, and
Kakhetian prince Alexander Chavchavadze (1786–1846). Reflecting the European
tastes of those members of the 19th-century Georgian aristocracy who were wealthy
and interested enough to travel, the grounds are laid out as a magnificent English
park. The approach to the House Museum is flanked by superb sentinels of cypress.
It leads to an array of exotic plants that partially obscure some of the Eastern decorative elements that grace the wooden balconies around the house. A splendid rose
garden within a garden maze is also in front. Among the many rarities brought to
this extensive park from all over the world is a sequoia.

HOUSE MUSEUM OF ALEXANDER CHAVCHAVADZE

A center of intellectual life, the house served as a salon for exiled Decembrists and
Mikhail Lermontov, together with members of his regiment, the Nizhegorodsky
Dragoons, whose headquarters were nearby. The house is mentioned in the writings
of Lermontov and Alexandre Dumas.

Chavchavadze's poetry marks the beginning of Georgian romanticism. It is work
fueled by the the country's disillusionment over its loss of independence. As such,
patriotism and many of the virtues, both poetic and personal, embodied in the work
of Rustaveli came to the fore.

The aristocratic Chavchavadzes were certainly among the most talented and
powerful families not just in Kakheti but in all of Georgia. Alexander's father,
Garsevan, who founded the famous winery on the property, was King Herekle's
ambassador to Russia. Alexander's daughter, Nina, married the Russian poet and
diplomat Alexander Griboyedov. A frequent guest here, he and Nina married in the
chapel in the park. Griboyedov met his end at the hands of an enraged mob in Iran.

The museum itself will be most meaningful to Russian and Georgian speakers
familiar with the work of Chavchavadze, since the collection is almost exclusively
devoted to his memorabilia and that of his family. In addition the rooms show what
the good life in Kakheti must have been like in the 19th century.

In the northeast corner of the park is the **Tsinandali Winery** built in the 19th
century by Alexander Chavchavadze's father. The wonderful brick edifice with its
lancet arches looks more like an Ottoman arsenal than a factory devoted to the
grape. This paradox is precisely what Georgia is all about. The winery is open the
same hours as the museum, but you must join a tour to see the vast cellars housing

a library of wines. The oldest wines go back to 1814. An inner courtyard and garden feature a statue of a plump and jolly Bacchus, and the passages are lined with large *kvevris* (earthenware jars in which wine is matured) and examples of the *uremi* (special wooden wagons used exclusively for the transport of grapes and wine)— both of which are frequently found in the paintings of Pirosmani. A banquet hall for feasts and wine tastings is also here and should, without too much difficulty, be put at your disposal for a leisurely tasting.

GURJAANI

From Tsinandali continue southeast on the same road for another 26 km (16 miles) to the town of Gurjaani. This road is known as the Kakhetian Wine Route, since one wine-producing village follows closely upon another with little discernible demarcation. Sophisticated oenophiles regard this route as heaven on earth. Gurjaani, the administrative center of this wine-producing area, has two sites of particular interest to the traveler: the House Museum of Nato Vachnadze, and the Church of Kvelatsminda of the eighth to ninth centuries.

HOUSE MUSEUM OF NATO VACHNADZE

Arriving at Gurjaani from Telavi, bear right at the roundabout beyond the central square and continue on the road to Tbilisi. Go another two km (1.2 miles) and then turn right, climbing a small hill for approximately one km (0.6 mile).

Of interest to Georgian cinema fans, the Nato Vachnadze museum chronicles the life of Nato Vachnadze the greatest Georgian actress of her day, having appeared in numerous films from the 1920s through the 1940s. The museum was opened on June 25, 1989, through the efforts of her two sons, the famous Georgian film directors Eldar and Giorgi Shengelaya. A single-story building on the left as you enter, houses memorabilia of her cinemagraphic career, including many stills from her films, as well as clippings and letters. The two-story building was her birthplace and contains family history and period furniture.

KVELATSMINDA

Coming on the road from Telavi toward the junction with the A302 to Tbilisi, turn right 250 meters (820 feet) before Gurjaani's town line. Follow the asphalt road uphill for 1.5 km (0.9 miles) to the fence at the top. Turn right to the gate marking this as a historic site. The road here runs through superb farm country where the timeless pursuits of husbandry give the scythe, the plow, the tethered sheep a pastoral magic.

A unique structure in Georgia because of its two domes, the Church of Kvelatsminda (eighth–ninth century) is a fascinating example of a transitional style

The charming house museum of Nato Vachnadze located in Gurjaani justifies a day trip into Kakheti from Tbilisi (photo by David Halford)

in Georgian architecture that borrows elements from two types of Georgian churches, as well as features from the secular, palace tradition. Conceptually it is an extremely complex building.

On a slope of the left bank of the Kakhtubnis (or Gurjaanis) Gorge, the church stands in a thicket that is a favorite picnic spot for villagers. The ground plan is that of the traditional three-aisled basilica. Three arcades of low massive pillars separate the naves in the north and south. The lateral naves are joined in the west by a vestibule. A narthex is at the extreme west end, and in the east is a horseshoe-shaped apse not visible from the exterior. The central nave comprises three equal squares. Two small octagonal drums rise over the east and west squares where they are crowned with domed vaults. As a result of the diminutive aspect of the domes and their inability to dominate the space as central cupola churches do, the impression of the "hall-type" church remains. The same applies to the exterior.

Above the lateral naves and the western vestibule are second-story barrel-vaulted galleries. These can be reached only from the outside. In the north and south these galleries run the length of the lateral naves and end in horseshoe-shaped altars.

*The two domes of the Church of Kvelatsminda are very unusual for a traditional
three-aisled basilica (photo by David Halford)*

Constructed to be self-contained and to allow someone inside to hear the services in
the central nave but not see them, these choruses might sometimes have served a
separate church function. The southern gallery was originally constructed with four
arcades to open outward, similar to a loggia, and was once directly over the southern portal and closed to the main aisle. A feudal lord would probably have used this
gallery to show himself to his subjects and to hold meetings. If so, the double cupola
over the central nave here would have worked beautifully to glorify his person by
hovering like two crowns over him. The emphasis on the southern façade comes
from the Byzantine tradition by way of Georgian palace architecture.

The division of space, in fact, is one of the most interesting elements of
Kvelatsminda, suggesting that this was a ruler's church. The external staircase indicates a hierarchical division wherein the prince and his retinue entered the upper
western gallery to show himself to his subjects, the congregants gathered below.
The western area was traditionally reserved for the worldly ruler, whereas the eastern altar was the spiritual realm devoted to Christ. The common people worshiped
in the central nave, lesser nobility in the lateral naves, and the ruler above, sometimes sealed off in private prayer in the north or south gallery.

The exterior of Kvelatsminda does not begin to suggest the complexity of the interior plan. The walls were constructed with even rows of fieldstones finished on the edges and trimmings with porous yellow tuff. Bricks were used for the two cupolas. Exterior decoration was never favored in Kakheti, and only the east wall gives any hint as to what's going on inside: in the central nave the two pairs of horseshoe arches, flanking each side of tall blind arcading that mark the central nave, stand one above the other. This serves to suggest the two stories of the north and south lateral naves, just as the uninterrupted sweep of the two middle arches indicates the unbroken height to the vaulting in the middle aisle. A window in the middle of the façade had once served as a pedestal for a monumental cross. This cross was converted in the 17th century to the midsection that delineates the two arches. The cross in the gable is a 17th-century restoration.

Other Trips from Telavi

Using Telavi as your base, a third day's touring through Kakheti could encompass the important historical and architectural monuments at Gremi, Nekresi, Ikalto, Alaverdi, and Kvetara.

GREMI
Located 19 km (11.8 miles) northwest of Telavi on the road to Kvareli, Gremi was the ancient capital of the Kakhetian Kingdom in the 16th century. Mentioned in ancient chronicles as a beautiful city of palaces, churches, baths, markets, gardens, and residential areas, the whole was destroyed by the invading Persian force of Shah Abbas in 1614.

THE CHURCH OF MTAVARANGELOZI
(THE ARCHANGELS MICHAEL AND GABRIEL)
That this church was built on the site of an earlier church is attested to by an interior fresco inscription in Greek over the western entrance: "The Holy Temple of Great Michael and Gabriel was built and restored by the efforts and labor of King Leon (Levan) on August 29, 1565 (7085), in the period of Father Superior Saba." A wonderful portrait of King Levan decorates the southern portion of the west wall. He wears a crown and holds a model of the church in his hands. He is giving the church to the Virgin Mary, who holds the Christ child on her knees. The inscription in Georgian reads, "King Levan is the builder." Levan's tomb is in the southwest corner of the church and is marked by the rostrum.

The frescoes throughout the church are of outstanding quality and represent a very schematic program of decoration that was completed in 1577. Among the many subjects depicted are the Death of the Virgin (west portal), the Emperor Constantine (north wall), and, from right to left, St. George and St. Saba (south wall). Many surfaces are badly defaced by graffiti. It is interesting to note that the letters of names are in both Russian and Georgian. A newly built wooden iconostasis prevents access to the altar. The church was reconsecrated in September 1989.

Mtavarangelozi employs the traditional plan of a cross-cupola church with two detached pillars in the west. The emphasis of the design is on the vertical, which is achieved through the tall and narrow octagonal drum that rises above the truncated east-west axis of the central aisle.

The church, like the neighboring dwelling tower, was made of brick, and the façade was decorated with relief decorations typical of the period. The belltower at Ninotsminda is also from this period, and the same decorative techniques were used.

The three-story dwelling tower is located southwest of the Church of the Archangels, so close to it that only a narrow passage separates the two. The first-floor chamber may, in fact, predate the church. The entrance is in the north, and a southern portal opens onto a small chamber in which a western door provides access to the stairs to the second and third floors. The tower served as King Levan's palace and the second and third floors were living quarters. The belfry at the northeast corner of the top floor is a later addition. You can ascend the tower and the view afforded of the Alazani Valley, the Greater Caucasus mountains, the remains of the town, and the close-set Church of the Archangels is well worth the climb.

Nekresi Monastery

Leaving Gremi, continue on the road to Kvareli for nine km (5.6 miles), where there is a sign for the monastery. Turn left onto the asphalt road indicated and continue for approximately three km (1.9 miles) to the foot of the mountain. You must proceed uphill on foot the rest of the way. Figure on walking along this dirt road for 45 minutes.

Beautifully situated within the dense forests of these foothills of the Caucasus, the site of Nekresi has an ancient provenance that even predates its early Christian origins. According to ancient sources, King Parnavaz (112–93 BC) founded the settlement sometime during his reign. In the fourth century AD, King Mirian strengthened the walls of the community and his son, Trdat, is credited with founding the first church here. It is one of the oldest Christian buildings still standing in Georgia. The importance of this cloister stems from the fact that it was chosen as one of the sites from which King Mirian waged his holy war to make Christianity the state religion. The fortunes of the cloister reflect this struggle.

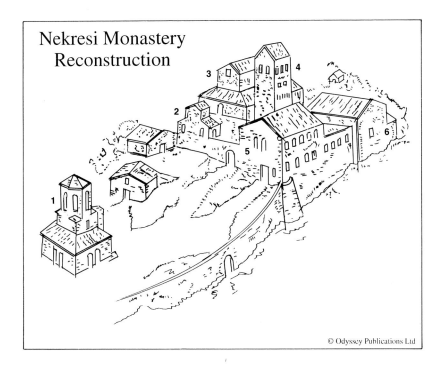

Nekresi Monastery Reconstruction

© Odyssey Publications Ltd

For the traveler, the gorgeous setting, its isolation and consequent peace, together with its unique structures, make Nekresi worthy of a pilgrimage. If permission can be arranged, take provisions and a sleeping bag and stay a night or two. It's the kind of place you will seriously entertain as being appropriate for a last resting place.

Neskresi became an especially important cultural and religious center in the middle of the sixth century with the arrival of the missionary Abibos, one of the 13 Syrian Fathers. Under his supervision as bishop, Nekresi flourished as a cloister and as a stronghold against the Persians' efforts to convert the local population to the practices of Zoroastrianism. (East Georgia at the time was under Iranian domination and ruled by an Iranian viceroy living in Tbilisi.) Abibos was finally captured by the Persians and died a martyr's death at their hands. He is largely credited with having secured the place of Christianity throughout Kakheti despite the efforts of foreign conquerors to replace it.

The complex consists of the following (consult the plan of the reconstruction above):

1. Fourth-century basilica, founded by King Mirian's son Trdat.
2. Three-church basilica, seventh century.

3. Bishop's Palace, eighth–ninth century, an important example of secular architecture, with service quarters on the first floor and a large hall on the upper level.
4. Refectory, behind the Bishop's Palace.
5. Bishop's tower, added to the east side of the palace in the sixteenth century.
6. Cupola church, eighth–ninth century.

Entering the complex from the northwest, the first structure you come upon is the cupola church built from the eighth to ninth centuries. Like Kvelatsminda, its contemporary in Gurjaani, it shows similar features of this transitional period in Georgian architecture. The attempt to combine the three-church basilica with the central-cupola structure finds expression here in the tall and slender drum that rises over the quadratic interior through the use of squinches in the west and horizontal stone slabs in the east. The external ambulatories in the north and south that end in altar niches in the east, are the visual equivalent of the three-church basilica's side naves. They join with an ambulatory in the west. A polygonal apse projects from the east. Entrance to the church is through a pair of arches in the west and south. The absence of light in the northern ambulatory and its spatial separateness suggest a special function: the place was designated to hold the coffins of deceased monks until their burial.

Walking through the complex to the southeast, you next come upon the ruins of the Bishop's Palace at the edge of the hillside. The high-arched windows of the second floor commanded a magnificent view of the Alazani Valley which you can share by standing above the ruins. You can still see an octagonal base for a pillar in the main chamber of the first floor. This served as one element in a system of beams that supported the second floor. Niches and fireplaces can be seen in the walls of the palace. Behind the palace is the one-story *marani*, the storage area for jugs of wine. Access to the four-story 16th-century tower within the palace complex was exclusively through the *marani*. Built as a defense against the frequent incursions of the Persians, it served as a residential tower similar to the one at Gremi. Large horseshoe-arched windows open on every side of the tower. The floors between stories were of wood. As the main vertical feature in the complex, the tower is an interesting example of the defensive architecture of the period. Still farther east, behind the *marani*, is the refectory. It has survived better than most of the civil buildings of the complex. Niches are still visible within.

Directly across from the Bishop's Palace in the north is the fourth-century church, one of Georgia's oldest surviving religious buildings. This church served as the focal point of the cloister and everything else developed around it. Founded by King Mirian's son Trdat, it is built of fieldstone. Though bearing most of the characteristics of a basilica, it differs in sufficient detail to make various scholars believe it was built from a written description of a basilica rather than a familiarity with an existing model. Others think the structure bears resemblance to the temples of Zoroastrianism, which were contemporary. It is built on a special base to provide for a crypt, a feature that is a key element in determining the antiquity of the structure. The central nave is unusually narrow and high. The eastern wall is completed by a horseshoe-shaped apse niche, which is not visible from the outside. Entrance to the church is through a door in the northern annex. A similar southern annex once existed but has since been destroyed.

The main church of the cloister is a three-church basilica of the seventh century dedicated to the Assumption of the Virgin Mary. It marks the second phase of construction within the cloister and is a traditional example of this architectural style. The separation of the two lateral naves from the central nave by walls was necessary to conduct a number of church services at different altars at the same time. These lateral churches were connected by a western vestibule. The fresco cycles within the main church were painted in the 16th century. They bear mostly Georgian and some Greek inscriptions. Among identifiable subjects are the portraits of King Levan and his wife Tinatin in the west corner of the south wall. Also on the south wall are the Last Supper, the Kiss of Judas, and the Lamentation. Above the altar is an enthroned Mary with the archangels Michael and Gabriel. In the west is the Crucifixion under which is the Dormition, taking up the entire length of the wall, then the Nativity of Theotokos and the Presentation in the Temple. On the north wall is the Resurrection, *Noli me Tangere*, and the Raising of Lazarus.

The monastery complex of Nekresi suffered attacks not only by Persians but also by the Lezghins of Daghestan, who raided it many times. It is interesting to note that the border with Daghestan is not more than 20 km (12.4 miles) away to the northwest. The monastery was ultimately destroyed in the 18th century.

Ikalto Monastery

Located eight km (five miles) to the west of Telavi on the road to Akhmeta in the village of Ikalto, a sign indicates the turnoff for this academy and cloister. It is 1.7 km (one mile) from the main road.

The monastery was founded in the second half of the sixth century by Zenon, one of the 13 Syrian Fathers. The importance of Ikalto as anything more than a local center of learning did not occur until the first quarter of the 12th century, when David the Builder founded a second academy here to give to east Georgia what Gelati

The 12th-century Academy at Ikalto Monastery

was accomplishing in west Georgia. To this end, King David sent Arsen Ikaltoeli from Gelati to assume the leadership. Among his students is supposed to have been Shota Rustaveli, the national poet of Georgia and author of *The Knight in the Panther's Skin*.

Although the academy is in ruins and the interior of the main Church of the Transfiguration was completely whitewashed in the 19th century, the church's exterior and the cypress grove in the cloister grounds make this a particularly charming spot, redolent with history.

The cloister complex consists of three churches, the ruins of the academy, and the refectory. The main church is dedicated to Ghvtaeba or the Transfiguration of Christ.

THE CHURCH OF THE TRANSFIGURATION OF CHRIST
Built in the eighth to ninth centuries on the site of an earlier church in which the founder of the monastery, Zenon, is buried, the Church of the Transfiguration has undergone many renovations since its construction. The cupola, in fact, was restored as recently as the 19th century, although it saw change in the tenth to 12th centuries. Due to the number of renovations and their extent, it is difficult to place this church within one clearly defined architectural style.

The cupola rises above the central hall on four freestanding pillars, the oldest example of this technique in Kakheti. The cupola has 12 facets with a window in each. The architectonic decorative devices above these windows and the colored stones around them bespeak the aesthetic of a much later era than that of the unadorned fieldstone and tuff of the walls.

The little belfry above the western entrance is a 19th-century contemporary of the cupola. Between the belfry and the western portico is a small second-floor living quarter for the Father Superior. The room has a window, which is in the center of the western vestibule. The altar apse in the east has a horseshoe shape, and beneath the altar window a seat is carved out for the Father Superior.

South of the Church of the Transfiguration are the small church of Kvelatsminda and the ruins of the refectory that was part of the academy complex built during the time of David the Builder (1089–1125). West along the southern wall of the complex are the two remaining buildings of the academy, destroyed in 1616 by the Persians under Shah Abbas. A plaque pays homage to Shota Rustaveli's study here.

East of the Church of the Transfiguration is a small church dating to the third quarter of the sixth century, dedicated to the Trinity (*Sameba*). Restorations have changed its original appearance so that now it is a basic rectangle with a gable roof; an exterior staircase in the west leads to a two-room cell.

The Cathedral of Alaverdi (Dedicated to St. George)

Alaverdi is 12 km (7.4 miles) north of Telavi. From Ikalto, continue two km (1.2 miles) on the road to Akhmeta before turning right onto an asphalt road. Follow this road northwest through superb vineyards for approximately another two km (1.2 miles) until you see the cathedral soaring grandly from the plain.

Situated two km (1.2 miles) from the Alazani River, this has been a holy spot since pagan times. Joseph of Alaverdi, one of the 13 Syrian Fathers, is credited with establishing the first church on this site, which was covered in forests then.

Built during the period of Georgian unification and expansion when large-scale building programs not only fulfilled a heavenly directive but also served to enhance Georgian prestige, the Cathedral of Alaverdi is part of the architectural tradition exemplified by the Church at Oshki (now in Turkey), Bagrat's Mother of God Cathedral in Kutaisi, and Sveti-tskhoveli in Mtskheta. Of these, the Cathedral of Alaverdi bears the greatest artistic kinship with Bagrat's Cathedral in Kutaisi, in terms of its general ground plan formulation.

The Cathedral of Alaverdi is the tallest church in Georgia. It is a triconch that differs in one distinctive element from the usual plan of these structures. Instead of the north and south apses projecting from the longitudinal axis, these apses are incorporated into the sides of the rectangle formed by the outer walls. This mitigates the pronounced effect of the cruciform in the exterior, although original ambulatories surrounding the north, south, and west sides would have produced the same result.

Alaverdi

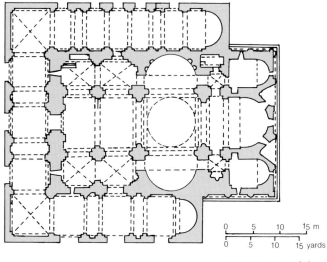

Today, only the western ambulatory remains. A central portico opens onto the long western arm of the church, which is flanked by lateral naves. Above, in the west, the chorus has a view of the central space through the arches of the gallery, though in a later restoration the north portion was completely sealed and in the south the openings were reduced. On each side of the altar apse are side conches that connect to the whole through narrow antechambers.

Although the configuration is complicated it does not detract from the simplicity, majesty, and monumentality of the interior because of the way in which it has been separated from the central scheme. This interior grandeur is achieved through the emphasis on verticality provided by the great height of the 16-window drum and cupola, and by the shallowness of the north and south apses that are obscured by the massive pillars that support the drum.

The Cathedral has undergone a number of restorations, most significantly between 1476 and 1495, during the reigns of King Nestan-Darejan, King Aleksandre, and Queen Anna, to repair damage caused by the Mongol invasion. At that time repairs to the walls, the drum, and the cupola were carried out with brick. The dimensions and proportion of the cupola remained the same as the original. An earthquake in 1742 necessitated additional restoration, which was begun in 1750 by Queen Tamara (not to be confused with the grand-daughter of David the Builder) and finished by her son Herekle II. Repair was primarily made to the vault, although numerous bays were also blocked up.

In the 19th century the north and south ambulatories were torn down. Also in this epoch, as part of the Russification program imposed on Georgian churches, all the interior frescoes were whitewashed. In 1967, work that continues to this day was begun to uncover frescoes from the 11th, 12th, 13th, and 15th centuries that once completely covered these walls. For example, the monumental portrait of the Virgin and Child can be seen in the altar apse, and the Ascension and the Raising of Lazarus in the southern conch.

The cathedral is constructed of porous tuff or travertine, the ubiquitous Kakhetian building material. The walls were whitewashed in the 18th century as a method to cover the differing building materials of various restorations and to create a greater structural unity. Like almost all Kakhetian churches, exterior decoration is kept to a minimum. Blind arcading, niches, and ornamental arches are used to help accentuate the structural lines and relieve the potential for severity created by the uninterrupted north and south walls.

The Fortress Walls and Other Buildings

The cathedral is surrounded by fortress walls built at the beginning of the 18th century. Certain sections were built in the 17th century, and others are of an even earlier date. Northwest of the cathedral, still within the fortress walls, are the ruins of the summer palace of the local governor of Shah Abbas I. Constructed in 1615 of brick, it comprised an octagonal room crowned with a cupola. Parallel to the north façade of the cathedral are the ruins of a *marani*, the building used to store wine jars. This building predates the fortress walls, as do the monastery lodgings, bishop's room, and refectory that run along the south wall of the fence. The refectory, west of the southern entrance, occupied the first floor of the two-story building. The vault of this room has some very interesting frescoes from the end of the 16th to the beginning of the 17th centuries. The belltower above the entrance is from the 19th century, and a passage in the fortress wall joins it to the refectory.

The view of white-walled, silver-domed Alaverdi towering out of the flat Alazani valley with the foothills of the Greater Caucasus mountains rising in the distance is one of the greatest visual moments Georgia affords. It stands as a powerful symbol of the technical and artistic achievements of the Georgian people. A major celebration takes place on September 14 in the cathedral precincts.

The Fortress of Kvetara

Take the road from Akhmeta west toward Tianeti for nine km (5.6 miles). Here the road branches. Go left on the upper road and climb for two km (1.2 miles), and left again for another one km (0.6 miles). Although it is out of the way, your efforts are

rewarded by one of the most extraordinary churches in Georgia: a jewel of a centralized dome church whose small dimensions do nothing to detract from the overriding impression of monumentality. This is a Napoleon of a church, and the surrounding forested hills outside the fortress complex make for a first-rate outing into the heart of the country.

Built by a local Kakhetian prince in the tenth to 11th centuries, the fortress of Kvetara existed to protect his territory from incursions by rival dukes in neighboring Kartli. Inside the area protected by extensive fortress walls was a palace that served as the prince's residence and ancillary buildings, as well as the exquisitely proportioned centralized dome church in the southeast corner of the complex. The ruined palace is an interesting and rare glimpse of secular architecture of the early feudal period. It predates the largest portion of the walls, going back to the eighth–ninth centuries. The ruins exhibit the typical two-story hall dwelling with service quarters on the ground floor and the residential area of the lord on the second, illuminated by arched windows. A vast quantity of blue enamel tile fragments scattered around the ruins suggests that the palace roof was covered in the same material as the church.

THE PALACE CHURCH OF KVETARA

Neither a description nor a photograph can quite capture the light and elegant refinement that emanates from this small church. Perhaps it is the blue-enamel tiles that grace the central dome and surrounding conches, or the white tuff or travertine that seems particularly malleable here, and vulnerable to the elements; perhaps it is its excellent state of preservation in a site whose walls and other dwellings have borne the brunt of the ravages of time. For whatever reason, no building in Georgia so completely reveals the perfect eye of the builder and allows us to enjoy what he saw without the additions and renovations of intervening generations.

The Church at Kvetara is a tetraconch with four narrow niches between the apses that almost bring their semicircle to closure with the grouping of three columns on each side. The altar apse has three windows, while each of the other apses has one. Entrance to the church is through the southern and western apses. The central space of the church is crowned by a cupola with six windows in its drum: one each in the east and west and two in the north and south. The interior of the church is preserved in pristine state, never having been restored.

From the exterior the arcading on the pentahedron apses is perfectly balanced with the decorative molding of the drum to render this the harmonious structure it is. The protrusions between the apses mask the basic tetraconch to intrigue the eye sufficiently and give the illusion of a much more complex structure.

The Palace Church of Kvetara is one of the most beautiful buildings in Georgia; it possesses an impressive monumentality despite its relatively small size

Tbileasy.

Getting to Tbilisi is now a lot easier. British Airways fly direct from London Heathrow Terminal 4 to the capital of Georgia three times a week. For bookings and reservations, please contact your local travel agent or British Airways booking office.

Operated by the independent carrier British Mediterranean Airways Ltd.

www.british-airways.com

BRITISH AIRWAYS
The world's favourite airline

Practical Information

Travel Agencies Specializing in Trips to Georgia

ARMENIA
AKN
16 Parpetsi Street, Yerevan
tel. (374 2) 565 184,
fax. (374 2) 561 325

AUSTRIA
ARR STUDIENREISEN
Landstrasser Haupstrasse,
A 1030 Vienna
tel. (43 1) 715 7531,
fax. (43 1) 715 7538

EGNATIA TOURS
Piaristengasse 60,
A 1080 Vienna
tel. (43 1) 405 5346,
fax. (43 1) 405 666 833

AZERBAIJAN
IMPROTEX TRAVEL
16 Samed Vurgun Street,
370000, Baku
tel. (994 12) 932 279,
fax. (994 12) 937 520

BELGIUM
VITAMIN TRAVEL
St. Gorikspiein 17, Brussels
tel. (32 2) 512 7464,
fax. (32 2) 512 6960

DENMARK
COAST TO COAST
Grunnegade 10,
DK 1107 Copenhagen
tel. (45) 3393 9305,
fax. (45) 3393 9304

VALLUGA TOURS
Hestemellestrade 3,
DK 1464 Copenhagen
tel. (45) 3393 5044,
fax. (45) 3314 4031

FRANCE
CLIO
34 rue du Hameau,
75015 Paris
tel. (33 1) 5368 8277,
fax. (33 1) 4250 4979

ESPRIT D'AVENTURE
13 rue Saint-Victor,
75005 Paris
Tel. (33 1) 8373 7800,
fax. (33 1) 4329 9632

TERRES D'AVENTURE
32 Montée du Parc, 69250-
Neuville/Saone, Paris
tel. (33 1) 0478 915 814,
fax. (33 1) 7891 5814

GERMANY
DERTOUR
Emil-von-Behring-Strasse 6,
60424 Fankfurt
tel. (49 69) 9588 3544,
fax. (49 69) 9588 3550

ERKA REISEN
Robert-Stolz-Strasse 21,
76646 Bruchsal
tel. (49 7251) 930 390,
fax. (49 7251) 930 392
e-mail: 101321.1274@-
compuserve.com

FRANKFURTER STUDIENREISEN
Neiderhofheimer Strasse 26,
6238 Hofheim am Taunus 1
tel. (49 61) 922 8833,
fax. (49 61) 922 5291

HAUSER
Marienstrasse 17,
80331 Munich
tel. (49 89) 235 0060,
fax. (49 89) 291 3714

KARAVANE STUDIENREISEN
Schorndorfer Strasse 149,
71638 Ludwigsburg
tel. (49 7141) 284 858,
fax. (49 7141) 284 859

OLYMPIA-REISEN
Siegburger Strasse 49,
D-53229 Bonn
tel. (49 228) 400 0336,
fax. (49 228) 466 932

VENTUS REISEN
Krefelder Strasse 8,
10555 Berlin
tel. (49 30) 393 2031,
fax. (49 30) 399 5587

GREECE
MANOS TRAVEL SYSTEM
Charleou Trikoupi 6-10
Atrium Center,
Athens 10679
tel. (30 1) 362 8077,
fax. (30 1) 362 7329

ITALY
CONWAY CULTURAL TRAVEL
Piazza S. Domenico 2,
40124 Bologna
tel. (39 51) 233 3716,
fax. (39 51) 220 723

JAPAN
JES
9-3 Rokuban-cho,
Chiyoda-ku, Tokyo
tel. (81 3) 3221 9121,
fax. (81 3) 3221 9120

M.O. AIR SYSTEM
14-9, Nishishimbasi,
Minako-ku, Tokyo
tel. (81 3) 3593 0432,
fax. (81 3) 3593 0484

PORTUGAL
EUROVIAGENS
Rua Jose Falcao 82,
4050 Porto
tel. (351 2) 314 525,
fax. (351 2) 320 822

RUSSIA
GEOGRAPHIC BUREAU
9 Arsenalnaia Street,
195009, St. Petersburg
tel. (7 812) 325 9448,
fax. (7 812) 325 8556

KIVI TRAVEL
Neglinnaya Street, 18/1,
Moscow
tel. (7 095) 209 1112,
fax. (7 095) 921 5613

SWITZERLAND
ALPIN TRAVEL
Postfach 14 CH-8880,
Walenstadt
tel. (41 81) 735 3434,
fax. (41 81) 735 2317

TURKEY
TURK EXPRESS
Cumhuriyet Caddesi, 47/1,
80090 Taksim, Istanbul
tel. (90 212) 235 9500,
fax. (90 212) 235 2313

U.K.
BRITISH MUSEUM
TRAVELLER
46 Bloomsbury Street,
London, WC1 3QQ
tel. (44 171) 323 8895,
fax. (44 171) 580 8677

CRICKETER HOLIDAYS
4 W. House, Beacon R.
Croborough, E. Sussex
tel. (44 1892) 664 242,
fax. (44 1892) 662 355

REGENT HOLIDAYS
15 John Street,
Bristol, BS1 2HR
tel. (44 117) 921 1711,
fax. (44 117) 925 4866
e-mail: regent@regent-holidays.co.uk

THE RUSSIA HOUSE LIMITED
37 Kingly Court, Kingly
Street, London, W1R 5LE
tel. (44 171) 439 1271,
fax. (44 171) 434 0813

U.S.A.
GEOGRAPHIC EXPEDITIONS
2627 Lombard Street,
San Francisco,
CA 94123
tel. (1 415) 922 0448
fax. (1 415) 346 5535
e-mail: info@geoex.com

MIR CORPORATION
89 South Washington
Street, Suite 210, Seattle,
WA 98104
tel. (1 206) 624 7289,
fax. (1 206) 624 7360

SVANETI TRAVEL
85 East Asia Row, Suite 12F,
Boston, MA 02110
tel. (1 617) 227 6547,
fax. (1 617) 227 0695

Accommodations

When Sokhumi fell in late 1993 (see page 225), 200,000 to 300,000 Georgians were forced to leave their homes in Abkhazia and flee from the war-torn region in search of safety and shelter. The Georgian government, having declared a state of emergency, was ill-equipped to handle the sudden influx of so many refugees to other regions of the country. These refugees were accommodated in very cramped conditions in hotels throughout Georgia. Most of them remain there to this day. The Intourist hotels of yore are therefore unavailable to travelers, with the exception of a floor or two sometimes made available to guests at the Ajara and Iveria Hotels in Tbilisi. But more congenial arrangements can probably be found. Long-time visitors to Tbilisi will be saddened to learn that the beautiful Hotel Tbilisi on Rustaveli Avenue was reduced to a shell during the street fighting that accompanied the ouster of Zviad Gamsakhurdia in 1992. At the time of writing, however, the façade is being restored and an American hotelier is attempting to purchase the site and what is left of the building.

Despite the refugee situation and the power and heating problems that the country is experiencing as it struggles toward recovery, the range of accommodations available to visitors to Tbilisi has never been better. Best known, of course, is the Sheraton Metechi Palace Hotel, a four-star hotel built by the Austrian Marco Polo group in 1991. The hotel has recently been purchased by Sheraton. It is the most expensive hotel in the country and has every possible amenity including a swimming pool. Whether you stay at the Metechi or not, it's a great place from which to make arrangements of every kind: car rental with driver, ticket purchases (for a 20 lari service fee), excursions. The British and Greek embassies, as well as the British Airways office, are also located here.

Betsy's is a hotel favored by many American travelers to Tbilisi. It's easy to understand why. The hotel is owned and run by American Elizabeth Haskell who has brought a tremendous sense of style to the furnishings of the rooms and the atmosphere as a whole. Antique Caucasian carpets are juxtaposed against modern furniture by the designer Guga Kotetishvili, and exhibitions of contemporary Georgian paintings often grace the walls. Much more intimate than the Metechi, closer to the center, and considerably less expensive, Betsy's is often booked far in advance. Her success has spawned other guesthouses with their own charms.

Most of the hotels and guesthouses listed here have their own generators, so the supply of heat, hot water, and electricity is not subject to the vagaries of

A view of downtown Tbilisi from the balcony of the Sachino Palace in the Avlabar Heights; the Iveria Hotel, now filled with refugees from Abkhazia, rises in the background (photo by David Halford)

the city's services. Most of the prices listed do not include 20 percent VAT. Unless specified, quoted prices include breakfast and dinner. The Sheraton Metechi Palace Hotel and Villa Berika take most major credit cards. Betsy's only accepts American Express. Most other hotels require cash payments, but this situation is changing as credit cards and traveler's checks gain ever greater acceptance. A general indication of price is given by the following, based on one person/one night occupancy:

A **Expensive** (US $120 and above)
B **Moderate** (US $80–120)
C **Cheaper** (less than US $80).

The code for Georgia is **995**; for Tbilisi, **32**.

ARSENA **B**
46 Arsena Street
tel. 32 05 03

BETSY'S **B**
21 Gogebashvili Street
tel. 98 95 53, 98 35 51,
98 29 37, 98 87 83,
fax. 00 12 37
e-mail: Betsy@2121.ge
Fifteen rooms. Suites available.

CHAVCHAVADZE **B**
35 Arsena Street
tel. 98 44 43

DODO'S **B**
31 Shanidze Street
tel. 22 66 79, 29 09 36,

fax. 23 40 93
Ten percent discount with
the mention of their
Internet site and with two-
week advance booking.

IA B
10 Iashvili Street
tel. 96 85 40

IBERIA INN A
10a Bakhtrioni Street
tel. 94 05 75,
tel./fax. 96 75 48
Dinner not included. Suites
available. Five percent
discount with the mention
of their Internet site.

ILIANI B
1 Weriko Anjaparidze Street
tel. 23 40 86, 29 22 85,
fax. 22 56 76
Dinner not included. Six
rooms with ensuite
bathrooms. Luxury rooms
available. Three percent
discount with the mention
of their Internet site.

JEJILI C
7 Gorgasali Street
tel. 99 95 37
Dinner not included. Four
rooms (three are doubles).

HOTEL KARTLI C
30 Barnow (Barnova) Street
380008 Tbilisi
tel. 98 29 66,
fax. 99 91 34

KOLKHETI B
31 Shanidze Street
tel. 23 40 93
Dinner not included. Seven
double rooms.

LUX B
47 Nutsubidze Street
tel. 39 71 94, 39 47 87,
93 91 62
e-mail: nino@homelux.ge

MORKINALI C
1,26 Maisis Square
tel. 22 15 10
Dinner not included.
Fifteen double rooms.
Luxury rooms available.

MTIS KALTA B
46a Odzelashvli Street
tel. 93 63 97
Dinner not included. Three
rooms with en suite
bathrooms.

MUZA C
27 Kostava Street
tel. 98 88 15, 98 88 17,
tel./fax. 93 32 65,
fax. 98 88 16
Meals not included.

Fourteen rooms (four
singles, four doubles, six
suites).

OWEN'S B
44 Petriashvili Street
tel. 23 14 42
Dinner not included.
Two rooms.

SHARMI B
11 Chakhrukhadze Street
tel. 98 63 48,
tel./fax. 98 53 33

THE SHERATON METECHI PALACE HOTEL A
20 Telavi Street, Issani
tel. 94 64 44,
fax. 95 61 35
Telex: 212248 abvtb su
Reservations can be made
in the US by calling
(800) 325-3535.
Dinner not included.

VILLA BERIKA A
9 Dzotsenidze Street, Third
district, Nutsubidze Plateau
tel. 30 38 03, 30 41 26,
30 44 38,
fax. 93 35 62
Some rooms have their own
bathrooms.

Finding accommodations outside of Tbilisi requires some preplanning. There is not as yet any formal network of guesthouses or B&Bs, so without connections it is virtually impossible to organize accommodations on one's own. The best thing to do is contact one of the two best travel agents in Tbilisi: Saba Kiknadze of Caucasus Travel, 5/7 Shavteli Street, tel. 98 74 00 or 98 73 99, or Rainer Kaufmann of Sak Tours, 43 Tamriko Tshovelidze Street (formerly Belinski Street), tel. 98 29 66 or 99 54 29. Both of these companies have their own network of guesthouses that are the best available in the area. Rainer Kaufmann of Sak Tours is said to be fanatical about Western-style toilets, and has installed many of them in the houses that he uses throughout the country. Caucasus Travel will probably be marginally more expensive than Sak Tours but they are specialists in trekking, skiing, and mountaineering, and can provide you with tents and guides as well as accommodations anywhere in the country. Caucasus Travel can also book you into the Sport Hotel Club Gudauri.

Saba Kiknadze is also involved in trying to start an enterprise called Folk Hotel Systems, building small guesthouses in the local style near historic sites. The first hotel he hopes to build is in Ushguli in Zemo Svaneti. Perhaps in the years ahead Georgia will have a network of hotels akin to Spain's *paradores*. Until this occurs you can expect to stay with local people who will welcome you into their homes, and who will prepare meals of their region for you.

Embassies of Georgia in other Countries

ARMENIA
5 Nalbandian Street, Erevan
tel. (88 552) 564 357,
fax. (88 552) 564 183
e-mail:
georgia@arminco.com

AUSTRIA
Marokkanergasse 16,
A 1030 Vienna
tel. (43 1) 710 3611,
fax. (43 1) 710 3610

AZERBAIJAN
Hotel Azerbaijan, 13/F
1 Azadlegi Avenue, Baku
tel. (99 412) 939 184,
fax. (99 412) 989 440
e-mail: georgian.buku.az

BENELUX COUNTRIES AND THE EUROPEAN UNION
47 Avenue Edmund
Mesens, 1040, Brussels,
Belgium
tel. (32 2) 732 8550,
fax. (32 2) 732 8547
e-mail:
0006853309@mcimail.com

FRANCE, SPAIN AND UNESCO
104 Raymond Poincaré
Avenue, 75116, Paris
tel. (33 1) 4502 1616,
fax. (33 1) 4502 1601

GERMANY
Bad Godesberg Am
Kurpark 6, Bonn, 53177
tel. (49 228) 957 5110,
fax. (49 228) 957 5120
e-mail: geobotger@aol.com

GREECE
24 Agiou Dimitriou Street,
P. Psychico, 15452 Athens
tel. (301) 671 6737,
fax. (301) 671 6722
e-mail: embassygeo@hol.gr

IRAN
36 Mottaghian Street,
Farmanieh, Tehran
P.B. 19575-37
tel. (9821) 229 5135,
fax. (9821)229 5136

ITALY
Piazza S. Edigio 7,
00153, Rome
tel. (39 6) 589 8677,
fax. (39 6) 589 8677
e-mail:
amb.georgia@agora.stm.it

KAZAKHSTAN
246 Gornaya Street,
Almaata, 480020
tel. (7 3272) 21 4930,
fax. (7 3272) 21 3881

RUSSIA
6 Paliashvili Street,
Moscow, 121069
tel. (7 095) 292 1107,
fax. (7 095) 202 4098

SWITZERLAND
N1, Rue Richard Wagner,
1202 Geneva
tel. (41 022) 010 1010,
fax. (41 022) 733 9033

TURKEY
Ulubey Sok. N.28,
Gaziosmanpasa, Buyuk Esat
Caddesi, Ankara
tel. (90 312) 447 1720,
fax. (90 312) 447 1724
e-mail: gab-o@servis2.net.tr

CONSULATE GENERAL
Gazipasa Cad. 20, Trabzon
tel. (90 462) 326 2226,
fax. (90 462) 326 2296

UKRAINE
12/F Hotel Kiev,
Grushevkogo Street, Kiev
tel. (380 44) 293 6976,
fax. (380 44) 293 6957
e-mail: root@georgia.kiev.ua

UNITED KINGDOM
3 Hornton Place
London W8 4LZ
tel. (44 171) 937 8233,
fax. (44 171) 938 4108

U.S.A.
(CONSULATE GENERAL)
1511 K Street NW, Suite
400, Washington, DC
20005
tel. (202) 393-5959,
fax. (202) 393-4537
e-mail: 73324.1007@--
compuserve.com

Restaurants

ANANURI
If you've parked by the
entrance to the fortress,
drive down the narrow road
along the battlements
toward the river. Make the
only left you can and then
the first right on what was
the old Military Highway. A
few yards from the
right-hand turn is an excellent shop for *khinkali*, the
Georgian meat dumpling.

BATUMI
Situated in the park on
Ninoshvili Street between
26th of May and the former
Marx Streets, SALKINO (tel.
32 965) is among the best
restaurants in town, with a
pleasant terrace and a view
of the sea. Try the *ochakhuri*,
a tasty meat and potato fry-
up, and *kapchonaya*, cured
roast pork.

An excellent *khatchapuri* cafe without a name is in the port, behind the terminal on Gogegashvili Street. It serves at low prices the Ajaran dish of cheese bread topped with egg.

THE MORVOKZAL (SEA STATION) RESTAURANT

is inside the terminal of the Port. It is fancier than most restaurants with a good reputation for fish dishes.

MTSKHETA

MTSKHETA RESTAURANT,

next to the Samtavro Monastery complex, is open 9 a.m.–midnight and serves a range of standard Georgian fare.

SALOBIO, located just over four kilometers (2.5 miles) south of Mtskheta on the old road to Tbilisi (follow the Mtkvari River), is the best place to eat in the area. Open 10 a.m.–10 p.m., this is a favorite spot for residents of Tbilisi, who come here to sit on stools at traditional low tables and eat red beans in clay pots, with scallions, and corn bread. Ask for *lobio* and

chadi. No liquor is served, but nice carbonated drinks made from a variety of herbs are very refreshing. Don't be put off by the green color of one of them. Fried cheese dumplings (*piroshki*) can also be ordered. Facing the building, the left side wing serves beer, *khatchapuri* (cheese bread), *khinkali* (meat dumplings), and kebabs. There's a little garden with waiter service or you can take out. You cannot bring food from one wing to the other. There is a new Salobio right on the M27 near Mtskheta, but it's not as good as this one. A trip to Mtskheta would not be complete without stopping here. It's the best value in all Georgia.

TBILISI

In Tbilisi, restaurants, cafés, and bars are opening and closing all the time. These are enterprises that lend themselves to a free market and the initiative of an individual entrepreneur or family. Akhvlediani (formerly Perovskaya) Street is a particularly good

example of this phenomenon. Many members of the intelligentsia who live on this street have turned the ground floors and basements of their private homes into shops and restaurants. Here you can buy the best cakes in Tbilisi, booze, stuffed toys, even suckling pig at almost any hour. THE GUINNESS BAR at number 16 is particularly famous. Chavchavadze Street, near the university, also boasts many new coffee bars and restaurants. Of course, these spots are excellent places to meet students. The restaurants and cafes listed below are some of the better-known places but many new ones are opening all the time. At the time of writing, main courses run about nine or ten lari.

ALVEBI, 1 Sandro Euli Street, tel. 30 09 69

ARAGVI, 1 Sanapiro Street, tel. 98 23 53, 93 44 23

BUDAPESHTI, 74 Chavchavadze Avenue, tel. 22 41 95

BUDWEISER BUSINESS CLUB: Bar and Restaurant, 41 Taboukashvili Street, tel. 98 55 53 Reasonable Georgian and Russian cuisine, modern decor.

CAFÉ LAGIDZE
37 Gorgasali Street
Justly named for its "Tbilisi Waters" (flavored soda waters), this is a sister café of the well-known Lagidze Cafe on Rustaveli Avenue. The soda waters come in an enormous variety; chocolate, plum, and lemon are the most popular. These cafés have fallen somewhat out of favor with the locals and are not as crowded as they once were.

CHINA RESTAURANT,
47 Leselidze Street
Near the synagogue, the chef of this restaurant is from Urumchi. Ideal for when you're looking for something different in Tbilisi.

DIPLOMATIC CLUB, 4/6 Mtkvari, tel. 99 76 62

DURUJI, 11 Leonidze Street, tel. 99 86 47

EKRANI, 11 Dzmebi Kakabadzeebi Street, tel. 99 86 47

EUROPA, 47 Kostava Street, tel. 94 07 77
A very popular restaurant, especially with the expat community.

GREEK CAFE SITAKI, 37 Kostava Street, tel. 99 67 53 Open 11 a.m.–11 p.m.

GUINNESS BAR (officially, Wheels Irish Bar), 16 Akhvlediani Street, tel. 98 87 33
An excellent place to meet members of the expat community in Tbilisi. Draft Guinness is served as well as a full menu. You can also make international telephone calls from here for 1.64–4 lari per minute depending on where you are calling. Great atmosphere.

HEINEKEN BAR, 17 and 23 Akhvlediani Street, tel. 98 69 06
Also at: 8 Chavchavadze Street, tel. 22 60 85 Open 24 hours.

IVERIA, 6 Inashvili Street, tel. 93 64 98

JURNALISTI, 3 Erekle Square, tel. 98 74 90

KAISER'S PUB,
2 Chavchavadze Avenue (near the university) Serves Murphy's Irish Stout. Good music in the evening.

KALAKURI, 2 Shavteli Street, tel. 93 31 47

KHEIVANI, 1 Gulia Street, Ortachala District, tel. 72 44 39

KRTSANISI, Station Square, tel. 72 42 31

LE CABERNET, 8 Kazbegi Street, tel. 22 58 65
A newly opened restaurant in the Vera district that specializes in French cuisine.

MTATSMINDA, tel. 93 33 31 Located on Mount Mtatsminda in the upper station of the funicular railway provides a magnificent view of the city. The food isn't quite up to the view but then such restaurants usually provide one or the other.

MUKHRANTUBANI,
29 Baratashvili Street,
tel. 99 59 04
Serves superb Georgian cuisine in a wonderful re-creation of a wealthy 19th-century home of Tbilisi.

NATALY CAFE AND BAR,
1 Melikishvili Street,
tel. 98 44 56
Open 24 hours.

NIKALA CAFE
22 Rustaveli Avenue,
tel. 99 82 83,
99 70 75
This restaurant evokes the world of Pirosmani the Georgian "Primitive" painter.

PALERMO, 67a Tsereteli Avenue, tel. 95 01 55, 35 47 70

PICNIC, 13 Akhvlediani Street, tel. 93 42 77
Excellent *khachapuri*, including *achma*, *megruli*, *penovani*, and *ajaruli*.

RAINER'S CAFE, 39 Barnov Street, tel. 99 54 29
Open 12 p.m.–11 p.m.
Six tables, owned by the German tour operator of Sak Tours. Pasta and other European cuisine.

RAMPA RESTAURANT,
19 Rustaveli Avenue,
tel. 93 20 00
Near the Theatre Institute, this restaurant serves European and Georgian dishes in a very elegant and romantic atmosphere.

RIONI, 70 Kostava Street,
tel. 36 75 06

SACHASHNIKO
RESTAURANT, 4 Nakashidze Street, tel. 99 58 57
Excellent Georgian cuisine in a friendly atmosphere.

SAKARTVELO, 14 Melikishvili Street,
tel. 22 14 45

STUTTGART, 2 Vazha Pshavela Avenue,
tel. 37 47 04
European and Georgian Cuisine.

SVANETI, 14 Chiaureli, Digomi District,
tel. 96 90 72, 51 98 72

USHBA, Georgian Military Highway, tel. 51 49 33

VIENNA-SARI RESTAURANT,
14 Akhvlediani (formerly Perovskaya) Street,
tel. 90 82 40
Live jazz from 9 p.m.–11 p.m. Partly owned by a New Jersey native, this restaurant evokes East and West with great charm.

ZUR GLOCKE,
17 Baratashvili Street,
tel. 92 19 16
German cuisine in a pleasant environment.

For homesick travelers with a sweet tooth:
BASKIN-ROBBINS ICE CREAM, 142 Agmashenebeli Avenue, tel. 95 56 56

Hotel Restaurants

BETSY'S, 21 Gogebashvili Street, tel. 98 95 53, 98 35 51
Dinner is served from 7.30 p.m.–9 p.m. in a beautifully furnished dining room. In summer, one can dine on a roof deck. Dinner and Sunday brunch cost US $15.

THE SHERATON METECHI PALACE HOTEL, 20 Telavi Street, Issani, tel. 94 64 44 This luxury hotel has two restaurants, two bars, and a nightclub. The Narikala Restaurant is open for breakfast. King Gorgasali Restaurant, with beautiful views of Tbilisi, is open for dinner and serves continental cuisine. Cafe Vienna is open 9 p.m.– midnight. The Piano Bar is open 6 p.m.–midnight. The Nightclub is open on Fridays and Saturdays 9 p.m.–3 a.m.

Museums

TBILISI
BEE-KEEPING MUSEUM
15a Guramishvili Street

I. GRISHASHVILI MUSEUM OF THE HISTORY AND ETHNOGRAPHY OF TBILISI
8 Sioni Street,
tel. 72 51 26

MUSEUM OF
CHILDREN'S ART
17a Shavteli Street

MUSEUM OF
GEORGIAN ART
1 Gudiashvili Street,
tel. 99 66 35, 99 99 09

MUSEUM OF GEORGIAN DRAMA, CINEMA, AND MUSIC
11 Herekle II Square

MUSEUM OF GEORGIAN FOLK AND APPLIED ART
6 Akhospireli Street

MUSEUM OF GEORGIAN FOLK ARCHITECTURE AND LOCAL LORE
Entrance: 74 Chavchavadze Avenue, in Vake Park
tel. 23 09 60, 22 63 02

MUSEUM OF THE HISTORY OF GEORGIAN MEDICINE
25 Kakheti Street,
tel. 93 69 83

PALIASHVILI MUSEUM
10 Bakradze Street

HOUSE MUSEUM OF NIKOLOZ BARATASHVILI
17 Chakhrukhadze Street,
tel. 99 06 99

HOUSE MUSEUM OF
I. NIKOLADZE
6 Rodeni Street,
tel. 22 23 31

HOUSE MUSEUM OF MOSE TOIDZE
1 Culukidze Street,
tel. 99 01 49

ELENE AKHVLEDIANI MEMORIAL MUSEUM
12 Kiacheli Street,
tel. 99 74 12

ILYA CHAVCHAVADZE MEMORIAL LITERARY MUSEUM
7 Javakhishvili Street,
tel. 95 70 78

LADO GUDIASHVILI MEMORIAL MUSEUM
11 Gudiashvili Street
Admission by
appointment only.

DAVID KAKABADZE MEMORIAL MUSEUM
11a G. Chanturia Street
Admission by
appointment only.

S. JANASHIA MUSEUM OF GEORGIA
3 Rustaveli Avenue,
tel. 99 80 22, 93 27 27

G. LEONIDZE GEORGIAN LITERATURE STATE MUSEUM

8 G. Chanturia Street,
tel. 99 86 67, 93 28 90

NIKO PIROSMANASHVILI STATE MUSEUM

29 Pirosmani Street,
tel. 95 86 73

TOY MUSEUM

6 Rustaveli Street

KARTLI

UPLIS-TSIKHE

Open 9 a.m.–6 p.m. daily.

SVANETI

HOUSE MUSEUM OF MIKHEIL KHERGIANI

29 Khergiani Street
Open 10 a.m.–6 p.m. daily.
No admission fee.

SVANETIAN HISTORIC AND ETHNOGRAPHIC MUSEUM

57 Stalin Street
Open 10 a.m.–1 p.m. and
2 p.m.–5 p.m. every day
except Monday.

IMERETI

THE CATHEDRAL OF KING BAGRAT (Mother of God Church)

Open 10 a.m.–6 p.m.

GEGUTI PALACE

Open daily morning to
evening.

GELATI MONASTERY

Open 10 a.m.–6 p.m. daily.

GEORGIAN ART GALLERY

8 Rustaveli Avenue
Open 11 a.m.–7 p.m. daily
except Monday.

THE KUTAISI STATE MUSEUM OF HISTORY AND ETHNOGRAPHY (BERDZENISHVILI)

1 Tbilisi Street
Open 10 a.m.–6 p.m. daily
except Monday.

BLACK SEA COAST

AQUARIUM

37 Ninoshvili Street,
Batumi.
Open 10 a.m.–6 p.m.

DOLPHINARIUM

37 Ninoshvili Street
Batumi

Shows at 12.30 p.m.,
3 p.m., 5.30 p.m. except
Monday.

MUSEUM OF AJARA

4 Jincharadze Street,
Batumi
Open 10 a.m.–7 p.m.

THE ABKHAZIAN STATE MUSEUM

22 (former) Lenin Street,
Sokhumi
Due to the current situation
in Abkhazia, museum hours
could not be verified.

THE BOTANICAL GARDENS OF THE ACADEMY OF SCIENCES OF GEORGIA

18 Chavchavadze Street,
Sokhumi
Open 9 a.m.–8 p.m.

THE HISTORICAL AND ETHNOGRAPHIC MUSEUM

1 David the Builder Street,
Sokhumi
Open 10 a.m.–5.30 p.m.
except Monday.

THE MONKEY COLONY

5a Baratashvili Street,
Sokhumi
Open 10 a.m.–5 p.m. daily.

MESKHETI

VARDZIA

Open 9 a.m.–2 p.m. and
3 p.m–6 p.m. daily.

KAKHETI

THE HISTORY AND ETHNOGRAPHIC MUSEUM

Open 9 a.m.–6 p.m. except
Monday.

THE HOUSE MUSEUM OF
ALEXANDER
CHAVCHAVADZE
Open 10 a.m.–2 p.m. and
3 p.m.–6 p.m. daily.

Tbilisi Practicalities

MAJOR BANKS

ABSOLUTE BANK
8 Ingorokva Street
tel. 98 53 75,
fax. 99 61 82

THE NATIONAL BANK OF
GEORGIA
3/5 Leonidze Street
tel. 98 31 95,
fax. 99 98 85

TBC BANK
11 Chavchavadze Avenue
tel. 22 06 61,
fax. 22 04 06

TBILCOMBANK
2 Shalva Dadiani Street
tel. 98 85 92,
fax. 98 53 97

TBILCREDIT BANK
79 Agmashenebeli Avenue
tel. 95 83 43,
fax. 95 72 50

UNITED BANK OF GEORGIA
37 Uznadze Street
tel. 95 83 43,
fax. 95 72 50

SULFUR BATHS

THE ORBELIANI
BATHHOUSE
2 Abano Street
tel. 72 26 33
Also called the Motley Bath
as well as Tsisperi Abano
(Blue Bath), this establishment is open every day 7
a.m.–10 p.m. There are
both public and private
bath facilities. For a
description of the building,
see page 108.

SULFUR BATH
35 Ketevan Tsamebuli
Street
tel. 74 23 46

CASINOS

ATINATI CLUB
73 Agmashenebeli Street
tel. 96 31 23

CASINO IVERIA
16 Inashvili Street
(Hotel Iveria)
tel. 98 24 63, 98 96 54

IMPERIAL CASINO
41 Gamsakhurdia Avenue
tel. 94 37 23, 94 37 21

COURIER SERVICES

DHL
tel. 99 95 68, 34 48 26,
34 03 93

FEDEX
tel. 29 27 06

UPS
tel. 92 03 44, 92 03 56

EMBASSIES

ARMENIA
4 Tetelashvili Street
tel. 99 01 26

AZERBAIJAN
4 Mukhadze Street
tel. 23 40 37

CHINA, PEOPLE'S
REPUBLIC OF
52 Barnov Street
tel. 93 12 76

FRANCE
15 Gogebashvili Street
tel. 93 42 10, 99 99 76,
95 33 75

GERMANY
166 Agmashenebeli Avenue
tel. 95 09 36

GREECE
Sheraton Metechi Palace
Hotel, Issani
tel. 93 89 81

HOLY SEE
(APOSTOLIC NUNCIATURE)
40 Jgenti Street
tel. 29 39 44

IRAN
16 Zovreti Street
tel. 98 69 90, 98 69 91

ISRAEL
61 Agmashenebeli Avenue
tel. 95 17 09, 96 44 57

RUSSIA
61 Agmashenebeli Avenue
tel. 95 59 11

TURKEY
61 Agmashenebeli Avenue
tel. 95 20 14, 29 23 19,
95 18 10

UKRAINE
61 Agmashenebeli Avenue
tel. 23 71 45

U.K.
Sheraton Metechi Palace
Hotel, Issani
tel. 95 54 97

U.S.A.
25 Atoneli Street
tel. 98 99 68, 98 99 67,
93 38 03
fax. 93 37 59

GEORGIAN MINISTRIES
AGRICULTURE AND
FOODSTUFFS
41 Kostava Street
tel. 99 62 61, 99 02 72

CULTURE
37 Rustaveli Avenue
tel. 99 02 85, 93 71 33,
93 34 26, 98 74 32

DEFENSE
22 University Street
tel. 30 31 63, 98 39 30, 99
61 92, 29 26 74, 99 81 12

ECONOMY
12 G. Chanturia Street
Tel. 23 09 25, 23 58 82,
98 23 59

EDUCATION
52 Uznadze Street
tel. 95 66 30, 95 70 10,
95 09 49, 95 09 64

FINANCE
70 I. Abashidze Street
tel. 22 68 05, 29 20 77,
22 68 05, 23 54 16

FOREIGN AFFAIRS
4 Chitadze Street
tel. 98 93 77, 98 93 88

HEALTH
30 K. Gamsakhurdia
Avenue
tel. 38 70 71, 37 79 06

INTERNAL AFFAIRS
10 Gulua Street
tel. 99 62 96, 99 10 49,
93 30 47, 99 80 50

JUSTICE
30 Rustaveli Avenue
tel. 93 27 21, 98 92 52,
93 62 54

MANUFACTURING
28 K. Gamsakhurdia Ave.
tel. 38 55 49, 38 50 28

NATURAL RESOURCES
68a Kostava Street
tel. 23 06 64, 36 73 40,
36 73 34, 36 05 68

SOCIAL PROTECTION,
LABOR AND EMPLOYMENT
2 Leonidze Street
tel. 93 69 68, 93 69 81,
93 65 81

STATE ADMINISTRATION
AND PROPERTY
64 Chavchavadze Avenue
tel. 29 48 75, 29 30 66, 29
27 93, 29 30 72, 29 00 04

TELECOMMUNICATIONS
2 Ninth of April Street
tel. 99 95 28, 98 43 43, 98
65 65, 93 45 45, 93 26 26

TRADE AND SUPPLY
42 Kazbegi Street
tel. 38 96 52, 38 96 23,
39 30 32, 39 40 29

TRANSPORTATION
12 Kazbegi Street
tel. 36 45 55

INTERNATIONAL
ORGANIZATIONS

AGRICULTURAL
COOPERATIVE
DEVELOPMENT
INTERNATIONAL (ACDI)
1 Marukhis Gmirebis Street
tel. 29 14 36, 29 25 03,
fax. 94 10 96
e-mail: acdi@acdi.ge

AMERICAN BAR
ASSOCIATION (ABA)
10a Chonkadze Street
tel. 93 25 04

ADVENTIST DEVELOPMENT
AND RELIEF AGENCY
(ADRA)
2 Lagidze Street,
Apartment 52
tel. 99 83 36

ACADEMY FOR
EDUCATIONAL
DEVELOPMENT (AED)
14 Paliashvili Street
tel. 23 10 77

AMERICAN-JEWISH JOINT
DISTRIBUTION COMMITTEE
35 G. Tabidze Street,
Apartment 48
tel. 99 89 92

ATLANTA-TBILISI HEALTH
PARTNERSHIP
30 K. Gamsakhurdia
Avenue
tel. 23 70 87

BCC EUROPEAN UNION
PROJECT
47 Kostava Street
tel. 98 76 19

CARE—INTERNATIONAL
IN THE CIS
42 Petriashvili Street
tel. 29 12 69, 29 19 41,
29 15 31, 29 13 78
fax. 29 43 07
e-mail: carecis@iberiapac.ge

CARITAS DENMARK
5 Marjanishvili Street,
Apartments 411 & 412
tel. 95 17 60

CATHOLIC RELIEF
SERVICES (CRS)
65 Zhiuli Shartava Street
tel. 94 20 73

THE CAUCASIAN
INSTITUTE FOR PEACE,
DEMOCRACY AND
DEVELOPMENT (CIPDD)
89/24 Agmashenebeli
Avenue
tel. 95 47 23,
fax. 95 44 97
e-mail:
cipdd@access.sanet.ge

CENTER FOR DISEASE
CONTROL (CDC)
1 Abasheli Street
tel. 93 89 64

CENTER FOR ECONOMIC
POLICY AND REFORM
(CEPAR)
12 Chanturia Street,
Suite 801
tel. 98 84 25, 98 84 50,
fax. 98 84 39
e-mail: gmp@gaecon.pvt.ge

CHILDREN'S AID DIRECT
9 Radiani Street
tel. 22 37 21

COUNTERPART
FOUNDATION
HUMANITARIAN
ASSISTANCE PROGRAM
(CHAP)
33 Zubalashvili Street
tel. 98 61 58

EURASIA FOUNDATION
20 Abashidze Street
tel. 22 56 88

EVANGELICAL MISSION
SOCIETY OF AMERICA
(EMSA)
3 Mtisdziri Street
tel. 95 78 90

EUROPEAN COMMUNITY
HUMANITARIAN OFFICE
(ECHO)
1/F, 31 Shanidze Street
tel. 29 09 36

FUND FOR DEMOCRACY
AND DEVELOPMENT (FDD)
5 Virsaladze Street
tel. 98 39 68

GLOBAL HEALING
21 Lubliana Street
tel. 22 59 04

HELSINKI CITIZENS
ASSEMBLY TRANSCAUCASIA
OFFICE (HCA)
5 Dariali Lane
tel. 96 15 14

EAST GEORGIA OFFICE
INTERNATIONAL
FEDERATION OF RED
CROSS AND RED CRESENT
SOCIETIES (IFRC)
15 Photi Street
tel. 95 09 45

THE INTERNATIONAL
COMMITTEE OF THE RED
CROSS
1 Dutu Megreli Street
Tbilisi
tel. (32) 93 55 11, 93 55
13, 93 55 15, 93 55 17
45 M. Kostava Street,
Kutaisi
tel. (231) 52 179
59 K. Gamsakhurdia Street,
Zugdidi
tel. (215) 22 949

INTERNATIONAL
EXECUTIVE SERVICE CORPS
(IESC)
19a Tabukashvili Street
tel. 23 21 18

INTERNATIONAL MONETARY
FUND (IMF)
7 Ingorokva Street
tel. 93 67 52

INTERNATIONAL
ORTHODOX CHRISTIAN
CHARITIES (IOCC)
4 Abashidze Street
tel. 22 20 20

INTERNATIONAL RESCUE
COMMITTEE (IRC)
6 Tabidze Street
tel. 22 70 24

INTERNEWS NETWORK
Georgia Regional Office
2 Kakabadze Street
tel. 98 83 24, 98 83 25,
99 60 13, 93 68 59,
fax. 93 50 66
e-mail:
dcampbell@iberiapac.ge,
gena@iberiapac.ge

ISRAEL-GEORGIA CHAMBER
OF BUSINESS
15 P. Iashvili Street
tel. 99 88 10,
fax. 99 85 57

MÉDECINS DU MONDE-
GREECE (MDM-GREECE)
76 Barnov Street
tel. 22 77 12

MÉDECINS SANS
FRONTIÈRES (MSF/HOL-
LAND)
9 Abasheli Street
tel. 22 06 78

MÉDECINS SANS
FRONTIÈRES (MSF/SPAIN)
1 T. Tabidze Street
tel. 23 59 94

NATIONAL DEMOCRATIC
INSTITUTE (NDI)
1 Larsi Street
tel. 93 58 30

OPEN SOCIETY GEORGIA
FOUNDATION (OSGF)
18 Abashidze Street
tel. 22 23 46

OPEN SOCIETY GEORGIA
FOUNDATION/INTERNATIONAL
STUDENT ADVISORY
CENTER (OSGF/ISAC)
82 Paliashvili Sreet
tel. 29 44 82

OXFAM
100 T. Tabidze Street
tel. 29 22 63

PREMIÈRE URGENCE
12 Dariali Lane
tel. 29 33 47

RAIL OPERATIONS CENTER
FOR CAUCASUS REGION
15 Tamar Mepe Avenue
tel. 23 71 80

SAVE THE CHILDREN
54 Mtskheta Street
tel. 22 77 24

TACIS GEORGIAN
ECONOMIC TRENDS
16 Zandukeli Street
tel. 93 91 61

TECHNICAL ASSISTANCE TO
THE COMMONWEALTH OF
INDEPENDENT STATES
(TACIS)
12 Chanturia Street
tel. 98 85 29

THE SALVATION ARMY
(TSA)
29 Abashidze Street
tel. 22 75 30

TURKISH INTERNATIONAL
COOPERATION AGENCY
(TICA)
61 Agmashenebeli Avenue
tel. 95 30 46/Branch
address: 4 Chitadze Street
tel. 98 54 39

UNITED NATIONS
CHILDREN'S FUND
(UNICEF)
UN House, Floor IV,
9 Eristavi Street
tel. 23 23 88, 25 11 30
e-mail:
cao-geco@unicef.org.ge

UNION OF COUNCILS
CAUCASIAN BUREAU
12 Tumanian Street
tel. 93 34 13

UNITED METHODIST
COMMITTEE ON RELIEF
(UMCOR)
8 Abasheli Street
tel. 23 16 38

UNITED NATIONS
DEPARTMENT OF
HUMANITARIAN AFFAIRS
(UNDHA)
9 Eristavi Street
tel. 94 31 63
e-mail: toby@undha.org.ge
tel. and fax. via Georgia
(995 32) 95 95 16
tel. and fax. via U.S.A
(1 908) 888-1554

UNITED NATIONS
DEVELOPMENT
PROGRAMME (UNDP)
Georgia Office
9 Eristavi Street
tel. 99 85 58, 94 11 25,
94 11 26
e-mail: fo.geo@undp.org.ge

UNITED NATIONS HIGH
COMMISSIONER FOR
REFUGEES (UNHCR)
2a Kazbegi Street
tel. 98 62 02

UNITED NATIONS
VOLUNTEERS (UNV)
9 Eristavi Street
tel. 99 85 58

UNITED STATES AGENCY
FOR INTERNATIONAL
DEVELOPMENT (UNSAID)
6 Orbeliani Street
tel. 98 99 67

WOMEN AID
INTERNATIONAL
31/33 Amagleba Street
tel. 99 79 48

THE WORLD BANK
Resident Mission Georgia
18a Chonkadze Street
tel. 94 22 13, 94 28 98
fax. 99 52 88; e-mail:
niakobis@worldbank.org

WORLD BANK PROJECT
Development and
Privatization of Georgian
Agriculture
41 Kostava Street
tel. 99 99 42

WORLD BANK PROJECT
Georgia Health Project
Coordination Unit
30 Gamsakhurdia Avenue
tel. 29 44 07

WORLD COUNCIL OF
CHURCHES
2/1 Erekle Square
tel. 94 16 49

WORLD FOOD PROGRAMME
35a Amagleba Street
tel. 95 99 51, 93 42 59,
93 44 92 ext. 126,
fax. 99 71 71 ext. 116
e-mail: CRO@unwfp.ge
Internet address: http:
/www.sanet.ge/unwfp.html

WORLD HEALTH
ORGANIZATION (WHO)
Medical University
tel. 39 84 66

WORLD WIDE FUND FOR
NATURE (WWF)
52 Rustaveli Avenue
tel. 99 81 50
tel./fax. 99 86 28

LEGAL RESOURCES
Insiders recommend the
following law firm in
Tbilisi. Both director Ted
Jonas and his partner
Constantine Rizhinashvili
speak excellent English:

GCG LAW GROUP
24 Rustaveli Avenue
tel. 93 64 22
fax. 93 27 52
e-mail: tedo@gcg.com.ge.

LIBRARIES
CENTRAL SCIENCE LIBRARY
2 Z. Chavchavadze Street
tel. 95 03 28

GEORGIAN NATIONAL
LIBRARY
5 Gudiashvili Street
tel. 98 75 91

MARKETS AND
SUPERMARKETS
CENTRAL MARKET
137 Tsinamzgrishvilis Street

SABURTALO REGIONAL
43 Shartava Street
Shopping in one of Tbilisi's markets (be it the large Central Market near the Railroad Station, the Saburtalo Regional market, or the smaller market in Orbeliani Square) certainly provides the greatest breadth of choice, the freshest produce at the best prices, and the most interesting experience.

For convenience, the three Super Babylon supermarkets listed below can't be beat. They are open 24 hours a day.

SUPER BABYLON
23 Kostava Street
tel. 99 06 64

7 Mardjanishvili Street
tel. 95 37 02

42 Chavchavadze Avenue
tel. 22 51 51

PHARMACIES
BATONI BONA
5 N. Nikoladze Street
tel. 93 32 21

ELENE PHARMACY
117 David Agmashenebeli Avenue
tel. 95 88 10

GEOPHARM
11 Kostava Street
tel. 99 67 71

UNIPHARM
In the mall under Republican Square

SWIMMING POOLS
SHERATON METECHI PALACE HOTEL
20 Telavi Street, Issani
tel. 95 42 70, 95 37 57, 95 73 76
(For hotel guests only)

VAKE SWIMMING POOL
49 Chavchavadze Avenue
tel. 22 61 00

VERE-TBLISI CENTRAL POOL
1 Kostava Street
tel. 99 82 31, 99 89 60, 99 70 18

THEATERS AND CONCERT HALLS
CIRCUS
Heroes' Square

THE GEORGIAN NATIONAL BALLET
123 Agmashenebeli Avenue
tel. 94 21 98, 95 42 91, 95 06 11, 95 51 83,
fax. 94 21 99

GEORGIAN STATE PHILARMONIC HALL
136 Agmashenebeli Avenue
tel. 95 95 20

GRIBOYEDOV RUSSIAN DRAMA THEATER
2–4 Rustaveli Avenue
tel. 93 43 36

MARJANISHVILI ACADEMIC DRAMA THEATER
8 Marjanishvili Street
tel. 95 24 25

MIKHAIL TUMANISHVILI FILM ACTORS' THEATER
127 Agmashenebeli Avenue
tel. 95 97 34, 95 39 27

PHILHARMONIC MAIN CONCERT HALL
1 Melikishvili Street
tel. 98 77 07

SARAJISHVILI
CONSERVATORY MAIN
CONCERT HALL
8 Griboyedov Street

(SHAUMYAN) ARMENIAN
THEATER
8 Ketevan Tsamebuli Street
tel. 74 16 56

SHOTA RUSTAVELI STATE
ACADEMIC THEATER
17 Rustaveli Avenue
tel. 99 85 87, 99 63 73

TBILISI CHILDREN'S
CENTRAL THEATER
127 Agmashenebeli Avenue
tel. 95 97 34, 95 39 27

TBILISI PANTOMIME STATE
THEATER
37 Rustaveli Avenue
tel. 99 63 14

TBILISI STATE
MARIONETTE THEATER
26 Shavteli Street
tel. 99 66 20, 98 65 93

Z. PALIASHVILI OPERA AND
BALLET THEATER
25 Rustaveli Avenue
tel. 99 03 45, 99 06 42

Practical information, such as telephone numbers and opening hours, is subject to change. We welcome updates, suggestions, corrections and comments:

**Odyssey Publications Ltd,
1004 Kowloon Centre,
29–43 Ashley Road,
Tsim Sha Tsui,
Kowloon, Hong Kong
tel. (852) 2856 3896
fax. (852) 2565 8004
e-mail:
odyssey@asiaonline.net**

Selected Further Reading

HISTORY AND POLITICS

ALLEN, W. E. D., *A History of the Georgian People*, Barnes & Noble, 1971.
This overview of Georgian history is written by a great English scholar of the Caucasus. The work serves as a nice introduction.

ARBEL, Rachel, and Lily Magal (Magalashvili)(co-editors), *In the Land of the Golden Fleece: The Jews of Georgia—History and Culture*, The Ministry of Defense Publishing House, Tel Aviv, 1992.
A collection of articles on the history of Jews in Georgia from ancient to present times.

AVES, Jonathan, *Politics in Contemporary Georgia*, Royal Institute of International Affairs.

BADDELEY, John F. *The Russian Conquest of the Caucasus*, Curzon Press Limited, 1997.
A reprint of Baddeley's classic account of the resistence of the north Caucasians under Shamil against the expansion of Tsarist Russia. Highly relevant to the developments of 1996.

BRAUND, David, *Georgian Antiquity: A History of Colchis and Transcaucasian Iberia, 550 BC–AD 562*, Oxford: Clarendon Press, 1994.
An important history of ancient Georgia, with an introduction to the substantial archaeological work that has been carried out in Georgia in recent decades.

BURNEY, Charles, and David Marshall Lang, *The Peoples of the Hills: Ancient Ararat and Caucasus*, Praeger, 1972.
A general introduction to Transcaucasia. This work places Georgia within a larger geographical, historical, and political context, especially with respect to Armenia.

CHERVONNAYA, Svetlana, *Conflict in the Caucasus*, Gothic Image Publications, 1994.
A Russian journalist's eyewitness account of the war in Abkhazia with much information on the deliberate conspiracy of destabilization in the region.

DAWISHA, Karen, Parrott and Bruce, (co-editors), *Conflict, Cleavage, and Change in Central Asia and the Caucasus (Democratization and Authoritarianism in Post-Communist Societies, No. 4)*, Cambridge University Press, 1997.
A chapter on Georgia provides a systematic analysis of politics, factionalism, party formation, and social and ethnic divisions.

EKEDAHL, Carolyn McGiffert, and Melvin A. Goodman, *The Wars of Eduard Shevardnadze*, The Pennsylvania State University Press, 1997.
Veteran observers of the Soviet system describe and analyse Shevardnadze's career.

GACHECHILADZE, Revaz, *The New Georgia: Space, Society, and Politics*, Texas A & M University Press, 1995.
Written by a leading Georgian scholar and published in 1995, this book consists of geographical and historical background on Georgia as well as an analysis of sociogeographical problems.

GOLDENBERG, Suzanne, *Pride of Small Nations: The Caucasus and Post-Soviet Disorder,* Zed Books, 1994.

An indispensable resource to anyone interested in the Caucasus.

LANG, David Marshall, *A Modern History of Georgia,* Weidenfeld and Nicolson, 1962.

For many years the most accessible book about Georgian politics and history, especially concerning independent Georgia, Communist Russia and the Stalin era. However, this book is now showing its age.

LANG, David Marshall, *The Georgians,* Praeger, 1966.

A comprehensive portrait of the Georgian people.

LANG, David Marshall, *The Last Years of the Georgian Monarchy,* 1658–1832, Columbia University Press, 1957.

A scholarly look at the fascinating period of Georgian history in which pressures from Iran and Turkey forced the Georgian nobility to look toward Russia for help.

LANSELL, Scott, *Republic of Georgia,* International Foundation for Election Systems.

ODOM, William E., and Robert Dujanic, *Commonwealth or Empire: Russia, Central Asia, and the Transcaucasus,* Brookings Institute, 1996.

An astute and up-to-date analysis of Moscow's attempt to regain control over the Transcaucasus and Central Asia.

NASMYTH, Peter, *Georgia Mountains and Honour,* Curzon Press Limited, 1998.

A new book that covers the country region by region, taking the form of a literary journey through the transition from Soviet Georgia to the modern independent nation state.

SHEVARDNADZE, Eduard, *The Future Belongs to Freedom,* Free Press, 1991.

The former First Secretary of the Communist Party of Soviet Georgia and the current President of Georgia explains his repudiation of communism, and his new political philosophy emphasizing democracy and universal human values.

SUNY, Ronald Grigor, *The Making of the Georgian Nation,* Indiana University Press and Hoover Institution Press, 1988.

The first full history of the Georgian nation in a western language to be published in more than a quarter-century.

WRIGHT, John, *The Georgians: A Handbook,* Curzon Press Limited, 1998

An indispensable resource to anyone interested in the Caucasus.

ART HISTORY

VELMANS, T., and Aplago A. Novello, *L'Arte della Georgia: Affreschi & Architcttura (The Art of Georgia: Frescoes & Architecture),* Jaca Books, 1996.

A beautifully illustrated book on Georgian art and architecture with equally excellent text.

TRAVEL

BITOV, Andrei, *A Captive of the Caucasus,* Farrar Straus Giroux, 1992.

In *Choosing a Location,* the second of two personal memoirs that make up this book, the author beautifully describes his travels in Georgia.

DUMAS, Alexandre, *Adventures in Caucasia*, Chilton Books, 1962.
A must for all travelers to Georgia. Dumas' vivid presentation of his experiences will serve as a useful touchstone for your own.

FARSON, Negley, *Caucasian Journey*, Penguin Travel Library, 1988.
Negley Farson shares anecdotes and fascinating descriptions from his journey to the Caucasus in 1926.

MACLEAN, Fitzroy, *To Caucasus: The End of All the Earth*, Little Brown, 1976.
A friend of Georgia for many years, Maclean shares his love and knowledge of the country as he relates his travels in Georgia in the mid-1970s.

NASMYTH, Peter, *Georgia: A Rebel in the Caucasus*, Cassell, 1992.
The account of a young British traveler's enthusiastic experience of his first time in Georgia.

PUSHKIN, Alexander, *A Journey to Arzrum*, Ardis, 1974.
An account of the great Russian poet's travels through the Caucasus on his way to Turkey via Tbilisi.

RUSSELL, Mary, *Please Don't Call It Soviet Georgia*, Serpent's Tail, 1991.
An idiosyncratic solo journey in 1990 by an Irish writer whose adventures constantly shatter the misconceived beliefs she held before traveling in Georgia.

SEVERIN, Timothy, *The Jason Voyage: The Quest for the Golden Fleece*, Arrow, 1986.
An intrepid British explorer sets sail from Greece to recreate Jason's voyage to Colchis (West Georgia) with his own band of contemporary Argonauts. He provides fascinating corroboration of the historical reality behind the legend of the golden fleece.

THUBRON, Colin, *Where Nights Are Longest*, Atlantic Monthly Press, 1984.
A beautifully written book in which Thubron devotes some chapters to traveling through parts of Georgia by car. His description of his time in Gori, Stalin's birthplace, is particulary fine.

WARDROP, Sir Oliver, *The Kingdom of Georgia*, Luzac & Company, first published 1888, reprinted in 1977.
Sir Oliver Wardrop (1864–1948) wrote this book at age 24. It provides a vivid picture of life in Georgia when it was part of the empire of Tsar Alexander III.

RELIGION

ALFEYEVA, Valeria, *Pilgrimage to Dzhvari: A Woman's Journey of Spiritual Awakening*, Bell Tower Press, 1995.
A Russian woman immerses herself in the religious life of a Georgian monastery.

CUISINE

GOLDSTEIN, Darra, *The Georgian Feast*, HarperCollins, 1993.
Over 120 wonderful recipes from various regions of Georgia. Insightful commentary on Georgia's culinary history and traditions.

MARGVELASHVILI, Julianne, *The Classic Cuisine of Soviet Georgia: History, Traditions, and Recipes*, Prentice Hall, 1991. More than a hundred traditional recipes accompanied by descriptions of the herbs and spices to be found in a Georgian bazaar.

LITERATURE

DUMBADZE, Nodar, *Granny, Iliko, Illarion and I*, Raduga Publishers, 1981.
The first novel by a Georgian writer that tells the story of an orphaned Georgian boy and his studies at Tbilisi University.

Iskander, Fazil, *The Gospel According to Chegam*, Vintage Books, 1984.
Interrelated short stories by Abkhazia's most famous writer set in a fictionalized Caucasian village.

PASTERNAK, Boris, *Letters to Georgian Friends*, Harcourt Brace, 1967.
The correspondence of the Nobel prize–winning poet and author with his Georgian friends, whose poetry he translated.

RAYFIELD, Donald, *The Literature of Georgia: A History*, Clarendon Press, Oxford, 1994.
An excellent introduction to Georgia's great literary tradition.

RUSTAVELI, Shota, *The Knight in the Panther's Skin*, translated by R. H. Stevenson, State University of New York Press, 1977.
This masterpiece of Georgian literature was written in the 12th century and is considered the Georgian national epic. Required reading for every traveler.

TOLSTOY, Leo, *Hadji Murad (from Great Short Works of Tolstoy)*, Harper & Row, 1967.
Tolstoy's brilliant novella describes the wilds of Daghestan, the war of Shamil against the Russian occupation of Transcaucasia, and court life in Tbilisi.

MOUNTAINEERING

SALKELD, Audrey, and José Luis Bermudez, *On the Edge of Europe: Mountaineering in the Caucasus*, The Mountaineers, 1993.
A collection of some of the best writing on climbing in the Caucasus written this century.

INDEX